# WATCHING THE JACKALS

**Georgetown Studies in Intelligence History**

Series Editors: Christopher Moran, Mark Phythian, and Mark Stout

Editorial Advisory Board
Ioanna Iordanou
Peter Jackson
Tricia Jenkins
Paul Maddrell
Paul McGarr
Kathryn Olmsted
Dina Rezk
Calder Walton
Michael Warner

**Titles in the Series**

*Canadian Military Intelligence: Operations and Evolution from the October Crisis to the War in Afghanistan*
David A. Charters

*Crown, Cloak, and Dagger: The British Monarchy and Secret Intelligence from Victoria to Elizabeth II*
Richard J. Aldrich and Rory Cormac

*Mission to Mao: US Intelligence and the Chinese Communists in World War II*
Sara B. Castro

*Spies for the Sultan: Ottoman Intelligence in the Great Rivalry with Spain*
Emrah Safa Gürkan. Translated by Jonathan M. Ross and İdil Karacadağ

# WATCHING THE JACKALS

## PRAGUE'S COVERT LIAISONS WITH COLD WAR TERRORISTS AND REVOLUTIONARIES

**DANIELA RICHTEROVA**

FOREWORD BY CHRISTOPHER ANDREW

GEORGETOWN UNIVERSITY PRESS / WASHINGTON, DC

© 2025 Georgetown University Press. All rights reserved. No part of this book may be reproduced or utilized in any form or by any means, electronic or mechanical, including photocopying and recording, or by any information storage and retrieval system, without permission in writing from the publisher.

The publisher is not responsible for third-party websites or their content. URL links were active at time of publication.

Library of Congress Cataloging-in-Publication Data

Names: Richterova, Daniela, author. | Andrew, Christopher M., writer of foreword.
Title: Watching the jackals : Prague's covert liaisons with cold war terrorists and revolutionaries / Daniela Richterova ; foreword by Christopher Andrew.
Description: Washington, DC : Georgetown University Press, 2025. | Series: Georgetown studies in intelligence history | Includes bibliographical references and index.
Identifiers: LCCN 2024011599 (print) | LCCN 2024011600 (ebook) | ISBN 9781647125134 (hardcover) | ISBN 9781647125141 (paperback) | ISBN 9781647125158 (ebook)
Subjects: LCSH: Czechoslovakia. Státní bezpečnost. | Terrorism—Middle East. | Terrorists—Middle East. | Intelligence service—Czechoslovakia. | Espionage—Czechoslovakia. | Czechoslovakia—Relations—Middle East. | Middle East—Relations—Czechoslovakia.
Classification: LCC HV6433.M5 R534 2025 (print) | LCC HV6433.M5 (ebook) | DDC 363.3250956—dc23/eng/20240916
LC record available at https://lccn.loc.gov/2024011599
LC ebook record available at https://lccn.loc.gov/2024011600

♾ This paper meets the requirements of ANSI/NISO Z39.48-1992 (Permanence of Paper).

26 25      9 8 7 6 5 4 3 2 First printing

Printed in the United States of America

Cover design by James Keller
Interior design by BookComp, Inc.

*Dedicated to all victims of hot and cold wars—
be they a subject of history or reigniting.*

# CONTENTS

List of Illustrations — ix
Foreword by Christopher Andrew — xiii
Preface — xvii
List of Abbreviations — xxi

    Introduction — 1

## PART I: THE FORMATIVE ERA

1. Czechoslovakia's Early Global Cold War — 25
2. A New Battleground — 57

## PART II: THE PLO

3. A Gordian Alliance — 77
4. Anatomy of an Intelligence Liaison — 95
5. Cruel Intentions — 113
6. A Very "Special" Relationship — 134
7. Training Palestinian Spies and Bodyguards — 147
8. Liaise, Watch, and Infiltrate — 164
9. Countering PLO Extremists — 180

## PART III: THE REJECTIONISTS

10. Keeping Things Semiofficial — 201
11. In the Gray Zone — 218
12. Countering the Rejectionists — 232

## PART IV: LES ENFANTS TERRIBLES

| | | |
|---|---|---|
| 13 | "My Name Is 'Carlos,' and I Am a Good Person" | 239 |
| 14 | Abu Nidal, the "Apostle of Palestinian Violence" | 267 |
| 15 | Anxious Hosts | 293 |
| | Conclusion | 319 |

*Afterword: A Note on Sources*   327
*Bibliography*   333
*Index*   343
*About the Author*   351

# ILLUSTRATIONS

MAPS

| | | |
|---|---|---|
| 0.1 | Central Europe in the mid-1980s | xi |
| 0.2 | The Middle East in the mid-1980s | xii |

ILLUSTRATIONS

| | | |
|---|---|---|
| 1.1 | Monument to V. I. Lenin in front of the Antonín Zápotocký Military Academy in Brno | 34 |
| 1.2 | Fidel Castro with Gustáv Husák, president and first secretary of the Czechoslovak Communist Party | 42 |
| 1.3 | Che Guevara driving a Czechoslovak tractor | 48 |
| 2.1 | Red Army Faction members in court | 59 |
| 2.2 | Hijacked planes blown up by PFLP guerrillas in northern Jordan | 63 |
| 3.1 | Yasser Arafat with Gustáv Husák | 78 |
| 3.2 | Yasser Arafat being greeted at Prague Airport | 83 |
| 4.1 | Abu Iyad, chief of the PLO's Joint Security Service | 96 |
| 4.2 | Ján Kuruc, the StB's rezident in Beirut and Cairo | 102 |
| 4.3 | Czechoslovak Ministry of the Interior | 107 |
| 5.1 | Czechoslovakia's minister of the interior, Jaromír Obzina, with Gustáv Husák | 114 |
| 5.2 | Anwar Sadat being assassinated during a military parade | 119 |
| 5.3 | President of the International Union of Students Jiří Pelikán with Yuri Gagarin | 123 |
| 5.4 | Fusako Shigenobu of the Japanese Red Army | 128 |
| 6.1 | An employee assembling a Czechoslovak pistol | 136 |
| 6.2 | Czechoslovak embassy in Amman | 138 |
| 7.1 | Beshara Traboulsi, PLO's Joint Security Service representative | 150 |
| 7.2 | Muslah Owni Abdulla, Fatah student in Czechoslovakia | 156 |
| 7.3 | Ahmad Mustafa Ahmed Mohammad, Fatah student in Czechoslovakia | 159 |

| | | |
|---|---|---|
| 8.1 | Abu Bakr, head of the PLO Office in Prague | 168 |
| 8.2 | Abu Hisham, head of the PLO Office in Prague | 171 |
| 9.1 | Abu Daoud walking through the Old Town of Prague | 184 |
| 9.2 | Abu Daoud before being forced to leave Czechoslovakia | 188 |
| 9.3 | Gunmen surround the blasted automobile of PLO security chief Ali Hassan Salameh | 191 |
| 10.1 | George Habash, leader of Palestinian Front for the Liberation of Palestine (PFLP) | 203 |
| 10.2 | Nayef Hawatmeh, head of the Democratic Front for the Liberation of Palestine | 207 |
| 10.3 | First secretary of the Communist Party of Czechoslovakia, Vasil' Biľak, with Minister of Foreign Affairs Lubomír Štrougal | 214 |
| 11.1 | Abu Bassam Sharif, PFLP spokesman | 221 |
| 11.2 | Abu Bassam Sharif's letter of acceptance for medical treatment in Prague | 226 |
| 13.1 | Young Carlos the Jackal | 241 |
| 13.2 | Carlos with his partner, Magdalena Kopp | 244 |
| 13.3 | Carlos in front of an advertisement for the movie *The Sting* | 251 |
| 13.4 | Carlos with associates at Prague Airport | 256 |
| 14.1 | Abu Nidal, founder the Abu Nidal Organization | 268 |
| 14.2 | Abu Bakr with his security escort in Prague | 282 |
| 15.1 | Abu Daoud walking the streets of Prague | 295 |
| 15.2 | Carlos's request for a Czechoslovak diplomatic visa | 300 |
| 15.3 | Layla Khaled, first female hijacker | 307 |

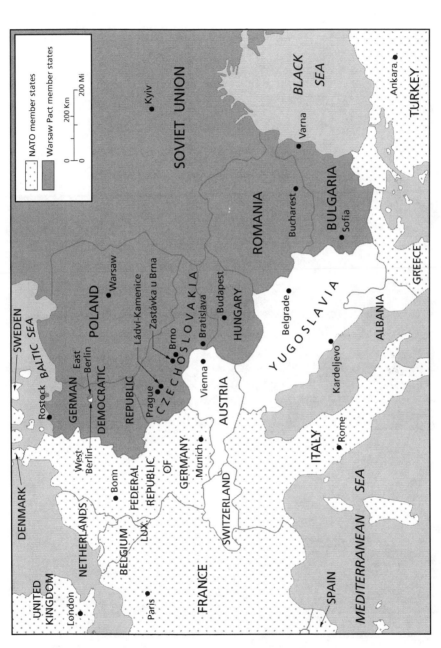

MAP 0.1. Central Europe in the mid-1980s

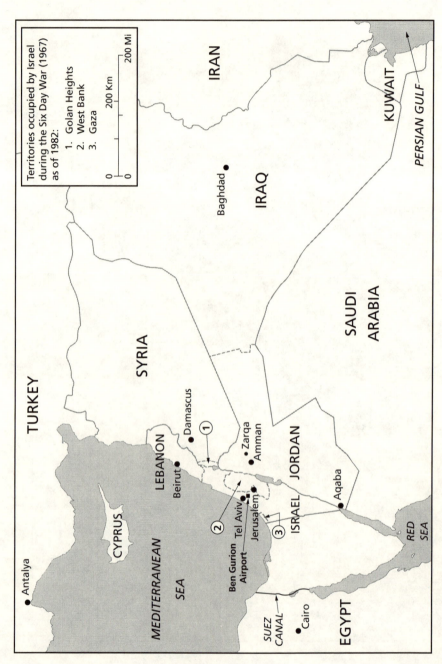

MAP 0.2. The Middle East in the mid-1980s

# FOREWORD

Daniela Richterova's main source for this pathbreaking book is the most important Cold War archive to become available in recent years: Archiv bezpečnostních složek (ABS; Security Services Archive), which houses the voluminous files of the Státní bezpečnost (StB; State Security Service), the domestic and foreign intelligence service of communist Czechoslovakia. About 99 percent of communist-era foreign intelligence files have now been passed on to the ABS—a higher proportion than in any other major intelligence archive in either the East or the West. Also remarkably, unlike the declassified files of the CIA, MI5, and other major Western agencies, none of the StB's once top-secret files have been redacted. In striking contrast, MI6 has yet to declassify any of its past files, though its documents sometimes turn up in other records.

Thanks to the ABS, we are now in the extraordinary position of knowing more about Czechoslovak intelligence operations and their impact on international events. Notably, these documents unveil Prague's operations against the United Kingdom at the height of the Cold War. British archives say as little about this important intelligence struggle as they do about another crucial chapter in Czechoslovak-British history—that of the two countries' cooperation on the eve of World War II. There are no accessible files in British archives, for example, about the secret MI6 operation on March 14, 1939, to fly the Czechoslovak foreign intelligence chief, František Moravec, to London with ten of his senior staff and their most important intelligence files. He later became the first foreign intelligence chief to be awarded the CBE. Since Moravec became a Cold War StB target in the United States, where he lived before his death in 1966, the best prospect of discovering more about his early relations with Western intelligence is probably in StB files.

Beyond expertly utilizing this rich new archival material, Dr. Richterova's *Watching the Jackals* speaks to key intelligence studies and international history debates. Her account of Prague's dilemmatic engagement with some of the most recognizable Cold War revolutionaries and terrorists enables us to better understand the myriad ways in which states use their intelligence agencies to engage with such controversial nonstate actors. This meticulous study of Czechoslovakia's approach to those she terms "Cold War jackals" shows that Prague's Communist Party representatives, diplomats, and spies often struggled when engaging—either cooperating or countering—groups that embraced terrorist methods.

*Watching the Jackals* reveals that the Soviet Bloc was far from a monolith. When it came to Cold War jackals, Prague's attitudes toward the likes of Abu Nidal and Carlos the Jackal often diverged from its more eccentric allies, such as the German Democratic Republic. Richterova's brilliantly researched and scrupulously fair book also puts the story of Prague's relations with jackals into broader Cold War context. It does so by scrutinizing the country's earlier interactions with African and Latin American revolutionaries in the 1960s, an approach that enables her to show the evolution of Prague's attitude toward these controversial, yet important, Cold War actors over time and space.

What Richterova's remarkable research has discovered in the ABS goes far beyond European and Soviet Bloc history. *Watching the Jackals* shows that StB files are an essential though neglected source for understanding Middle Eastern events and dynamics. It reveals much about the secret lives of some of the best-known revolutionaries and terrorists committed to the Palestinian cause, chief among them PLO chairman Yasser Arafat, the Venezuelan Carlos the Jackal, feared Black September commander Abu Daoud, and the leader of the Cold War's most lethal terrorist organization, Abu Nidal. While doing so, it also details their relations with powerful Arab states, including Saddam Hussein's Iraq, Hafez al-Assad's Syria, and Muammar Qaddafi's Libya.

*Watching the Jackals* is almost certainly far better at identifying the flaws in StB intelligence reports than the KGB was at the time. It finds that the StB was regularly confused by the changes in cover names and travel documents used by pro-Palestinian revolutionaries and terrorists. Even after the world's most publicized terrorist, Carlos the Jackal, had visited Prague five times, StB reports continued to refer to him as an "Arab." For some years, the StB also believed Abu Daoud was a member of Carlos's group. In reality, he was a member of the PLO faction Fatah and former commander of Black September, which had been responsible for the terrorist attack on Israeli athletes at the Munich Olympics.

Richterova's pioneering interviews with former Communist Party representatives, diplomats, and StB personnel help to account for these and other errors. It tends to be assumed that monitoring terrorist activities and networks during the later Cold War was bound to be a major intelligence priority in both West and East. In Prague, however, counterterrorism was not usually a popular posting in the StB. Ladislav Csipák recalls, "When I, as a 'greenhorn' was given this agenda, everyone [else] was happy that they did not receive this new task.... They threw me into the water and told me to swim." Richterova also quotes the comments of the former head of the counterterrorism department in postcommunist Czechoslovakia: "They [the StB] were no Middle East experts. What they knew they largely learned from their Arab agentura [agent network]."

Finally, *Watching the Jackals* highlights issues of trust in state-nonstate alliances—an important but thus far understudied phenomenon. Despite its many public protestations of friendship and support, Prague never fully trusted Arafat and his key security envoys. It continued to be nervous of what the StB called his "ideological volatility," reflected in the PLO's annoying flirtations with the West. Richterova's artful account of the extraordinary story of Prague's relations with Cold War jackals is as enticing as it is important for understanding the role intelligence plays in totalitarian states and in their liaisons with unpredictable friends and foes.

*Christopher Andrew*
*Official historian of MI5 and coauthor of* The Mitrokhin Archive:
The KGB in Europe and the West
*Cambridge, UK*
*November 2023*

# PREFACE

This book is the result of a decade of research. In the early 2010s, I was part of a London-based think tank's effort to investigate European Union member states' attitudes toward the Israeli-Palestinian conflict. An initial review revealed that much was assumed yet little was known about Central Europe's historical ties to the Middle East. Intrigued and ready for a new intellectual adventure, I decided to turn this interest into an academic inquiry. By 2014 I had embarked on a doctorate at the University of Warwick focused on Czechoslovakia's relations with violent Middle Eastern nonstate actors and, more broadly, on state-nonstate intelligence alliances.

My research took me to exotic places: dusty archives in Central Europe, Atlanta, Simi Valley, and Kew Gardens. It led me to seek out former diplomats, communists, and spies enjoying their retirement in the Czech countryside; the German Black Forest; the leafy suburbs of Washington, DC; and the sprawling British metropolis. I was also able to track down several victims of terrorist attacks or machinations carried out by the communist State Security Service or Middle Eastern terrorists. None of this would have been possible without key people and institutions that assisted me throughout the years.

The first among equals is Richard J. Aldrich. As my PhD supervisor-turn-mentor, Richard has offered strategic guidance and tactical support. While doing so, he taught me that patience, a bit of sun, and good humor can get you further than you would think. Equally, there would be no book without "the Peters"—two Czechoslovak-born scholars with impeccable knowledge of the country's Cold War history, firsthand knowledge of the intelligence world, and matchless insight into the archival records that the crumbling communist regime left behind upon its demise. I am grateful for their trust, time, and motivation.

I am particularly grateful to Georgetown University Press senior acquisitions editor Donald Jacobs and the editors of the series Georgetown Studies in Intelligence History—Christopher Moran, Mark Phythian, and Mark Stout—for believing in this project, providing exceptionally helpful feedback, and for seeing this project through. My thanks also belong to the press's fantastic production team and copy editor Don McKeon for his meticulous attention to detail and invaluable contributions to refining the manuscript.

Throughout the past decade, many colleagues and friends at the University of Warwick, Brunel University London, and King's College London provided much-needed support and guidance and engaged in conversations that helped improve my thinking and writing on this topic. Together with them, many others provided generous assistance and advice that enabled me to think through the problems addressed in this book: Egemen Bezci, Pauline Blistene, Irina Borogan, Patrick Bury, Rory Cormac, Philip H. J. Davies, Melina Dobson, Huw Dylan, David Easter, Jules Gaspard, David Gioe, Dorothea Gioe, Michael Goodman, Elena Grossfeld, Christian Gustafson, Mark Harrison, Kjetil Hatlebrekke, Jan Koura, Mark Kramer, Magda Long, Thomas Maguire, Sarah Mainwaring, Paul McGarr, Christopher Moran, Mikuláš Pešta, Thomas Scheuer, Radek Schovánek, Karel Sieber, Andrei Soldatov, John Taylor, Natalia Telepneva, Damien Van Puyvelde, Steven Wagner, and Petr Zídek. I am also grateful to my early academic mentors who, two decades ago, first inspired me to pursue archival research on the Holocaust and Middle Eastern peace negotiations: Ahron Bregman, Andrej Findor, Ján Hlavinka, Katarína Hradská, Ivan Kamenec, Eduard Nižňanský, and Monika Vrzgulová.

I would also like to thank the anonymous reviewers as well as colleagues and friends who took the time to read this manuscript. Their observations and suggestions helped improve my work considerably. Debates and exercises with my students also pushed the boundaries of my analysis.

One of the perks of being an "espionage academic" is the ability to regularly interact with former practitioners. These men and women with decades of experience in national security strategy, intelligence tradecraft, and counterterrorism—in many cases from the Middle East—were incredibly generous with their time. They helped me think through some of the more complicated issues associated with state interactions with violent nonstate actors. Although most wish to remain anonymous, I am nevertheless indebted to them for their interest and insightful observations.

The time I spent sifting through Cold War–era records in Central Europe, London, and across the United States was a fascinating and often breathtaking experience. I am forever indebted to the wise and welcoming staff of these archives. There would be no book without the assistance of the staff of the ABS in Prague, the National Archive of the Czech Republic, and the Archive of the Ministry of Foreign Affairs of the Czech Republic. I would also like to thank the ABS and the Czech Press Agency (ČTK) for allowing me to use photographs that help bring the stories told in this book to life.

Equally, my work would not have an academic home were it not for Christopher M. Andrew, who, in an effort to unveil the missing dimension, founded the field of intelligence studies.[1]

My thanks also belongs to the Faculty of Social Science and Public Policy Publication Subvention Fund at King's College London for providing generous support for the book. Additionally, this book would not have been possible without the generous financial support of the University of Warwick, which entrusted me with a Chancellor's Scholarship and supported my research via the Transatlantic Fellowship Award. I also benefited from the generous UK Research and Innovation fund awarded for a joint research and practitioner training project led by Patrick Bury, "Transformation of Transatlantic Counter-Terrorism, 2001–25."

I would also like to thank the audiences at the various conferences—most important the Intelligence Studies Section at the International Studies Association and the Cambridge Intelligence Seminar, where I presented and tested earlier versions of some of the chapters that make up this book. Their observations helped improve my work by spotting various conceptual and methodological weaknesses during the earlier stages of my research. Nonetheless, all errors and mistakes in this book are mine alone.

Short segments of the chapters on Carlos the Jackal and Abu Daoud previously appeared in two academic journals. I wish to thank the editors and publishers of *Surveillance and Society* and the *International History Review* for allowing me to use and expand on several sections of these articles in this book. I am also indebted to my coauthors, Natalia Telepneva and Mikuláš Pešta, for allowing me to use documents on Prague's relationship with Africa, which they collected for our joint piece published as part of the special issue of the latter, "The Secret Struggle for the Global South: Espionage, Military Assistance and State Security in the Cold War." My gratitude also goes to Jonathan Boseley and Yusuf Ozkan for their research assistance.

Friends, both old and new, had a profound impact on the final product of my doctoral study. Without their support, good spirits, frankness, and assistance at all hours of the day, this book would not exist. Miroslav Joachim Skovajsa served as my "Q," providing invaluable technical support and security backup during crucial interview and data-collection stages. My other lifelong friends and their families encouraged and nurtured me throughout the process: Miška and Roman; Verča and Aaron; Miro and Deedee; Aňa, Viktor, and Jaro; Katka, Milan, and Leo; Ilke and Simon; Sarah and Kevin; Federica and Jorge; Monika and Marko; Magda, Jelena, and Mia; Patrick; Kubo; Kovo; Maťo; Bára; Karla; Andrejka; Michaela; and Zuzana. Their friendship and our valuable conversations mean a great deal to me.

My family has been my foundation stone throughout this process. Their encouragement, advice, wisdom, and impeccable translation and journalistic skills have been invaluable. My mom, Adriena; my father, Milan; and my sister, Katarína (and her beautiful family), have made all the difference.

Finally, a note on names: Names have been romanized following modern conventions to avoid ambiguity and sometimes exclude diacritics. Original source material, where Arab names are spelled phonetically in Czech, has been in some instances changed to reflect more conventional renderings.

## NOTE

1. For more on what Andrew and David Dilks called "the missing dimension," see Christopher Andrew and David Dilks, *The Missing Dimension: Governments and Intelligence Communities in the Twentieth Century* (London: Macmillan, 1984).

# LIST OF ABBREVIATIONS

| | |
|---|---|
| ABS | Archiv bezpečnostních složek (Security Services Archive) |
| ANC | African National Congress |
| ANM | Arab Nationalist Movement |
| ANO | Abu Nidal Organization |
| BND | Bundesnachrichtendienst (Federal Intelligence Service) |
| CIA | Central Intelligence Agency |
| CSSR | Czechoslovak Socialist Republic |
| ČTK | Czech Press Agency |
| DFLP | Democratic Front for the Liberation of Palestine |
| DGI | Dirección General de Inteligencia (General Directorate of Intelligence) |
| DRC | Democratic Republic of the Congo |
| DST | Direction de la surveillance du territoire (Directorate of Territorial Surveillance) |
| ETA | Euskadi Ta Askatasuna (Basque Homeland and Liberty) |
| FCO | Foreign and Commonwealth Office |
| FLN | Front de libération nationale (National Liberation Front) |
| FRELIMO | Liberation Front of Mozambique |
| GDR | German Democratic Republic |
| INO | Index nežádoucích osob (Unwanted Persons Index) |
| JRA | Japanese Red Army |
| JSS | Joint Security Service |
| KANU | Kenya African National Union |
| KGB | Komitet gosudarstvennoy bezopasnosti (Committee for State Security) |
| KTS | kandidát tajné spolupráce (candidate secret collaborator) |
| MfS/Stasi | Ministerium für Staatssicherheit (Ministry for State Security) |
| MI5 | Security Service |
| MK | uMkhonto we Sizwe (Spear of the Nation) |
| Mossad | popular name for the Institute for Intelligence and Special Operations |

| | |
|---|---|
| MPLA | People's Movement for the Liberation of Angola |
| NATO | North Atlantic Treaty Organization |
| OAS | Organization of American States |
| OPEC | Organization of the Petroleum Exporting Countries |
| PAIGC | African Party of Independence of Portuguese Guinea and Cape Verde Islands |
| PFLP | Popular Front for the Liberation of Palestine |
| PFLP-EO | Popular Front for the Liberation of Palestine–External Operations |
| PIRA | Provisional Irish Republican Army |
| PKK | Kurdistan Workers' Party |
| PLO | Palestinian Liberation Organization |
| Securitate | Departamentul Securității Statului (Department of State Security) |
| SIGINT | signals intelligence |
| SIS | Secret Intelligence Service (also colloquially known as MI6) |
| StB | Státní bezpečnost (State Security Service) |
| USD | US dollars |
| ÚSTR | Ústav pro studium totalitních režimů (Institute for the Study of Totalitarian Regimes) |
| ÚZSI | Úřad pro zahraniční styky a informace (Office for Foreign Relations and Information) |
| VAAZ | Vojenská akademie Antonína Zápotockého (Antonín Zápotocký Military Academy) |
| ZAPU | Zimbabwe African People's Union |

# Introduction

In June 1977, less than five years after the Munich Olympics massacre, the International Olympic Committee held a session at Prague's most luxurious hotel—the brutalist, newly built Hotel Intercontinental. As the committee members assembled in the Czechoslovak capital, a forty-year-old, unusually tall man sporting a fashionable pair of thick-rimmed glasses checked into the same hotel on the Vltava River. He had arrived on an Algerian passport under the name "Amara Salem," claiming to be visiting the Czechoslovak capital for business. Soon the domestic branch of Czechoslovakia's notorious State Security Service (Státní bezpečnost, or StB) learned that Amara Salem was no ordinary businessman. He was, in fact, Abu Daoud, the infamous commander of the 1972 Munich Olympics massacre, which led to the death of eleven Israeli athletes and a protracted hostage drama seen by almost one billion viewers worldwide. He was responsible for one of the most infamous terrorist attacks of the Cold War era.[1]

Abu Daoud's presence in Prague made the StB's blood run cold. Petrified of violence erupting on its territory, the security service was desperate to find out what brought one of the world's most wanted terrorists to Czechoslovakia and, most crucially, whether it was a mere coincidence that he had arrived in Prague just as the International Olympic Committee began its annual proceedings there. Anxious to learn more about the villainous visitor, the StB turned to its agent network and swiftly deployed its surveillance teams to track him. Prague was watching Abu Daoud's every move.[2]

\*\*\*

During the latter part of the Cold War, the paths of spies, terrorists, and revolutionaries often crossed. In the late 1960s, a new wave of terrorism began dominating the Cold War security space and news headlines. Groups of Palestinian, West German, Venezuelan, American, and Italian nationals hijacked airplanes, blew up consulates, and took high-profile hostages in efforts to draw attention to their myriad causes. Some were led by a desire to achieve their own statehood, others to change the world or promote their ideology. Not unlike wild jackals, the perpetrators of international terrorism of the late Cold War era were territorial about their beliefs and causes, chose their targets with much precision, and attacked in packs. Much like the fictional "Jackal"—the protagonist of Frederick Forsyth's 1971 bestseller *The Day of the Jackal*—Cold War terrorists were enigmatic, prone to targeting high-ranking officials and symbolic targets, and feared by powerful governments.[3]

As the operations of "Cold War jackals" became more frequent and sophisticated, Western states—which were prime targets of these contemptible attacks—started looking for culprits responsible for this growing threat. Their intelligence agencies laboriously tracked the movements of these terrorists and revolutionaries, looking for breadcrumbs that would lead them back to potential supporters. Moscow and its allies in the Soviet Bloc were often alleged to be main backers of these groups. After all, Cold War jackals and communists seemed to hate the West with similar passion.

Concerns about Soviet Bloc backing of Cold War jackals were not unfounded. They were fueled by mounting evidence suggesting that these terrorists and revolutionaries visited, received training, or, in some cases, even settled down in East Central Europe. In fact, in the late 1970s and 1980s, the region did become a favorite destination for these controversial individuals. A well-trained intelligence officer strolling through the streets of Prague, Budapest, East Berlin, or Warsaw could observe hushed discussions between Middle Eastern diplomats and some of the most notorious of the Cold War jackals. A careful people-watcher about town could spot these infamous figures wining and dining in luxurious hotels, bars, and restaurants. And a watchful hospital patient could see men and women with bullet or shrapnel wounds receive treatment at renowned Soviet Bloc medical facilities.

This all presented a conundrum for Western politicians, diplomats, and spies. Why did these dangerous individuals frequent Central European capitals? Did the communist governments invite them, or did they arrive there on their own accord? Were they all provided with the same level of support, or did they distinguish between the moderates and extremists? If so, where did Soviet Bloc governments draw the line between those they aligned with and those they countered? What kind of support were they willing to provide and to what end? Most crucially, what role did their infamous security and intelligence services play in managing these complicated interactions?

Recent scholarship suggests that the links between Soviet Bloc states and Cold War jackals were remarkably diverse. The policies that bloc states adopted toward these actors were not uniform but instead reflected each country's unique interests, concerns, and capabilities. On the ground, the reality of these highly clandestine interactions was also much more complex and fluid than many in the West thought at the time. The way in which the Soviet Union, East Germany, Poland, Bulgaria, and others interacted—in some cases actively supporting, in others tolerating or countering violent nonstate actors—was often haphazard and at times paradoxical. The Soviet Bloc was a far cry from the monolith it was widely considered to be.[4]

The story of Czechoslovakia's relationship with Cold War jackals, however, has remained untold. Although preliminary research on some groups and operations began to emerge several years ago,[5] we are still missing the big picture—a comprehensive history of Prague's engagement with Cold War revolutionaries and terrorists. Thanks to thousands of recently released diplomatic and intelligence files coupled with interviews with communists, diplomats, and spies, we are now able to start unraveling this tangled story of Prague's relations with some of the most prominent jackals—a story that shows how Czechoslovakia gradually developed its own policy toward these violent nonstate actors and underscores the complexities and challenges inherent in state interactions with them.

The main focus of this book is Czechoslovakia's relationship with Cold War jackals associated with the Palestinian cause. It primarily interrogates Prague's diplomatic, security, and intelligence liaisons with these high-profile terrorists and revolutionaries. The book traces Prague's complex dealings with them from the 1960s, when the country first started engaging with nonstate actors who employed terrorist methods, until the end of the Cold War. It explores how Czechoslovak communists, diplomats, and spies interacted with these groups on two fronts: in the Middle East—specifically Jordan, Lebanon, Syria, and Libya—and on Czechoslovak territory. To cover both sides of the story, it utilizes a unique cache of foreign intelligence as well as domestic security documents.

The book's first substantive section presents an in-depth account of Prague's long-standing alliance with the Palestinian Liberation Organization (PLO) led by Yasser Arafat, one of the most recognizable political figures of the twentieth century. It shows that while this clandestine relationship was incredibly complex—covering areas of intelligence exchange, training, arms deals, and joint operations—it was ultimately characterized by a mismatch in expectations, objectives, and modi operandi. Furthermore, it was plagued by mutual suspicion and manipulation, which led Prague to keep its liaison partner under close watch, penetrate its ranks, and ultimately expel some of its most extreme members and associates.

Its second substantive section explores Prague's attitude toward some of the most notorious figures of the Cold War terrorist underworld, who broke away from the more mainstream Palestinian factions. These enfants terribles included high-profile terrorist outfits such as the Abu Nidal Organization (ANO), which turned against moderate Palestinian groups after they embraced diplomacy, and the group led by Carlos the Jackal, one of the most notorious terrorists of the late Cold War. It shows that from the onset Prague was reluctant to align with these radicals. In fact, it displayed substantial anxiety about their stay in Czechoslovakia and gradually developed ways of infiltrating and pushing them out in a way that would enable it to mitigate potential risk.

This book primarily focuses on understanding how the communist state used the StB—the joint domestic and foreign intelligence organization—to manage these intricate relations. It argues that Czechoslovak decision-makers deployed the StB in multifarious ways. Prague used its spies, multitooled like a Swiss Army Knife, to pursue a full spectrum of policies and approaches toward Cold War jackals. At times, it deployed them to forge clandestine alliances with more moderate, politically significant factions. In other instances, when it came to those whom Prague deemed radical, its officers were tasked to do quite the opposite—to monitor, block, infiltrate, manipulate, and, eventually, oust some of the most notorious figures from its territory.

Nevertheless, the StB's tool kit was not always sharp enough to manage these complicated and fluid interactions. While employing its multitool approach, Prague often faced dilemmas and challenges. It found Cold War jackals to be unpredictable partners and foes. Moreover, it considered them difficult to control and, in some cases, even dangerous. In fact, the Czechoslovak intelligence and security apparatus—reputed for its tight grip on the local population living within the walls of the communist state—was not always adequately equipped, trained, or staffed to deal with these nebulous foreign targets effectively. Consequently, interactions between Czechoslovak spies and these violent nonstate actors were inherently uncomfortable, profoundly anxious, and at times suspenseful.

Gradually, Czechoslovakia sharpened the many tools in its arsenal, refining and enhancing the StB's capability to deal with these mercurial actors. Prague's spies learned how and when to apply the various tools available to them. While they learned how to best calibrate liaison with their allies, they also developed a set of approaches designed to quell those violent nonstate actors deemed dangerous, without provoking retribution or incurring reputational damage. Czechoslovakia's approach to these jackals could be best described as a risk-management, counterterrorism style.

Fundamentally, this book is about the various ways in which states use their spies to pursue covert policies at home and abroad, especially in relation to violent nonstate actors, and how governments employ intelligence as part of statecraft and as a form of power. It also explores the way totalitarian states engage with terrorists and revolutionaries who might share their political goals yet subscribe to different ideologies or employ controversial tactics. Based on primary source material, it analyzes the dilemmas and challenges that intelligence practitioners faced when navigating these complicated relations set against the background of Cold War competition. And, crucially, it exposes the red lines that they did not dare to cross as well as the moments when they turned a blind eye.

The book is primarily an analysis of how the Czechoslovak government and its communist leaders, diplomats, and spies engaged with Cold War jackals. It is not a book about the Palestinian people, nor is it designed to be a political, military, security, or intelligence history of the PLO.[6]

## THE SOVIET-SPONSORED TERRORISM PLOT

The issue of Soviet Bloc interactions with terrorists and revolutionaries was no ivory tower debate. In the closing decade of the Cold War, it became one of the most controversial and divisive issues in US foreign policy. As the attacks and operations mounted by Cold War jackals became more frequent and daring, certain conservative American politicians, journalists, and terrorism experts became increasingly convinced that international terrorism—largely directed at Western European and US targets—had to be orchestrated by America's ideological adversaries. In fact, many argued that Moscow had instrumentalized international terrorism as a weapon against the West.[7]

Key proponents of this school of thought were part of the Reagan administration. Chief among them was Ronald Reagan's secretary of state, retired general Alexander Haig, who, several years prior to his appointment, narrowly escaped an attempt on his life by the Red Army Faction, a German Marxist terrorist group. While reportedly in good spirits shortly after the attack—joking with the press, "I thought I should go out with a bang, but this is too much"—the attack fundamentally reshaped Haig's outlook on terrorism.[8] In January 1981, at his first press conference as secretary of state, Haig argued that the Soviet Union is "involved in conscious policy, in programs, if you will, which foster, support and expand this activity [international terrorism] which is hemorrhaging in many respects throughout the world today."[9] Although later admitting that first-rate intelligence on this issue was scarce, he effectively singled out Moscow and its allies as the leading force behind Cold War–era international terrorism.[10]

Haig's very public accusation triggered a major dispute that opened fault lines between US intelligence professionals, diplomats, and incoming political appointees, some finding the evidence about Moscow's support for terrorists inconclusive, others siding with the newly appointed secretary of state. Major Beltway battles broke out over who was a terrorist and who was a freedom fighter and over whether the Soviet Union and its allies were arming and training the Palestinian and Southern African groups largely engaged in national liberation or those Palestinian, German, and Italian factions known for their exclusive use of international terror. Horns were also locked over the role their intelligence and security services played in these schemes and, most crucially, whether they discouraged or encouraged these actors to use terror to attack the West.[11]

The nature of Czechoslovakia's relationship with revolutionaries and terrorists was at the heart of this heated debate. As a key ally of Moscow and one of the world's most renowned arms producers, Czechoslovakia's connections to Cold War jackals were closely scrutinized and monitored by Western governments. In the 1970s Richard Dearlove, then a junior British Secret Intelligence Service (SIS, also colloquially known at MI6) case officer stationed in Prague and later rising to become "C," chief of the SIS, reported from his post in Prague on the PLO's efforts to set up a political alliance with the communist country.[12] In the 1980s the Central Intelligence Agency (CIA) and the Defense Intelligence Agency quarreled over whether "training of terrorists" had taken place in Soviet Bloc states, including Czechoslovakia.[13] Prague was a key suspect in the West's search for a culprit responsible for the Cold War wave of international terrorism.

Several journalistic books penned during this era helped perpetuate Haig's Soviet Bloc–sponsored terrorism theory. No author was more influential than Claire Sterling—an American journalist based in Italy—with her controversial 1981 book *The Terror Network*. Void of primary document evidence, it hinted at a broad international terrorist conspiracy, arguing that Moscow "took an avuncular interest in terrorist 'adventurers' of every alarming shade. . . . Practically every other sort of armed guerrilla group bent on destroying the vital centers of multinational imperialism has been able since then to count on a discreetly sympathetic ear in Moscow."[14] According to the reporter, all of these groups became "elite battalions in a worldwide Army of Communist Combat."[15]

Despite her shifting argument and frequent inconsistencies, the book's persuasive tone and confidence in largely unsourced claims led many in the incoming Reagan administration to believe that the media was on to something that the intelligence community had missed. Often it ignored cautions and qualifications offered by its professional analysts and official advisers. Crucially, Reagan's CIA director, William J. Casey, ridiculed his own agency's reports, clearly demonstrating more faith in Sterling's account. "Read Claire Sterling's book," Casey told his analysts, "and forget this mush. I paid $13.95 for this, and it told me more than you bastards whom I pay $50,000 a year."[16]

None of the numerous analytical reports produced by the US intelligence community during this time substantiated the "terror network" theory. Although they did find that Moscow and its allies liaised with what most agreed were "national liberation movements"—such as the African National Congress (ANC) and the PLO—evidence of orchestrated support for the more extremist groups and factions was at best "inconclusive."[17] By the mid-1980s other states—such as Libya, Syria, and Iran—took the limelight away from the alleged link between the Soviet Bloc and international terrorism. Nevertheless, we still hear the echoes of this theory down the years. Some practitioners as well as scholars continue to assume that during the Cold War Moscow and its allies vigorously supported international terrorism in an orchestrated fashion.[18] In a way, the narrative that the Soviet Bloc supported Cold War terrorists has become a part of Cold War folklore.

This is hardly surprising, given that primary sources on this subject have been few and far between. State relations with terrorists and revolutionaries are inherently secretive and notoriously difficult to study. There are good reasons for this. To survive in illegality and achieve operational success, violent non-state actors must remain under the radar and avoid leaving a paper trail. States are likewise shy about their dealings with controversial entities, fearing reputational damage, condemnation, or embarrassment. Furthermore, state secrecy about contacts with terrorists is often reinforced by the fact that they tend to contradict official government policies.[19] Thanks to the thick veil of secrecy tightly wrapped around state-terrorist relations, until recently we have seen little evidence and scholarship assessing these links.

Over the past decade, this has changed. Thanks to newly declassified intelligence files from the former Soviet Bloc, scholars have challenged Reagan-era efforts to depict Cold War–era terrorism as a type of covert warfare unleashed from the East. While most recent work shows that Moscow as well as most Soviet Bloc states had indeed created diplomatic as well as clandestine relationships with the PLO, most notably Fatah and some of its Marxist factions, there is no evidence thus far of these governments working in concert to encourage or direct international terrorist campaigns.

This new scholarship, therefore, undermines the idea of a monolith. It shows that each Soviet Bloc country followed its own tempo and reasons for engagement with Cold War jackals. Moreover, it also illuminates how these policies changed over time. Whereas some states had created alliances with certain groups, their Soviet Bloc partners often took a different—sometimes opposing—stance. The German Democratic Republic (GDR) was perhaps the most adventurous of all when it came to Cold War terrorists and revolutionaries. The country's Ministry for State Security (MfS, better known as the Stasi) provided weapons to various Palestinian factions and limited assistance to the groups led by Abu Nidal and Carlos the Jackal.[20] Nicolae Ceaușescu's Romania was rather choosy about its associations. While its Department of State Security, colloquially known as the Securitate, never collaborated with Abu Nidal and, in fact, incurred an attack by the group, it did forge a short-lived yet intense relationship with the Carlos Group, which it hired to strike its opponents abroad.[21] We also know that Polish military intelligence developed a business relationship with the ANO, which provided the regime in Warsaw with Western weapons and electronics.[22]

Nevertheless, not all of Moscow's allies were ready to forge relationships with Cold War jackals other than the PLO, and many in fact displayed a more cautious approach. For instance, Bulgaria showed more resistance and indeed reluctance to create such operational alliances.[23] Hungary was also not an enthusiastic terror supporter but rather a reluctant host to the ANO and Carlos the Jackal, who were allowed to set up a base there while being closely watched by the country's secret police and periodically asked to leave.[24] While Yugoslavia was a member of the Non-Aligned Movement, Western states often talked about Belgrade's relationship with the jackals in the same breath as they did about the Soviet Bloc. We now know that Yugoslavia was also no ardent terror supporter. In fact, new evidence suggests that it was a rather unwitting host, as it took Belgrade years to realize Carlos had set up a base there, and once it did it refused to establish an alliance with him.[25]

This book tells the story of the missing puzzle piece: Czechoslovakia's relationship with Cold War jackals. It shows that much like its other partners in the Soviet Bloc, Prague treaded its own path with regard to these groups. While it did follow the bloc's wider policy goals regarding the Palestinian umbrella organization, it received little guidance when it came to the other jackals. Accordingly, it developed its own unique way of engaging with these actors, one that was often in contrast with how they were treated by other bloc capitals. This shows that the Soviet Union was no master coordinator of an international terror network, that it did not impose a blueprint for relations with the jackals that had to be equally adopted by all bloc states, and that each of Moscow's allies organically developed its own approach to international terrorism, which varied from group to group and changed over time. In fact, these were complex and often haphazard relations frequently characterized by anxiety.[26]

Despite these recent revelations, there remain important blind spots. While intelligence archives in most of the former Soviet Bloc are becoming increasingly open, those in Moscow are yet to be made available to researchers scrutinizing the Soviet Union's engagement with Cold War jackals via the KGB (Komitet gosudarstvennoy bezopasnosti; Committee for State Security) or other services. Thanks to recent research we know that apart from striking a political and security alliance with the PLO in the late 1960s, Moscow attempted to use one of the fringe Palestinian groups as contract kidnappers and killers.[27] There is, however, limited evidence detailing Moscow's approach to other nonstate actors such as the terrorist outfits led by Abu Nidal or Carlos the Jackal. Future research will thus need to determine which Cold War jackals Moscow allied with, under what circumstances, and which ones it chose to counter.

## SMALL POWERS, BIG QUESTIONS

The story of Czechoslovakia's relationship with Cold War jackals contributes to broader debates about the international history of the Cold War. It also prompts us to rethink the dynamics within the Soviet Bloc and how small-to-medium powers make foreign policy and national security decisions.

Traditionally, historians of the Cold War have focused on high-profile events and high politics centered on the Washington-Moscow dynamic. Recently, however, we have seen a shift to a more global perspective on the ideological conflict and on the categories of the actors who made history. This is epitomized by Odd Arne Westad's *The Global Cold War*, which highlighted the fact that the conflict manifested itself in quite different ways across the globe: yes, there was frosty peace in Europe, but there were also close-call, short-of-war crises in Cuba and the Middle East and a plethora of vicious wars (e.g., in Vietnam and Angola). Moreover, his work underscored the fact that events were not solely shaped and impacted by great-power alliances, such as those between Western allies or the Warsaw Pact, but also by West-South and East-South interactions.[28]

Alongside Westad's call for a more global and nuanced interpretation of the Cold War, there has also been increased interest in the role of junior partners during the Cold War—either small and middle-size states such as East Germany, Cuba, Czechoslovakia, and Syria or nonstate actors such as the PLO and the ANC. This is based on a growing appreciation of the fact that not only great powers but also their smaller allies have their own agency and interests that drive their actions.

Most famously, Tony Smith's essay "New Bottles for New Wine" argued that the contest between the East and the West can be better understood if we appreciate the "critical ways" junior partners helped to intensify or moderate this "epic struggle"—the way that the periphery impacted the "central dynamics" of the conflict. Smith also calls for a more colorful and realistic portrayal of key actors of Cold War events—the Mandelas, the Castros, the Ulbrichts, and Wałęsas—who generated often paradoxical and complicated legacies. He encourages scholars who do have access to newly released Cold War archives to not portray them as heroes or villains but to appreciate the fluidity of their politics and actions.[29] Smith's pericentric approach to studying the Cold War—which highlights the agency and impact of junior partners on its nature—ultimately argues that an important driver of why superpower involvement and competition spread across the globe was the "deliberate policies of junior actors in the international system, which in effect pulled Moscow and Washington into situations they might otherwise have avoided."[30]

This book is a response to both calls—for a more global and less superpower-centric international history of the Cold War. By reconstructing the history of Czechoslovakia's diplomatic, security, and intelligence interactions with various Middle Eastern terrorists and revolutionaries, it explores how junior state and nonstate actors deliberately moderated, intensified, or expanded the conflict. On the one hand, it shows the agency of Cold War jackals—how they energetically courted Moscow and its allies and, in some cases, succeeded in gaining the Soviet Bloc's support. It also explains how terrorists and revolutionaries descended on Eastern European capitals as part of their struggle against the

West and how they forged alliances with key Middle Eastern allies but also what made them break away from key patrons such as Libya's Muammar Qaddafi and Syria's Hafez al-Assad.

On the other hand, it shows how Prague made decisions about whom to align with and whom to keep out in the cold. Although its policies toward third world revolutionaries were coordinated with Moscow,[31] as we shall see, Prague gradually developed its own red lines with respect to these unpredictable allies. When it came to the more radical of Cold War jackals, in the absence of an all–Soviet Bloc policy Czechoslovakia was forced to design its own way of dealing with them, which often considerably differed from that of its closest allies, such as East Germany and Poland.

Overall, by focusing on Cold War revolutionary politics, this book shows when junior states followed hegemonic interests and when they trotted their own paths with regard to international terrorists and revolutionaries. While doing so, it assesses how small and medium states contributed to the globalization of political violence and terrorism and, moreover, how they used their military, security, and intelligence services to further their foreign policy objectives.[32] Simultaneously, we get an insider's look at the numerous challenges and dilemmas junior partners faced while engaging in overt and covert liaisons with unfamiliar allies from around the globe. And we can understand the lengths that small powers are willing to go to show solidarity, attempt political influence, and satisfy the foreign policy goals of their hegemons.

This focus on small and medium states also contributes to a more holistic understanding of the Soviet Bloc. Although traditionally viewed as a homogeneous alliance of ideological and loyal partners, recent scholarship has started to undermine this idea of a monolith.[33] By detailing where Prague followed Moscow's guidance and where it forged its own path, this book shows that not all was decided in Moscow. It demonstrates that while Prague received and followed Soviet strategic guidance, when it came to its security and intelligence policies many of these were decided locally, often curbed by Prague's worries about such associations besmirching its reputation. In other words, Prague was not just Moscow's willing executioner. It had its own agency, which left a footprint on the international story of revolutionaries and terrorists.

This contributes to our understanding of how Moscow's junior partners conducted themselves as foreign and domestic security actors. It also shows the often-complicated dynamics of cohabiting in an ideological bloc with other small and medium states—each with their own interests and motivations.[34] Additionally, it also highlights the fact that Soviet Bloc governments and their national security apparats were not the omnipotent systems with unlimited capability that the regime made them out to be.[35] Instead, their intelligence services struggled with adapting to new targets and threats, much like their opposite numbers in the West.

Overall, this book situates Prague's policy toward revolutionaries and terrorists within discussions about the nature and drivers of the Cold War as well as into the context of the Soviet Bloc's policy toward the third world.

## ARCHIVES AND INTERVIEWS

This book draws on thousands of Czechoslovak communist-era foreign policy, intelligence, and security records collected across five Czech and Slovak archives, most crucially the Security Services Archive in Prague (Archiv bezpečnostních složek, or ABS), which holds millions of records of the Czechoslovak communist-era secret service, the StB.[36] Despite the importance and accessibility of this archive, its material has not yet been widely utilized in academic works available in the English language. Furthermore, this is the first book based on the voluminous recently declassified collections on the Middle East and international terrorism.

The general public and researchers were first given significant access to StB documents in 2007. This was the result of a set of laws that enabled unprecedented access to these materials. These saw a blanket declassification of all communist-era security and intelligence documents created prior to the dissolution of Czechoslovakia on December 31, 1992. What is more, they allowed for these documents to be presented in their original form—without redaction. In the same year, to enable further research based on these records, the government established the Institute for the Study of Totalitarian Regimes (Ústav pro studium totalitních režimů, or ÚSTR)—a research outfit dedicated to the study of the Nazi occupation of the Czech lands (1938–45) and the Czechoslovak communist regime (1948–89)—as well as the ABS, which became the main repository for all security and intelligence files pertinent to these periods.[37]

This opened the floodgates and saw the Czech Republic's intelligence and security community, which was until then the guardian of StB secrets, pass on millions of pages of files to the ABS. In fact, in 2007 and 2008 the Czech foreign intelligence service handed over 97 percent of all material it had inherited from the StB's foreign intelligence branch, the First Directorate. The remaining files were kept in the metaphorical vaults of the Czech Republic's intelligence service as they were deemed either crucial for the service's future work or too sensitive. The most delicate of all were documents detailing so-called live issues—operations, activities, or the work of officers and agents who switched allegiance and continued to work for the postcommunist secret state.

Unsurprisingly, most files on the Middle East and international terrorism were part of the too-sensitive-to-release 3 percent. In the late 2000s most domestic security files on this topic were also still kept under lock. In other words, in 2013, when this research commenced, there was little to go on. Soon afterward, however, following further careful assessment, the Czech security and intelligence community began releasing core files on this delicate subject to the ABS.[38] Accordingly, this author was fortunate to be the first to view many of these voluminous and freshly declassified files and sift through them as they were brought into the archive reading room on heavy-duty trolleys. Over the next decade, I processed all core files pertinent to Czechoslovakia's relations with Middle Eastern nonstate actors—namely, those on the PLO and its various splinter groups.

Arguably, this collection of materials on Middle Eastern terrorists and revolutionaries is one of the most complete anywhere in the world. First, its volume and extent are impressive. To date, the ABS has released hundreds of thousands of pages of documents detailing Prague's interaction with Cold War jackals. These are made up of foreign intelligence as well as domestic security files of various kinds: large thematic files, often focused on a specific target (an embassy or intelligence service) or a theme (such as "international terrorism") as well as detailed personal files of officers, informants, or targets. These collections contain fascinating documents, including minutes of high-level and back-channel negotiations, correspondence between the headquarters in Prague and its *rezidenturas* (intelligence outposts based at diplomatic missions) around the globe, including Lebanon, Syria, and Jordan as well as surveillance reports and photos detailing the exciting as well as the mundane from the lives of Cold War jackals.[39] This breadth of documents—especially those on Prague's foreign intelligence operations—is exceptional, even in comparison to records of other former Soviet Bloc states.

Second, this collection contains documents on international terrorism not only from Czechoslovakia but also materials produced by Hungarian, East German, Bulgarian, Polish, and Soviet intelligence and state security services. Arguably, the content of these files constitutes a unique crossroads of information generated by multiple security services east of the Iron Curtain. Third, due to the Czech Republic's liberal legislation pertaining to communist-era documents, all information in these files generated before February 15, 1990, the official date of the StB's dissolution, is unredacted. This is in stark contrast with most other archives around the globe, which tend to remove personal data and information deemed as sensitive—a process often downgrading the utility and legibility of these important historical materials. The exceptionally liberal archival legislation has not been without criticism and challenge.[40] Nevertheless, it enables the researcher to not only assess context and high policy but also to follow tactical leads crucial to the understanding activities pursued by nonstate actors.

While in its last weeks in power, the Czechoslovak communist regime engaged in StB file destruction; core documents on Cold War terrorism were largely left intact and remain remarkably complete.[41] Accordingly, Professor Christopher Andrew, the founder of British intelligence studies, describes the

ABS as "one of the most important Cold War archives to become available in recent years."[42]

Thanks to this impressive body of primary material, we are now able to study the complicated state-nonstate interactions in a new way. Most of what we knew about Czechoslovakia's interactions with the jackals has been based on external assessments from Western governments and from defectors—StB officers who escaped Czechoslovakia in the latter part of the Cold War.[43] Today, however, access to files that include diplomatic and intelligence reports, minutes of meetings, top-secret assessments, memos, and surveillance reports allows us to study such multilayered alliances "from within." Thanks to these unredacted files, we get a glimpse inside the minds of ministers, heads of services, case officers, and agents as well as their Middle Eastern partners and targets.

We are also able to observe internal debates among different foreign policy and security actors frequently tainted by doubts, hesitations, and conflicts in respect to their nonstate liaison partners. This dynamic suggests that these totalitarian systems were more pluralistic than we thought and not well-oiled bureaucracies following a singular party line. Furthermore, thanks to informants' reports, signals intelligence intercepts, and documents confiscated from Cold War jackals, we get a front-row seat to the decision-making processes of these enigmatic groups.

Archives, however, do not always tell the whole story. No matter how far we dig, there will always remain important crevices between the official record and reality (or multiple realities) as experienced by key actors. To bridge the two, or represent both, this book also rests on two dozen interviews conducted with former Czechoslovak intelligence officers, diplomats, and Communist Party representatives who witnessed Prague's attempts to navigate the disorderly world of terrorist and revolutionary diplomacy. These are complimented by interviews with national security and intelligence practitioners from the United States and the United Kingdom and a French national security judge. Their firsthand experience with Cold War jackals helps us understand how key Western states grappled with international terrorism during the formative years of transatlantic counterterrorism. Although some interviewees cannot be named, their contribution to this book is no less important.[44]

## A TERMINOLOGICAL MINEFIELD

Writing about violent nonstate actors is a terminological challenge. Groups perpetrating violence in the name of political goals have variously been referred to as freedom fighters, guerrillas, insurgents, revolutionaries, and terrorists. Decades-long attempts by politicians and scholars to settle on meaningful and universally accepted definitions of these terms have frequently been described as futile. This assessment is not entirely fair. Thanks to these exhaustive multi-stakeholder debates, we now know that these terms are inherently subjective and have a better understanding of the factors that lead to this biased approach.[45]

This subjectivity has largely been generated by the fact that each belief system, regime, and ideology chooses to define the term "terrorist" or "freedom fighter" in the context of its own political interests and security needs—perceived or real. Accordingly, states typically publicly condemn their nonstate opponents or enemies as "terrorists," whereas allies with familiar political or ideological aims are treated with more tolerance and attributed one of the less pejorative terms typically used to denote substate actors engaged in politically led violence, such as "freedom fighters" or "revolutionaries."[46]

With the rise of international terrorism in the 1960s and state efforts to introduce national counterterrorism legislation, definitions became even more important. Accordingly, states affected by or fearing potential terrorist attacks invested considerable brainpower in devising definitions of terrorism—suited to their interests, historical experience, and current threats. The high ideological polarization of the Cold War had an impact on these definitional debates. Labels were largely ascribed to groups based on ideological and strategic proximity. This created parallel universes of definitions of "terrorism"—each suiting a particular "them and us" narrative.

Ideology also shaped the Czechoslovak definition of "terrorism." In the early 1980s, Czechoslovak spies were taught that the term "terrorism" was considered "an exceptionally brutal and violent form of subversive activity" politically motivated and primarily aimed at "damaging the socialist state and order"—that is, mostly Communist Party representatives who were considered "frontrunners of socialism."[47] Ultimately, terrorism was a violent expression of the class struggle, either enacted domestically or internationally with the aim of instilling public fear.[48]

Crucially, however, terrorism was strictly divided into domestic and international. Domestic terrorism included activities such as death threats to state and party officials and vandalizing their property. Attacks on StB officers could also fall under this purview. Equally, dissidents could also be accused of plotting terrorist operations if caught distributing antiregime signs and leaflets. In this respect, terrorism was seen as an extension of psychological warfare, and perpetrators of such acts were led to them by their "hatred toward representatives of this regime" and the "socialist establishment." While the Communist Party carefully crafted the definition of "domestic terrorism," this never really materialized.[49] Nevertheless, we see that it was used largely to label opponents of the communist regime.

Prague's definition of international terrorism was much less developed. Although from the mid-1970s onward the StB was acutely aware of the presence of Cold War jackals on its territory and referred to many of them as "international terrorists," the state security apparatus never clearly defined the phenomenon. While left undefined, the regime did consider foreigners from countries where terrorism was widespread—most important, students from capitalist and developing countries—as a potential threat.[50] With respect to targets, Prague thought embassies of foreign diplomatic missions, Czechoslovak diplomatic missions abroad, government representatives, foreign dignitaries, airplanes and airports, ships, and economically important objects were most likely terrorist targets.[51]

The term "terrorism" was initially rarely used in the context of Palestinian operations. When it came to armed Palestinian campaigns in the Middle East—mostly against Israel—these were termed "military operations" or "armed struggle against the occupier" via partisan and sabotage/subversive means. In 1970 the terms "subversive," "diversion," and "extremist" were also preferred when it came to describing some of the Palestinians' most daring operations and hijackings.[52] By 1977, however, the Czechoslovak deputy minister of interior clearly defined a "terrorist" as someone who "engages in terrorist/diversion operations including hijackings," suggesting a semantic shift when it came to Palestinian operations.[53] By the time Prague struck an intelligence alliance with the PLO, key Czechoslovak officials openly mentioned terrorism at meetings with top Palestinian representatives—perhaps to implicitly communicate to their partners that Prague was done with using euphemisms.

The PLO and its main faction, Fatah, were not considered a terrorist franchise. They were "the representative of the Palestinian people," argued Prague, "leading a national liberation struggle with the goal of attaining full self-determination and the creation of an independent state on a territory, which will be liberated from Israeli aggression."[54] Although occasionally Prague did admit that there were extremist elements among the numerous Palestinian nonstate actors, we also see attempts to shift blame for such manifestations of "extremism." For instance, a 1970 ministerial document claimed that "Israel, Western imperialist circles and other enemies of a peaceful solution to the Middle East crisis try to make use of Palestinian extremism—to emphasize the impossibility of a just political solution of the crisis and to solidify Israel's position on the occupied territories."[55]

So-called extremist international terrorist groups, however, were a separate category. Prague feared these could target foreign visitors, delegations, embassies, or foreign aircraft on Czechoslovak territory. In the late 1970s "Carlos's terrorist group" was the StB's main concern.[56] Its "political nature" and "ideological profile," the StB argued, were extremist.[57] Similar concerns were raised later, when Abu Daoud, the Munich massacre commander, and members of the ANO entered Czechoslovakia. Gradually, they were largely denoted as "terrorists."

It is not the goal of this book to determine which Cold War jackals should be labeled "terrorists" and which should go down in history as "revolutionaries." Throughout the literature on the Palestinian armed struggle, these factions have been variably referred to as national liberation movements, terrorists, revolutionaries, guerrilla, or paramilitary groups. Perhaps to highlight this dichotomy, the book's subtitle refers to "terrorists and revolutionaries."

To avoid this terminological minefield, in this introduction and first two chapters of this book, the PLO and its factions are referred to as "violent nonstate actors." Terms "terror" and "terrorism" are used here interchangeably to define the tactics they chose to use during various operations directed at noncombatants or critical infrastructure targets, including hijackings, kidnappings, assassinations, car bombs, select shootings, and sabotage operations.[58] Using the term "terrorism" to refer to tactics will enable us to discuss key terrorist incidents while avoiding generalizations and complex ideological traps. In the later chapters, which deal directly with Czechoslovakia's attitude toward individual groups and factions, the book adopts Prague's terminology to denote each group. As we go along, the book will illuminate how Prague arrived at these distinctions and, ultimately, where it drew the metaphorical line between terrorists and revolutionaries.

## STRUCTURE

Chapter 1 of this book provides an overview of the formative era of Prague's engagement with violent nonstate actors. It explores the security and intelligence assistance the communist country provided mostly to African revolutionaries during the 1950s and 1960s and how it helped facilitate Cuba's international revolutionary programs. Chapter 2 depicts the ascent of Cold War international terrorism in the late 1960s and early 1970s by introducing key actors and providing a tour d'horizon of key incidents of international terrorism. It shows the inherently international nature of this terrorist wave and depicts the evolution of this threat during the closing decades of the Cold War. Crucially, it provides context to further chapters, which discuss Prague's reaction to these events and relations with key perpetrators.

Chapters 3 to 9 provide an in-depth analysis of Prague's political, security, and intelligence alliance with the PLO, specifically Yasser Arafat's Fatah faction. They show that Czechoslovakia adopted a multipolicy approach to the Palestinian umbrella organization, on one hand striking a close liaison with Arafat's men while on the other surveilling, infiltrating, and ultimately countering some of its more extreme and dangerous elements. Chapters 10 to 12 focus on the Rejectionists—two of the numerous factions that periodically left and reunited with the PLO and Fatah throughout the latter part of the Cold

War. They provide an overview of the cautious political and security approach Prague adopted toward these factions and how it used the StB to engage in so-called gray zone liaison with one of their top men.

Chapters 13 and 14 explore how Prague deployed the StB to surveil, infiltrate, and ultimately expel some of the most notorious terrorist figures of the Cold War associated with Carlos the Jackal and the ANO. The final substantive chapter, 15, critically assesses StB's Swiss Army Knife approach to Cold War jackals and draws parallels with approaches of Western European states at the time.

## NOTES

1. Václav Pokorný (X.S[práva]/3), August 8,1979, "Návrh na zavedení svazku signální: Abu Daoud," ABS [Archivu bezpečnostních složek]-728008 MV.
2. Pokorný.
3. Frederick Forsyth, *The Day of the Jackal* (London: Hutchinson, 1971).
4. See essays on this in Adrian Hänni, Thomas Riegler, and Przemyslaw Gasztold, eds., *Terrorism in the Cold War: State Support in Eastern Europe and the Soviet Sphere of Influence*, vol. 1 (London: Bloomsbury, 2021); and Adrian Hänni, Thomas Riegler, and Przemyslaw Gasztold, eds., *Terrorism in the Cold War: State Support in the West, Middle East and Latin America*, vol. 2 (London: Bloomsbury, 2021).
5. Karel Pacner, *Československo ve zvláštních službách: Díl IV* (Prague: Themis, 2002); Michal Zourek, "Operation MANUEL: Prague as a Transit Hub of International Terrorism," *Central European Journal of International & Security Studies* 9, no. 3 (2015); Daniela Richterova, "The Anxious Host: Czechoslovakia and Carlos the Jackal 1978–1986," *International History Review* 40, no. 1 (2018): 108–32; Natalia Telepneva, "'Code Name SEKRETÁŘ': Amílcar Cabral, Czechoslovakia and the Role of Human Intelligence during the Cold War," *International History Review* 42, no. 6 (2020): 1257–73; Daniela Richterova, "Terrorists and Revolutionaries: The Achilles Heel of Communist Surveillance," *Surveillance & Society* 16, no. 3 (2018): 277–97; Mikuláš Pešta, "Reluctant Revolutionaries: Czechoslovak Support of Revolutionary Violence between Decolonization and Détente," *Intelligence and National Security* (2022): 1–17; Pavel Žáček, *Ruce světové revoluce: Carlos, mezinárodní terorismus a Státní bezpečnost, 1976–1989; Edice dokumentů* (Prague: Akademia, 2022).
6. The closest we have come to such an account is Yezid Sayigh's seminal work *Armed Struggle and the Search for State: The Palestinian National Movement, 1949–1993* (Oxford: Clarendon, 1997). That said, this book also draws on memoirs of key Palestinian figures.
7. See the genesis of this thinking in Lisa Stampnitzky, *Disciplining Terror: How Experts Invented "Terrorism"* (Cambridge: Cambridge University Press, 2013); A. Hänni, "Introduction," in Hänni, Riegler, and Gasztold, *Terrorism in the Cold War*, vol. 1, 1–4.
8. John Vinocur, "Gen. Haig Unhurt as Car Is Target of Bomb on Road to NATO Office," *New York Times*, June 26, 1979.
9. "Excerpts from Haig's Remarks at First News Conference as Secretary of State," *New York Times*, January 29, 1981.

10. "Haig's Commanding Start," *Time*, February 23, 1981, https://www.cia.gov/reading room/docs/CIA-RDP90-00552R000201720005-6.pdf.
11. For an overview of these Beltway battles, see Bob Woodward, *Veil: The Secret Wars of the CIA, 1981–1987* (London: Simon & Schuster, 1987); and Adrian Hänni, "When Casey's Blood Pressure Rose: A Case Study of Intelligence Politicization in the United States," *Intelligence and National Security* 31, no. 7 (2016).
12. Richard B. Dearlove (Prague), May 16, 1975, "Visit to Prague by Yasser Arafat, 5–6 May," TNA (The National Archives) FCO 28/2695.
13. Central Intelligence Agency (CIA), "Soviet Support for International Terrorism and Revolutionary Violence," SNIE 11/2-81, https://www.cia.gov/library/reading room/docs/DOC_0000272980.pdf.
14. Claire Sterling, *The Terror Network: The Secret War of International Terrorism* (New York: Berkley Books, 1981), 12–13. Other books authored by former practitioners or journalists further contributed to the zeitgeist on international terrorism at the time: Stefan Possony and L. Francis Bouchey, *International Terrorism: The Communist Connection* (Washington, DC: American Council for World Freedom, 1978); Samuel T. Francis, *The Soviet Strategy of Terror* (Washington, DC: Heritage Foundation, 1981); Claire Sterling, *The Time of the Assassins* (New York: Holt, Rinehart & Winston, 1983); Ray S. Cline and Yonah Alexander, *Terrorism: The Soviet Connection* (New York: Crane Russak, 1984); Roberta Goren, *The Soviet Union and Terrorism* (London: Allen & Unwin, 1984); and Uri Ra'anan, Robert L. Pfaltzgraff Jr., Richard H. Shultz, Ernst Halperin, and Igor Lukes, eds., *Hydra of Carnage: International Linkages of Terrorism; The Witnesses Speak* (Lexington, MA: Lexington Books, 1986). See a good critical overview of the rising class of terrorism experts in the latter part of the Cold War in Stampnitzky, *Disciplining Terror*.
15. Sterling, *Terror Network*, 15.
16. Woodward, *Veil*, 125–26; Melvin A. Goodman, *Failure of Intelligence: The Decline and Fall of the CIA* (Lanham, MD: Rowman & Littlefield, 2008), 178.
17. See, for instance, CIA, "Soviet Support for International Terrorism and Revolutionary Violence," CIA, SNIE 11/2-81, https://www.cia.gov/library/readingroom /docs/DOC_0000272980.pdf.
18. Stella Rimington, *Open Secret: The Autobiography of the Former Director-General of MI5* (London: Arrow Books, 2001), 146; Daniel Byman, *Deadly Connections: States That Sponsor Terrorism* (Cambridge: Cambridge University Press, 2005), 1; Paul Wilkinson, *Terrorism versus Democracy: The Liberal State Response*, 3rd ed. (London: Routledge, 2011), 26–27.
19. This dichotomy was perhaps most famously demonstrated during the Margaret Thatcher era, when the British prime minister vowed never to negotiate with terrorists, while authorizing a secret MI6 back channel with the troublesome Provisional Irish Republican Army. Thatcher, in common with many other leaders, repeatedly declared that she would "never" talk to terrorists. Wilkinson, *Terrorism versus Democracy*, 80. On Thatcher and her resolve "never" to negotiate with the PIRA, see Margaret Thatcher, *The Downing Street Years* (London: HarperCollins, 1993), 83–87.
20. For instance, see the GDR's relationship with the PLO in Lutz Maeke, *DDR und PLO: Die Palästinapolitik des SED-Staates* (Berlin: De Gruyter Oldenbourg, 2017).
21. Liviu Tofan, *Sacalul Securitatii. Teroristul Carlos in solda spionajului romanesc* (Iași, Rom.: Polirom, 2013).

22. Przemysław Gasztold-Seń, "Międzynarodowi terroryści w PRL-historia niewymuszonej współpracy," *Pamięć i Sprawiedliwość* 21 (2013): 275–315; Przemysław Gasztold-Seń, "Between Geopolitics and National Security: Polish Intelligence and International Terrorism during the Cold War," in *Need to Know: Eastern and Western Perspectives*, Studies in Intelligence and Security, ed. W. Bułhak and T. Wegener Friis, 137–62 (Odense: University Press of Southern Denmark, 2014); Przemysław Gasztold-Seń, *Zabójcze układy: Służby PRL i międzynarodowy terroryzm* (Warsaw: Wydawnictwo Naukowe PWN, 2017).
23. Jordan Baev, "Infiltration of Non-European Terrorist Groups in Europe and Antiterrorist Responses in Western and Eastern Europe (1969–1991)," in *Counter Terrorism in Diverse Communities*, ed. Siddik Ekici, 58–74 (Amsterdam: IOS Press, 2011).
24. Balázs Orbán-Schwarzkopf, "Hungarian State Security and International Terrorism in the 1980s," in Hänni, Riegler, and Gasztold, *Terrorism in the Cold War*, vol. 1, 123–42.
25. Gordan Akrap, "Yugoslavia, Carlos 'the Jackal' and International Terrorism during the Cold War," in Hänni, Riegler, and Gasztold, *Terrorism in the Cold War*, vol. 1, 167–84.
26. See essays on this in Hänni, Riegler, and Gasztold, *Terrorism in the Cold War*, vols. 1 and 2; Jussi M. Hanhimäki and Bernhard Blumenau, eds., *An International History of Terrorism: Western and Non-Western Experiences* (Abingdon, UK: Routledge, 2013).
27. Christopher Andrew and Vassili Mitrokhin, *The World Was Going Our Way: The KGB and the Battle for the Third World* (New York: Basic Books, 2005); Isabella Ginor and Gideon Remez, "The KGB's Abduction Programme and the PFLP on the Cusp between Intelligence and Terrorism," in Hänni, Riegler, and Gasztold, *Terrorism in the Cold War*, vol. 1, 21–39; Adrian Hänni, "Introduction," in Hänni, Riegler, and Gasztold, *Terrorism in the Cold War*, vol. 1, 5–7.
28. Odd Arne Westad, *The Global Cold War: Third World Interventions and the Making of Our Times* (Cambridge: Cambridge University Press, 2007).
29. Tony Smith, "New Bottles for New Wine: A Pericentric Framework for the Study of the Cold War," *Diplomatic History* 24, no. 4 (2000): 567–91.
30. Smith, 572.
31. This book adopts a broad definition of the term "third world" that denotes geographical areas—Latin America, Africa, the Middle East, and Asia—of Cold War superpower competition. See more in Artemy M. Kalinovsky and Sergey Radchenko, "Introduction: The End of the Cold War in the Third World," in *The End of the Cold War and the Third World*, ed. Artemy M. Kalinovsky and Sergey S. Radchenko (London: Routledge, 2011), 1–20. The term will also be used interchangeably with "developing world."
32. For instance, see Egemen Bezci, *Turkish Intelligence and the Cold War: The Turkish Secret Service, the US and the UK* (London: Bloomsbury, 2019).
33. Philip E. Muehlenbeck and Natalia Telepneva, eds., *Warsaw Pact Intervention in the Third World: Aid and Influence in the Cold War* (London: I. B. Tauris, 2018).
34. Hope M. Harrison, *Driving the Soviets up the Wall: Soviet–East German Relations, 1953–1961* (Princeton, NJ: Princeton University Press, 2011); Sheldon Anderson, *A Cold War in the Soviet Bloc: Polish–East German Relations, 1945–1962* (London: Routledge, 2018); Laurien Crump, *The Warsaw Pact Reconsidered: International Relations in Eastern Europe, 1955–1969* (London: Routledge, 2015).

35. See more on the Soviet Bloc intelligence semblance of omnipresence versus reality in Kieran Williams and Dennis Deletant, *Security Intelligence Services in New Democracies: The Czech Republic, Slovakia and Romania*, Studies in Russia and East Europe (London: Palgrave, 2000), 32.
36. The five archives are the Security Services Archive (Archiv bezpečnostních služeb, or ABS), the National Archive (Národní archív, or NA), the Archive of the Ministry of Foreign Affairs of the Czech Republic (Archiv Ministerstva zahraničných věcí ČR, or AMZV), the Military Historical Archive (Vojenský historický archív, or VHA), and the National Memory Institute (Ústav pamäti národa, or ÚPN).
37. The ABS manages civilian as well as military documents produced by intelligence/security organizations, the Ministry of Justice, and law enforcement. Petr Kaňák, "Cesta ke zpřístupnění dokumentace československé rozvědky" (unpublished manuscript, 2023), private archive; "Zákon o Ústavu pro studium totalitních režimů a o Archivu bezpečnostních složek a o změně některých zákonů," *Sbírka zákonů, Zákony pro lidi*, https://www.zakonyprolidi.cz/cs/2007-181.
38. At the time of writing, 1 percent of StB files continue to be retained by the Czech republic's foreign intelligence service, ÚZSI (Úřad pro zahraniční styky a informace). Kaňák, "Cesta ke zpřístupnění dokumentace."
39. See the overview of different file categories in Jan Koura and Petr Kaňák, "Czechoslovak Foreign Intelligence Files," *International Journal of Intelligence and Counter-Intelligence* 37, no. 2 (2024): 21–22.
40. "O archivech StB rozhodl na Ústavním soudu jediný hlas," Echo24, January 11, 2017.
41. See more on this in Afterword: A Note on Sources.
42. Christopher Andrew, Cambridge Intelligence Seminar, Corpus Christi College, October 13, 2017.
43. Josef Frolik, *The Frolik Defection: The Memoirs of a Czech Intelligence Agent* (London: Leo Cooper, 1975); Jan Sejna, *We Will Bury You* (London: Sidgwick & Jackson, 1982); Ladislav Bittman, *The KGB and Soviet Disinformation: An Insider's View* (Washington, DC: Pergamon-Brassey's, 1985).
44. See more in Afterword: A Note on Sources.
45. For debates on definitions of terrorism, see Luis de la Calle and Ignacio Sánchez-Cuenca, "What We Talk about When We Talk about Terrorism," *Politics & Society* 39, no. 3 (2011): 451–72; Bruce Hoffman, *Inside Terrorism* (New York: Columbia University Press, 2006); and Frank Foley, *Countering Terrorism in Britain and France: Institutions, Norms and the Shadow of the Past* (Cambridge: Cambridge University Press, 2013).
46. On the subjectivity of the term "terrorism," see Martha Crenshaw, "The Subjective Reality of the Terrorist: Ideological and Psychological Factors in Terrorism," in *Current Perspectives on International Terrorism*, ed. Robert O. Slater and Michael Stohl (London: Palgrave Macmillan, 1988), 12–46. For more on the utility of definitions of terrorism, see Gilbert Ramsay, "Why Terrorism Can, but Should Not Be Defined," *Critical Studies on Terrorism* 8, no. 2 (2015): 211–28.
47. The term "terrorism" is used interchangeably with the term "terror" in Czechoslovak documents on the subject.
48. Federální ministerstvo vnitra, *Základy bezpečnostní služby II: Základní úkoly StB* (Prague: Federální ministerstvo vnitra, 1981), 18–9; 28–30.
49. Milan Beluský (XIV.S), August 31, 1982, "NÁVRH na založení objektového svazku "TERORISMUS"," ABS-24113/2.

50. Beluský.
51. Ján Hanuliak (I. Nám[ěstek] ministra vnitra ČSSR), February 18, 1977, "Zpráva o situaci na úseku problematiky terorismu v ČSSR," ABS-HFSB, a.č. H-720/II.
52. MZV [Ministerstvo zahraničních věcí] (8.t.o. [teritoriální odbor])—Kolégium ministra, March 26, 1970, "Věc: Informace o palestinském hnutí odporu," A-MZV [Archiv Ministerstva zahraničních věcí], 8.TO-T, 1970-1974, Ka 1.
53. Hanuliak, February 18, 1977.
54. Bohuslav Chňoupek (Ministr zahraničních věcí), n.d., 1976, "Důvodová zpráva," ABS-19324/2.
55. MZV (8.t.o.)—Kolégium ministra, March 26, 1970, A-MZV.
56. II.S/5-SNB [Sbor národní bezpečnosti], January 29, 1980, "Současná situace a charakteristika mezinárodního terorismu a hlavní úkoly orgánů po linii II.S-SNB," ABS-19324/1.
57. Karel Vrba (Náč. II.S)–Ján Kováč (I. Nám. ministra vnitra ČSSR), August 21, 1981, "Zvláštní informace," ABS-19324/3.
58. On the most widely used definitions, see Hoffman, *Inside Terrorism*, chap. 1. See more on terrorism as a tactic in Wilkinson, *Terrorism versus Democracy*, 17.

# PART I
# THE FORMATIVE ERA

# 1

# Czechoslovakia's Early Global Cold War

In the small hours of Christmas Day 1964, Mohammad Ali stormed out of his room in the Hotel Kosodrevina in Czechoslovakia's Low Tatra Mountains and ran into the downstairs restaurant. Here he found the source of his anger—the hotel's operations manager. Without a warning, Ali delivered the first blow. What happened next was a blur. The manager collapsed onto the wooden floor under Ali's punch, Ali's drunken friends rushed to his defense, shocked hotel employees watched the drama unfold, and agitated international guests, awoken by the brawl, rushed downstairs to demand that the fighting stop.

The steadily growing number of spectators was disconcerting, especially for one man present at the scene, a Major Forstinger. He was not at this little mountain chalet for pleasure but to accompany Ali and several other mysterious-looking foreigners on their Christmas vacation. As the group's chaperone, Forstinger had one job: to ensure his men stay under the radar. But now that all eyes were on Ali, it was clear he had failed. Although Ali was no world heavyweight boxing champion, it was obvious that this conspicuous South African Muslim knew how to fight. Moreover, intoxicated and agitated, he was now shouting and loudly boasting to the reluctant spectators about his revolutionary credentials. Czechoslovakia's sabotage and guerrilla training program for uMkhonto we Sizwe (MK), the underground armed wing of the South African Communist Party and the ANC, was about to be blown.[1]

In the late 1950s and 1960s, communist Czechoslovakia engaged in covert liaison and provided financial, military, and intelligence assistance to third world revolutionaries. A crucial part of this venture was a clandestine training program that Prague delivered to more than a hundred fighters. This boutique covert assistance scheme was designed to improve the capacity of and gain political leverage over mostly African nonstate actors—national liberation movements and so-called nongoverning political parties. By doing so, Prague hoped to accelerate the fall of colonialism and to create alliances across the developing world. This was about helping the Soviet Bloc get a foothold in the region. It was also as much about keeping the West down and out as it was about ensuring that future postcolonial third world elites would gravitate toward the bloc—be it out of genuine fondness or a sense of obligation.

Running this operation was, however, no easy feat. Although Prague was an early and enthusiastic supporter of third world revolutionaries, it was not entirely fit for the job. While the Czechoslovaks tried to build close ties with top third world revolutionaries, trust and control proved difficult to establish. Crucially, Prague struggled to deliver well-calibrated training programs and achieve a level of deniability, which would avoid putting the country's reputation, business interests, and trainee lives in jeopardy. In many ways, Prague's engagement with nonstate actors in this early Cold War period and the challenges it presented informed its later approach to the Middle Eastern jackals who appeared on the world stage at the end of the 1960s.

## "COLOUR THE GLOBE OUR SHADE OF RED"

In the mid-1950s the superpowers became increasingly interested in expanding their influence. With Europe firmly divided between the East and the West and eager to avoid direct confrontation possibly resulting in a nuclear crisis, the superpowers took their Cold War to the third world. The Soviet Union, looking to fight "imperialists and colonialists," and the United States, ready to take on "international communism," adopted a set of ideological and economic strategies that would make them worthy contestants in the competition over the developing world.[2] According to historian Odd Arne Westad, to prove the utility and applicability of each party's ideology, "they needed to change the world."[3]

And it was the newly independent actors in the third world that provided a suitable stage for this ideological struggle. In search of both recognition and aid, many of these countries (re)emerging from behind the veil of colonization sought weapons from superpowers to solidify their power domestically as well as regionally. By the 1970s developments unfolding throughout the third world, whether in Chile, Cambodia, Iran, or the Democratic Republic of Congo (DRC), could not be viewed as peripheral but instead became crucial for the wider conduct of the Cold War.[4]

The Soviet Union's policy toward the third world was complex, inconsistent, and often paradoxical. As a matter of practical foreign policy, Moscow's interest in the third world began during the Nikita Khrushchev era.[5] With a shift from previously preferred armed interventions to a focus on government-to-government links with countries in the third world, military and economic assistance became key to Moscow's fight against colonialism and imperialism. At the famed February 1956 Twentieth Congress of the Communist Party of the Soviet Union, Chairman Khrushchev reportedly boasted, "They [third world countries] now have no need to go begging to their oppressors for modern equipment. They can obtain such equipment in the socialist countries." This new third world foreign policy triggered reforms within the Soviet Union's government infrastructure. Accordingly, academic institutes focusing on the third world were set up to deepen understanding of these countries. The Communist Party established two new departments focusing on international affairs and foreign communist parties. Moreover, the country's intelligence community, the KGB as well as the GRU, the Soviet Union's military intelligence outfit, were reorganized to help facilitate this new policy.[6]

In the early 1960s, competition over influence in the third world became essential to the Soviets and the existence of socialism.[7] Under the leadership of Leonid Brezhnev from 1964 to 1982, Moscow stepped up its involvement across Africa, the Middle East, Asia, and Latin America.[8] Gradually, however, it also learned that its interests could swiftly be undercut by local developments, such as the overthrow of Moscow's protégés or some of their key clients turning against the superpower. This was a hard education for the leaders of the Soviet Union, showing them that they could not exercise unlimited influence over the third world. As a consequence, by the 1980s the Soviet Union and its allies became more selective about their support and would not back just any "progressive" government or force. To deploy significant assistance, they would need to be confident that the recipient regime was a stable and dedicated ally.[9]

In the 1950s and 1960s, Moscow's allies followed suit, setting up their own paths to engagement "with" and "in" the third world. As East Germany's former head of foreign intelligence, Markus Wolf, later admitted, the bloc's desire to engage was about earthly interests but also very much about ideology: "Although we examined strategic, economic, and military factors before becoming involved in a developing country, we, like the West, saw our activities primarily as part of a greater struggle for influence and an attempt to colour the globe our shade of red."[10]

Adding to the complexities, in the 1950s and 1960s Moscow and its allies also forged alliances with various third world national liberation movements, which roughly fell into three categories: anticolonial movements, such as those in Zimbabwe and Mozambique; separatists, including the Eritreans and the Kurds; and a mixed form of national liberation movements, not strictly anticolonial but neither separatist, which included the ANC and the PLO. Most Soviet Bloc support was channeled to anticolonial movements.[11]

Moscow and its allies did not follow a single authoritative model in their relations with national liberation movements. Their level of commitment and control varied, ranging from opposition through propaganda support to proxy intervention, advisers, and even large-scale Soviet intervention. The nature and degree of engagement was determined by a number of factors: internally by ideology, organization, composition, leadership, or means of struggle and externally by Sino-Soviet competition; local, regional, or global factors; East-West relations; or Soviet relations with the ruling government.[12]

Ideologically, many of the newly established movements in the developing world were drawn to the Soviet Union. Most third world rebellions, seeking moral and intellectual legitimacy against a background of colonialism, were leftist but not necessarily communist. Some were pushed further eastward by their former colonial metropole trying to make them choose sides in the Cold War. Accordingly, at the end of the 1960s, there was a decided turn toward Marxism among leaders of developing countries and within liberation movements. This was triggered by a further set of factors: disillusionment with postcolonial leadership, which in some cases had become autocratic; the assumed fairness of Marxism-Leninism, which was in line with the goals of their revolutions; and international events, including the performance of the United States in Vietnam and the international ramifications of the Cuban Revolution.[13]

Moscow extended a mixture of overt and covert support to global revolutionaries. On the surface, it presented itself as a prominent and loud advocate of select third world states—supporting them politically and diplomatically and providing further humanitarian and financial support. Simultaneously, at the United Nations and other international forums, it advocated for national liberation movements and their just fight against oppressive colonizers. It invited them into student organizations, pursued cultural ties, and educated the third world elite.[14] Under the surface, Moscow also provided significant support by way of covert liaison, supply of arms, and military and intelligence equipment as well as training to its partners in the developing world.[15]

These were risky liaisons as these national liberation movements often operated in unstable regions and environments, supplies had to be delivered in the utmost secrecy, and alliances were often shifting. Nevertheless, Moscow took these risks because the potential benefits presented an incredible opportunity to create new alliances and project its own influence over the continent. Providing covert financial, military, and intelligence support in time of need was seen as a gateway into the hearts and minds of new leaders across the developing world.

Although there was no master plan, Moscow's approach to the third world was to be done in conjunction with its "junior partners," which, Khrushchev envisioned, should play more independent roles on the world stage.[16] To enhance the power of the Soviet Bloc, he encouraged Eastern European allies to pursue an "activist foreign policy" in the third world.[17] Czechoslovakia soon became Moscow's most willing junior partner in its global pursuit of allies.

## ASSISTANCE TO THIRD WORLD REVOLUTIONARIES

Czechoslovakia was well positioned to take up this challenge and had just the right mix of credentials to help Moscow project its influence across the developing world. First, it had the right connections. During the interwar period, thanks to being highly industrialized and becoming one of the world's key arms producers, Prague established economic and diplomatic relations with an impressive number of countries in Asia, Africa, and Latin America.[18] Owing to this legacy, in the 1950s and 1960s Prague had more embassies and consulates in the West and across the third world than Moscow. Second, during decolonization, Czechoslovakia's "small-state" status appealed to leaders of developing nations who were somewhat suspicious of superpowers.[19] Accordingly, in the 1950s and 1960s Prague became the go-to capital for many leaders from Africa, Asia, and Latin America looking for guns, know-how, and cash.[20]

Third, the Czechoslovak foreign intelligence service operating under the umbrella of the StB—the First Directorate—was ready and willing to join Moscow's global covert initiatives and campaigns. Since its establishment in the early 1950s, the service had closely allied its own goals with those of the Soviet Union and tailored its covert operations accordingly. This close alignment meant that Prague engaged in global operations designed to benefit Moscow and the Soviet Bloc.[21]

So, not only was Czechoslovakia the best-connected of Moscow's junior partners and viewed positively across the third world—it was also willing and ready to engage in operations beyond its own national foreign policy objectives in favor of Moscow's greater good.[22] This made the country exceptionally well placed to also join Moscow's battle for the "hearts and minds" of third world leaders. Similar logic led Prague to support nonstate actors in their fight against colonial regimes as well as those political parties it was keen to see in power. It was about forging alliances with potential future elites, about supplying matériel and expertise that could help them achieve power and about influencing the way they viewed the ideological struggle between the East and the West.

Prague began liaising, financing, arming, and training third world (mostly African) revolutionaries in the late 1950s. For the next decade, this small-scale covert venture would deliver thousands of dollars, provide tons of explosives and weapons, and train a variety of mostly African nonstate actors. These programs were regarded as a means of projecting "long-term influence on the thinking of foreign nationals," which would hopefully impact the further progressive direction of these nations, where the military often stood at the epicenter of power.[23]

The recipients of Prague's aid could roughly be divided into two categories: national liberation movements and nongoverning parties. When it came to the former, Prague's covert support was provided to three movements that were fighting against Portuguese colonial empire: the African Party of Independence of Portuguese Guinea and Cape Verde Islands (PAIGC), the People's Movement for the Liberation of Angola (MPLA), and the Liberation Front of Mozambique (FRELIMO). Furthermore, Prague hosted members of two Southern African groups: the MK and the Zimbabwe African People's Union (ZAPU). Prior to independence, it also provided covert assistance to the Front de libération nationale (FLN; Algerian National Liberation Front) and gave a one-off donation of matériel to the Front for the Liberation of Occupied South Yemen (FLOSY). The latter category comprised nongoverning communist parties, namely, the Iraqi Communist Party and the Kenya African National Union (KANU).[24]

These liaisons with Prague were in most part instigated by the nonstate actors. Typically, they would approach and request assistance from Czechoslovak Communist Party representatives (in Czechoslovakia or at international events), diplomats, or intelligence officers stationed abroad. The way some alliances with African groups came about could be rather haphazard. According to Eduard Kukan, a Moscow-educated Africanist who served in the 1960s as a junior diplomat in the Sub-Saharan Africa Department at the Czechoslovak Ministry of Foreign Affairs, sometimes more tactical and earthlier factors tipped the scales. Support for African revolutionaries could be determined simply by how they impressed a certain Communist Party bureaucrat or diplomat. Kukan, who started his four-decade-long diplomatic career in Zambia, recalls, "Here, all these groups—ZAPU, ZANU, ANC, SWAPO, FRELIMO—had a little village where they had their offices in small shacks. We, Soviet Bloc diplomats (without coordinating with each other), would set up meetings with them and invite them for dinners. Some of them remained friends for life—the president of Mozambique, the minister of foreign affairs of Angola, top representatives of the ANC. So, these contacts were sometimes quite random and accidental."[25]

While the beginnings may have been haphazard, the final decision on which group to support was ultimately a strategic one made in close coordination with Moscow. During this time, third world assistance seekers had to fit strategic criteria, such as demonstrating a track record of good relations with Soviet Union and sufficient distance from its rivals, most notably China. On the national level, a number of institutions were key to Prague's foreign policy and hence its support for national liberation movements. The ultimate decision-maker was the Politburo of the Central Committee of the Czechoslovak Communist Party, populated by the party's general secretary (usually also the country's president), select ministers, and Communist Party officials. The party's foreign policy decisions were crafted by the powerful International Department of the Communist Party, which practically called the shots at Prague's Ministry of Foreign Affairs—nothing being approved without its consent. According to Kukan, who served at the Czechoslovak foreign ministry for over two decades and later became Slovakia's foreign minister, "Every time I prepared materials for the government, these needed to be discussed with the Central Committee of the Communist Party, and this had to be explicitly stated in the document. Otherwise, no one would read it."[26]

The country's assistance to third world revolutionaries was carried out by two key players. The First Directorate—Prague's foreign intelligence branch—was fundamental to this effort. It existed as part of the StB—a mammoth, fluid, and multifaceted institution—which was divided into multiple "directorates" (*správy*). With the First Directorate overseeing foreign intelligence, other directorates focused on counterintelligence against domestic and foreign enemies, surveillance, and technical and signals intelligence. Furthermore, the StB presided over the passports and visas agenda, investigations, training, and education.

The First Directorate was intimately connected with its counterparts in Moscow. In fact, to oversee the more junior services within the Soviet Bloc, Moscow sent so-called advisers to key institutions in East Central European capitals. KGB advisers sent to the Ministry of Interior, also known colloquially as "Mr. P,"[27] served in different branches of the intelligence and security apparatus and were there to exercise control and facilitate liaison but also to collect information from its ally and engage in joint operations against enemy targets. Their privileged status enabled them access to sensitive information on operations and identities of StB collaborators and informers, and they were also able to influence the StB's plans and activities.[28]

In the mid-1950s, Prague's First Directorate became a global service. By 1968 it had set up rezidenturas in thirty-nine countries across the globe. As its mandate grew, so did its ranks. Whereas in 1953 the First Directorate had 360 employees, fifteen years later this number almost quadrupled to 1,236, with 352 officers stationed abroad.[29] Apart from fighting the "principal adversary"—a term used to primarily denote the United States but also its close allies the United Kingdom, France, and West Germany as well as so-called imperialist organizations such as the North Atlantic Treaty Organization (NATO) and the European Community—the First Directorate gradually emerged as a self-proclaimed guardian of the third world from Western influence. Its statutes bound it to undermine the influence of "imperialist powers" in these "underdeveloped nations" as well as to provide support to the "national liberation movement," which involved assistance for nonstate groups.[30]

The Ministry of Defense also played an important supporting role with regard to third world revolutionaries. While not in charge of forging or managing these alliances, it was the provider of most weapons and military equipment that was sold or gifted to African nations and national liberation movements. Moreover, it ran its own training venture in Czechoslovakia.[31] Remarkably, despite running in parallel, these military assistance programs for revolutionaries were largely separate from the security and intelligence ventures run by the Ministry of the Interior, with no regular interaction among cadets. In fact, at times the Defense Ministry lamented that cooperation with the Interior Ministry was "unsuitable" and argued that "there would be no harm" in knowing more about the security and intelligence training programs and experience. This perhaps underlined the standing of these two institutions with regard to third world revolutionaries, with the Ministry of the Interior and its officers clearly playing a leading role.

Support provided to these groups was a multistage endeavor. Typically, Prague first provided its liaison partners with a supply of cash and weapons. This "special material"—a Soviet Bloc euphemism for arms and military gear—gifted to nonstate actors was usually a mixture of pistols, rifles, anti-tank rockets, grenades, knives, explosives, and mines. Some groups would also be provided with more elaborate military or communication equipment. Although we do not know the total amount of weapons Prague supplied to its third world nonstate partners during this era, the records of individual orders give a good indication of how much Prague was willing to commit in one go.

In 1965 the Communist Party Politburo gave a green light for its First Directorate to deliver the following to ZAPU: five hundred rifles, two hundred pistols, five hundred submachine guns, fifty light machine guns, five heavy machine guns, one thousand attack grenades, one ton of TNT and detonation equipment, and twenty magnetic compasses.[32] Typically, these were not new, cutting-edge weapons, but older, decommissioned items largely captured during World War II and held in the reserve of the Ministry of the Interior. To achieve deniability, Czechoslovakia was keen to provide mostly foreign weapons and ammunition without manufacturer designation.[33] Moreover, it tried to further conceal its involvement by, in some cases, using middlemen. As at the time Tanzania was somewhat of a hub for national liberation movements from across the continent, its Ministry of Defence played an important role in Prague's covert supplies to these groups. While Prague would deliver the cargo to the port of Dar es Salaam, Tanzanian officials would help distribute these weapons to appropriate national movements that were at the time based on their territory.[34]

In addition to providing weapons, Prague—often in sync with Moscow—ran covert operations in support of third world states and nonstate actors in Africa, which included building networks of clandestine contacts across the continent.[35] To achieve more influence but also help build capacity of friendly leaders, during this time the First Directorate sent their officers as advisers to three African nations and one nonstate actor, PAIGC.[36] Furthermore, when it came to leaders of African nonstate revolutionary groups, Prague's spies also sought to create relations with key players.

Czechoslovakia's most prized intelligence relationship among African revolutionaries was that with PAIGC's founder and general secretary, Amílcar Cabral, one of the most recognizable African revolutionaries of the era. As part of this arrangement, Prague gained insight into African revolutionary politics, and Cabral received the financial and military assistance his movement needed.

This was, however, no hierarchical arrangement but one that resembled liaison rather than a typical handler-informer relationship. As recent scholarship shows, while Prague's aid to Cabral was significant, this gave the First Directorate little leverage over the West African revolutionary group. Cabral often disagreed with Prague's advice on military strategy—most notably when his primary contact, a Czechoslovak intelligence officer, contact suggested PAIGC use sabotage to assert its standing.[37] While Prague struck the alliance at a crucial time in PAIGC's campaign and provided significant support, it failed to get the upper hand. Exerting power and control over third world revolutionaries was an elusive prospect—a lesson the First Directorate would learn time and time again.

Most recipients of Czechoslovak special material also received training— in most cases in Czechoslovakia. Based on rough estimates, approximately 120 cadets were trained as part of this covert assistance scheme in the 1950s and 1960s.[38] Initially, this venture seemed quite ad hoc as the mostly African cadets were trained in safe houses scattered across Czechoslovakia. By 1963 this approach became more centralized as foreign cadets were taught guerrilla tactics and later security tradecraft at the Central School of the Ministry of the Interior—briefly named the Felix E. Dzerzhinsky Central School (Ústřední škola Felixe Edmundoviče Dzeržinského)—in Prague-Vinoř.[39]

In parallel with this Interior Ministry track, from 1961 to 1965 the Czechoslovak army also ran a top-secret training venture. This was housed at the Antonín Zápotocký Military Academy (Vojenská akademie Antonína Zápotockého, or VAAZ), the country's main military higher-education facility, in Brno, a key local metropole. In 1960 Prague's army established the Faculty of Foreign Studies at VAAZ, which became the main site for a large-scale for-profit training program for third world state militaries, including those of Egypt, Indonesia, Syria, Afghanistan, Guinea, Uganda, and Cuba.[40] In parallel with this impressive program for state actors, the Faculty of Foreign Studies was also responsible for covertly training nonstate actors, a program run on a strict pro bono basis.

Both the military and the First Directorate trained their third world clients in sabotage and guerrilla warfare. With most courses being six to twelve months long, this gave instructors enough time to deliver theory as well as engage in exercises that entailed learning how to operate weapons and gear supplied to the groups by Czechoslovakia. Cadets were taught how to navigate different terrain with as well as without navigation equipment. They were shown how to assemble and operate pistols, rocket-propelled grenades (RPGs), and hand grenades and engage in hand-to-hand combat. Moreover, they were trained in using multiple types of explosives on various targets behind enemy lines. Much of this training was practical, but most courses also involved theoretical modules and exposed the cadets to direct and indirect ideological education.[41]

ILLUSTRATION 1.1. Monument to V. I. Lenin on Lenin Boulevard in front of the Antonín Zápotocký Military Academy in Brno, 1975. *Czech Press Agency, ČTK / Korčák Vít*

The overall objectives of this covert training scheme were thus partly professional and partly political. On one hand, the foreigners were invited to travel halfway around the globe to improve their command of sabotage, guerrilla warfare, and security/intelligence tradecraft. This was meant to enable them to operate the Czechoslovak weaponry gifted to their organizations as well as improve their guerrilla warfare and sabotage skills. On the other, the months-long training in Czechoslovakia was also an exercise in indoctrination. During their stay, Prague's military and security instructors would use direct and indirect ways to promote socialism, nudge foreign trainees to adopt socialist principles and ways of thinking, and bring them back to their units at home. The goal was to "fully win them over to our side."[42]

## BEST-LAID PLANS

This cunning plan of fully winning over revolutionaries from the developing world, however, proved to be no easy feat. Prague's performance as a sabotage and guerrilla warfare instructor bore mixed results. Although many of the training courses were evaluated as "successful" on paper, the venture was plagued by various challenges. Crucially, the Czechoslovak military academy tasked with training third world partisans had little experience with training in unconventional warfare. Accordingly, the early days were tough as it had to develop this expertise on the go. Instructors, whose expertise was in conventional warfare, were largely armchair experts in partisan strategy and tactics. They also lacked adequate textbooks and had to rely on Western writing on irregular warfare to educate themselves as well as their cadets. Gradually, however, Prague developed its own partisan syllabus and expertise.[43]

Prague's competence was further questioned when it was found to be teaching similar content to groups that operated in very different political and operational environments.[44] This was, however, not purely Prague's fault. Often, the VAAZ military academy had little time for course preparation and often had limited, if any, information about the incoming groups of trainees. Due to the ad hoc nature of this covert enterprise and the inherently disorganized character of revolutionary politics, it did not know exactly when their partisan cadets would arrive, how many, and what kind of training they required or were suitable for. This made it virtually impossible to design well-tailored courses prior to the trainees' arrival and assessment.[45]

In terms of qualifications and military skill, Czechoslovakia's training courses attracted a very eclectic group of people. Some had formal education, while others were illiterate. Some were experienced fighters or soldiers, while others were complete novices. And some were politically conscious, while others not so much. Accordingly, with each incoming group, Prague had to make some difficult choices with regard to its curriculum, calibrating it in a way that would best help cadets achieve the desired or, in some cases, at least a minimal level of proficiency. Illiteracy was one such problem that would prove to have significant impact on cadets' performance and military training experience. When an eight-member group of PAIGC members arrived at the VAAZ military academy, their lecturers realized half of the cohort was illiterate. This significantly slowed down the course. Indeed, Czechoslovak instructors had to drop several core classes, including a weeklong resilience-building training course.[46] The Ministry of the Interior struggled with similar difficulties.[47]

Other challenges also plagued the covert program. Many cadets were completely new to combat. Prior to their arrival in Czechoslovakia, they had worked in noncombat resistance roles—for instance, in recruitment or propaganda—and had little understanding of guerrilla warfare.[48] If they were ready to learn, Prague redesigned its increasingly more professional programs to meet them where they were. Nevertheless, not all arrivals seem to have traveled to Czechoslovakia enthusiastically or even voluntarily. Some appeared to have been problematic cadets sent by their organizations to attend these guerrilla training programs halfway around the world in order to be "reeducated."[49]

While they were training these diverse groups on their territory, the Czechoslovaks also subjected them to ideological education. There were two ways of indoctrinating the cadets. Some groups were subject to "direct political education," by which they would attend lectures on Marxism-Leninism, the evolution of the socialism, or the evils of capitalism. Others were exposed to "indirect political education," which would entail trips to local factories and agricultural plants, films about the virtues of socialism or the Czechoslovak anti-Nazi resistance during World War II, and group discussions of these events. Most nonstate actors trained in Czechoslovakia received both direct and indirect political education.

In most cases, the Czechoslovak instructors used the English-language version of a Soviet textbook called *Fundamentals of Marxism-Leninism* to expose cadets to the principles of a communist regime. In an effort to turn them to this ideology, they discussed concepts key to Marxism at dedicated ideology lessons. The course leadership saw potential converts as very useful propagators of socialism abroad.[50] Some cadets were, however, not open to ideological conversion. With respect to some of the members of the South African MK, Prague had doubts whether the political and ideological principles they were taught had any impact at all. In fact, as they were discharged, the military academy wondered whether in the future it might be more feasible to first educate the South Africans in ideology and only then proceed to military training—using it as a reward for first achieving a more strategic alignment.[51]

Some groups not only resisted ideological indoctrination but also revolted against the strict military discipline typical for such training programs. In comparison with the Angolan MPLA and KANU participants, the MK cadets were considered the most impulsive. Their problems frequently had to be addressed by people high up in the faculty as well as other partner organizations.[52] Ultimately, in 1965, when the Faculty of Foreign Studies was discharging a group of ten MK revolutionaries, they lamented that these were not the enlightened, tough, courageous, and patient fighters for the "rights of the colored" that Prague thought they would be. The group had such major discipline issues that one of its cadets had to be sent back home. This was not a completely unusual occurrence even with the state actors, but as nonstate numbers were much smaller, expulsions were more visible, caused disruption to the course, and had more palpable impact on the morale and reputation of the group.[53]

Finally, although this venture was not designed to generate profits for Prague and was sold as an "act of solidarity," Czechoslovakia soon realized that such altruistic support came at a rather high financial cost. Although the final budget of Prague's solidarity programs remains elusive, we know that the Defense Ministry estimated cost for forty-five nonstate actor cadets was roughly today's equivalent of $1.7 million.[54] Accordingly, fierce interinstitutional battles over who would continue financing this expensive covert program ensued among the key ministries involved. While necessary in terms of security, the small-group format—which sometimes saw a cohort of two or three—was seen as uneconomical. For a nine-month training of two partisans, Prague spent today's equivalent of $200,000.[55] This raised eyebrows and caused concerns about the sustainability of the top-secret program.

## (IM)PLAUSIBLE DENIABILITY

In addition to the operational challenges associated with running multiple covert programs for third world revolutionaries, Prague was concerned about deniability. There were good reasons for Moscow and Prague to run these programs covertly—reputation, business interests, and trainees' lives were at stake. From the early years of its liaison with third world violent nonstate actors, Czechoslovakia took its reputation quite seriously. Although it was an enthusiastic supporter of the national liberation struggle in the diplomatic realm, direct military and intelligence interference in vicious wars of national liberation was quite another thing. Prague did not want to be named and shamed for contributing to atrocities or any large-scale attacks conducted by their nonstate allies.

Enjoying significant global status, the Czechoslovaks feared condemnation, especially in international political arenas such as the United Nations, where unmasking and highlighting Prague's engagement could be used to discredit the entire Soviet Bloc as well as its numerous peace initiatives. Prague was particularly worried about the potential wrath of those colonial powers who were still clutching on to the remnants of their empires in the third world. One such exposure of Prague's arms-dealing enterprise occurred in 1959 when the country's main arms export company, Omnipol, sold almost six hundred tons of weapons and ammunition to the Algerian FLN during its almost decade-long independence war with France, using Morocco as the middleman. Only moments prior to the cargo's arrival in Casablanca, French authorities intercepted the Czechoslovak ship *Lidice* carrying the contraband. The incident resulted in a diplomatic standoff with Paris, public condemnation, and termination of the careers of prominent Czechoslovak diplomats and the head of Omnipol.[56]

Prague also feared public scolding from Portugal for its assistance to national liberation movements active in its colonies. For instance, while training Angolan

MPLA fighters, Czechoslovakia was particularly concerned about the Portuguese government finding out about the clandestine venture and triggering an anti-Czechoslovak campaign at the United Nations.[57] International backlash of such magnitude could impact Prague's campaigns against the West—namely, make its condemnations of international aggression by the United States and other capitalist countries seem hypocritical.

Furthermore, publicity around these covert programs was also not good for business. Although the Soviet Union and Czechoslovakia had clear favorites when it came to wars of national liberation, this did not mean that the Soviet Bloc would automatically cease economic ties with their clients' oppressors. For instance, throughout the time Prague was training South African antiapartheid MK fighters, it was slow to reduce trade with Pretoria's increasingly brutal apartheid regime. Despite the death of dozens in 1960 in what became known as the Sharpeville massacre and the subsequent state of emergency that led to thousands of detentions and the outlawing of the ANC as well as other antiapartheid organizations, it took Prague another five years to end its diplomatic and economic relations with South Africa. This measure put an end to today's equivalent of $22.6 million of annual profit for Czechoslovakia.[58]

Keeping its solidarity programs under wraps was also necessary to protect the trainees from the governments they were at war with. Prague knew it was taking sides in what were often vicious conflicts and arguably contributing to their escalation by providing one side with the means to fight these wars and the ideology to fuel them. It was also aware of how colonial governments viewed its unacknowledged assistance to national liberation movements: "Undoubtedly, the trainees' stay in Czechoslovakia was an important experience and, in many ways, quite likely contributed to increasing their hatred for the current regime in SAR [South African Republic]. The very fact that they studied in the CSSR [Czechoslovakia] makes them no. 1 enemies of the regime."[59]

Moreover, Moscow and Prague understood that most of their clients' partisan organizations—such as the MK and the MPLA—were banned in their homelands. Naturally, then, they feared that if the Portuguese or South African governments were able to track down details about its training courses, they would be in a better position to arrest trainees returning to their nations or territories to rejoin the national liberation struggle. In fact, Prague was warned about this by a group of MK cadets it was hosting. They lamented that the future of MK's foreign trainings was uncertain due to a recent arrest of a nine-member group of partisans returning from training in Ethiopia while crossing the border back into South Africa.[60] This fear of getting caught was felt particularly strongly by those cadets who were seasoned members of their local resistance organizations and had previously been arrested for antigovernment activity.[61] They were already on their governments' radar and had to take special care when rejoining the struggle. The highly publicized 1963–64 Rivonia Trial, which led to Nelson Mandela's decades-long incarceration, sent a clear message to his followers that Pretoria was ready to prosecute and deliver harsh sentences to those engaged in the antiapartheid struggle.

Achieving deniability, however, was not an easy feat. Routes from Africa and Latin America to Central Europe at the time were treacherous enough for regular travelers. But when traveling incognito, extra precautions had to be taken to avoid exposure. Accordingly, when relocating from places such as Tanzania or the Middle East without arousing suspicion or leaving a trace, revolutionaries had to follow labyrinthine routes designed to shake off a potential tail. To prevent leaks and ensure deniability, some cadets were kept in the dark as to their final destination until the last possible moment.

Such trips could be exceptionally precarious. A two-man MK cell trained at the VAAZ military academy had a particularly difficult time keeping its mission secret and returning to Africa. After the completion of their course in February 1963, the men were sent back to Tanzania via London. Their travel plans were, however, disrupted by two vigilant British border police officers who found it suspicious that these "students," who had just flown in from Prague, did not have a Czechoslovak visa in their passport. As their answers failed to satisfy the British officials, the duo was interrogated and their bags searched. This revealed irreversible proof that the two men were members of the South African resistance: a letter from Oliver Tambo, the future president of the ANC, written on the organization's letterhead and discussing details of foreign training. This was enough for them to be denied entry. Although the British seemed to have sympathized with their struggle, they were adamant about not letting these two revolutionaries onto Her Majesty's soil and gave them two options: get on the next flight to Prague or be sent directly to South Africa. The MK fighters' cover story was clearly weak, and hence if sent straight to South Africa, they were sure to face trouble at the border, if not arrest.[62] And so they chose to return to Prague where they would spend several frustrating months waiting for the Czechoslovak government and their South African comrades to find a safe way of getting them to Tanzania. This was a traumatizing experience for the MK cadets and one that made Prague even more cautious about the perils of such covert operations. To avoid similar threats of exposure, Prague pledged to train future South African groups in counterintelligence and secrecy.[63]

The covert assistance program had to be kept secret not only abroad but also on Czechoslovak territory. News of sabotage and guerrilla training could spread fast, especially among foreign journalists, diplomats, and international students studying in Central Europe. Czechoslovakia thus adopted measures aimed at keeping things quiet. First, it attempted to keep the revolutionaries studying at the military's foreign faculty separate from all the other students from the third world, who were sent to Brno for training as part of an overt business and military assistance program for states. Second, cadets were admitted under false nationalities and identities. Members of the Angolan MPLA were registered under Guinean identities; the South Africans traveled under Tanzanian passports. Nevertheless, both measures proved deniability to be implausible. Despite strict orders not to mingle, the revolutionaries made friends with cadets from Egypt and Afghanistan who were not part of the covert venture. Moreover, thanks to a series of quite awkward encounters, the Kenyans discovered that their new "Tanzanian" friends could not speak Swahili and in fact knew very little about their alleged homeland. They quickly concluded that their fellow trainees were indeed South Africans.[64]

Equally, Prague tried to keep the presence of third world revolutionaries secret from the local population. But this strategy also proved imperfect, especially when cadets left for vacation outside the clandestine facility. At no point was this more apparent than during that fateful night when Mohammad Ali and his colleagues found themselves in the middle of the very public scandal in the Hotel Kosodrevina. The brawl with hotel employees—which ensued after Ali was found consorting with a (possibly underage) female member of the hotel staff—attracted attention from dozens of international guests staying at the holiday retreat in the middle of the snowy mountains. Fearing further exposure, the trainees' Christmas vacation was immediately cut short, and Ali was removed from the course. The incident taught Prague that if cadets displayed signs of disobedience, it was better to send them home early rather than wait for them to expose the operation publicly at a later stage.[65]

Overall, Prague's assistance to African revolutionaries revealed that engagement with controversial nonstate actors from halfway around the globe was a rather taxing exercise, characterized by lack of control and anxiety about possible exposure and blowback. Czechoslovakia's involvement in another clandestine venture run from the Western Hemisphere would evoke similar uneasiness.

## A REVOLUTIONARY LIFELINE

In addition to arming and training African national liberation movements, Prague assisted nonstate actors staging revolutions in their homelands in various other ways. Most famously, throughout the 1960s Czechoslovakia enabled its Cuban allies to use its territory for transporting hundreds of Latin American revolutionaries to and from the isolated island. Much like its other ventures, Prague's engagement in this covert operation was tainted by challenges, anxiety, and fear of reputational damage.

In December 1962 the deputy head of the Cuban intelligence service, Carlos Chaín Soler, turned to the Czechoslovak *rezident*—the senior officer heading

Prague's intelligence outpost based at its embassy in Havana—to ask for assistance with transporting seven members of the Venezuelan Communist Party, who had just completed their guerrilla training in Cuba, back to Caracas. It was shortly after the Cuban Missile Crisis, which had brought the superpowers to the brink of war and resulted in a harsh embargo being imposed on the communist nation. Cuba was isolated, with Czechoslovak State Airlines being one of the few carriers connecting the island to the rest of the world. Prague's rezidentura acted swiftly and, with endorsement from Moscow, administered the group's transit back home via Central Europe.[66] This one-off favor eventually turned into an almost decade-long transnational covert operation. For the next seven years Czechoslovakia served as a lifeline for Cuba's international revolutionary venture. It served as a logistical crossroads for over a thousand Latin American and some Middle Eastern revolutionaries en route to or from Cuba, where they attended political, ideological, security, and military training.

Castro's commitment to spreading revolution across the Western Hemisphere and, indeed, the globe was apparent from the outset of his reign. Soon after he overthrew the Fulgencio Batista regime in 1959, it was clear that Cuba's new government was keen to export the revolutionary ethos and skills that enabled its seizure of power. Castro's first love was the Algerian National Liberation Front. In 1961 his government sent weapons to aid the FLN in its struggle against France and provided medical care for the wounded. Soon Havana extended its support to other revolutionaries, especially those fighting against the Portuguese colonial empire in Africa.

Nevertheless, Latin America soon became Castro's main priority. From the early 1960s onward, Cuba became something of a headquarters for communists and revolutionaries from the Western Hemisphere. To strengthen the national liberation movement in Latin America and enable a low-intensity guerrilla conflict that would set off a socialist revolution, the regime in Havana regularly organized meetings, conferences, and training programs for Latin American revolutionaries looking to emulate Castro's revolutionary victory. It hosted thousands of communist armchair revolutionaries as well as battle-hardened guerrillas from across the Americas—Colombia, Ecuador, Peru, Venezuela, Guatemala, and Argentina.[67]

Running this international covert training program was no easy task. Getting to and from Cuba in the early 1960s was treacherous, especially for those looking to keep their links to Castro's regime secret. The island's isolation had further increased after the 1962 Cuban Missile Crisis. The miscalculated attempt by Soviet leader Nikita Khrushchev to secretly place nuclear missiles on Cuban territory just over 150 kilometers from US soil not only brought the two superpowers dangerously close to nuclear war but also created a wider operational fiasco for the Soviets and infuriated the Castro regime. As a result of the

ILLUSTRATION 1.2. Fidel Castro (*left*) being welcomed during an official visit to Czechoslovakia, with the president and first secretary of the Communist Party of Czechoslovakia, Gustáv Husák, June 21, 1971. *ČTK / Mevald Karel*

crisis, Cuba faced a blockade that entailed the suspension of most air links to the island. Although air connections with Mexico and Madrid remained, travelers were closely watched upon arrival and passenger lists handed over to Western intelligence services.[68]

Accordingly, Havana was desperate to find alternative routes. To prevent Cuba's defection from the Soviet camp, Moscow offered concessions, one of which was the bloc's logistical assistance to Castro's program for international revolutionaries. Accordingly, Moscow and Prague became the logistical lifelines to the Cuban covert operations. Revolutionaries en route to or from Cuba stopped over in the communist cities to change passports, take a break, or lie low until it was safe to return to their home countries.

Although Moscow initially kept its distance from the Castro regime, Prague was an early and enthusiastic supporter.[69] Czechoslovakia was the first Soviet Bloc country to open an embassy in Havana. In 1960 and 1961 Prague secretly printed new banknotes, minted new coins, and delivered them to Cuba by sea. It further helped jump-start the Cuban economy by purchasing products not key to the Czechoslovak economy—for example, importing Cuba's sugar despite itself being the world's leading producer of beet sugar. Prague also helped Cuba internationally. In January 1961 when the United States broke off diplomatic relations, Czechoslovakia became Havana's representative in Washington and later in other Latin American countries.[70] In the same year, a direct air connection was set up between Prague and Havana—the first one between Latin America and Eastern Europe.[71]

Crucially, Prague's commitment to Cuba also extended to the military and security realms. By the early 1960s Czechoslovakia was training Cuban fighter pilots and artillery and infantry officers on its territory.[72] In 1960 it set up a rezidentura in Havana, which became central to the country's operations in Latin America. As a part of this arrangement, Prague gave Havana much-needed intelligence about the United States and Cuban exiles. In fact, in 1961 the chief of Cuban intelligence (Dirección General de Inteligencia, or DGI), Gen. Manuel Pineiro Losada, reportedly considered the Czechoslovak intelligence agency superior in performance to the KGB.[73] Jealous about the Prague-Havana special relationship, by late 1961 Moscow put a stop to it by making Prague's liaison with Cuba entirely subordinate to the KGB.[74] Nevertheless, these formative years of the Prague-Havana intelligence liaison arguably laid the foundations for Czechoslovakia's engagement in Cuba's daring operation to ignite revolution across Latin America.

Czechoslovakia fulfilled a very specific, technical role in this delicate operation. When guerrillas traveled to Havana via Prague, their travel documents would be administered by a Cuban intelligence officer operating under the cover of a Cubana Airlines representative.[75] On their way back, the Czechoslovaks would be in charge. For things to really fall into place, Prague closely liaised with Havana and adhered to strict secrecy. No one was to know that the First Directorate was part of the operation, which the StB soon dubbed Operation Manuel.[76]

Prior to each group's departure, the Czechoslovak rezidentura in Havana received lists of travelers and times of arrivals, which would be sent to StB headquarters in Prague. To facilitate the smooth transfer of these revolutionaries at Prague Airport, the StB deployed a handful of its officers. These men in plain clothes were first and foremost responsible for ensuring that the incoming revolutionaries had correct documentation. Upon their arrival in Prague, undercover StB officers were sent to meet them either at the airport or in a designated restaurant. There the StB confiscated the fake Cuban passports that had enabled the revolutionaries to fly from Havana to Prague incognito. From this point on, the revolutionaries would travel on their genuine passports via several other transit countries. Such circuitous routes were designed to shake off any traces of their transit or stay in Czechoslovakia.

Although for some revolutionaries Czechoslovakia was solely a flight transit location, others stayed for a layover or a short break. In these instances Prague's involvement became ever more sophisticated. In some cases Czechoslovak authorities provided emergency health assistance; in others they made sure that the temporary guests had enough financial resources in the right currency to get by. Adequate accommodations—usually set up in StB's safe houses or one of Prague's hotels—would also be provided.[77] Although hosting sometimes unruly guests took considerable effort, Prague bore little of the financial burden. In fact, the entirety of Operation Manuel was funded by Cuban intelligence.[78]

From 1962 to 1969 the StB helped administer the transfer of 1,179 Latin American revolutionaries. Based on Michal Zourek's meticulous research, we now know that most were from Venezuela (236), followed by Argentina (177), the Dominican Republic (122), Guatemala (100), Colombia (79), Peru (76), Brazil (48), Ecuador (41), Paraguay (38), El Salvador (36), Honduras (35), Haiti (35), and Panama (28). In addition to the Latin Americans, however, in the last years of Operation Manuel, Prague became aware that other nationals were also flying to and from Havana. In 1967 under the code name Operation Ramadan, twelve Iranians passed via Prague after completing an eight-month-long guerrilla training in Cuba. A year later, a group of Eritreans flew in the other direction.[79]

This was a remarkable venture as Prague exercised no control over which of Castro's revolutionaries came onto its territory or whether they stayed or not. In fact, the StB rarely knew the identity of the revolutionaries who used the country as a lifeline to their comrades and mentors in Havana. Czechoslovakia's willingness to provide free rein to Cuban services on their territory was a demonstration of notable trust or perhaps of commitment to its strategic allies in Moscow and Havana. This was surprising behavior for a state known for keeping a tight grip on its territory and population.

Much like most covert endeavors, Operation Manuel was plagued with shortcomings. First, Prague found the Cubans chaotic, inflexible, and unresponsive to criticisms. This impacted the venture in many ways. There were issues with travel documents, unannounced arrivals of groups or individuals, and a general lack of situational awareness on the part of the revolutionaries who often left Cuba carrying promotional materials, Cuban spirits, or Cuban cigars.[80] Czechoslovak involvement in the operation was, however, also not without its flaws. This was apparent early on, upon the arrival of the very first group of "Manuelistas." When the Venezuelan revolutionaries arrived in Prague, they found no one waiting for them at the airport. The telegram informing Prague's foreign intelligence about their arrival reached the Prague headquarters one day too late. Thinking on their feet, the revolutionaries thus checked into the landmark Hotel Intercontinental and contacted the Cuban embassy in Prague, which alerted the appropriate authorities.[81] Although there was little else they could have done in this precarious situation, this strategy was not ideal because it exposed their stay and potentially the operation to an unnecessarily large amount of people.

Second, as with regard to African revolutionaries, Czechoslovakia was concerned about deniability. In fact, in 1963 Prague's minister of the interior, Lubomír Štrougal, called for greater secrecy over the operation as the news of Czechoslovakia's involvement was clearly spreading and there was word that the communist country was becoming "a central gateway for guerrillas." These efforts were largely futile, however, as the West was keenly watching. By 1967 the StB was sure that "CIA agents" were monitoring travelers from Cuba at Prague Airport and informed their Cuban counterparts about this worrying development. Around the same time, more and more revolutionaries who passed through Prague were arrested in their homelands. Moreover, the Organization of American States (OAS) established a committee on Cuban guerrilla politics.[82] Havana's program of exporting the revolution was now under a spotlight.

Prague's anxiety grew further as it found out more about the beneficiaries of the operation. By 1965 a number of Manuelistas had been murdered and arrested.[83] Remarkably, the StB did not learn of this from its Cuban counterparts but rather from its own assets or guerrillas passing through its territory. In the mid-1960s Prague was further agitated when it accidently learned about defections of key Cuban intelligence officers who could disclose further information about its involvement. It was also concerned about the defections of former Manuelistas. These worries became a reality in the latter half of the 1960s when a Dominican participant defected and an Eritrean participant attempted to escape to the West while in Prague—the latter sharing details of Operation Manuel with the Swiss embassy there in the hope of securing asylum.[84]

Issues with deniability had a real impact on Prague. Throughout the 1960s Czechoslovakia's role in the operation was exposed at various forums, and in some cases repercussions followed. For instance, in the summer of 1967 Cuban subversive activities were hotly debated at a meeting of the OAS as guerrilla activities in Latin America—namely, Bolivia, Guatemala, and Nicaragua—intensified. The Venezuelans were at the helm of this anti-Castro campaign, accusing Cuba of training groups responsible for political murders and a recent attempt to overthrow Venezuelan president Raúl Leoni with the help of weapons provided to Cuba by Czechoslovakia. In protest against Prague's involvement, Venezuela significantly restricted its visa regime for Czechoslovaks.[85]

Another blow came in 1969 when the Brazilian guerrilla José Duarte dos Santos was arrested in Brazil and testified about passing through Prague on his way from Cuba and receiving false documents from Czechoslovak nationals. This angered the Brazilian government and undercut Prague's commercial interests in this key Latin American state. Brazil refused to open a branch of the Czechoslovak Commercial Bank in Rio de Janeiro and a Czechoslovak State Airlines office in São Paulo, and it boycotted celebrations of the fiftieth anniversary of the countries' diplomatic relations. In October 1969, in what arguably became the most dramatic demonstration of this anti-Czechoslovak sentiment, a bomb was placed in front of the Czechoslovak embassy in Rio de Janeiro. This was a red line for Prague that triggered an unprecedented chain of events that included the Czechoslovak government sending an official note of protest to Havana explicitly refusing to serve as its revolutionary lifeline for Brazilian guerrillas engaged in subversive activities.[86]

As Operation Manuel matured, Prague was also skeptical about the impact of Havana's guerrilla politics on Latin America. The Latin American revolutionaries passing through Czechoslovakia were a mixed bag. Although some were experienced revolutionary leaders or communist party representatives, others were young, urban, leftist intellectuals or rural figures, often illiterate farmers.[87] During the early 1960s most revolutionaries were representatives of Latin American communist parties, whereas in the latter half of the decade the men and women secretly passing through Prague were largely associated with radical left-wing groups. Arguably, this shift was driven by discontent on the part of the Soviet Bloc and Latin American communist parties with Cuban revolutionary policies. As a result, they took a step back from the operation, which created more space for far-left groups eager to engage in antigovernment armed struggle upon their return from Cuba.[88]

This worried Prague for a host of reasons. It considered the latter category of revolutionaries to be of "lower intelligence" and questioned their commitment to the international revolutionary movement. For Prague a testament of their lesser value was the fact that upon their return from Cuba and Prague, many of these "second-rank" revolutionaries were killed in battle or captivity.[89] Denoting Cuba's policy as "adventurous"—a stamp of disapproval in the East—Prague noted that there was insufficient popular support for the Castro-sponsored revolution across the continent and likened his unrealistic efforts to those of the communist Chinese. In fact, the First Directorate was keen to distance itself from this sizable operation. It argued that "the assistance provided by the Czechoslovak intelligence service under Operation Manuel does not imply an acceptance of its political content and it forms only a minor and insignificant part of their intelligence work."[90]

Despite these concerns, Prague could not see a clear and obvious way out. To entirely extract itself from the operation would require severe steps: putting a stop to the DGI's operations on Czechoslovak soil and cutting off air traffic with the island. This would surely anger the Cubans and significantly cool down, if not sever entirely, relations with Havana. Strategically, this was not an option. Partial extraction was also not feasible. The StB knew that had it told the Cubans that they were to no longer participate in the covert operation, Havana would continue to send revolutionaries through Czechoslovak territory. This time, however, it would be done behind the StB's back.[91]

By late 1969, as Prague hesitated and weighed its options, Cuba's assistance to Latin American national liberation movements began winding down. By March 1970 it came to a complete halt. Havana probably put an end to this ambitious plan due to growing criticism, isolation, and the limited impact of its ambitious revolutionary plan as well as the high costs associated with running an international revolutionary hub. Instead, it opted for establishing economic and political relations with states across Latin America.[92]

Overall, Operation Manuel was characterized by anxiety and lack of control. Although Prague was concerned about being the logistical lifeline for this sizable operation, nevertheless for strategic reasons it provided support for almost a decade. Ultimately Prague's disengagement from the operation was led by its growing dissatisfaction with Cuba's program and the increased risk and reputational damage that it brought. It was a mismatch, an alliance of necessity rather than choice—and one that exposed the complexity of treading the delicate boundary between clandestine support for strategic allies, foreign policy objectives, and business interests.

## "NOWHERE MAN"

While Prague ran Operation Manuel, Operation Ramadan, and the top-secret training programs for African revolutionaries, in the 1960s Czechoslovakia also served as an unwitting and temporary host for various individuals associated with the international revolutionary ethos. In contrast to the popular conception that the StB closely monitored and controlled all movement on its territory, various actors escorted by Cuban intelligence managed to move in and out of the country under false identities without alerting Prague's watchers or leaving much of a paper trail.

In March 1966 a thirty-eight-year-old, dark-eyed man arrived in a small apartment in the Holešovice district of Prague. He was heavily disguised, wearing prosthetic teeth designed to change the shape of his jaw, an undershirt that made him look like a hunchback, shoes with lifts that gave his five-foot-seven-inch figure more gravitas, and heavy spectacles. Although according to his Uruguayan passport the visitor's name was Ramón Benítez, we now know that this was all a cover.[93]

The man, who would stay in Czechoslovakia unbeknown to the StB for four months, until July 1966, was none other than Ernesto "Che" Guevara—the most recognizable revolutionary of the twentieth century.[94] When Guevara appeared in Prague, he was in between revolutionary missions. In early 1965 the Argentine-born guerrilla traveled to the DRC to support the Marxist Simba rebels, led by followers of the late Patrice Lumumba, who were staging an uprising in the east of the country. Famously, Guevara's mission to bring the revolution

**ILLUSTRATION 1.3.** Ernesto "Che" Guevara seated on a Czechoslovak Zetor tractor at ZKL Brno during an official visit to Czechoslovakia on October 27, 1960, as president of the National Bank of Cuba. *ČTK / Bican Emil*

to the DRC ended in failure. By autumn 1965 he had to leave the country and hide at the Cuban embassy in Dar es Salaam, under the close protection of Cuba's secret service.[95]

Although allegedly Guevara wanted to deploy to yet another hot spot right away, he was persuaded to lie low in a safe, calmer place before embarking on a new mission. Czechoslovakia was apparently such a place. Moreover, thanks to the DGI's free rein on Czechoslovak territory and the special regime at the airport set up to facilitate Operation Manuel, getting Guevara into the country unnoticed was a relatively easy task. Accordingly, Prague became the place where Guevara spent his last spring.[96]

Guevara arrived in Czechoslovakia in March 1966 along with Ulises Estrada, a comrade in arms from the combat mission in the DRC. They lived in modest conditions, in a small safe house a short stroll from Prague's Vltava River. According to Estrada, there was no hierarchy. The two revolutionaries shared cooking and cleaning duties and deliberately had chosen this humble place to perfect their cover. Soon, however, it became apparent that lying low required a different setup. The famous revolutionary would have to avoid walking around the largely ethnically white Prague with the tall, black Ulises. After Estrada was sent back to Cuba, others joined Guevara in Czechoslovakia, possibly to start planning his next mission. His next adventure would take him back to Latin America where he would stage his final revolutionary attempt, in Bolivia.[97]

To accommodate this more sizable group, Guevara relocated to a larger dwelling in a much more secluded location, outside of Prague in the small, sleepy town of Ládví-Kamenice, southwest of the capital. The family house he stayed in was no vacation home. Built in the 1930s for Jaroslav Krejčí, a Nazi collaborator and later prime minister of the Protectorate of Bohemia and Moravia during World War II, it had been nationalized after the 1948 communist putsch and handed over to the StB. Conveniently tucked away, the rather austere villa was used by the StB to house or train so-called illegals—officers sent abroad under deep cover.[98]

In 1963, as part of the intelligence liaison with Cuban intelligence, the villa was "lent" to Castro's men. For all intents and purposes, it became a Cuban safe house. Throughout this time, a number of Manuelistas stayed in this very house. Crucially, in 1964 the Cuban DGI used it to accommodate and train a certain Tamara Bunke—an East German national turned Cuban illegal. During her time in Ládví-Kamenice, Tamara (also known as "Tania") was trained by her DGI handler, José Gomez.[99] This likely was in preparation for her next mission in which, much like the one Guevara had prepared for in this particular location two years later, would be her last.

During his time in Czechoslovakia, Guevara remained busy planning his upcoming mission to Bolivia. He knew the country well from a stay in 1953, when he witnessed it seething with revolutionary fervor triggered by a recent coup staged by thousands of working-class citizens. In the spring of 1966, local communists assured Guevara's associates that now—thirteen years later—the country was again ripe for revolutionary change and that all they needed to topple the military-backed regime of President René Barrientos was Cuban support.[100] Therefore, Guevara and the men who came to stay with him in Czechoslovakia spent their time there planning the Bolivia mission. Furthermore, during his stay Guevara wrote more than two hundred pages of notes on political economy and historical materialism. Allegedly, this unfinished tract revealed him to be a harsh critic of the Soviet model of socialism.[101]

When not planning, the revolutionaries passed their time with a variety of amusements. Some days they went hiking, played volleyball, or engaged in a soccer match. Other days they combined business with pleasure and held target practice in the backyard of the safe house. Guevara's companions also recall playing canasta and chess with the revolutionary strategist who would, at times, let them win. Although they had only two vinyl records, these were played on repeat. Guevara had a strong preference for the South African singer/songwriter Miriam Makeba but gradually also grew fond of the Beatles, quite possibly humming to their recently released "Nowhere Man"—a song about a man with no direction or worldview. In April 1966 Guevara's wife, Aleida, joined him in Czechoslovakia.[102]

The Argentinian revolutionary's three-month stay in Czechoslovakia ended on July 19, 1966, when, allegedly responding to Fidel Castro's plea, he returned to Cuba. Guevara would stay until October, when he set off on his ill-fated Bolivian mission via a treacherous journey that involved a brief stopover in Prague.[103] He entered Bolivia incognito as he had Prague earlier that year. Guevara altered his appearance by shaving off his beard and much of his hair and sporting spectacles. He arrived in La Paz on November 1, 1966, with a false Uruguayan passport and soon met up with Tania—the Cuban illegal agent who had lived in the Ládví-Kamenice villa two years prior to Guevara's secret stay. She provided him with a cover story and appropriate documentation—that of a special envoy of the OAS on a mission to conduct research on the social and economic conditions in rural Bolivia.[104]

As we know, this cover did not help save Guevara's life. A year later, he was caught by the Bolivian army, arrested, and ultimately shot. His death remains a matter of much speculation and controversy. Today, however, we know more about his stay in Prague than ever before. We know that he spent the last spring of his life in Czechoslovakia planning his next mission and writing the foundations of what was to be his next philosophical tract. We also know that his visit was perhaps one of the most notable examples of the free rein Prague gave to its Cuban allies in the 1960s and a demonstration of how far Czechoslovakia was willing to go to aid a strategic ally. Indeed, his incognito stay in the communist country undermines the academic consensus that communist states were in strong control of their territory and aware of all personal movements.

\*\*\*

In theory Prague was an early and enthusiastic supporter of national liberation movements and revolutionaries in the third world. Its amicable approach to revolutionaries was largely motivated by the zeitgeist of the decolonization era,

Soviet Bloc alliance politics, and strategic interests in key regions. In tandem with Moscow, Czechoslovakia was keen to see the old colonial powers fail and new allies, such as Cuba, succeed. In reality, however, Prague found its interactions with the 1960s revolutionaries challenging and, at times, counterproductive or even dangerous.

From the onset, Prague's intelligence, sabotage, and guerrilla warfare training for African national liberation movements faced various hurdles. While it gradually managed to overcome some of these problems, the unpredictability of the venture coupled with deniability concerns continued to plague the enterprise. Moreover, Prague also painfully learned that asserting power and control over third world revolutionaries was an elusive prospect—a lesson the First Directorate would be reminded of time and time again.

Its engagement in Operation Manuel was no less problematic. Although Prague, alongside Moscow, was keen to help a strategic ally that had suffered a setback as a consequence of the miscalculated Cuban Missile Crisis, it became gradually uneasy about its role in this venture. Prague distrusted the revolutionaries who passed through its territory and found transatlantic coordination of the venture difficult and the potential diplomatic and business blowback burdensome—so much so that following diplomatic reverses due to its engagement in the Cuban-run operation, it explicitly asked to be left out. Overall, when it came to revolutionary politics, Prague was caught between strategic interests and tactical concerns.

By the end of the 1960s Prague's engagement with third world revolutionaries wound down.[105] Some of its African clients had achieved independence or power. Cuba had abandoned its ambitious yet costly revolutionary ventures. But there were also domestic reasons for this shift. The August 1968 invasion of Czechoslovakia by Warsaw Pact armies, the subsequent Soviet occupation, and the so-called *normalizace* (normalization) of the communist regime put an end to the "golden years" of Prague's foreign operations. The following decade was largely devoted to consolidating the regime and cleansing the Communist Party and its security apparatus of those who had openly supported the discredited Prague Spring.[106]

It was not until the second half of the 1970s that Czechoslovakia gradually started renewing its global outreach, albeit on a more modest scale. During the closing decade and a half of the Cold War, Prague would not return to Africa in full force. In fact, the only nonstate actor it would ever again establish clandestine liaison with would be the PLO. While Prague's engagement with Arafat's men would bear many of the hallmarks and challenges of its earlier assistance programs, it would be different in important ways. Crucially, this time around, Prague would be more vigilant and particular about which groups it would align with and which it would leave out in the cold.

## NOTES

1. "Návrh na odeslání posluchače Ameen Mohamed Ali K 141 B pro hrubou nekázeň," January 11, 1965, VHA, f[ond], MNO (Ministerstvo národní obrany), 1965, Ka 232.
2. "Návrh na odeslání posluchače," 2–3. On the engagement in the third world of other global players, such as China, see Samuel S. Kim, ed., *China and the World: Chinese Foreign Relations in the Post–Cold War Era* (Boulder, CO: Westview, 1994).
3. Westad, *Global Cold War*, 4–5.
4. For instance, see how the KGB chairman suggested sponsoring large-scale anticolonial uprisings to distract the West during the 1961 Berlin Crisis in Telepneva, "Code Name SEKRETÁŘ," 1262.
5. Galia Golan, *The Soviet Union and National Liberation Movements in the Third World* (London: Routledge, 1988), 1.
6. Westad, *Global Cold War*, 58, 67–68.
7. Westad, 72.
8. Golan, *Soviet Union and National*, 1.
9. Robert Cassen, ed., *Soviet Interests in the Third World* (London: Sage Publications, 1985), 1–3.
10. Markus Wolf and Anne McElvoy, *Man without a Face: The Autobiography of Communism's Greatest Spymaster* (London: Jonathan Cape, 1999), 263.
11. Golan, *Soviet Union and National*, 3, 268.
12. Golan, 8–9.
13. Westad, *Global Cold War*, 108–9, 97–98.
14. Constantin Katsakioris, "The Lumumba University in Moscow: Higher Education for a Soviet–Third World Alliance, 1960–91," *Journal of Global History* 14, no. 2 (2019): 281–300.
15. Galia Golan, "Moscow and Third World National Liberation Movements: The Soviet Role," *Journal of International Affairs* 40, no. 2 (Winter/Spring 1987): 309.
16. Westad, *Global Cold War*, 39–67; Austin Jersild, "The Soviet State as Imperial Scavenger: 'Catch Up and Surpass' in the Transnational Socialist Bloc, 1950–1960," *American Historical Review* 116, no. 1 (2011): 109–32.
17. Csaba Békés, "The Warsaw Pact and the Helsinki Process, 1965–1970," in *The Making of Détente: Eastern and Western Europe in the Cold War, 1965–75*, ed. Wilfried Loth and Georges-Henri Soutou (London: Routledge, 2010).
18. Aleš Skřivan, "Zbrojní výroba a vývoz meziválečného Československa," *Ekonomická revue* 9, no. 3 (2006): 19–31; Jiří Dufek and Vladimír Šlosar, "Československá materiálně technická pomoc Izraeli," in *Československo a Izrael v letech 1947–1951: Studie*, ed. Jiří Dufek (Brno: Ústav pro soudobé dějiny AV ČR v nakl. Doplněk, 1993).
19. See more in Jan Koura and Robert Anthony Walters, "'Africanos' versus 'Africanitos': The Soviet-Czechoslovak Competition to Protect the Cuban Revolution," *International History Review* 43, no. 1 (2021).
20. See more in Daniela Richterova, Mikuláš Pešta, and Natalia Telepneva, "Banking on Military Assistance: Czechoslovakia's Struggle for Influence and Profit in the Third World, 1955–1968," *International History Review* 43, no. 1 (2021).
21. Petr Cajthaml, "Profesionální lháři: Aktivní opatření čs. rozvědky do srpna 1968," *Sborník Archivu Ministerstva vnitra* 4 (2006): 31–32. Cajthaml argues that not all Soviet Bloc countries allied their foreign intelligence objectives so closely to those

of Moscow. For instance, he argues that Polish active measures were largely limited to their national interests.
22. This trend continued until 1967 and 1968 when Prague gradually started losing Moscow's trust due to the gradual liberalization of Prague's communist regime.
23. "Rozbor plnění plánu technické pomoci za období od 1. ledna 1966–30. června 1966," n.d., VHA, f. MNO 1966, Ka 245.
24. On Czechoslovak relations with Africa and the Middle East, see Peter Zídek and Karel Sieber, *Československo a subsaharská Afrika v letech, 1948–1989* (Prague: Ústav mezinárodních vztahů, 2007); Petr Zídek and Karel Sieber, *Československo a Blízký východ v letech, 1948–1989* (Prague: Ústav mezinárodních vztahů, 2009); and Philip Muehlenbeck, *Czechoslovakia in Africa, 1945–1968* (New York: Palgrave Macmillan, 2016). On Prague's relationship with the PAIGC, see Telepneva, "Code Name SEKRETÁŘ."
25. Eduard Kukan, interview by the author, August 24, 2017.
26. Kukan.
27. *P* being the first letter of the Czech word for adviser, *poradce*. The first Soviet advisers to the Ministry of the Interior arrived in Prague shortly after the communist takeover in 1948. These fifty-odd men played a crucial role in this era, most notably engaging in the infamous political show trials. Gradually their numbers decreased and by 1962 had dropped to ten. Jiřina Dvořáková, Zdeňka Jurová, and Petr Kaňák, *Československá rozvědka a pražské jaro* (Prague: Ústav pro studium totalitních režimů, 2016), 12–13.
28. Dvořáková, Jurová, and Kaňák, 12–13.
29. Petr Blažek and Pavel Žáček, "Czechoslovakia," in *A Handbook of the Communist Security Apparatus in East Central Europe, 1944–1989*, ed. Krzysztof Persak and Łukasz Kamiński (Warsaw: Institute of National Remembrance, 2005), 104.
30. Petr Zídek, *Československo a francouzská Afrika, 1948–1968* (Prague: Libri, 2006), 26.
31. Zídek, 36.
32. Jaroslav Šilhavý (Náč. vnitřní správy MV)–Josef Houska (Náč.I.S), November 1, 1965, ABS-81029.
33. "Odhad potřeby výzbroje a výstroje pro pomoc bezpečnostním složkám rozvojových zemí a organizacím národně osvobozeneckého hnutí na léta 1966/68," November 10, 1965, ABS-81029; "Záznam o jednání se s.pplk. Němcem, náčelníkem KÚ, dne 21.VII.65," July 21, 1965, ABS-81029; Martin Smíšek, *Czechoslovak Arms Exports to the Middle East*, vol. 1 (Warwick, UK: Helion, 2021), 20–21.
34. "Přehled speciální pomoci poskytnuté národně osvobozeneckému hnutí," May 4, 1966, ABS-81029.
35. See more on the First Directorate's role in the DRC in Natalia Telepneva "Cold War on the Cheap: Soviet and Czechoslovak Intelligence in the Congo, 1960–3," in Muehlenbeck and Telepneva, *Warsaw Pact Intervention in the Third World: Aid and Influence in the Cold War* (London: I. B. Tauris, 2018), 125–47.
36. Three nations were Guinea, Mali, and the Republic of Congo (a.k.a. Congo-Brazzaville). Zídek, *Československo a francouzská Afrika*, 27.
37. Telepneva, "Code Name SEKRETÁŘ," 13–14; Natalia Telepneva, *Cold War Liberation: The Soviet Union and the Collapse of the Portuguese Empire in Africa, 1961–1975* (Chapel Hill: University of North Carolina Press, 2022). For Czechoslovak liaison/collaboration with African leaders, see Natalia Telepneva, "Mediators of Liberation: Eastern-Bloc Officials, Mozambican Diplomacy and the Origins

of Soviet Support for Frelimo, 1958–1965," *Journal of Southern African Studies* 43, no. 1 (2017); and James R. Brennan, "The Secret Lives of Dennis Phombeah: Decolonization, the Cold War, and African Political Intelligence, 1953–1974," *International History Review* 43, no. 1 (2021): 153–69.
38. See an overview of cadets trained by the Ministry of the Interior: "Přehled speciální pomoci poskytnuté národně osvobozeneckému hnutí," May 4, 1966, ABS-81029.
39. Plk. Houska (Náč. I.S MV), "Věc: bezpečnostní kurz pro PAI GC," April 27, 1963, ABS-11853.
40. For more about the for-profit venture, see Richterova, Pešta, and Telepneva, "Banking on Military Assistance."
41. "Přehled speciální pomoci poskytnuté národně osvobozeneckému hnutí," May 4, 1966, ABS-81029. For a specific course outline provided to PAIGC cadets, see "SVODKA o průběhu kursu za období 17-30.8.1961," n.d., ABS-11853. During this time, the Ministry of the Interior also trained state actors in state security, intelligence, and law enforcement. These included cadets from Uganda, Congo-Brazzaville, Indonesia, Mali, and Guinea, to name but a few.
42. Pplk. A. Janovec (Náč. Ústřední školy MV F. E. Dzeržinského Praha)–Mjr. Voldřich (Správa kádru MV), "Tématický plán pro zahraniční kurs PAI—předložení návrhu," July 16, 1963, ABS-11853.
43. "Zhodnocení činnosti za rok 1964 v akcích 137 and 141," VHA, f. MNO 1963, Ka 362.
44. "Zpráva o kontrole kurzu 141," n.d., VHA, f. MNO 1963, Ka 361.
45. "Technická pomoc straně Africký národní svaz Keňi. Akce 137," n.d., VHA, f. MNO 1963, Ka 362.
46. "Závěrečná zpráva o průběhu kursu státní bespečnosti pro posluchače Portugalské Guineje," n.d., ABS-11853.
47. Plk. Houska (Náč. I.S), "Věc: bezpečnostní kurz pro PAI GC," April 27, 1963, ABS-11853.
48. "Zjištěné skutečnosti o nových posluchačích zahraniční fakulty VAAZ v Brně—akce 141," March 1961, VHA, f. MNO 1963, Ka 361.
49. B. Chrastil (Náč. ZF VAAZ)–plk. Foršt (Náč. oddel. gener. štáb čsl. armády), "Věc: informace o posluchači K-141 Samuel Dube," VHA, f. MNO 1963, Ka 362.
50. "Zhodnocení činnosti za 1.pololetí, 1964," June 9, 1964, VHA, f. MNO 1963, Ka 362.
51. "Ukončení akce 141—Tanzanie," June 17, 1965, VHA, f. MNO 1963, Ka 361.
52. "Zhodnocení činnosti za rok 1964 v akcích 137 a 141," VHA, f. MNO 1963, Ka 362.
53. "Ukončení akce 141—Tanzanie," June 17, 1965, VHA, f. MNO 1963, Ka 361.
54. The original sum was CZK 2.3 million. All sums in CZK have been converted into US dollars (USD) first and subsequently adjusted to USD inflation in 2022. Whenever the year is unclear, the average exchange rate over the relevant period and the midpoint inflation index was used. CZKs are converted using the real economic CZK/USD rate, not the official Czechoslovak government rate. The source for the real economic CZK/USD rate is the Czech National Bank (https://www.historie.cnb.cz/cs/menova_politika/prurezova_temata_menova_politika/1_ekonomicky_vyvoj_na_uzemi_ceske_republiky.html). The source for the Consumer Price Index used in the inflation adjustment is the Minneapolis Fed (https://www.minneapolisfed.org/about-us/monetary-policy/inflation-calculator/consumer-price-index-1913-). "Technická pomoc Kenji a Zanzibaru," n.d., VHA, f. MNO 1961, Ka 453.
55. Original sum CZK 250,000. "Pomoc národně osvobozeneckému hnutí v Jižní Afrike, Akce 141 (Tanganjika)," n.d., VHA, f. MNO 1963, Ka 362.

56. Zídek, *Československo a francouzská Afrika*, 78–82; Lenka Krátká, "'Astounding It Is, What Lidice Carries': The Transport of Czechoslovak Weapons for the Algerian National Liberation Front in 1959," *International Journal of Maritime History* 33, no. 1 (2021): 54–69.
57. "Technická pomoc národně osvobozeneckému hnutí v Angole, Akce 133 Guinea," n.d., VHA, f. MNO, Ka 362.
58. Original sum CZK 30 million. Muehlenbeck, *Czechoslovakia in Africa*, 46–47. For other examples of business trumping strategic and intelligence interests, see Jan Koura, "A Prominent Spy: Mehdi Ben Barka, Czechoslovak Intelligence, and Eastern Bloc Espionage in the Third World during the Cold War," *Intelligence and National Security* 36, no. 3 (2020): 5.
59. "Ukončení akce 141—Tanzanie," June 17, 1965, VHA, f. MNO 1963, Ka 361.
60. "Další technická pomoc národně osvobozeneckému hnutí v Juhoafrické republiky," June 16, 1964, VHA, f. MNO, 1963, Ka 361.
61. "Další technická pomoc národně."
62. "Příloha k čj. [nečitelno]," n.d., VHA, f. MNO, 1963, Ka 362.
63. "Zhodnocení činnosti za 1. pololetí, 1964," June 9, 1964, VHA, f. MNO 1963, Ka 362.
64. "Technická pomoc národně osvobozeneckému hnutí v Angole, Akce 133 Guinea," n.d., VHA, f. MNO, Ka 362.
65. "Návrh na odeslání posluchače Ameen Mohamed Ali K 141 B pro hrubou nekázeň," January 11, 1965, VHA, f. MNO, 1965, Ka 232.
66. Michal Zourek, "Czechoslovakia and Latin America's Guerrilla Insurgencies: Secret Services, Training Networks, Mobility, and Transportation," in *Towards a Global History of Latin America's Revolutionary Left*, ed. Tanya Harmer and Alberto Martín Álvarez (Gainesville: University of Florida Press, 2021), 34–35.
67. To date, the most authoritative accounts of the operation are Prokop Tomek, "Akce MANUEL," *Securitas Imperii* 9 (2002): 325–32; and Zourek, "Czechoslovakia and Latin America's."
68. Zourek, "Czechoslovakia and Latin America's," 33.
69. See more on the history of Prague's economic and military cooperation with the continent, which enabled Prague to set up close relations with reform-minded and left-leaning regimes, in K. Březinová, "Turbines and Weapons for Latin America Czechoslovak Documentary Film Propaganda in the Cold War Context, 1948–1989," in *Cold War Engagements: Czechoslovakia and Latin America, 1948–1989*, ed. Mitchell Belfer and Kateřina Březinová, special issue of *Central European Journal of International and Security Studies* 7, no. 3 (September 2013).
70. Zourek, "Czechoslovakia and Latin America's," 28, 31.
71. Michal Zourek, "Zusammenarbeit tschechoslowakischer und kubanischer Geheimdienste: der geheime Aufenthalt von Ernesto Che Guevara," in Prague Papers on the History of International Relations—Univerzita Karlova, Filozofická fakulta, 2018), 72, https://praguepapers.ff.cuni.cz/wp-content/uploads/sites/16/2018/10/Michal_Zourek_69-83.pdf.
72. Richterova, Pešta, and Telepneva, "Banking on Military Assistance."
73. Koura and Waters, "'Africanos' versus 'Africanitos," 72.
74. Zourek, "Czechoslovakia and Latin America's," 32.
75. Prokop Tomek, "Dům, v němž bydlel i Guevara," *Paměť a dějiny* (March 2016): 31.
76. The full set of files detailing "Operation Manuel" can be found in ABS-807230.
77. Tomek, "Akce MANUEL," 328.

78. Zourek, "Czechoslovakia and Latin America's," 37.
79. Michal Zourek, "Operation MANUEL: Prague as a Transit Hub of International Terrorism," *Central European Journal of International & Security Studies* 9, no. 3 (2015): 86, 93.
80. Zourek, "Czechoslovakia and Latin America's," 50, 83.
81. Tomek, "Dům, v němž bydlel," 31.
82. Zourek, "Czechoslovakia and Latin America's," 50, 57.
83. One such case was that of Roque Dalton, a Salvadoran poet, communist activist, and partisan who was arrested and interrogated by US intelligence about dealings in Cuba as well as Czechoslovakia. The questioning revealed operational knowledge of the venture. Jiří Piškula, "Roque Dalton García: Básník, bohém a partyzán očima tří tajných služeb," *Paměť a dějiny*, January 2014.
84. After disclosing their intentions, the trainee was arrested and deported by the Cubans via Moscow back to Damascus. Zourek, "Czechoslovakia and Latin America's," 51–52; Zourek, "Operation MANUEL," 46.
85. Zourek, "Operation MANUEL," 53.
86. Zourek, "Czechoslovakia and Latin America's," 57–58.
87. Tomek, "Akce MANUEL," 331.
88. Zourek, "Operation MANUEL," 48.
89. Zourek, "Czechoslovakia and Latin America's," 46–48, 84.
90. Zourek, 55.
91. Tomek, "Akce MANUEL," 330.
92. Zourek, "Czechoslovakia and Latin America's," 31.
93. Zourek, "Zusammenarbeit tschechoslowakischer," 73–74.
94. Zourek and Tomek both agree that the StB was not aware that Guevara was staying in Czechoslovakia. Tomek, "Dům, v němž bydlel," 33; Zourek, "Zusammenarbeit tschechoslowakischer."
95. See Guevara's firsthand account of his time in the DRC in Che Guevara, *The African Dream: The Diaries of the Revolutionary War in the Congo* (New York: Random House, 2001).
96. Zourek, "Zusammenarbeit tschechoslowakischer," 72.
97. Zourek, 75.
98. Tomek, "Dům, v němž bydlel," 34, 36.
99. Tomek.
100. Sidney Jacobson and Ernie Colón, *Che: A Graphic Biography* (New York: Hill & Wang, 2009), 148.
101. Zourek, "Zusammenarbeit tschechoslowakischer," 77, 81.
102. Zourek, 76–78.
103. There is some dispute about the exact stopovers en route to Bolivia. Zourek, "Zusammenarbeit tschechoslowakischer," 81.
104. Jacobson and Colón, *Che*, 155.
105. Zídek and Sieber, *Československo a subsaharská Afrika*.
106. For more on the impact of the Prague Spring on the StB and the First Directorate, see Dvořáková, Jurová, and Kaňák, *Československá rozvědka a Pražské jaro*.

# 2

# A New Battleground

Shortly after midnight on July 23, 1968, the crew of El Al Flight 426 requested some hot drinks. It had been an exhausting day marked by delays and technical problems. They had just embarked on a three-hour flight from Rome to Tel Aviv. It was going to be a long night, and the crew needed a boost. As the stewardess walked into the cockpit with the refreshments, things took an unexpected turn. Within a matter of seconds, she was pulled back by two armed men who stormed the cockpit. After a series of dramatic twists and turns, which saw one of the crew get assaulted and a trainee pilot resort to violent flight maneuvers in the hope of knocking down the intruders, the captain finally turned to the attackers and asked, "What is our destination?" The attacker answered, "Algiers!"[1]

This event was unlike the other international hijacking incidents of the 1960s. The seizure of El Al Flight 426 by the Popular Front for the Liberation of Palestine (PFLP) was not simply an attempt to divert a plane to an alternative destination—a practice that became oddly prevalent during the early years of mass commercial air travel, especially in the United States.[2] The PFLP hijacking turned into a forty-day hostage drama during which the hijackers held the crew and selected Israeli travelers in Algeria while negotiating the release of Arab prisoners from Israeli jails.[3] By attacking a symbol of their chief enemy, an Israeli airline, and forcing Israel to de facto recognize the group by engaging in protracted negotiations over a hostages-for-prisoners deal, the PFLP attracted unprecedented media attention and achieved the release of its fellow fighters.[4] It represented a sea change in Palestinian resistance tactics and the nature of civilian aviation as well as a shift in state perception of threats. Crucially, it marked the onset of what became known as Cold War international terrorism.

The advent of Cold War–era international terrorism was swift and forceful. It emerged at the end of the 1960s as the national liberation struggle in Africa was winding down, as Arab states suffered a crushing defeat by Israel in the 1967 Six-Day War, and as students worldwide took to the streets to protest the Vietnam War and establishment politics. In many ways, it echoed terrorisms from previous waves and eras: it was perpetrated by nonstate actors; driven by political, doctrinal, or territorial objectives; enabled by the latest technological innovations; and characterized by symbolic and shocking acts of violence firmly positioned outside conventional rules of war.[5] Yet in important ways it was also different: it was distinctively international, highly visible, and deeply personal.

This two-decade sequence of international terrorist attacks was born out of two distinct strands of violence: ethnonationalist, largely led by domestic or regional political grievances, and neo-Marxist, triggered by a desire for a utopian world order. The ethnonationalist groups turned to political violence shortly after World War II in an effort to achieve independence or end discrimination. Winston Churchill's and Franklin D. Roosevelt's wartime declarations of respect for the right of all people to choose their own government reflected postwar anticolonial enthusiasm for self-determination and independence.[6]

Soon afterward, the British and French were forced to withdraw from key strongholds by violent campaigns. In the late 1940s, the Jewish Irgun Zvai Le'umi (National Military Organization) and the Lehi/Stern Gang (Lohamei Herut Yisrael, or Freedom Fighters for Israel) staged terrorist attacks against the British that certainly hastened London's retreat from Palestine. In 1954 the FLN instigated a revolt against French rule of Algeria. By 1962 the French were retreating from North Africa. These campaigns were soon followed by other local ethnonationalist struggles—most prominently the campaign in Northern Ireland by the Provisional Irish Republican Army (PIRA),[7] the violent effort against the Spanish government by the Basque separatist group Euskadita Ta Askatasuna (ETA; Freedom for the Basque Homeland), and the myriad Palestinian groups staging attacks against Israel.

In parallel, ideologically driven, mostly leftist boutique terrorist outfits emerged across Western Europe and the United States—the Italian Red Brigades, the German Baader-Meinhof Gang (also known as the Red Army Faction) and 2 June Movement, the French Action directe, and the American Weather Underground—and the obscure Japanese Red Army and the Marxist-Leninist Armenian Secret Army for the Liberation of Armenia (ASALA). Most of these groups emerged from some of the more radical segments of the student protests of the late 1960s and adopted terrorist tactics to further their anticapitalist and Marxist-Leninist agendas or simply to cause chaos. Various international events contributed to their rise, chiefly the protracted and gruesome Vietnam War. Although the political drivers for attacks perpetrated by the ethnonationalists and ideologically driven groups were different, they all attempted to join and capitalize on the international revolutionary ethos of the times.[8]

Motivations, strategies, and tactics varied considerably. Some groups had a clear nationalistic or Marxist-Leninist agenda, others claimed allegiance to various causes, and, in some cases, their politics were not entirely clear. Certain outfits were purely focused on using terrorist tactics such as hijacking,

ILLUSTRATION 2.1. Horst Söhnlein (*left*) and founder of the Red Army Faction Andreas Baader joke around with unlit cigars as other group members, Thorwald Proll and Gudrun Ensslin, look on during the opening of their arson trial in Frankfurt am Main, West Germany, October 14, 1968. *ČTK / AP / Peter Hillebrecht*

kidnapping, sabotage, or assassination. Others were seasoned guerrilla fighters in their own homelands, who—due to lack of progress in their cause or internal rivalries—decided to take their local anticolonial struggle to the global stage and adopt terrorist tactics. Some guerrilla groups crossed the Rubicon from guerrilla warfare to domestic or international terrorism only temporarily; for others, international terrorism was their bread and butter.

Cold War terrorism was international in a number of ways. The perpetrators constituted an inherently international milieu of operatives from across the globe. Typically, multinational terrorist cells orchestrated some of the most notorious hijacking and hostage campaigns of the late 1970s. For instance, the 1975 raid on the headquarters of the Organization of the Petroleum Exporting Countries (OPEC) was led by a Venezuelan who commanded a group of Arabs and Germans; some Palestinian-led operations were carried out by Japanese Marxists, who were deemed to attract less suspicion than Arab nationals when attempting to attack Israeli targets.[9] Perpetrators moved across international borders, using fake identities and travel documents from multiple countries. Their targets were also inherently international. Plane, ship, and train hijackings were guaranteed to engage multinational passengers, embassy takeovers and hostage takings were aimed at highly symbolic targets embedded in foreign states, and attacks on popular civilian or critical infrastructure would also see multinational victims—be they discotheque goers or oil refinery staff. Furthermore, terrorist attacks were often directed at high-level representatives of international organizations, such as NATO and OPEC, as well as international high-profile events, such as the Olympic Games. In cases of plane hijackings, third countries often became involuntarily engaged in the process, and negotiations followed.

Mid-twentieth-century technological advancements further amplified the internationalism of this new terror wave. Civilian aviation was on the rise, with many thousands of people of various nationalities crossing international boundaries for the first time. Remarkably, however, security measures were not moving at the same pace, leaving the crews and passengers vulnerable to hostile assaults. The combination of high-visibility targets with lax security was a magnet for those ready to use violence to highlight their cause. Accordingly, plane hijackings became the staple tactic of Cold War international terrorism. They were what assassinations were to the late nineteenth-century anarchists and what suicide bombings were to become to al-Qaeda.[10] A close second were hostage-takings and kidnappings. The advent of international broadcasting and satellite coverage also made such targets increasingly appealing and performative.

Arguably, the ascent of the twenty-four-hour media cycle also had an impact on the nature and longevity of such attacks. More often than not, these were no brief moments of terror but instead theatrical ordeals that lasted days, weeks, and in some cases over a month. The Red Brigades held Italy's former prime minister, Aldo Moro, hostage for fifty-four days before he was executed by the left-wing terrorist group.[11] The Israeli crew and passengers of El Al Flight 426 were held in captivity for an exhausting five weeks. This agony was prolonged for a reason. The goal was to maintain public attention for as long as possible and force states to negotiate. This attention-seeking strategy, however, had advantages for those captured by these groups. It added an extra incentive not to kill hostages on hijacked planes or at besieged diplomatic missions. As American terrorism expert Brian Jenkins observed, "terrorists in the 1970s and 1980s wanted a lot of people watching, not a lot of people dead."[12] When killings during attacks did occur, in most cases they were highly symbolic. Ultimately, the shock, fear, and alarm that these attacks sought to generate was also designed to be felt internationally.

From the outset, Palestinian guerrillas were the flag-bearers of international terrorism. Not only was one of its factions responsible for the first hijacking demarking this international terrorism wave, but since the late 1960s Palestinian groups have undeniably dominated the international terrorist scene. According to an audit of terror incidents conducted by the RAND Corporation—an

American think tank created to conduct research for the Pentagon—from 1968 to 1980 Palestinian groups perpetrated 331 terror attacks, anti-Castro terrorist groups came second with 170 operations, and Irish and Turkish groups combined came in third with 115.[13] Overall, despite the fact that a number of these high-profile terrorist events failed to achieve their specific objectives, terrorism expert Bruce Hoffman argues that they secured their strategic goal of "demonstrating how long-standing but hitherto ignored or forgotten causes can be resurrected and dramatically thrust onto the world's agenda through a series of well-orchestrated, attention-grabbing acts."[14]

## THE ASCENT OF PALESTINIAN INTERNATIONAL TERRORISM

The use of terrorism as a tactic by Palestinian groups first emerged as an alternative following the catastrophic defeat of conventional Arab armies by Israel in the 1967 Six-Day War. Witnessing traditional Arab armies fail, a number of Palestinian groups opted for a strategy of attacking civilians—predominantly in the Middle East and across Western Europe. This turning point came less than five years after the PLO's creation. Set up in 1964, the PLO was an umbrella organization for the dispersed Palestinian people, initially aimed at eliminating the state of Israel and establishing an Arab state on the territory of the former Mandatory Palestine. Made up of numerous—often extremely fissiparous—parties and clusters, it gradually came to resemble a state, with an elected chairman; an executive committee; a parliamentary body; its own social, cultural, security, and intelligence branches; and an army.[15]

Although Yasser Arafat was not the PLO's first chairman, shortly after he took over in the late 1960s he became almost synonymous with the Palestinian cause. Despite many challenges, the kaffiyeh-wearing Arafat managed to stay at the helm of the PLO until his death in 2004. Born in 1929 to Palestinian parents in Cairo, Arafat lost his mother at a young age. He was brought up by various family members, including his mother's family, whom he came to live with for four years in the heart of the Old City of Jerusalem—only a stone's throw away from the Al-Aqsa Mosque, which would become the scene of many Palestinian-Israel confrontations.[16]

Arafat—also later known as Abu Ammar—studied engineering at what would later be known as Cairo University. During his studies, he embraced Arab nationalism, became an activist, and smuggled weapons into what was then Mandatory Palestine. By 1948, when the first war between the Jews and Arabs broke out, the young engineer took up arms alongside the Muslim Brotherhood to fight against the establishment of the State of Israel, allegedly rowing across the Suez Canal in a small boat with only one weapon to share with his two comrades. While much of Arafat's life, including his alleged first contact with combat, remains shrouded in mystery—largely imposed by Arafat himself—this experience had a fundamental impact on his future career.[17]

Following the war Arafat returned to Cairo and became active in student politics by becoming the head of the General Union of Palestinian Students. By 1957 he had left for Kuwait, then also under British rule, where he briefly worked as a schoolteacher and a road engineer. In two years, however, he firmly stepped into the realm of armed struggle, founding Fatah with two close friends—Salah Khalaf (Abu Iyad) and Khalil al-Wazir (Abu Jihad)—who became key military and security players within the PLO until their assassinations at the tail end of the Cold War. Fatah, initially designed as a purely Palestinian armed group without direct Arab government backing, dominated the PLO for all of Arafat's career. Based in numerous Arab states, Fatah staged cross-border attacks and raids against Israel. In its first two years of existence, the faction staged over sixty incursions into the Jewish state. Most, however, were unsuccessful, exposing the group's lack of aptitude. Despite these early failures, throughout the 1960s Arafat's profile grew, and in 1969 he was elected chair of the Palestinian National Council, a move that effectively made him the kingmaker of Palestinian politics for the following four decades.[18]

From the onset, the PLO suffered from acute cognitive and ideological dissonance. Its largest faction—Fatah—was primarily concerned with armed struggle against Israel. Its second most powerful player, the PFLP, was rather more interested in the idea of a world revolution by way of terrorism, and the PFLP's splinter group the Democratic Front for the Liberation of Palestine (DFLP) was also dedicated to Marxism-Leninism and openly used terror tactics. Al Saiqa was set up by Damascus to counterweight the Egypt-sponsored Fatah, and for the same reason Iraq sponsored the Arab Liberation Front.[19] Hence, from its inception, the PLO was a platform of ideologically heterogeneous groups, loyal to different Middle Eastern governments. Like so many exile movements, they were often destined to be cards rather than players.[20]

These factions also harbored divergent views on how to wage the struggle against Israel. Although some were initially more hesitant, even critical, about taking the struggle beyond Israel's boundaries and about adopting tactics such as sabotage, assassination, and hijacking to raise awareness and force its enemies to take them seriously, most did migrate their struggle onto the global stage. Gradually, in addition to sporting official structures, the factions that constituted the PLO also set up clandestine infrastructures devoted to staging fringe covert operations and dramatic terrorist attacks on the international stage. The two-decades-long Cold War campaign of international terrorism perpetrated by Palestinian factions was characterized by key turning points—events that signaled important strategic or tactical shifts.

A New Battleground    63

ILLUSTRATION 2.2. Empty hijacked planes blown up by PFLP guerrillas at a desert airstrip in northern Jordan known as Dawson's Field, September 12, 1970. *ČTK/Profimedia*

In the late 1960s and early 1970s, the PFLP—the PLO's second-largest faction—was responsible for staging pathbreaking attacks, each of which would up the ante and attract more attention. Two years after its 1968 hijacking of El Al Flight 426, which effectively inaugurated the Cold War wave of international terrorism, the PFLP staged another landmark event. On September 6, 1970, it executed the most monumental airplane hijacking in Cold War history. On the same day, which became known as "Skyjack Sunday," the Palestinian faction captured two American and one Swiss aircraft. The first two planes were seized over Europe and flown to an old British military base near Zarqa in Jordan known as Dawson's Field. The third airliner was diverted to Cairo, where it was destroyed after the crew and passengers were forced out. Several hours later, the fourth hijacking attempt, focused on an El Al flight from Amsterdam to London, ran into trouble. After one of the hijackers was shot dead by El Al air marshals, the other, Layla Khaled, by now an icon of the Palestinian resistance, was taken into British custody.[21] In an effort to secure her release, on September 9 a fifth plane—a British Overseas Airways flight from Bombay—was hijacked and flown to Dawson's Field. Three days later, as a show of strength, the three empty planes were blown up in the Jordanian desert. While some hostages were let go, others remained and would later be exchanged for Palestinians imprisoned in Switzerland, the United Kingdom, and West Germany.[22]

Turning Jordan into a hijacking zone triggered major retaliation and brought the Middle East to the brink of yet another war. King Hussein had been growing increasingly irritated by various Palestinian factions operating on and from his territory against Israel even prior to the spectacular terrorist event, and Skyjack Sunday was the tipping point. On September 15, he mobilized his troops against the unwelcome Palestinian groups operating on Jordanian territory.[23] Four days later, in an effort to aid the Palestinians, Syria invaded northern Jordan. Soon, matters escalated even further when the United States gave Israel the green light to bomb the Syrian army in northern Jordan. If King Hussein had fallen, the fate of the surviving hostages still held by the PFLP would have become even more complicated. Ultimately, despite all parties having their swords drawn, by late September a number of concessions were granted to the PFLP, and the crisis came to an end.[24]

During the ensuing civil war, the Jordanian army confronted and ousted the PLO and its factions from the kingdom. This was a traumatic event for the Palestinian resistance movement. Arafat lost the base from where his fighters mounted attacks on Israel, further weakening the position of Fatah, which had thus far refrained from major international terrorist attacks. Although it had first attacked Israel in January 1965, Fatah was in fact initially critical of the PFLP's international terror campaign, favoring a full-on guerrilla war against Israel from Jordanian territory and arguing that such terror tactics gave the world the "wrong image of the Arab cause."[25]

Nevertheless, Arafat could not deny that these international operations generated traction. By the early 1970s the PFLP's international terrorist campaign was grabbing headlines, generating an international debate about Palestinian issues and frustrating governments from the United States to Israel. Its key rival, Fatah, could not remain idle. With the increasing popularity of other PLO factions, Arafat feared losing control of the PLO. His hands were further tied as Arab governments prohibited the PLO from mounting attacks on Israel from their territory.[26] Therefore, the loss of their base in Jordan and feeling outperformed by other Palestinian factions prompted some Fatah representatives to adopt a new strategy. They temporarily took the mantle from the PFLP and adopted terrorism tactics.

In 1972 an amorphous network of Palestinian commandos called Black September, set up by Arafat's closest allies and named after the civil war that got them evicted from Jordan, perpetrated an attack that became the Cold War's 9/11. Shortly after four on the morning of September 5, 1972, an eight-member Black September squad climbed over the Olympic Village fence on the outskirts of Munich and headed for the living quarters of Israeli athletes. After killing two members of the Israeli team during the takeover, nine others were taken hostage. With the world watching, the commandos engaged in protracted negotiations with West German authorities. The Palestinians requested the release of over two hundred of their fellow nationals from Israeli prisons, further releases of five Red Army Faction terrorists—including its founding parents, Andreas Baader and Ulrike Meinhof—and a guarantee of safe passage.

The pressure was high, and the German negotiation strategy uncoordinated and poorly managed, ultimately resulting in an amateurish attempt to trap and subsequently confront the Palestinians at a local airport. Twenty hours into the drama, all of the Israeli hostages, five Palestinians, and one West German policeman were dead. The hostage-taking episode had unfolded before a television audience of almost a billion around the globe.[27]

Munich's impact on the Palestinian struggle was paradoxical. On one hand, it seriously damaged the "righteousness" of the Palestinian cause. On the other, it provided the Palestinian issue with more public exposure than any other event perpetrated in its name. It also provoked unprecedented retaliation by Israel. Initially the country's forces bombarded PLO bases in Lebanon and Syria, downed three Syrian military aircraft, and killed dozens of civilians. In a further show of strength, on September 16, Israel led three armored columns into southern Lebanon, in what was one of the largest military interventions in the region, flattening 130 houses suspected of harboring PLO fighters. Finally, a third phase of retaliation was approved by Israeli prime minister Golda Meir—a covert operation aimed at avenging Munich and paralyzing the Palestinian leadership. During this highly controversial campaign, code-named Wrath of God, which stretched over two decades, the Mossad, Israel's foreign intelligence agency, was estimated to have assassinated ninety targets, mostly in Western Europe.[28]

According to Bruce Hoffman, it was no coincidence that less than two years after Munich, the PLO began gaining international recognition. In 1974 Arafat spoke before the United Nations General Assembly, the PLO was given observer status, and by the end of the 1970s the nonstate entity had secured diplomatic relations with more countries than its archrival Israel. Once they had acquired this new status, it seemed that the Palestinians gradually began moving from international terrorism to international diplomacy, no longer wanting to taint their image with high-profile international violence.[29]

Not all groups associated with the Palestinian cause were, however, ready to cease their international terror campaigns. Some continued to use violence as their main currency. Chief among them was a radical offshoot of the PFLP set up by Wadi Haddad, the mastermind of the PFLP's earlier terrorist operations. He went solo in the early 1970s when the PFLP's politburo denounced international terrorism operations. In 1975 his new terrorist venture—called Popular Front for the Liberation of Palestine–External Operations (PFLP-EO)—decided to push the boundaries again and stage a spectacular operation in the heart of Europe.

On December 21, 1975, the OPEC headquarters in Vienna became the scene of this high-profile hostage-taking drama. The commando squad was led by the Venezuelan Ilich Ramírez Sánchez—the now infamous "Carlos the Jackal"—who had cut his terrorist teeth by staging operations in the name of the Palestinian cause. Killing two people on-site, Carlos's group abducted forty-two participants of the oil-rich OPEC countries' meeting and, after a treacherous journey, flew them to Algiers. Although Carlos was clearly instructed by Haddad to kill the Saudi Arabian oil minister and the Iranian interior minister, eventually all hostages were released in return for an alleged multimillion-dollar ransom. For disobeying Haddad's orders to kill the two ministers, Carlos was expelled from the PFLP-EO. He then launched his own terrorist franchise, which would go on to perpetrate further attacks across Western Europe.[30]

The latter half of the 1970s was dominated by two daring events orchestrated by Haddad's PFLP-EO: the 1976 Entebbe affair and the 1977 hijacking of a Lufthansa Boeing 737 to Mogadishu, Somalia.[31] Both instances of hijacking saw increasingly professional counterterrorism units kill most of the hijackers and secure the release of most of the passengers. Target states were catching up with the terrorists. At Entebbe, the Israeli special forces unit Sayeret Matkal flew over numerous enemy states to free over a hundred hostages held by Palestinians and Germans at Uganda's main airport. Although three hostages were killed, and the mission's commander, Yoni Netanyahu, was fatally shot in the opening minutes of the operation, overall the rescue operation was heralded as a success. At Mogadishu, a year later, where another joint Palestinian-German group landed a hijacked West German Lufthansa aircraft, the drama was ended by a surgical operation carried out by the West German counterterrorism group GSG 9, backed up by the Somali armed forces and advised by the SAS, a special operations unit of the British Army.[32] Ultimately Entebbe and Mogadishu were blows to Haddad's reputation for mounting successful attacks against Western targets. They further highlighted how disastrous the use of terror eventually proved to be for the Palestinian cause—with most of its operatives dead, incarcerated, or their covers blown.[33]

The last decade of Cold War international terrorism was characterized by both continuity and change. The first half of the 1980s witnessed old-school attacks by some of the terrorists who had made their names in the previous decade. The gang loyal to Carlos the Jackal—who broke away from the PFLP-EO after the 1975 OPEC raid—continued to attack symbolic targets, some in the name of their state sponsors, others to achieve release of their incarcerated comrades.[34] The Abu Nidal Organization—one of the PLO's most vicious breakaway groups, known for equal hatred of all things Israeli and mainstream PLO—staged high-profile attacks, mostly in Western Europe.[35] Its targets and tactics very much resembled terrorism of the 1970s, but they were on a much smaller scale than the spectacular 1970s hijackings and hostage-taking dramas.

The purpose of their terrorist campaigns had also shifted. Whereas in the 1960s and 1970s international terrorism was largely employed as a means of attaining strategic political goals, by the 1980s many terrorists had given up on politics and increasingly saw terrorism as a way of making a living. Their attacks became less about a "cause" and more about personal vendettas and commercial interests. In fact, groups led by Carlos the Jackal and Abu Nidal were increasingly used as proxies by various Arab regimes, including Syria, Iraq, Iran, and Libya. As part of this shift that arguably felt like the privatization of terrorism, Middle Eastern states would hire these agile international groups to attack or liquidate their opponents abroad. This shift undermined the remnants of political justification that had been used to explain their controversial tactics only a decade earlier. It took the revolution out of international terrorism and brought private state interests and money in.[36] Terrorism was now viewed as a type of covert warfare—enabling less powerful states to take on their dissidents living abroad or much larger rivals without risking direct confrontation.[37]

## GRASPING THE NEW THREAT LANDSCAPE

As spectacular airplane hijackings and hostage dramas started dominating the headlines in the early 1970s, Prague had good reasons to follow these events closely. Historically, Czechoslovakia had close ties with many of the Middle Eastern states at the center of these dramatic events. It had a heavy economic footprint in the region—it sold weapons and built sizable infrastructure projects across Syria, Iraq, Yemen, and Egypt.[38] It also hosted a significant Arab diaspora on its territory. These were either students from friendly Arab states pursuing civilian degrees in medicine, engineering, or the arts or cadets enrolled in the country's military academy.[39] The communist nation also hosted Middle Eastern émigrés—Iraqi or Syrian communists who had fled their countries in fear of persecution.

Middle Eastern Arab states also shared an enemy with Prague and its Soviet Bloc allies. Following the Six-Day War, when Israel took over sizable territories from its Arab neighbors, Moscow and Prague cut off diplomatic relations with the Jewish state. Furthermore, communist states were known for their long-term campaigns again Zionism, which resulted in discrimination of the Jewish populations living on their territory.[40]

Watching Palestinian "partisans" or "guerrillas," as Prague referred to them in these early days of international terrorism, take their struggle against Israel to the global stage was a game changer. The Czechoslovaks, however, were not sure what the Palestinians' endgame was. At this stage, Prague had little to no contact with Yasser Arafat, his friends, or his rivals within the Palestinian movement. Accordingly, in the early 1970s the Czechoslovak state and Communist Party representatives were curious to better understand the growing threat of international terrorism. What caused this shift in Palestinian strategy and tactics? Why did they decide to go global? Was this a threat mostly manifesting itself in the West? Or could they also turn against the East? Was Israel likely to attack Soviet Bloc states hosting Palestinian guerrillas? Were Arabs living in Europe being used for these operations? Prague would rely on its diplomats and spies to provide answers to these complex questions.

Since the PLO's rise to prominence in the late 1960s, Prague's diplomats had been closely watching developments within the Palestinian umbrella organization—observing its relations with Arab states and keeping track of its tactics. As the PLO's national liberation struggle progressed into the 1970s, these envoys were keen to understand what caused the shift toward these high-profile and controversial international terrorist operations. In autumn 1971 they observed that "radicalization and fragmentation" of the movement went hand in hand. Finding the culprit responsible for undermining the movement's unity was not hard. Prague clearly observed that it was thanks to the Jordanian government's "physical and material liquidation" of PLO bases on its territory— the so-called Black September operation carried out in the aftermath of Skyjack Sunday—that the Palestinian factions resorted to "illegal tactics and operations." The diplomats considered this shift problematic because, as Prague's envoys observed, it led to uncoordinated individual operations, which included several attempts to hijack Jordanian planes and bomb attacks as well as assassination attempts against Arafat.[41] Overall, Prague's diplomats were skeptical about the utility of such methods and by the summer of 1972 referred to them as "individual operations aimed at inflicting terror."[42]

While Prague tried to understand the new wave of political violence, its communist-era propaganda also tried to pin the late Cold War wave of international terrorism on its adversaries. The root cause of terrorism was the crisis of capitalism in the West, the envoys argued, and it was thanks to this environment that extremism and terrorism thrived. Prague also suspected the so-called reactionary West of trying to direct this wave of terrorism toward socialist countries to "negatively affect the security situation" in the Soviet Bloc.[43] In other words, much like the Reagan administration ten years later, Prague attempted to blame its ideological adversaries for the new terror threat.

By autumn 1972, after the shock of the Munich Olympics massacre, the diplomats took an even stronger stance against the new tactic, arguing that "the interests of the PRM [Palestinian resistance movement] are being harmed by terrorist operations of this kind, such as for example the tragic incident in

Munich." Simultaneously, rarely letting an opportunity to criticize their Cold War rivals pass, they argued that such tactics are "widely used by imperialist and mostly Zionist propaganda against Arabs in general and especially the Palestinian resistance movement."[44]

Overall, however, in the early 1970s Prague's diplomats mostly viewed Palestinian terrorism as part of a bigger problem faced by the Palestinian resistance movement. They considered this a consequence of the harsh clampdown on the Palestinians by the pro-Western Jordanian government and blamed other, so-called reactionary Arab states and Israel for the movement's lack of unity, which Prague saw as another key contributor to its adoption of these harsh methods of political violence.

Whereas the diplomats were mostly concerned with tracing the root causes of the increasingly radical tactics of the Palestinian resistance movement, Prague's spies in the Middle East were closely monitoring the wider security implications of Palestinian terrorist attacks in the region. Less than two weeks after the gruesome attack at Lod Airport (renamed Ben Gurion Airport in 1973)—in which the Japanese Red Army, as a PFLP proxy, disembarked from an incoming flight and killed twenty-six individuals using Czechoslovak-made automatic weapons concealed in violin cases—Prague's rezidentura in Beirut was told by its sources that Israel was preparing to retaliate against Palestinian strongholds in Lebanon and Syria. While the conflict did not further intensify, the crisis was a symbol of how swiftly the Middle Eastern conflict could ignite.[45]

Soon Prague received further reports of possible regional escalation. Their Soviet counterparts suggested that Israel was training special commandos to kidnap one of the Palestinian strongmen who had blessed PFLP's terror campaign in the early 1970s—George Habash. According to what the KGB described as a reliable source, the PFLP leader was to be seized by the special unit and held hostage to prevent further high-profile terrorist attacks.[46] Although these specific warnings did not materialize, they were a good indication of what was to come. After the 1972 Munich massacre, Israel did indeed retaliate on an unprecedented scale by hitting civilian and military targets across Lebanon and Syria as well as setting in motion a protracted assassination campaign of key PLO representatives.

Prague's early approach to the Palestinian use of terrorist tactics was equivocal. It was a combination of lukewarm condemnation and blame-shifting. On one hand, its diplomats argued that the "interests of the Palestinian resistance movement are harmed by terrorist attacks, such as the tragic incident in Munich."[47] At meetings with partners they would even go as far as to explicitly condemn the use of terrorism by Palestinians. On the other hand, however, such condemnations would typically be accompanied by various caveats. At one such meeting with their Polish counterparts, the head of the Middle Eastern Department of the Ministry of Foreign Affairs told his partners, "We denounce terrorist attacks, which are rather harmful, and we also cannot rule out the involvement of Israel's 'long fingers' in these acts"[48]—suggesting the Jewish state was in fact instigating or orchestrating terrorist attacks in the name of the Palestinian struggle in devious false flag operations. In the same breath, Prague's diplomats condemned Palestinian violence and blamed it on the Palestinians' archrivals.

In the early years of Palestinian international terrorism, Prague did not feel directly threatened. Although occasionally it did receive thirdhand unverified information suggesting that some Palestinian elements might be keen to also attack targets in the Soviet Bloc, it did not seem to consider them a real threat.[49] It continued to keep its calm even when, on September 28, 1973, an obscure yet significant terrorist attack occurred aboard a train only moments after it left Czechoslovakia and entered Austrian territory. Staged by the Syrian-sponsored Palestinian group Al Saiqa, three Soviet Jewish emigrants traveling from Moscow to Israel via a transit camp close to Vienna were taken hostage in a passenger car. A Slovak railway worker who was on duty that day in Marchegg recalled the event forty-five years later: "I remember the shooting. I was outside, checking the train with an Austrian colleague. Austrian customs officials were the first to board the train. And all of a sudden we heard our Austrian colleague, Weleba, shouting. I saw the barrel of a Kalashnikov sticking out of the car carrying Russian Jews. We all ran in different directions. I hid behind the building and watched the drama unfold."[50] After protracted negotiations, the group's key demand—closing down the transit camp for Jews on Austrian territory—was met by Austrian prime minister Bruno Kreisky.[51]

As the 1970s progressed, however, Czechoslovakia's approach toward Cold War jackals became much better defined. Gradually it established a political and intelligence alliance with the PLO. It also became better at recognizing and managing risks posed by other groups that started descending on its territory in the latter part of the decade. To this end it used its top diplomats and spies, who, much like a Swiss Army Knife, served a number of functions. While in some cases they were used to foster alliances with Cold War jackals, at other times they were deployed to manage risk or oust those Prague deemed bad actors. Czechoslovakia's interactions with the jackals were as fascinating as they were treacherous.

# NOTES

1. Oded Abarbanell, "Hijacking to Algiers—Part 1," in *Stories of My Family and from the Dawn of Flight in Israel* (blog), May 8, 2013, https://odedabarbanell.wordpress.com/2013/03/08/hijacked-to-algiers-part-1/.

2. Although the PFLP's operation was unprecedented in its political undertone and execution, airplane hijackings were not an entirely new phenomenon. Since the late 1950s dozens of mostly American aircrafts were hijacked over US soil and diverted to Cuba, either by Cuban exiles or revolutionaries looking for a cheap ride to Havana. For more, see Timothy Naftali, *Blind Spot: The Secret History of American Counterterrorism* (New York: Basic Books, 2005), 19–25.
3. BBC, "History of Airliner Hijackings," BBC News, October 3, 2001, http://news.bbc.co.uk/1/hi/world/south_asia/1578183.stm.
4. Hoffman, *Inside Terrorism*, 63–80; Wilkinson, *Terrorism versus Democracy*, 63–64.
5. For an overview of nineteenth- and twentieth-century terrorism waves or strains, see David Rapoport, "The Four Waves of Rebel Terror and September 11," *Anthropoetics* 8, no. 1 (Spring/Summer 2002); Hoffman, *Inside Terrorism*, 1–64; Leonard Weinberg, "A History of Terrorism," in *Routledge Handbook of Terrorism and Counterterrorism*, ed. Andrew Silke (London: Routledge, 2019).
6. See the text of the Atlantic Charter, which promised self-determination: Franklin D. Roosevelt and Winston S. Churchill, "The Atlantic Charter," August 14, 1941, Avalon Project, Yale Law School, https://avalon.law.yale.edu/wwii/atlantic.asp.
7. The PIRA, often simply referred to as the "Provisional IRA," became the dominant republican paramilitary group during the conflict in Northern Ireland known as the Troubles. It carried out numerous bombings, shootings, and other attacks in Northern Ireland and across the United Kingdom, aiming to end British rule in Northern Ireland and establish a united Ireland. "The IRA" is a broader term encompassing various iterations of the Irish Republican Army throughout history.
8. Arguably this zeitgeist also led to the emergence of groups elsewhere on the globe claiming revolutionary credentials—such as the Colombian M-19, infamous for its 1985 Palace of Justice siege; the Uruguayan Tupamaros; and the Maoist Sendero Luminoso in Peru—as well as revolutionary pushback in Asia.
9. Thomas Riegler, "When Modern Terrorism Began: The OPEC Hostage Taking of 1975," in *Handbook of OPEC and the Global Energy Order: Past, Present and Future Challenges*, ed. Dag Harald Claes and Giuliano Garavini (London: Routledge, 2020).
10. See more on the evolution of terrorist doctrines and tactics in Rapoport, "Four Waves of Rebel Terror."
11. Richard Drake, "The Aldo Moro Murder Case in Retrospect," *Journal of Cold War Studies* 8, no. 2 (2006): 114–25.
12. Wilkinson, *Terrorism versus Democracy*, 7.
13. From the RAND Terrorism Incident Database, which covers only international terrorist incidents, in Hoffman, *Inside Terrorism*, 64, 309.
14. Hoffman, 65.
15. See more on its evolution in Sayigh, *Armed Struggle*; Jillian Becker, *The PLO: The Rise and Fall of the Palestine Liberation Organization* (Bloomington, IN: AuthorHouse, 2014); Paul Thomas Chamberlin, *The Global Offensive: The United States, the Palestine Liberation Organization, and the Making of the Post–Cold War Order* (Oxford: Oxford University Press, 2012); and Helena Cobban, *The Palestinian Liberation Organisation: People, Power and Politics*, vol. 10 (Cambridge: Cambridge University Press, 1984).
16. Tony Walker and Andrew Gowers, *Arafat: The Biography* (London: Virgin, 2003).

17. Barry Rubin and Judith Colp Rubin, *Yasir Arafat: A Political Biography* (New York: Oxford University Press, 2003), 11–36.
18. Rubin and Rubin, 11–36.
19. Christopher Dobson, *Black September: Its Short, Violent History* (London: Macmillan, 1974).
20. Yossi Shain, *The Frontier of Loyalty: Political Exiles in the Age of the Nation-State* (Ann Arbor: University of Michigan Press, 1989), 26.
21. "I Made the Ring from a Bullet and the Pin of a Hand Grenade," *Guardian*, January 26, 2001.
22. Christopher Dobson and Ronald Payne, *The Terrorists: Their Weapons, Leaders and Tactics* (New York: Facts on File, 1982), 233; Naftali, *Blind Spot*, 41–48. For firsthand accounts of the hijacking, see David Raab, *Terror in Black September: The First Eyewitness Account of the Infamous 1970 Hijackings* (New York: St. Martin's, 2007).
23. Naftali, *Blind Spot*, 48–49.
24. Although members of some Palestinian factions would stay behind to fight the Hashemite regime until the summer of 1971. For more on the Jordanian Civil War, see Sayigh, *Armed Struggle*, 262–81.
25. Simon Reeve, *One Day in September: The Full Story of the 1972 Munich Olympics Massacre and the Israeli Revenge Operation "Wrath of God"* (New York: Arcade, 2000), 27, 31, 34.
26. Reeve, 27, 31, 34.
27. For thorough accounts of the Munich attack as well as its aftermath, see Aaron J. Klein, *Protiúder: Mníchov*. Bratislava: Slovenský spisovateľ, 2005.
28. Klein, *Protiúder*. For more on Operation Wrath of God, see Ronen Bergman, *Rise and Kill First: The Secret History of Israel's Targeted Assassinations* (New York: Random House, 2018), chaps. 9–14.
29. Hoffman, *Inside Terrorism*, 68–70.
30. John Follain, *Jackal: The Complete Story of the Legendary Terrorist, Carlos the Jackal* (New York: Arcade, 1998), 79–98, 102; Bassam Abu Sharif and Uri Mahnaimi, *Best of Enemies: The Memoirs of Bassam Abu-Sharif and Uzi Mahnaimi* (Boston: Little, Brown, 1995), 163–65. For a detailed account of the raid, see Colin Smith, *Carlos: Portrait of a Terrorist* (London: Deutsch, 1995), 171–244.
31. "Hanseatisches Oberlandesgericht Urteil im Names des Forlkes in der Strafsache Gegen Souhaila Sami Andrawes Sayeh," court judgment in criminal case against Souhaila Sami Andrawes Sayeh, November 27, 1996, author's private archive, 9. For further information on the hijacking crisis, see Bernhard Blumenau, *The United Nations and Terrorism: Germany, Multilateralism, and Antiterrorism Efforts in the 1970s* (Basingstoke, UK: Palgrave Macmillan, 2014), 74–86; and T. Geiger, "'Landshut' in Mogadischu: Das Außenpolitische Krisenmanagement der Bundesregierung Angesichts der Terroristischen Herausforderung 1977," *Vierteljahrshefte fur Zeitgeschichte* 3 (2009): 413–56.
32. Mark A. Carolla, "Operation 'Magic Fire': A Case Study in Collaborative Threat Assessments and Risk Analysis of the German Bundesgrenzschutz GSG-9 Rescue of the Lufthansa Boeing 737-200 'Landshut' Hostages in Mogadishu, October 1977" (diss., Aviation Institute, George Washington University, 2007); Richard J. Aldrich and Rory Cormac, *The Black Door: Spies, Secret Intelligence and British Prime Ministers* (London: Collins, 2016), 340–41.
33. Smith, *Carlos*, 266; Andrew and Mitrokhin, *World Was Going Our Way*, 254.

34. To date, the best biography of Carlos the Jackal remains John Follain's *Jackal*.
35. For most authoritative accounts of the Abu Nidal Organization, see Yossi Melman, *The Master Terrorist: The True Story of Abu Nidal* (New York: Adama Books, 1986); and Patrick Seale, *Abu Nidal: A Gun for Hire* (New York: Random House, 1992).
36. Blumenau, *United Nations and Terrorism*, 193–94; Leonard Weinberg, *The End of Terrorism?* (New York: Routledge, 2012), 103–4.
37. Hoffman, *Inside Terrorism*, 17–18.
38. Dušan Ulčák, interview by the author, September 8, 2015. For more on Prague's diplomatic relations with the Middle East and North Africa, see Zídek and Sieber, *Československo a Blízký východ*; Jan Adamec, "Czechoslovak-Syrian Relations during the Cold War," in *Syria during the Cold War: The East European Connection*, ed. Przemyslaw Gasztold-Sen, Massimiliano Trenin, and Jan Adamec (Fife, UK: University of St Andrews Centre for Syrian Studies, 2014); Motti Golani, "The Historical Place of the Czech-Egyptian Arms Deal, Fall 1955," *Middle Eastern Studies* 31, no. 4 (1995): 803–27; and Guy Laron, "Logic Dictates That They May Attack When They Feel They Can Win: The 1955 Czech-Egyptian Arms Deal, the Egyptian Army, and Israeli Intelligence," *Middle East Journal* 63, no. 1 (Winter 2009): 69–84.
39. Daniela Hannová, "Problémoví elegáni: Arabští studenti v Praze v 50. a 60. letech 20. století," *Auc Historia Universitatis Carolinae Pragensis* 54, no. 2 (2016): 105–25; Richterova, Pešta, and Telepneva, "Banking on Military Assistance."
40. Nora Levin, *The Jews in the Soviet Union since 1917: Paradox of Survival*, vols. 1 and 2 (New York: New York University Press, 1990).
41. Tajovský (8.t.o.), October 13, 1971, "Informace o současném stavu palestinského hnutí odporu," A-MZV, T-1970-1974, 8.t.o., Ka 1/111.
42. Tajovský (8.t.o.), June 28, 1972, "Informace ZÚ Ammán o situaci v palestinském hnutí odporu," A-MZV, T-1972-1973, Jordansko, Ka 1, 127/311.
43. Vladimír Stárek (Náč.X.S-FMV)–Jaroslav Hrbáček (Náčelník II.S-FMV), July 4, 1979, "Důvodová zpráva k návrhu nařízení ministra vnitra ČSSR pro činnost SNB a HS PS OSH na úseku boje proti terorizmu," ABS-HFSB, a.č. H-720/3.
44. M. Vojta (MZV, 8.t.o.), October 23, 1972, "Návštěva s. ministra Chňoupka v SFRJ—dílčí podkladové materiály /BSV, EAR, ADLR, Eriopie. Palestinské hnutí odporu.," A-MZV, T-1970–1974, 8.t.o., Ka 1/112.
45. Seman (Beirut, I.S/47), June 14, 1972, ABS-12470/103.
46. J. Zajíc (Náč. odboru 17)–I.S/47, July 4, 1972, "Výcvik protipalestinské záškodnické skupiny v Izraeli," ABS-12470/103.
47. M. Vojta (MZV, 8.t.o.), October 23, 1972, "Návštěva s. ministra Chňoupka v SFRJ-dílčí podkladové materiály/BSV, EAR, ADLR, Eriopie. Palestinské hnutí odporu.," A-MZV, T-1970–74/8.t.o., Ka 1/112.
48. "Zpráva o konzultacích mezi 8.t.o. FMZV a 5.t.o. MZV PLR," January 12, 1974, A-MZV, T-1970–74/8.t.o., Ka 1.
49. Mjr. F. Domkař (I.S/47), May 17, 1973, "Vyjádření odboru 47 I.Správy FMV k otázce příprav akcí organizace "Černé září" proti zastupitelským úřadům socialistických zení," ABS-12470/000.
50. Milan K., interview by the author, September 13, 2017.
51. There is some debate about how much the StB knew about the attackers' intentions to hijack the train in question. Documents available to date do not unequivocally confirm or deny whether Prague had prior knowledge about the attack, but they

do show that Prague knew about the attackers' presence on its territory shortly prior to the hijacking incident. For more on the hijacking drama, see Paul Thomas Chamberlin, "Schönau and the Eagles of the Palestinian Revolution: Refugees, Guerrillas, and Human Rights in the Global 1970s," *Cold War History* 12, no. 4 (2012): 595–614; Federal Chancellery, *Events of September 28th and 29th 1973: A Documentary Report* (Vienna: Federal Chancellery, 1973); Peter P., interview by the author, September 4, 2015; and "Krajská správa ZNB Bratislava, 'Prepadnutie Čs. vlaku—Marchegg,'" 1973, ÚPN, f. R 012, 51/30; "Khaldi Cheikh," ABS-6088; and "Husejn Raad," ABS-10733.

# PART II
# THE PLO

# 3

# A Gordian Alliance

Dear Comrade Arafat, a great patriot and fearless leader of the heroic Palestinian people.... I would like to again assure you and the Arab people that you have the full support of the Czechoslovak people for your difficult and fully legitimate struggle. Your revolution, your struggle, is also our struggle. It is an integral part of the revolutionary fight for peace, security, justice and social progress in the world. This is why we attach great importance to our relations.[1]

On April 18, 1983, the Czechoslovak president, Gustáv Husák, used these words to toast the Palestinian leader during one of his official visits to Prague.[2] Arguably, as a former anti-Nazi partisan and political prisoner, Husák empathized with the armed struggle and revolutionary ethos epitomized by the PLO. Although Czechoslovakia was no superpower, the Palestinians were keen to forge an alliance with it because they saw its small-size status as an advantage. Not burdened by imperial legacies, responsibilities, and protocols, it could perhaps become the flag-bearer of a much more open policy toward the Palestinians. What is more, due to its status as a global arms dealer, it was a well-known country with global outreach.[3]

We now know, however, that Arafat's road to Prague was long. Despite President Husák's warm toast suggesting his country's unequivocal support for the Palestinian struggle, it took considerable time for the PLO to create official relations with Czechoslovakia. Although representatives of the Palestinian umbrella organization started courting Prague in the mid-1960s, it took almost another decade for Arafat to establish direct relations with the communist state. During the first decade of the PLO's existence, 1964 to 1974, the Soviet Bloc's attitude toward the controversial nonstate actors was marked by reluctance and stalling.[4] Hamstrung by alliance politics, Prague waited until Moscow made the decisive move to provide assistance to Arafat's organization. Moreover, it was hesitant about creating an alliance with controversial nonstate actors involved in high-profile acts of international terror.

**ILLUSTRATION 3.1.** Yasser Arafat with Gustáv Husák during official talks at Prague Castle, April 18, 1983. *ČTK / Kalina Michal*

Once established, the PLO's diplomatic relationship with Prague was hard work. Although by the mid-1970s, following the PLO's pivot to diplomacy, Prague warmed to Arafat and gradually expanded and intensified its relations with the PLO, major cracks in the relationship soon appeared. During the last decade of the Cold War, lack of unity, flirtation with the West, and distrust of Arafat made Prague's diplomatic relationship with the Palestinians a complicated affair—so much so that in the mid-1980s, along with other Soviet allies, Czechoslovakia temporarily suspended its relations with the PLO.

## HESITANT BEGINNINGS

The PLO first tried to strike an alliance with Czechoslovakia in the mid-1960s, well before its heyday. In August 1965 the then chairman of the PLO, Ahmad al-Shuqayri, met with the Czechoslovak ambassador in Beirut and expressed interest in forging ties with socialist countries, hoping they would provide military supplies and training for its cadets. Although by that time the PLO had already established offices in Washington, New York, Geneva, Belgrade, and Beijing, it was now looking to extend its presence into the Soviet Bloc.

Prague's reaction to al-Shuqayri's courtship was unenthusiastic and cautious, with the country's diplomats arguing that "establishing direct ties would be a delicate political issue." At this stage, reactions of other socialist countries had also been rather reserved. While Prague waited to receive further instructions from Moscow, it considered its options. If the PLO delegation was touring other socialist states, argued Foreign Minister Václav David, Prague could invite it for an unofficial visit, which would promote low-profile contacts and hold exploratory talks on possible assistance. This would, however, stop short of outright political or military support and focus on providing stipends for Palestinian students. Such a visit would demonstrate goodwill but not commitment.[5]

Eventually Moscow instructed Prague not to facilitate such a meeting with the PLO because the movement's relationship with socialist states remained unclear. If the PLO was to bring up the subject of a visit again, it advised, Prague should follow Moscow's approach—use the Czechoslovak Solidarity Committee to handle the visit and seek "Soviet opinion" on whether to provide military supplies to the PLO via its state-owned arms companies.[6] Through its sources in Cairo, Prague knew the PLO would readily accept a visit to Czechoslovakia as it had intense interest in the country's weapons, some of which were deemed especially suitable for guerrilla warfare, as well as in forging a long-term political and military alliance. Prague, however, avoided meeting the Palestinians until a clear policy was laid down by Moscow.[7]

After the Six-Day War of 1967, when the Arab nations suffered a humiliating defeat at the hands of Israel, Moscow gradually started seeing value in the enigmatic Palestinian resistance movement, not least due to its own deteriorating relations with Israel, having suspended diplomatic relations due to the war. Czechoslovakia also happily observed positive shifts in the movement's development and scope. Most important, it responded warmly to the PLO's increasing activity in the occupied territories as well as in Israel proper and to the fact that its armed struggle was able to generate tensions within Israel and challenge its military and police apparatuses.[8]

In March 1969, a month after Yasser Arafat was elected chairman of the PLO, the organization was promised assistance at an initial, low-profile meeting in Moscow that included military training and arms supplies via Egypt.[9] It took, however, another year for Arafat to embark on his first official visit to Moscow. Remarkably, Prague only found out from the Egyptian newspaper *Al Ahram* that a Fatah delegation would soon hold its first meeting with the Soviets in Moscow. Dumbfounded, Prague hastily sent a classified telegram to its embassies in Moscow and Cairo, asking its envoys to verify this information: "In case the findings are affirmative, attempt to find out on what level will the meeting be held and what it will be about. . . . Find out whether the Soviet side has been informed about Palestinian objectives in respect to other socialist countries and what it thinks about potential coordination of our approach." Noting that thus far Moscow's attitude toward Palestinian resistance groups has been "relatively cold," Prague observed that, if true, the PLO-Soviet meeting marked "a fundamental change in their mutual relations."[10] Obviously left in the dark by the Soviets, the Czechoslovak ambassador in Moscow soon met with the secretary of the Soviet Committee for Solidarity with Countries in Asia and Africa—the so-called Solidarity Committee—a front organization set up to facilitate Soviet contacts with third world movements. There the Soviet representative assured his Czechoslovak counterpart that during the upcoming meeting with the PLO, the Soviets would stick to the course agreed on by six socialist states—hinting at a joint approach to the issue. Moreover, he reiterated that, thus far, the Palestinians had not received direct Soviet military support but had only been passed supplies via Cairo.[11]

Finally, in February 1970, after some Soviet hesitation, and with assistance from Egyptian president Gamal Abdel Nasser, Arafat visited Moscow. This represented a fundamental turning point in Soviet-PLO relations, ensuring that the PLO received political and material support from the superpower. Although the Soviets first supplied the PLO with arms via its Middle Eastern allies, by 1972 it was receiving direct deliveries. These were largely similar to those Moscow provided to other anticolonial national liberation movements: tanks, light weapons, and SA-7 surface-to-air missiles.[12]

Undoubtedly, by now Moscow considered the PLO an important political resistance movement worthy of Soviet support. Nevertheless, it also saw it as a means to achieving three strategic goals. Within the context of the Palestinian-Israeli conflict, the PLO could be Moscow's "ticket" into this important process that would likely shape Middle Eastern politics and geography for decades to come. In addition to that, it could serve as a useful ally to exercise military pressure on Israel and, by extension, on the Soviet Bloc's "principal adversary"—the United States. On a more global level, turning the PLO Palestinian umbrella group into an ally could also result in pushing China out. This was particularly important because Beijing was now Moscow's great rival, with wider ambitions in the Middle East and an early and enthusiastic supporter of the PLO. Support for the PLO also complemented the Soviet Union's self-appointed role as the guardian of national liberation movements in the third world.[13] This support was, however, not entirely selfless. As with the national liberation movements in Africa, Moscow worked hard to create ties with Palestinian representatives to influence their internal affairs and turn them into active pro-Soviet advocates in the Middle East.[14]

While Moscow looked to achieve these goals, Arafat's visit to the Soviet Union raised some concern there, chiefly in respect to the PLO's lack of unity and its uneasy relationship with Moscow's key Arab allies, most prominently Syria. Nevertheless, Moscow decided to support the movement "in those efforts we consider legitimate"—using armed struggle to oust an aggressor and confront Israeli expansion. At the same time, however, it vehemently refused to support "irresponsible proclamations" by some of the PLO's previous representatives, such as those made by former chairman al-Shuqayri, who stated, "We will throw Israelis into the sea," as well as demands calling for a unified Palestinian state built according to the 1947 borders.[15]

Overall, even after having created an official channel with the PLO, Moscow remained skeptical. The Czechoslovaks were told by Aleksandr Dzasokhov, head of the Solidarity Committee, who would rise in the 1990s to become the deputy of the State Duma of the Russian Federation that hosted Arafat, "We feel that complications will emerge in the near future. Political solutions to the Middle Eastern question will lead to a conflict with the Palestinians. That is why our relations are handled through our committee."[16] The Palestinians were thus to be kept at arm's length from the Communist Party.

During Arafat's ten-day visit, Prague also shifted its perspective on the PLO. Despite enduring reservations that echoed those of Moscow, Prague's rationale for supporting the PLO was threefold. Primarily, Czechoslovakia chose to liaise with the PLO because it was a key and "internationally recognized" player in the Middle East, with an "anti-imperialist" mind-set and mass support of the Palestinian population. In other words, the PLO was now too important to ignore. Second, Moscow and its Soviet Bloc allies were well aware of the ideological tensions and conflicts taking place within the PLO at the time. Hoping to influence these power struggles to their advantage, Prague argued that "without establishing direct and regular contacts [with the PLO], socialist countries will not be able to influence the movement" and paralyze other "dangerous" influences, including those of "reactionary Arab states" and "imperialist intelligence agencies" as well as China.[17] Accordingly, partnership with the PLO was also about projecting influence and direction—especially when it came to the PLO's relationship with Arab states, many of which were key Soviet Bloc allies.

While in the early 1970s Czechoslovakia started engaging in more regular contact with the PLO, it was not until several years later that its strategy became more clearly defined. The year 1974 was a turning point crucial to PLO recognition. Throughout the year, Arafat made it clear that he was interested in making a transition from a partisan to a political leader. He was keen to let his potential allies in Central Europe know about his shift to diplomacy and ask for their support in the PLO's path to further recognition. In September 1974 the PLO chief wrote to First Communist Party Secretary Husák, informing him that "the PLO decided to intensify its diplomatic and political activity" and extend its scope to the political-diplomatic realm, as opposed to its predominantly military-driven politics. Husák responded enthusiastically and, wishing to reward this more diplomatic path, promised Arafat Czechoslovakia's support for the PLO's efforts to have the Palestinian issue discussed at the upcoming UN General Assembly.[18]

Further political successes followed. At the October 1974 Arab League summit in Rabat, Morocco, leaders of twenty Arab states unanimously passed a resolution declaring the PLO the "sole legitimate representative of the Palestinian people."[19] One month later, Arafat delivered his historic speech at the UN General Assembly in which he publicly, yet not unequivocally, declared his openness to a peaceful solution: "Today I have come bearing an olive branch and a freedom-fighter's gun. Do not let the olive branch fall from my hand. I repeat: do not let the olive branch fall from my hand."[20] The UN reacted to this public proclamation by awarding the PLO nonstate observer status, further increasing the organization's importance in the international domain.

During the first decade of its existence, the PLO had managed to rise from obscurity to gaining international recognition. This included an intensification of relations with the Soviet Union as well as its East Central European allies. Prague, Moscow's most willing junior partner, would play an important role in this process.

## GREAT EXPECTATIONS

Recognition of the PLO by the Arab League and UN was an important impetus for Prague to shift gears and give it the recognition it longed for. In May 1975 Arafat made his first official visit to Czechoslovakia as PLO chairman.[21] There he met the country's top leaders: the pragmatic lawyer and anti-Nazi resistance leader who became Czechoslovakia's longest-standing president and first secretary of the country's Communist Party, Gustáv Husák; Foreign Minister Bohuslav Chňoupek; and the tailor-turned-secretary of the Presidium of the Central Committee of the Communist Party of Czechoslovakia (ÚV KSČ), Vasiľ Biľak, whose post made him one of the kingmakers of Czechoslovak foreign policy, particularly when it came to national liberation movements.[22]

In hindsight, this visit represented a milestone in Czechoslovak-PLO relations. Crucially, in 1976 it led to the establishment of the so-called PLO Office—a permanent PLO representation that would play an important and at times controversial role in Prague's security and intelligence liaison with Arafat's men.[23] Largely funded by the Czechoslovak Communist Party, the office was led by the special representative, who was granted diplomatic privileges and two assistants. The PLO Office was part of the PLO's Political Department, which, in consultation with Arafat, approved all major decisions.

Officially the PLO Office was accredited by the Czechoslovak Solidarity Committee—the Communist Party's front organization set up to facilitate relations with allied national liberation movements and other nonstate actors, including the PLO. Josef Krejčí remembers frequent meetings with PLO representatives during his time as the Solidarity Committee's executive secretary

ILLUSTRATION 3.2. Yasser Arafat being greeted by the first secretary of the Communist Party of Czechoslovakia, Vasiľ Biľak, at Prague Airport during his first official visit to Czechoslovakia, May 5, 1975. *ČTK / Hajský Libor*

(1977–83) and effectively serving as Arafat's majordomo during several of his visits. It was his job to chaperone the PLO leader and his large, heavily armed entourage to meetings with Czechoslovak powerbrokers.[24]

Prague opened the PLO Office for symbolic as well as practical reasons. On one hand, it viewed the PLO representation as "the first step to its [the PLO's] international legal recognition by the CSSR and creating new conditions for intensifying mutual cooperation in all areas."[25] Its establishment was seen as a strong sign of Czechoslovakia's support for the Palestinian cause. On the other hand, Prague also had practical reasons for hosting Palestinian representatives on its territory. As their bilateral relations expanded, the office oversaw the growing population of Palestinian students enrolled at the country's universities.[26] During the 1970s, an estimated 100 to 150 Palestinians pursued university studies in Czechoslovakia annually, mostly funded by stipends from the Czechoslovak Communist Party, the government, or international organizations.[27]

The PLO Office also helped coordinate Prague's material support to the PLO. This came in the form of medical and other aid for dozens of Palestinians—including hospital stays for wounded Palestinian fighters and material and financial help—which from 1976 to 1980 amounted to $1.7 million.[28] This included medicine, blankets, shoes, and food. In the following years, further material and financial support would follow. Most crucially, after the 1982 Israeli invasion of Lebanon, the PLO was given the equivalent of $9 million, and fifty wounded fighters were transported to Czechoslovakia for medical treatment.[29] In addition to humanitarian assistance, the PLO Office also organized cultural and social gatherings for the growing Palestinian diaspora.

But Prague was by no means a pioneer in this respect. By June 1975 Arafat's organization had established seventy-four official representations around the world. They were based in most Arab states; key Western capitals, including New York, Ottawa, Tokyo, London, Paris, Geneva, Madrid, and Rome; and across the third world, ranging from Brazil to Kenya, Uganda, India, Malaysia, and China.[30] Each one of these offices had a different status. For instance, the Palestinian representation in Washington was officially designated the PLO Information Center. By the mid-1970s, most Soviet Bloc countries also made their relations with the Palestinians official. The setup was similar to Prague's: PLO Offices in the Soviet Union, Bulgaria, and East Germany were generously funded and supported by the host countries' communist parties.[31]

Gradually, as the PLO became more visible and prestigious, Czechoslovakia's relations with it came to resemble relations between two international legal entities. In April 1980 the PLO Office was granted diplomatic privileges and immunities, elevating the PLO representation to something close to an embassy fully funded by the Czechoslovak government and the Communist Party.[32] Three years later, Prague further elevated its status, this time to a full diplomatic mission, with the ambassador accredited at the Ministry of Foreign Affairs.[33] Overall, by the early 1980s the PLO had made significant advances in its global diplomatic offensive, which included setting up key posts across the Soviet Bloc.

## STUMBLING BLOCKS

Despite this unprecedented political recognition, there were considerable stumbling blocks throughout the entire lifetime of this alliance. These centered on Prague's concerns about the PLO's limited ability to reign in its multiple, often warring factions as well as about Arafat's persistent efforts to gain Western recognition and support.

Prague was concerned about the Palestinian organization's chronic lack of unity and the infighting displayed by its key factions from the outset. The first major inter-PLO rifts materialized in 1974—the year when Arafat turned to diplomacy and adopted a more reconciliatory tone toward Israel at the Arab League summit in Rabat. This triggered a revolt from most PLO factions, including George Habash's PFLP and Abu Nidal's Fatah–Revolutionary Council (also known as the Abu Nidal Organization), who opposed a political solution. Soon they united themselves within the so-called Rejectionist Front, enthusiastically supported by Iraq.[34]

Throughout the 1970s and 1980s the PLO would break up and reunite with notable frequency. This worried Prague. The PLO's lack of unity meant diminishing prospects of a Palestinian state. "The PLO is effectively not a Palestinian umbrella organization," lamented Czechoslovak diplomats stationed in Amman, as every faction is "doing whatever it wants and is loyal to whomever is providing them with support." Also, they reflected, the prospect of a progressive Palestinian state—should it ever come into being—was minimal.[35] This fragmentation did not allow for any one of these factions to propose a convincing plan for solving the Palestinian issue. In fact, as the more cynical analysts in Prague speculated, most Palestinian factions might prefer this state of affairs "as this makes them legitimate representatives of the Palestinian people and, as a consequence, they receive sizable financial support for doing nothing." Indeed, if the Palestinian issue were ever resolved, most of them would lose their leadership positions and solid income and "would actually have to do something for a living."[36] A divided Palestinian movement made the prospect of an Israeli-Palestinian settlement, in which Moscow was keen to play a leading role, ever more elusive. It also made attempts to in any way shape or control the PLO futile.

Furthermore, rifts in the PLO worried Prague because they typically had a destabilizing effect on the organization. After such shakeups, new organizations would emerge—each more difficult to read than the next. These new entities would often seek Soviet Bloc support and try to play potential donors against each other. Finally, due to the fact that Arab countries often sided with different Palestinian factions, disunity amplified these frictions even further. Occasionally, these shifting alliances transformed into open confrontations—for instance, when Syria attempted to overthrow Arafat in the early 1980s.[37]

The second big issue that haunted Czechoslovak communists was the PLO's persistent flirtation with the West, what Prague referred to as "ideological volatility." By 1975 several US politicians had met with Arafat, including former Democratic Party presidential nominee and senator George McGovern, Republican senator Charles Percy, and the chairman of the Senate Foreign Relations Committee, William Fulbright. Prague's diplomats closely followed these encounters and concluded that "it seems that the Palestinians have a favorable stance toward such contacts, especially those which are expected to bring some sort of advantages or support for the movement." Moreover, they noted that in addition to official contacts, there were "unpublished" meetings between "al-Fatah and US State Department or special services representatives," hinting at a clandestine relationship between Washington and Arafat's men.[38]

Most likely this was a reference to the liaison channel set up by the CIA's legendary case officer Bob Ames and the "Red Prince," Arafat's right-hand man Ali Hassan Salameh, active from the late 1960s to the early 1970s.[39] According to Douglas London, who spent over three decades as a CIA operations officer, this relationship with the PLO did not end after Salameh's death in 1979 but continued all the way to the end of the Cold War:

> The agency had a long-standing relationship with al-Fatah. The Israelis did not like it and at times killed US contacts in the organization, but overall the US–al-Fatah relationship with Arafat's faction was beneficial, evolved, and improved—especially in the mid [to] late 1970s and in the 1980s. The contact was good when they were still in Lebanon and afterward when the leadership moved to Tunis. This was not all that "clandestine," but both parties benefited from it being rather discreet and provided each a means to promote the two-state solution.[40]

Accordingly, as the Czechoslovak diplomats suspected, since the early years of his tenure as PLO chairman, Arafat had established a relationship with the United States, and by 1979 Arafat had made further advances in the West. Spain and Portugal officially hosted the PLO chairman on a high political level as did the representatives of the Socialist International, Willy Brandt and Bruno Kreisky, which the Soviet Bloc loathed. Furthermore, the Palestinians were also in close contact with China, which was providing support ranging from food to weapons and various types of military training. According to Prague's estimates, in 1978 Beijing provided the PLO with material assistance worth today's equivalent of $360 million—a sum that grossly overshadowed the bloc's much more modest contribution.[41] Throughout the 1980s, the PLO's outreach to Soviet adversaries would remain a concern and impact Arafat's trustworthiness in the eyes of his Soviet Bloc partners.

This was further complicated by the fact that Prague did not trust Arafat. The Czechoslovak communists considered him a Center-Right pragmatist, eager to align with reactionary Arab regimes, the United States, and other capitalist countries in order to secure a Palestinian state. This was an unwelcomed scenario, and Prague believed that Syria could well be the only ally in the Middle East capable of slowing down this pro-Western trend and using its leverage over the PLO to prevent its gradual defection to the West. Somewhat ironically, the Czechoslovak communists were critical of Arafat's undemocratic manner when running the PLO. Although on paper the PLO's top decision-making organs were populated by representatives of various PLO factions, Arafat's Fatah faction was the de facto kingmaker of the organization.[42]

Moreover, Arafat was known for making unilateral, and sometimes erratic, decisions without wider consultation or consent. Prague frowned on this imbalance and Arafat's dominance within the PLO, but it had to work with the cards that it had been dealt. Accordingly, it tolerated Arafat as the strongman of the PLO, hoped to use its leverage with the organization to influence him in the right direction, and, while doing so, maintain relations with other Palestinian organizations in case the balance shifted.[43] In other words, Prague tolerated Arafat but was not going to put all its eggs into one basket.

All these issues concerned Prague, but they never really threatened the long-term alliance. In February 1985, however, Arafat made a move that thrust the PLO and its alliance with the Soviet Bloc into a profound crisis. Despite the opposition of the organization's key factions and his closest associates, the PLO chairman decided to sign a pact with one of his archnemeses, King Hussein of Jordan. The so-called Amman Accord was a joint commitment to a set of principles for achieving peace with Israel and represented a remarkable blow to the PLO's independence with regard to the peace process. By consenting to it, Arafat bound Palestinian statehood to a confederation with Jordan and agreed to negotiating for peace as part of a joint Jordanian-Palestinian delegation. This unexpected decision singlehandedly realized one of Prague's worst nightmares: the PLO had officially aligned with a pro-US state that was, traditionally, opposed to Soviet Bloc interests in the region. By doing so, it set off the most significant rift to date with other PLO factions and key Arab allies, chiefly Assad's Syria.[44]

Unsurprisingly, then, the move led to a freeze in the PLO's relations with the Soviet Bloc. This was not a decision taken lightly, but Moscow was furious. Two weeks after the signing of the Amman Accord, Soviet Bloc diplomats based in

Syria assembled at the Soviet embassy in Damascus. Their host's harsh words echoed the Kremlin's sentiment. Soviet ambassador Feliks Fedotov argued that the main reason for the lack of unity and in fact "a threat to efforts by progressive forces to achieve a just settlement in the ME [Middle East] is the nonprincipled, opportunistic and treacherous leadership of the PLO headed by Arafat." Letting out his anger at the PLO chairman, Fedotov told his counterparts that Arafat had lied to Moscow, Prague, and Berlin. What is worse, he speculated that Arafat had coordinated this move with Zionists, Western Europe, and the United States. Socialist states should now all strive to "unmask and condemn Arafat's opportunistic and treacherous politics" while encouraging the PLO to remain united. In Moscow's eyes, Arafat had crossed a red line.[45]

## MAKING AMENDS

In February 1986, almost exactly a year after its signing, the Amman Accord officially collapsed. Shortly before King Hussein announced the suspension of Jordan's diplomatic coordination with the PLO, Arafat sent his top diplomat for a tour of the Soviet Bloc.[46] Faruq al-Qaddumi's job was to make amends, restart relations with Moscow and its allies, present them with Arafat's version of events, and resume aid. In a meeting with Czechoslovak foreign minister Bohuslav Chňoupek, the Palestinian clarified the nature of the crisis within the PLO and clearly held Syria responsible. Chňoupek pushed back by emphasizing that the Palestinian resistance movement needed to cooperate with all progressive and anti-imperialist forces in the region—most prominently Damascus. Peace in the Middle East could be achieved only via an international conference that would include the Soviets and the PLO, not via separate political initiatives. Although Prague expected the PLO to show more humility about the Amman Accord fiasco, al-Qaddumi's visit fulfilled its ultimate goal: the renewal of top-level Czechoslovak-PLO dialogue. Prague, however, did not immediately resume its assistance. It decided to wait and see what was going to be Arafat's next move, especially with regard to his geopolitical orientation.[47]

As Czechoslovakia renewed its alliance with the PLO, it also took on a new role. Alongside Moscow, Prague became the site of PLO reunification efforts. In the latter part of the 1980s, representatives of warring Palestinian factions met in Prague to negotiate and make amends. Furthermore, Palestinian representatives used the Czechoslovak capital as a safe place to meet with representatives of the Israeli Communist Party.

In February and March 1986, Abu Jihad and Abu Iyad—Arafat's top deputies—traveled to Prague twice to participate in a "Palestinian summit." The meetings with representatives of Fatah, the DFLP, the Palestinian Communist

Party, and Al Saiqa were regarded as top-secret because—according to some insider sources—the Palestinians knew that the Mossad was very interested in Abu Jihad's whereabouts.[48] These worries were not exaggerated: both of Arafat's deputies would soon be assassinated—Abu Jihad in 1988 and Abu Iyad three years later.

The Prague meetings exposed major internal cleavages. The Palestinian Communist Party was not ready to negotiate unless Fatah condemned the Camp David Accords, continued to foster close relations with the Jordanian king, who was a staunch anticommunist, or refused to improve its relations with Syria.[49] Somewhat ironically, by early September 1986 meetings of the Palestinian factions in Prague were being facilitated by the Israeli Communist Party under the leadership of Tawfiq Toubi.[50] The Israeli government had passed a decree banning the Israeli Communist Party from any form of negotiations with the PLO as such, together with its individual factions. The Central Committee of the Israeli Communist Party, however, decided to publicly defy this order and facilitate a meeting between the Palestinian factions, minus the PFLP.[51]

Prague remained at the center of these important conversations. Eventually, the warring Palestinian factions—Fatah, the DFLP, and the Palestinian Communist Party—publicly announced they had reached a compromise and that the PLO was withdrawing from the Amman Accord with Jordan. This became known as the Prague Declaration.[52] Two months later Fatah representatives tried to replicate this success and use Prague as a venue for reuniting with the PLO's second-largest faction, the PFLP. In mid-November 1986 Arafat's deputy, Abu Jihad, met the PFLP's founder, George Habash, at the PLO Office in Prague. Here, they discussed rapprochement after a three-year break in contact. Forty-eight hours later, they both flew to Moscow, where the talks continued.[53] Although we do not know whether these negotiation rounds held in Soviet Bloc capitals helped move the stubborn faction leaders toward unity, in April 1987 PLO unity was officially restored at a Palestinian National Council meeting in Algiers. The more radical factions, however, remained in opposition to the agreement, including the feared ANO. Algiers was not the terminus of the road to Palestinian unity. During the coming years, further important negotiations of Palestinian factions would be held in Prague.[54]

By December 1987, when the First Intifada began, the Palestinian leadership was faced with a whole new set of challenges. This was the most significant and widespread grassroots uprising in the occupied territories since the establishment of Israel. Prague recognized this momentous development and, almost instantly, approved aid worth $200,000 today for Palestinians in refugee camps in the West Bank and Gaza. The package, mostly medicine and food, was flown to Cyprus, where it was collected by representatives of the PLO and the United Nations Relief and Works Agency for Palestine Refugees in the Near

East.[55] From 1981 to 1988, Czechoslovakia donated food, medicine, clothes, and ambulances to the PLO worth $1 million today.[56]

On June 27, 1988, six months into the Intifada, Yasser Arafat visited Prague, heading a Palestinian delegation made up of four factions. At the meeting he requested further elevation of the PLO's status.[57] The Palestinian leader's request was met soon afterward. On September 8, 1988, the Czechoslovak government elevated the PLO representation to a diplomatic mission.[58] Two months later, on November 15, Palestine declared independence, which was almost immediately recognized by Moscow and its allies. Defending the move, Prague argued that this step was a reaction to a new situation in the Middle East caused by a mass uprising of the Palestinian people on territories occupied by Israel.[59] It wanted to help Arafat cease the momentum.

In 1989 Prague continued to serve as a meeting place for the fissiparous Palestinian factions. During this pivotal year, when the PLO also began direct negotiations with the United States in Tunisia, Arafat was a frequent visitor to Czechoslovakia.[60] While communism gradually began to crumble across East Central Europe, Arafat continued to meet key representatives of the Palestinian, Israeli, and Lebanese communist parties in Prague. His last trip to communist Czechoslovakia took place a month prior to the Velvet Revolution. During the visit, Arafat signed an agreement of cooperation with Prague, which, however, never came into effect because it was overtaken by the end of the Cold War.[61]

***

The initial years of the PLO's approaches to the Soviet Bloc and Prague were marked by hesitation and stalling. The communist states warmed to the PLO only gradually, after it publicly embraced a diplomatic path. The thirteen-year-long diplomatic relationship between Prague and the PLO was often beset by challenges and substantial disagreements. The PLO's lack of unity, its attempts to defect to the West, and Arafat's erratic political strategy represented key stumbling blocks to political alliance.

In 1985 these problems coalesced into a crisis that led to a freeze in high-level political and diplomatic relations. The Soviet Bloc's behavior during such friction points also showed that although its partnership with the PLO was serviceable for emphasizing communist states' revolutionary credentials and keeping their foothold in the Middle East, it was never designed as a vehicle to take over its strategic interests in the region. Furthermore, it revealed to Prague that Arafat and the PLO were no puppets. They had their own agency, interests, and other alliances they wished to pursue. While the Soviet Bloc's wrath at Arafat's Amman Accord miscalculation arguably had some moderating effect on his ultimate decision to withdraw from the deal, Czechoslovakia's attempts to reign him in or influence Arafat's decision-making never materialized.

Prague's intelligence and security liaison with the PLO was intimately linked to the tempo of their political relationship. Unsurprisingly, then, once its clandestine component was launched in 1979, it revealed multiple cracks in the fragile alliance.

## NOTES

1. G. Husák (Prezident ČSSR), April 18–19, 1983, "I. pracovní varianta návrhu přípitku s. G.Husáka na večeři na počest Jásira Arafáta," NA-A ÚV KSČ, Gustáv Husák/840-9075.
2. Michal Macháček, *Gustáv Husák* (Prague: Vyšehrad, 2017).
3. B. Pištora (8.t.o.), November 27, 1970, "Palestinské hnutí odporu," A-MZV, T-1970-74/8.t.o., Ka 1.
4. For a more, see Galia Golan, *Soviet Policies in the Middle East: From World War Two to Gorbachev*, vol. 2 (Cambridge: Cambridge University Press, 1990); and Roland Dannreuther, *The Soviet Union and the PLO* (London: Macmillan, 1998).
5. Václav David (Ministr MZV)–Antonín Novotný (Prezident ČSSR), September 3, 1965, NA, A-ÚV KSČ, f. AN-Zahraničí, Vztahy ČSSR-Libanon 2/6-16.
6. MZV (8.t.o), January 22, 1970, "Záznam k šifře Novák 28/9," A-MZV, T-1970-4/8.t.o., Ka 1.
7. Novák-MZV, January 19, 1970, "Telegram z Káhiry," A-MZV, T-1970-74/8.t.o., Ka 1.
8. "Materiály k situaci na BSV. Palestínske hnutí odporu. III.," February 15, 1970, NA, A-ÚV KSČ, f. GH, OOP, k 839.
9. Novák-MZV, "Telegram z Káhiry."
10. Benda-MZV (8.t.o.), January 5, 1970, "Cesta delegace al Fatáh do Moskvy," A-MZV, T-1970-74/8.t.o., Ka 1.
11. M. Havlásek, January 12, 1970, "Záznam o návštěvě s. M. Havláska v sekretariátě Sovětského výboru solidarity zemí Asie a Afriky," A-MZV, T-1970-74/8.t.o., Ka 1.
12. Golan, *Soviet Union and National*, 288.
13. Golan, *Soviet Policies in the Middle East*, 110.
14. I.S/47, May 11, 1978, "Podklady pro SIR: Současný stav a perspektivy řešení palestinské otaázky," ABS-12470/011.
15. Miloslav Vacík (ÚV NF ČSSR), June 27, 1970, "Průběh a výsledky návštěvy delegace Sovětského výboru solidarity zemí Asie a Afriky v ČSSR," NA, ÚV NF ČSSR-Výbor solidarity, Ka 26.
16. Vacík. The original spelling of "Dzasokhov" in Czechoslovak documents is "Dzasochov." See more on Dzasokhov in "Aleksandr Dzasokhov," Russian International Affairs Council, https://russiancouncil.ru/en/aleksandr-dzasokhov/.
17. "Materiály k situaci na BSV. Palestínske hnutí odporu. III.," February 15, 1970, NA, A- ÚV KSČ, f. GH, OOP, k 839.
18. Gustáv Husák (Prvý tajomník ÚV KSČ)–Jásir Arafat (Předseda OOP), September 26, 1974, NA A-ÚV KSČ, 1945-1989, Praha-Gustáv Husák, Ka 841.
19. "Základní údaje o palestinském hnutí odporu /PHO/. Podklady k návštěvě," March 25, 1983, NA A-ÚV KSČ, f. GH, OOP, k 840.

20. Yasser Arafat, "Speech to the UN General Assembly in New York," November 13, 1974, https://al-bab.com/documents-section/speech-yasser-arafat-1974.
21. Bohuslav Chňoupek (Ministr FMZV), n.d. 1975, "Důvodová zpráva," ABS-19324/2.
22. Biľak played a pivotal role in deposing the reformer Alexander Dubček in 1968. For more on this, see Peter Jašek, *Biľak: Zradca alebo kolaborant?* (Bratislava: Marenčín PT, 2018); Vasiľ Biľak, *Až po mé smrti* (Prague: BVD, 2014); and Vasiľ Biľak, *Paměti Vasila Biľaka: Unikátní svědectví ze zákulisí KSČ* (Prague, Agentura Cesty, 1991).
23. "Oficiální přátelská návštěva předsedy VV OOP J. Arafáta v ČSSR ve dnech April 18–19, 1983. Základní údaje o palestinském hnutí odporu /PHO/," n.d. 1983, NA A-ÚV KSČ, f. GH, Ka 840.
24. Josef Krejčí, interview by the author, September 16, 2015.
25. Krejčí.
26. "Jednání s předsedou Organizace pro osvobození Palestiny Jásirem Arafatem. Podklady k návštěvě," April 28, 1975, NA A-ÚV KSČ, f. GH, OOP, Ka 840; "Vyjádření MPO/1 k návrhu materiálu pro vládu ČSSR, týkajícímu se kanceláře OOP," August 22, 1975, A-MZV, To-T, 1975-1979/Palestina, 128/111.
27. "Vyjádření MPO/1 k návrhu materiálu." To compare, in 1972 there were approximately six thousand Palestinians living in West Germany, most of whom were students. Klein, *Protiúder*, 117–18.
28. The sum is noted in Czechoslovak crowns as CZK 6 million.
29. Original sum of CZK 4 million. "Styky ČSSR—OOP. Podklady k návštěvě," March 25, 1983, NA A-ÚV KSČ, f. GH, OOP, Ka 840.
30. V. Smíšek–MZV (8.t.o.), June 19, 1975, "Současný stav v palestinském hnutí," A-MZV, To-T, 1975-79/Libanon, 115/111.
31. Remarkably, in some cases it took the PLO more than a year to begin setting up its offices. "Jednání s předsedou Organizace pro osvobození Palestiny J.Arafatem. Podklady k návštěvě," April 28, 1975, NA A-ÚV KSČ, f. GH, OOP, Ka 840; Bohuslav Chňoupek (Ministr MZV), n.d. 1975, "Důvodová zpráva," ABS-19324/2; "Jednání s předsedou Organizace pro osvobození Palestiny Jásirem Arafatem. Podklady k návštěvě," April 28, 1975, NA A-ÚV KSČ, f. GH, OOP, Ka 840.
32. Bohuslav Chňoupek (Ministr FMZV), April 1980, "Návrh na sjednání dohody o výsadách a imunitách zastoupení Organizace pro osvobození Palestiny v ČSSR," NA-A, ÚPV-F, Ka 102-431/2; Vláda ČSSR, "Usnesení vlády Československé socialistické republiky," April 24, 1980, NA-A ÚPV ČSSR-ČSFR-usnesení vlády č.144/1980.
33. Prior to this, the PLO was granted diplomatic status by key Soviet Bloc allies. Vláda ČSSR, February 24, 1983, "Usnesení vlády Československé socialistické republiky," NA-A ÚPV-ČSSR/ČSFR, 40/1983.
34. "Oficiální přátelská návštěva předsedy VV OOP J.Arafáta v ČSSR ve dnech 18–19.4.1983. Základní údaje o palestinském hnutí odporu /PHO/," n.d. 1983, NA-A ÚV KSČ, f. GH, Ka 840.
35. K. Hotárek (ZÚ Ammán)–FMZV, May 10, 1975, "Věc: Vývoj v řešení palestinské otázky," A-MZV, To-T-1975-79/Jordánsko, 127/111.
36. K. Hotárek (ZÚ Ammán)–FMZV, August 8, 1975, "Věc: Řešení krize na BSV—zpráva," A MZV, To-T-1975-79/Jordánsko, 127/111.
37. Hotárek (ZÚ Ammán)–FMZV, 121.

38. V. Smíšek–MZV (8.t.o.), June 19, 1975, "Současný stav v palestinském hnutí," A MZV, To-T, 1975–1979, Libanon, 115/111.
39. Kai Bird, *The Good Spy: The Life and Death of Robert Ames* (New York: Broadway Books, 2014).
40. Douglas London, interview by the author, September 13, 2022.
41. Original sum of $80 million. All sums in US dollars adjusted to 2022 inflation. The source for the Consumer Price Index used in the inflation adjustment is the Minneapolis Fed, https://www.minneapolisfed.org/about-us/monetary-policy/inflation-calculator/consumer-price-index-1913-. V. Smíšek–MZV (8.t.o.), June 19, 1975, "Současný stav v palestinském hnutí," A-MZV, To-T-1975-79/Libanon, 115/111; "Organizační struktura palest. hnití odporu," n.d., ABS-12470/106.
42. "Organizační struktura palest. hnití odporu," n.d., ABS-12470/106.
43. "Organizační struktura palest."
44. Sayigh, *Armed Struggle*, 578.
45. Dušan Ulčák (ambassador in Damascus), February 28, 1985, "Blesk," ABS-12470/101.
46. Sayigh, *Armed Struggle*, 587.
47. Bohuslav Chňoupek (Ministr zahr. věcí), February 7, 1986, "Zpráva o průběhu a výsledcích návštěvy člena Výkonného výboru a vedoucího politického oddělení Organizace pro osvobození Palestiny Farúka Kaddúmího v ČSSR," NA-A ÚPV-ČSSR/ČSFR, 38.
48. Karel Fiřt (Náč.II.S-SNB), February 21, 1986, "Návštěva funkcionářů OOP v Praze—požadavek k přijetí bezpečnostních opatření," ABS-19324/5. See also the reference to this meeting in Zídek and Sieber, *Československo a Blízký východ*, 253, and Informant Zeman, February 27, 1986, "Nové jevy v jordánsko-palestinských vztazích a sbližování OOP—informace," ABS-24113/12.
49. Informant Mušír, March 19, 1986, "ABU IJAD, představitel bezpečnostních složek OOP a Al Fatahu—návštěva v ČSSR a ohlasy na tuto návštěvu mezi členy KS Palestiny," ABS-19324/6.
50. Informant Adam, September 8, 1986, "KS Izraele—poznatky, účast na mezipalestinských jednáních v ČSSR jako zprostředkovatel," ABS-19324/6.
51. Informant Adam.
52. "Palestine Chronology, 16 August–15 November 1986," *Journal of Palestine Studies* 16, no. 2 (Winter 1987): 215–32; Zídek and Sieber, *Československo a Blízký východ*, 256.
53. Informant Mušír, November 18, 1986, "ABU JIHAD, gen.tajomník OOP—účel cesty to ČSSR," ABS-19324/6; Informant Návštěvník, November 24, 1986, "Zájem dopisovatelky AFP v Praze o jednání posílení jednoty palestinského lidu, které se uskutečnilo dne 20.11.1986 v Praze -poznatek," ABS-19324/6; Informant Novák, November 24, 1986, "Jednání představitelů palestinského hnutí odporu na našem území," ABS-19324/6.
54. Zídek and Sieber, *Československo a Blízký východ*, 256; Kotora (ZÚ Bagdad), June 22, 1987, "Telegram z Bagdadu," ABS-19324/7.
55. Original sum of $78,000. "Poskytnutí československé pomoci palestínskemu lidu na okupovaných územích z Fondu míru a solidarity NF ČSSR," NA-A KSČ-ÚV-02/4, S94/89-kinf1.
56. Original sum of CZK 5.6 million. MZV, 8.To-1980-1989.
57. Zídek and Sieber, *Československo a Blízký východ*, 256–57.

58. Vláda ČSSR, September 8, 1988, "Usnesení vlády Československé socialistické republiky," NA-A ÚPV-ČSSR/ČSFR, 252/1988.
59. Vláda ČSSR, November 18, 1988, "Usnesení vlády Československé socialistické republiky," NA-A ÚPV-ČSSR/ČSFR, 307/1988.
60. Vláda ČSSR, November 18, 1988.
61. Vláda ČSSR, November 18, 1988, 258–59.

# 4

# Anatomy of an Intelligence Liaison

The first steps toward intelligence and security liaison between Prague and the PLO were taken three years after the establishment of the PLO Office in Czechoslovakia. In late June of 1979 a short, heavily bespectacled Palestinian man flew from Berlin to Prague. The visitor was Abu Hisham, a senior envoy of the PLO's Joint Security Service (JSS)—an enigmatic security organization largely made up of Fatah loyalists and led by Abu Iyad, Arafat's number two in Fatah. The Palestinian arrived in Prague to shape the contours of what would become the Prague-PLO intelligence and security alliance.[1]

In the first year of the liaison, things moved rather slowly and centered on information exchange. The Palestinians provided Prague with steady reports on US relations with Arab allies, Middle Eastern developments, and counterterrorism cooperation among West European states.[2] Although not high-grade intelligence, the reports showed good faith, and for now this was enough for Prague to consider liaison with the PLO security service "useful."[3] It was so much so that by summer 1980 Prague had designated a First Directorate officer at its rezidentura in Beirut as the PLO's main contact point.[4] By autumn it was providing security training to a multifaction group of thirty Palestinians at one of its educational facilities in Slapy, one hundred kilometers south of Prague.[5]

## MAKING IT OFFICIAL

Although things were progressing steadily, a brief March 1981 visit by one Abu Iyad marked a tectonic shift in this clandestine alliance, which would determine its structure for years to come. A former philosophy teacher born Salah Khalaf in Jaffa in 1933, Abu Iyad was one of the founders and most senior representatives of Fatah. Allegedly of mixed Jewish-Palestinian heritage, from the late 1960s he headed some of the PLO's first security and intelligence elements and soon became the head of the JSS. Shadowy, well-informed, soft-spoken, and wearing safari suits favored by African leaders, Abu Iyad exuded natural authority. With a sharp brain and extensive field experience, he was Yasser Arafat's

96    Chapter 4

ILLUSTRATION 4.1. A smiling Abu Iyad, standing behind Yasser Arafat, after a meeting with French prime minister Michel Rocard, August 29, 1990. Six months later, Abu Iyad would be assassinated by his bodyguard, allegedly acting in the name of Abu Nidal.
ČTK / Profimedia / Pierre Guillaud

fixer—a confident negotiator trusted with Fatah's deepest secrets and most clandestine missions.[6]

Although evidence is scarce, in the early 1970s Abu Iyad was widely considered to be the hidden hand behind Fatah's brief yet vicious campaign of international terror, which followed its expulsion from Jordan. He is alleged to have been a key figure in the Black September network, coordinating its most daring attacks, including multiple efforts to assassinate King Hussein and the infamous 1972 Munich Olympics massacre.[7] Using the terrorist group as a proxy largely to attack Jordanian and Israeli targets, Abu Iyad soon topped the Mossad's assassination list.[8] As Arafat's number two, he was just the right man to bolster and expand the developing security and intelligence liaison with Prague.

When the authoritative Abu Iyad arrived in Prague in March 1981, he knew he had to present his security organization in the best light possible. Accordingly, when he sat down with his counterparts at the Ministry of the Interior, he boasted of the PLO's intelligence capabilities. Apart from political counterintelligence, he assured his hosts that "the PLO Security Service does not only defend—it also attacks." With an *agentura*—a web of secret collaborators—and rezidenturas all around Western Europe and in Israel, he told his hosts, the PLO's JSS had prevented many military attacks by Israel. While the JSS maintained relations with Arab security services, Abu Iyad was now working hard to forge liaison with socialist states. In fact, he assured the Czechoslovaks that his service enjoyed excellent relations with the USSR, East Germany, and other Soviet Bloc countries and considered the United States the leader of "the enemy camp."[9]

While Abu Iyad's hosts listened attentively to his pitch, they were eager to draw some lines in the sand. Likely aware of Abu Iyad's alleged links to terror, the minister of the interior, Jaromír Obzina, warned the Palestinian strongman, "We do not condone the use of individual or group terror as a part of the struggle. We do, however, support the struggle against imperialism and a popular war for liberation. Such fights we unequivocally support." Furthermore, the minister stressed that Czechoslovakia would not allow any terror or violence on its territory: "We do not, however, want an open conflict with terrorist organizations. We will not allow them to enter our territory.... Anyone who would engage in terrorism on our territory will be sentenced to death."[10] Clearly worried about inter-Palestinian violence spreading across the country, Obzina asked that the JSS provide Prague with lists of terrorists—arguably hinting at the more radical elements within the PLO and other offshoot organizations. To reciprocate, Prague would offer the PLO all it knew about Carlos the Jackal.[11]

Sensing that Prague was fishing for a guarantee, Abu Iyad assured his hosts that the PLO was a proponent of armed struggle, not terrorism. He added, however, that the organization "does need to fight for its territory 'gun in hand.'" Clearly eager to evade discussing the issue of terrorism per se, the Palestinian strongman emphasized that Soviet Bloc support for the Palestinians' struggle was key. Furthermore, he pushed back by arguing that the PLO was often a victim of disinformation, especially with regard to terrorist attacks, which, he maintained, were organized by "someone else with the goal of discrediting the PLO."[12] Abu Iyad's strategy of fending off accusations of terrorism were denial mixed with blame-shifting.

In respect of Carlos, Abu Iyad was keen to show his hosts that the JSS was a step ahead of them. Accordingly, he told them about the infamous terrorist's associations with Iraq and Syria. Moreover, he assured Obzina that the JSS was surveilling Carlos and had him "under control" to prevent him from perpetrating terror in the PLO's name. Abu Iyad also tried to calm his counterpart down by suggesting that Carlos's reputation much exceeded his actual capabilities.[13]

Although the leadership of the Ministry of the Interior seemed satisfied with his pitch, the lower ranks were concerned. When the officers of the Active

Measures Department met to discuss this new partnership, they urged caution, flatly stating that "in the CSSR [Czechoslovak Socialist Republic] basically no one really knows any details about the PLO JSS"—about its structure, its personnel, or about how secure it is from infiltration by the Mossad and intelligence services of reactionary Arab states. In other words, the PLO security was an unknown entity and could thus not be automatically trusted. Accordingly, the seasoned operators suggested a more careful approach: the rezidentura in Beirut should continue to manage contact with the JSS and, for now, only exchange information on agreed-on topics. Liaison on the more sensitive active measures—operations aimed at spreading disinformation or discrediting opponents—should only be pursued once trust is established. For now, due to an "absolute lack of background information," special joint operations with the JSS were "out of the question."[14]

Despite these reservations, after the three-day clandestine negotiations, Obzina and Abu Iyad agreed on a blueprint for their liaison: intelligence exchange, active measures, joint operations, arms supplies, and security training were all part of the package. This was going to be a two-track partnership, with meetings and consultations taking place in Prague as well as Beirut. On Prague's end, the liaison would be tightly managed by the ministry's International Relations Department, the interior minister's main outfit for all things foreign, with the StB's First Directorate playing a key role. On the PLO side, the relationship would be maintained by JSS representatives based in Beirut and some elements also by the PLO Office in Prague. The First Directorate's rezident in Beirut would set up an intense liaison schedule—meeting his PLO contact every week or two at JSS headquarters located in the Palestinian section of the war-torn city.[15]

Three months later a Palestinian delegation arrived in Prague to put flesh on the bones of the initial agreement and, arguably, to allay some of Prague's concerns. This time, the delegation was led by Abu Ayman, who would become a permanent fixture of this liaison until its final months.[16] The enigmatic Palestinian was well prepared and ready to give his hosts a better sense of the JSS, mainly when it came its structure and goals. Accordingly, he offered a tour d'horizon of his organization: although created in 1973 in Lebanon as a multi-faction initiative, most of its leadership came from Fatah, with Abu Iyad at its helm. Functionally, the service was divided into four departments: Security and Information, International Relations and Cooperation, Executive-Military, and Foreign Operations. Its overall mission was to protect the Palestinian liberation movement, fight against "Zionist centers and institutions," and support international revolutionary movements with training and arms.

As way of introduction, Abu Ayman also told his hosts about his own role within the organization. Recently he became the head of the JSS's Department for International Relations and Cooperation, taking over from Abu Hisham—the

Palestinian who first set up the Prague-PLO intelligence liaison relationship back in 1979. The JSS had a unique position, Abu Ayman explained, because, despite being funded also by reactionary Arab regimes, it secretly fought against them. Although this may have been an attempt to show that the PLO service was sitting on the correct side of the ideological Cold War fence, it also underscored its political duplicity—a key concern for Prague and Moscow when it came to supporting the Palestinians. Nevertheless, the Czechoslovak men in gray suits did not blink.[17]

Further underscoring the uniqueness of the JSS, Abu Ayman explained that thanks to the Palestinian diaspora, the service enjoyed many opportunities globally. Eager to show that secrecy was important to him, he emphasized that only four people were indoctrinated on all the details of the Czechoslovak-PLO agreement: Yasser Arafat; his deputy and the godfather of this agreement, Abu Iyad; Abu Ayman himself; and his predecessor, Abu Hisham.[18] If they were to carry out joint operations, however, the Palestinians would cast an even deeper veil of secrecy confined to only Arafat, Abu Iyad, and himself. This was a relief for the Czechoslovaks, who were clearly very cautious about keeping this liaison secret, not least because of a recent very public statement by the Italian foreign minister about Prague training Palestinian terrorists.[19]

Abu Ayman's monologue seemed to satisfy his hosts. With all the pieces having fallen into place, Prague was ready for the liaison to accelerate. As the alliance progressed, however, multiple challenges and hurdles emerged.

## LIAISON IN CRISIS AND WAR

The ultimate hurdle was the political environment in which the intelligence alliance was embedded. Since its foundation in 1965, the PLO was based and operated from the so-called frontier Arab states. This was key to its mission—staging guerrilla attacks on Israeli soil from neighboring Egypt, Jordan, Syria, or Lebanon. At first it settled in Jordan, only to be ousted by King Hussein during the Black September events of 1970. From there the PLO moved to Lebanon, where it stayed for twelve years until Israel invaded its northern neighbor in 1982. Subsequently, much of the Palestinian leadership settled down in Tunisia, but some—acutely aware that proximity to Israel was crucial to their cause—tried to recreate a stronghold in Syria or a return to Lebanon.

These waves of Palestinian exodus took a heavy toll on Prague's clandestine relationship with the PLO. Due to forced relocations, the Palestinians often lost access to hard-won agent networks and political circles. Trust between Palestinian and Czechoslovak liaison officers also suffered when the former had to escape, often in dramatic circumstances. Moreover, during the 1980s Beirut and Damascus—main points of clandestine Prague-PLO contact during the decade—were dangerous and difficult operational environments marked by frequent bombings, raids, and other crises that further complicated the running of the alliance.[20]

In 1979, at the start of its liaison with Prague, the JSS was based in Beirut. During this time Lebanon was an especially volatile place. Since 1975 the multiethnic nation—made up of Sunni Muslim and Maronite Christian majorities and Shia Muslim and Druze minorities—had been embroiled in a barbarous civil war. Adding to this complexity, the country hosted thousands of Palestinian refugees and, since 1970, was also the home of the PLO. Political, ethnic, and religious tensions were running high. Key regional powers, including Syria and Israel, had stakes in the civil war and the future makeup of the Lebanese leadership.[21]

Despite the dire security situation in Lebanon, the PLO had no intention to leave the country. Its deep-seated presence was, however, suddenly threatened in June 1982 when Israel's defense minister, Ariel Sharon, orchestrated an invasion of Lebanon under the pretext of securing northern Israel from PLO attacks.[22] By June 15 the Israel Defense Forces were at the gates of Beirut, bombarding Palestinian positions in the west of the city. Amid various UN and US interventions aimed at stopping hostilities, negotiations began over what happened next. Arafat and his men were adamant about staying in Beirut, much like they had been about staying in Amman prior to their 1970 forced exodus.[23] In fact, during the summer of 1982, top PLO envoys pleaded with the Soviets as Beirut was being shelled, asking them to intervene and ask Syria to follow. Reportedly, Moscow refused and persistently advised the Palestinians to leave the besieged city.[24]

Clearly outnumbered and without enough political support to stay, the Palestinian leaders and fighters decided to cut their losses and leave Beirut. This was, however, no easy logistical feat for the PLO and its security bureau. Accordingly, they turned to their allies for help. In a remarkable show of faith, the JSS entrusted the Czechoslovak rezidentura in Beirut with one of its greatest treasures: its security archive. Perhaps by then the PLO was aware that Israeli forces had been confiscating documents from Palestinian outposts in the occupied south.[25] If Arafat's secrets fell into the hands of its fiercest adversary, this would be both an operational and public relations disaster.

By entrusting Prague with their secrets, the Palestinians displayed significant trust in their new liaison partner in a time of crisis. By providing this sanctuary, Prague showed readiness to step in and support the JSS in times of need. Nevertheless, this display of what seemed like a touching combination of trust and loyalty was short-lived. As soon as the unsealed boxes arrived at the embassy, the Czechoslovaks informed the Soviet KGB rezident in Beirut who, without much hesitation, swiftly copied key materials. The headquarters in Prague instructed its own rezident to do the same.[26]

By the end of summer 1982, Arafat and his men had been evacuated from Beirut. This effectively marked the end of the first phase of Czechoslovak-PLO liaison. Prague and its Palestinian counterparts had to reinvent their alliance under new, strenuous conditions. Reestablishing contact was no easy feat. In early September 1982, Prague learned that the enigmatic Abu Ayman was now in Damascus.[27] Although eager to reestablish direct communication via telephone, Prague decided to wait for him to travel to Czechoslovakia for a critical meeting, where they could discuss a way forward.

Abu Ayman, however, did not show up, due to reportedly undergoing medical treatment in Bulgaria. Meanwhile, the fighting in Lebanon was increasingly fierce. In September 1982 Bashir Gemayel—Lebanon's Maronite president-elect—was assassinated by the Syrian Social Nationalist Party. This triggered yet more violence. Most notably, several days later hundreds of Palestinian civilians were killed in the two largest refugee camps in Beirut, Sabra and Shatila, by members of the Maronite Catholic Phalangist militia, with Israeli assistance. The massacre caused an international outcry and signaled that things would get worse before they got better. Prague's foreign intelligence branch was growing increasingly impatient, arguing that the reassessment of its strategy and objectives in the Middle East was hinging on discussions with its Palestinian counterpart. In November Prague sent one of its most experienced Middle Eastern hands, the First Directorate officer Ján Kuruc (alias Mináč), to Sofia to meet Abu Ayman.[28]

In a secure facility at the Czechoslovak embassy in Bulgaria, Kuruc and Abu Ayman reconnected and discussed the dramatic events that had forced the PLO and its JSS into exile. The Palestinian told his counterpart that the security service had been hit hard by the forced eviction from Lebanon and was restructuring. For now, its core cadres would remain in Damascus under the leadership of Abu Iyad, and it was hoping to be fully up and running in two or three months. Operating from Damascus would, however, be nothing like Beirut, Abu Ayman lamented. Due to Arafat's fraught relationship with Hafez al-Assad, the JSS would need to operate in a highly cautious and clandestine way to prevent penetration and leaks. They simply did not trust the Syrian regime and, in the long run, had every intention of returning to their previous base where they could operate at full capacity.[29]

The Palestinian security men remained hopeful that a comeback was possible, a belief that was strengthened by increased public support for the Palestinians following the ousting. This growing prestige, Abu Ayman argued, boosted their international network of collaborators in Lebanon and Western Europe. Perhaps to show Kuruc that the JSS had not lost all its contacts in Lebanon, the Palestinian ensured him that it had cells and left-behind units in the country, which they would soon reactivate. Finally, Abu Ayman highlighted the

ILLUSTRATION 4.2. Ján Kuruc joined the StB's First Directorate in 1972 and served as rezident in Beirut and Cairo. *ABS-3135/46*

importance of the Prague-PLO alliance during these tough times. He told the Czechoslovak officer that the PLO was eager to further deepen this relationship and noted that the StB's willingness to safeguard the JSS archive was but one demonstration of this increasing closeness. However, to further commit, his service first needed to finalize its reform. Following that, Abu Ayman would restore this liaison by visiting Prague and using the Damascus rezidentura as a primary point of contact.[30]

While the Middle Eastern liaison track was suspended and Abu Ayman was preoccupied with adapting the JSS to a new reality, Prague started engaging more with the JSS envoy based at the PLO Office in Prague, the relatively junior Beshara Traboulsi, who always sported a thick black mustache. In November 1982 Ján Kuruc met Traboulsi in Klášterní vinárna, a cozy little wine bar in the heart of the city. Here the First Directorate officer explained that the StB was eager for Abu Ayman and his boss, Abu Iyad, to visit Prague as soon as possible.[31] While Prague had sympathy for the JSS's difficult situation, it was keen to get firsthand insight about the unfolding crisis from its Palestinian partners.

Traboulsi agreed to pass on the message but also used this opportunity to sound out Kuruc about how much Czechoslovakia was willing to help the JSS during these hard times. It has now become clear that the service simply was not able to operate normally in Damascus. Its relocation to the Syrian capital was, Traboulsi argued, largely "for show"—an attempt to demonstrate unity and cooperation. To escape this difficult operational environment, the PLO service was now relocating its personnel to other Arab and European countries. Accordingly, Abu Ayman considered relocating to Bulgaria or, in fact, Czechoslovakia. Kuruc immediately recognized this as an attempt to sound out whether Prague was ready to host the JSS. Although it was not his call, he used Traboulsi's extended hand to again urge that a high-level meeting in Prague was necessary.[32]

In March 1983 the exiled JSS leader Abu Iyad finally made it to Prague to shed light on the events that had led to the PLO's expulsion from Lebanon. He told his hosts a tale of betrayal by key Arab allies during Israel's 1982 invasion of Lebanon. Despite Syrian promises to deploy thirty thousand soldiers who would fight "like partisans" side by side with the Palestinians, this never materialized. Likewise, months before the confrontation, when the Palestinian leadership discussed with Muammar Qaddafi the eventuality of war, the Libyan leader promised to provide the movement with modern weaponry. This, however, also never came through.[33]

While dissing key Arab statesmen, Abu Iyad also gave his hosts a summary of the JSS's performance during the 1982 summer hostilities. While the Palestinians held their positions in Beirut for over eighty days, the JSS focused on liquidating traitors and spies recruited by Israel within Palestinian and Lebanese ranks. Together with allied Lebanese security services Abu Iyad's outfit reportedly killed more than two hundred enemy agents. Overall, Abu Iyad was satisfied with the performance of his men and awkwardly thanked Prague for training them: "I am happy to inform you that PLO JSS firmly stood their ground and those who have been trained in CSSR had great success. Although some of them fell in battle."[34]

Primarily, however, the PLO strongman traveled to Prague to recalibrate the security agreement in the face of new facts on the ground. Prague vowed to expand its training for Palestinian cadets and was eager to focus on signals intelligence (SIGINT) capabilities. This was a necessity, Prague thought, as the PLO's communication security was chronically weak—a problem especially pronounced under the systematic control of Syrian security services. Crucially, Prague gave a green light for extra JSS personnel to settle down in the capital and operate from an StB safe house. This was perhaps Prague's answer to Traboulsi's earlier inquiry about Czechoslovakia's openness to hosting a JSS outpost. The designated apartment would contain the JSS archive and serve as an office for the incoming PLO security men. By doing so, Prague effectively agreed to become one of the PLO's security strongholds in Europe. Furthermore, considering the recent leaks pertaining to their collaboration, they explicitly agreed on sharing information with third parties only with mutual consent.[35] Five years into the liaison, Prague and the PLO were still setting up rules of engagement.

Over in Damascus, liaison between Abu Ayman and his Czechoslovak contact continued. Although the two sides met regularly at the embassy under the pretext of Abu Ayman fixing visas for his colleagues, the quality of this on-the-ground element of the liaison hit an all-time low. Abu Ayman's "briefings" of the senior Czechoslovak officer sounded more like emotionally tainted personal observations and not sound assessments. The rezident was also concerned about his liaison partner's safety and the infiltration of Syrian special services operatives. Although Abu Ayman typically brushed off this well-meaning professional advice, by October 1983 the pressure had intensified, and most JSS representatives left Damascus. The regional element of Prague's liaison with the PLO was thus void once again. It would have to find yet another way to establish regular contact in the Middle East.[36]

## BACK TO BEIRUT

Throughout 1984 Prague's liaison with the PLO was solely based on occasional meetings in Prague and an unreliable enciphered connection to the JSS's outposts abroad. By December 1984, however, the JSS had managed to reinstate its network of collaborators and presence in Beirut. As its presence there was unofficial, the PLO's operations in Beirut were highly clandestine and had to be kept from Lebanese authorities. Accordingly, the head of this underground PLO branch in Beirut, Tawfiq Tawari—in Lebanon under nonofficial cover as a construction company representative—was hard to pin down. Czechoslovak and Soviet spies based in Beirut were equally frustrated by this lack of on-the-ground contact.[37]

Soon, however, Tawari reemerged and finally met his StB counterpart. At this meeting they set up a new modus operandi for collaboration. The priority was to avoid the watchful eyes of the Lebanese security service and other hostile groups operating in Lebanon, such as Hezbollah and its rival Shia militia group, Lebanese Resistance Regiments, better known as Amal. Accordingly, meetings could no longer take place at the Czechoslovak embassy but rather were held at new secure locations. A detailed plan was thus devised, complete with addresses of safe houses, preset meeting times, dates, and pickup spots. Tawari even arranged for a young female operative to drive the Czechoslovak intelligence officer to their next meeting.[38]

Confident about this new setup, Tawari vowed the JSS would continue providing valuable intelligence about Prague's principal adversaries and Middle Eastern developments. This information was to come from the PLO's agent network embedded in Lebanese political and security institutions, which, he emphasized, the PLO thanked with high financial rewards. He would do this in two ways: verbally brief his Czechoslovak contact in Beirut and hand over copies of documents in Arabic. Finally, worried about meeting his Soviet contacts due to the increased surveillance of their embassy and staff in Beirut, Tawari suggested that his Czechoslovak contact become their middleman—handing over extra copies of documents for his Soviet counterpart.[39]

In April 1985, after a yearlong break, Tawari and his StB contact resumed their on-the-ground liaison by putting in motion one of their rendezvous plans. At a designated time, the Czechoslovak case officer met Tawari's contact at a location near the embassy. When he saw a young woman dressed in black standing next to a green BMW, he knew this was his cue. In a matter of minutes, the StB officer jumped into the car and was soon en route to the Barbir quarter, which, on a good day, was a welcoming place for foreigners. However, that evening, it was firmly under the control of the Hezbollah and Amal militias, which the PLO was desperately trying to avoid. Just before the night fell, they arrived at a nondescript flat occupied by a Palestinian family. This was the new safe house designated for the Prague-PLO liaison.[40]

Tawari went straight to the point, delivering a swift briefing on US facilities and activities in the region and handing over documents about the feared Lebanese State Security Service. To reciprocate, he asked the Czechoslovak officer to help deliver the same documents to his JSS colleagues in Prague, who would make sure the material got to Tunis, where most of the PLO leadership currently resided.[41] Prague's officers were now not just liaison partners, middlemen for the Soviets, but also couriers for JSS branches in Lebanon, Czechoslovakia, and Tunisia.

The meeting with Tawari in this inconspicuous Palestinian safe house marked the end of Prague's on-the-ground liaison with the JSS. Soon afterward, the security situation in Lebanon deteriorated even further. The Lebanese government launched yet another operation against the Palestinians and other militias on its territory. Indeed, the situation became so bleak that the Czechoslovak and Soviet rezidenturas in Beirut both worried that Tawari was either under heavy surveillance or would soon be dead. To preempt any trouble with the Lebanese authorities, the Soviets advised their Czechoslovak colleagues stop meeting him altogether. The KGB had already ceased contact with the Palestinian and, in fact, out of caution sent his immediate handler back to Moscow.[42]

At the end of May 1985, two months after his last meeting with the Czechoslovak liaison officer, Tawari reappeared. In an act of desperation, he asked his Czechoslovak contact for help—to allow him a several-day refuge at the diplomatic mission. Realizing the risks, the StB officer flatly refused this plea, arguing that the embassy building was not a secure-enough location. The Soviets seconded this approach, claiming that under the current political and security circumstances in Lebanon, diplomatic privileges might not be respected—hinting at the possibility that, if taken in, Tawari's pursuers could retaliate against the Czechoslovaks or attempt to capture him.[43]

We now know that Prague's intelligence liaison with the JSS came to an end in 1985, seven years after it began. Arguably, however, security concerns on the ground were only a contributing factor. Bigger, strategic issues were primarily responsible for the termination of the Czechoslovak-PLO alliance and for Prague distancing itself from Tawari. Several months prior to his plea, in February 1985, Yasser Arafat made a decision that almost cost him his career.

Without proper authorization from the Central Committee of Fatah, the PLO chairman signed the Amman Accord with the king of Jordan.

Abu Iyad, the father of the Prague-PLO liaison, was one of Arafat's key opponents on this issue. Acutely aware that the move had not only infuriated Syria but also upset the Soviet Bloc and could thus cost the PLO its most treasured alliances, he made a damage-control visit to Prague. This was aimed at assuring his Czechoslovak counterparts that there was still a voice of reason within the PLO, working hard to nullify the controversial accord. Although Abu Iyad stopped short of calling Arafat a traitor, he did accuse him of making serious mistakes and ignoring opposition from his trusted allies. He asked his liaison partners in Prague to prevent a further crisis by posing as middlemen between the Palestinians and Hafez al-Assad. In fact, he asked that none other than Czechoslovakia's president, Gustáv Husák, visit Syria and personally press Assad to meet with a PLO delegation.[44]

The Czechoslovaks never officially stepped into this dispute as mediators. By May 1985, according to available documents, the Prague-PLO intelligence liaison was disrupted.[45] While the Middle Eastern track of this alliance would not recover, in the final years of the Cold War high-level JSS representatives reconnected with their counterparts and continued to meet them in Prague.

Overall, the alliance was a precarious affair consistently undermined by the volatile political and security situation in the Middle East, the PLO's internal disputes, and Arafat's miscalculations, which, at times, clashed with the Soviet Bloc's strategic interests. In addition to high politics, however, it also suffered from design flaws that complicated its existence.

## DESIGN FLAWS

Challenges to the Prague-PLO intelligence arrangement emerged from the beginning, and many could be characterized as fundamental flaws in its design. Although key principles of the liaison were repeatedly discussed, they were never codified in an official liaison document. This might have been a step too far for Prague. Although the PLO was increasingly showing signs of statehood and international recognition, in the late 1970s and early 1980s it was still a nonstate actor known for—increasingly rare yet highly controversial—links to terrorism. Moreover, it was fickle and, at times, fell out with the Soviet Bloc's key allies in the Middle East. Prague had to be cautious about making the long-term promises and commitments that typified such official liaison arrangements.

This absence of written liaison rules, however, was often problematic when it came to running the alliance. This was further exacerbated by the labyrinthine setup of this arrangement. With the Interior Ministry's International Relations Department being largely in charge of meetings with Palestinians in

ILLUSTRATION 4.3. The headquarters of the Czechoslovak Ministry of the Interior sporting the slogan "For Socialism and Peace" and flying the Czechoslovak and Soviet flags, October 1971. *ČTK / Macháček Jan*

Prague and the First Directorate running liaison in the Middle East—Beirut and later Damascus—issues soon emerged. In 1983 the First Directorate lamented that its representatives were not always invited to meetings with Palestinians or familiarized with conclusions of discussions held in Prague under the auspices of the Interior Ministry's International Relations Department. It argued that this felt as if there were two, not one, liaison channels with the PLO. In an effort that perhaps resembled a bureaucratic version of land grabbing rather than a genuine attempt to solve a problem, the First Directorate suggested taking over most of the liaison. Unsurprisingly, this was rejected by the more powerful International Relations Department serving the minister.[46]

While these bureaucratic issues persisted, other, more acute red flags soon emerged. Chief among them was the varied quality of information provided by the Palestinians as part of this arrangement. While information exchange represented the PLO's key contribution to the partnership, from early on it was clear that what they were providing to Prague was hardly cutting-edge intelligence.

In fact, shortly after Abu Iyad's inaugural visit to Prague, Czechoslovak spies complained that the information they were receiving from the JSS represented more of a burden and a distraction than anything else and a rather financially taxing one.[47] A year later the Czechoslovaks were still not happy. They lamented that the "operative value of collaboration in Beirut is currently low."[48]

Over in Lebanon, officers liaising with Abu Ayman also noticed that the Palestinians were being economical with their information. After one such liaison meeting in Beirut, veteran StB officer Ján Kuruc likened his Palestinian liaison partner's briefing to a summary of local newspaper headlines. This was, however, not just pure negligence or lack of preparation. When another man present went into more detail on US military installations in Egypt, his colleague cut him off, telling him to leave the rest for another meeting. This suggested that the Palestinians were rationing the information they were providing to Prague. Arguably, this strategy was adopted so as not to provide all their relevant information at once but instead to spread it out and thus hopefully give the semblance of a steady flow. Alternatively, perhaps there was some information that the Palestinians did not want to pass on.[49]

In 1983 Prague conducted an audit of its liaison with the PLO. In true Eastern European fashion, the Interior Ministry made no attempt to sugarcoat how it felt about the alliance. Four years after Czechoslovakia's first security contact with the PLO, Prague concluded that "the results of this collaboration do not, for now, fulfill the original objectives and expectations." Largely it blamed this on the increasingly difficult political situation in the Middle East, which forced the Palestinians into exile and hence undermined the functioning of the JSS. Prague also recognized the difficulty of operating under close surveillance in Damascus. At the same time, however, the Czechoslovaks engaged in some self-criticism and recognized their own shortcomings. Crucially, they admitted that the setup of this liaison was far too official, which "prevented establishing closer relations with representatives of the PLO JSS as well as gaining their trust and respect."[50]

The bureaucracy accompanying Prague's approach was also flawed. During talks in Prague, the Palestinians would usually meet the representatives of the International Relations Department, tasked with managing the multifaceted PLO-Prague clandestine relationship, and then have separate meetings with representatives of the First Directorate in charge of collection and operations. Although Prague tried to coordinate better, this setup was inherently flawed. Moreover, the dual-track nature—which saw liaison meetings take place both in Prague and in Beirut (and later Damascus)—further complicated things. Prague's men in the Middle East were not always kept up to speed with what was discussed in Prague and were not given sufficient authority to react flexibly to their partners' urgent inquiries and needs.[51]

Furthermore, Prague was not sure how "tight" this liaison really was—whether it was acceptable for Prague to send documents delivered by the Palestinians for translation to Moscow. The current pace of translation facilitated by the headquarters in Prague was clearly slow and ultimately undermined the utility of these reports. Having identified these flaws, Prague was keen to relaunch and deepen this collaboration at the upcoming meeting with Abu Iyad. To prove trust of the PLO Service to their Czechoslovak counterparts, the Ministry of the Interior decided to offer the Palestinians a highly sensitive training course in enciphered communication.[52]

Finally, throughout the lifespan of the Prague-PLO alliance, it became apparent that each side had different expectations and ideas about what the role of a liaison partner entailed. Clearly, the Palestinians saw themselves as equal partners worthy of special attention and treatment. This was evident from the Palestinian liaison representative's persistent efforts to push the boundaries and ask for favors. In May 1983, when the PLO was temporarily exiled in Damascus, Abu Ayman asked his Czechoslovak liaison partner for permission to use the communist country's diplomatic license plates. The intelligence officer swiftly denied this request, although his Palestinian counterpart maintained that other countries such as Algeria, Tunisia, and Morocco had allowed this.[53]

On a more granular level, there seemed to be some discord in characterizing Czechoslovakia's partnership with the PLO. For the most part, Abu Ayman was treated as a liaison partner—participating at high-level meetings with Ministry of the Interior and foreign intelligence representatives in Prague and the Middle East. Nevertheless, the First Directorate officers on the ground—in Beirut and Damascus—consistently referred to him as an "agent" code-named Areza.[54] This dichotomy of language and approach suggests that old-style intelligence services struggled to adapt their practices shaped by predominantly state-to-state interactions to nontraditional partners.

Overall, while both sides invested considerable effort in setting up the framework and modus operandi of this intelligence liaison arrangement, bureaucratic hurdles frustrated the effort. Furthermore, the difference between tradecraft methods and competences also proved problematic for the partnership. What is more, trust gradually eroded as Palestinian partners provided information that seemed indistinguishable from open-source information or was recycled from other sources.

\*\*\*

Since the launch of their intelligence and security collaboration in 1979, Prague and the PLO agreed to collaborate in a number of areas. It was not, however, until 1981 when their intelligence liaison was fully defined and made official during the pivotal visit of Arafat's deputy, Abu Iyad, to Prague. The liaison being very much a work in progress, its many rules and principles were developed on the go.

From the beginning there seemed to be genuine will on both sides to collaborate. The Palestinians promised to tap into their rich contacts and agent networks in the Middle East. During times of crisis, Prague provided support to the JSS. Especially after the organization was ousted from Lebanon, Prague agreed to effectively host a PLO security outpost on its territory. While the PLO would never enjoy the free rein that Prague gave the Cubans in the 1960s, and, as we shall see, it did keep the Palestinians under close watch, this was a great help to the struggling PLO partner service. There were, however, red lines that Prague would not cross. These included harboring JSS representatives at their embassy in Beirut during heightened security crises.

Overall, running such a complex set of interactions with an unruly partner operating in a war zone was no easy task. The structure, quality, and tempo of this liaison seemed to have been largely impacted by the tumultuous nature of Middle Eastern politics, which would periodically push the PLO into exile and hence undermine its intelligence capability. Bureaucratic challenges and competition within the Czechoslovak Ministry of the Interior also complicated this relationship. And, finally, the Soviet Bloc's strategic interests and anxieties put an end to the state-nonstate alliance shortly after Arafat made the fateful decision to ally himself with the king of Jordan.

## NOTES

1. Miloš Hladík (Náč.I.S)–(I.S/47), July 2, 1979, "Funkcionář bezpečnostní služby OOP Abu HIŠAM—zpráva," ABS-12470/108.
2. D. Hronec (Kancelár sekr. NMV ČSSR)–Karel Vrba (Náč.II.S), November 21, 1979, ABS-19324/3.
3. M. Miloš Hladík (Náč.I.S)–Ján Kováč (Náč. Ministra vnitra), September 5, 1979, ABS-12470/103.
4. K. Vrba (Náč.II.S)–Ondrej Dovina (Náč.I.S SNB), July 3, 1980, ABS-38165/12.
5. Josef Závada (Náč.I.S/47)–Emil Hradecký (Náč. OMS), November 11, 1980, "Věc: Bezpečnostní kurs členů OOP—poznatky," ABS-12470/108.
6. Seale, *Abu Nidal*, 40, 42.
7. Abu Iyad denied his involvement in the Munich massacre, but some of his former fellow fighters from the PLO and Black September confirm his prominent role in the organization.
8. Klein, *Protiúder*, 190. See also Abu Iyad's autobiography: Abu Iyad and Eric Rouleau, *My Home, My Land: A Narrative of the Palestinian Struggle* (New York: Times Books, 1981).
9. Josef Vlček (Náč. OMS, Kanceláře MV ČSSR), March 26, 1981, "Informace o přijetí delegace Sjednocené bezpečnostní složky Organizace pro osvobození Palestiny, vedené jejín předsedou Abu AJADEM ve dnech 9-13.3.1981 v ČSSR," ABS-90078.

10. Vlček.
11. Vlček.
12. Vlček.
13. Vlček.
14. Seman, June 15, 1981, "Záznam jednání s představitele Sjednocené bezpečnostní služby OOP Abu AYMAN em v Praze v dnech 9.-11.6.1981. Příloha 5.," ABS-12470/108.
15. Vlček, March 26, 1981, "Informace o přijetí."
16. Ján Kuruc (Bejrút-I.S), March 20, 1981, "Záznam zo schôdzky," ABS-12470/108.
17. Seman, "Záznam jednání s představitele AYMAN."
18. Although he did admit that the head of the PLO Office, Abu Bakr, and the JSS officer stationed at the office, Beshara Traboulsi, were also aware of the general contours of the deal.
19. Seman, "Záznam jednání s představitele AYMAN."
20. At this time, Prague did not have a rezidentura in Tunisia.
21. For more on the war in Lebanon, see David Hirst, *Beware of Small States: Lebanon, Battleground of the Middle East* (London: Faber, 2011).
22. For a full debate on the various reasons that led Israel to invade, see Laurie Eisenberg, "History Revisited or Revamped? The Maronite Factor in Israel's 1982 Invasion of Lebanon," *Israel Affairs* 15, no. 4 (2009): 372–96.
23. See more on PLO decision-making during the invasion in Rashid Khalidi, *Under Siege: PLO Decisionmaking during the 1982 War* (New York: Columbia University Press, 2013).
24. Bílek (Bejrút-I.S), August 17, 1982, Přijatá šifrovka, ABS-12470/107.
25. Some were published shortly thereafter—for example, in *PLO in Lebanon: Selected Documents*, ed. Raphael Israeli (London: Weidenfeld & Nicolson, 1983).
26. Bílek (Bejrút-I.S), June 22, 1982, "Přijatá šifrovka," ABS-12470/107.
27. Hlad, n.d., "Záznam," ABS-12470/108.
28. See Kuruc's personal files: ABS-KP-3135 and ABS-30006.
29. Ján Kuruc (I.S/47), October 14, 1982, "Záznam ze služební cesty v BLR ve dnech 8.-11.10.1982," ABS-12470/108.
30. Kuruc.
31. Vápeník (I.S/47), November 18, 1982, "Záznam ze schůzky," ABS-12470/108.
32. Vápeník.
33. J. Vlček (Náč. OMS, Kanceláře MV ČSSR), March 17, 1983, "Informace o průběhu a výsledcích návštěvy delegace SBS OOP, vedené předsedou Abu Ayadem, v ČSSR ve dnech 7-10.3.1983," ABS-12470/108.
34. Vlček.
35. Vlček.
36. See meetings of Abu Ayman with First Directorate case officer January–October in ABS-12470/108.
37. Bílek (I.S/47), December 4, 1984, "Věc: jednání s delegacy SBS-OOP," ABS-12470/108; Ayman (Bejrút-I.S), March 23, 1985, "Ke spolupráci se SBS," ABS-12470/110.
38. Ayman (Bejrút-I.S), April 12, 1985, "Přijatá šifrovka," ABS-12470/110.
39. Ayman.
40. Ayman (Bejrút-I.S), May 6, 1985, "Ke spolupráci se SBS OOP," ABS-12470/110.
41. Ayman, May 6, 1985; Ayman (Bejrút-I.S), April 16, 1985, "Přijatá šifrovka," ABS-12470/110.

42. Ayman (Bejrút-I.S), April 23, 1985, "Přijatá šifrovka," ABS-12470/110.
43. Ayman (Bejrút-I.S), May 31, 1985, ABS-12470/110.
44. Emil Hradecký (Náč.OMS)–Karel Sochor (Náč.I.S), May 8, 1985, "Současná situace v OOP—informace," ABS-12470/011.
45. The paper trail documenting Prague's on-the-ground liaison with the JSS ends here. Although it is possible that documents detailing further liaison will be found in coming years, a more likely scenario appears to be that the Middle Eastern track of Prague's intelligence liaison ended at this time and that, following the lull caused by Arafat's signing of the Amman Accord, Palestinian representatives engaged in occasional security coordination via their contacts in Prague.
46. (I.S/47), March 31, 1983, "Věc: Vyjádření odboru čý k výsledkům jednání s delegací SBS OOP," ABS-12470/108.
47. Jaromír Kolouch (I.S/36), June 8, 1981, "Záznam k jednání na OMS FMV dne 3.6.1981," ABS-12470/108.
48. Seman (I.S/47), December 30, 1981, "Jednání s představitelem SBS OOP."
49. Ján Kuruc, "Záznam ze schodzky," January 7, 1981, ABS-12470/108.
50. Karel Sochor (Náč.I.S)–Jaromír Obzina (Ministr vnitra), February 23, 1983, ABS-12470/108.
51. K. Sochor (Náč.I.S)–J. Obzina (Ministr vnitra), February 23, 1983, ABS-12470/108.
52. Sochor-Obzina.
53. Ján Kuruc, "Záznam ze schůzky," May 18, 1983, ABS-12470/108.
54. Kuruc.

# 5

# Cruel Intentions

Despite the various hurdles and inherent design flaws, the breadth of the Prague-PLO liaison was ambitious. On paper, the unlikely partners agreed to collaborate on a full spectrum of intelligence and security activities, ranging from information exchange to active measures, agent recruitment, and joint operations. During their meetings in Prague, Beirut, and Damascus, they exchanged information about Middle Eastern leaders and events and discussed plans of joint operations and possible new alliances. The reality, however, was somewhat more complicated.

## AGAINST THE PRINCIPAL ADVERSARY

A common adversary was the glue that held the Prague-PLO intelligence alliance together. During the pivotal March 1981 visit of the head of the JSS, Abu Iyad, to Prague, both sides vowed to cooperate on weakening the principal adversary—namely, the "imperialists" (the United States and Western Europe) and the "Zionists" (Israel and its supporters).[1] The Czechoslovak minister of the interior, Jaromír Obzina, pledged that Prague would supply the Palestinians with intelligence on operations of "imperialist intelligence services" aimed against the Palestinian movement. Crucially, Prague vowed to focus on activities of Israeli intelligence in Europe, especially in neighboring Austria.[2] In June 1981 Prague did warn the PLO about "Zionist operations" during the upcoming congress of the International Union of Socialist Youth in Vienna, which Arafat was planning to attend. Upon receiving this warning and eager to avoid "Zionist provocation," Arafat canceled his attendance.[3] Such warnings, however, were few and far between. Prague acknowledged this by admitting that its possibilities for collecting information relevant to the PLO were limited.

Throughout the lifespan of the clandestine alliance, more information flowed in the other direction. In fact, it was the PLO's principal currency or contribution to this clandestine partnership. From the early stages of the partnership, Arafat's men vowed to provide Prague with information on the strategic goals of the United States and other NATO member states in the Middle

113

ILLUSTRATION 5.1. Czechoslovakia's longtime minister of the interior, Jaromír Obzina (*second from right*), standing to the right of the country's most famous singer, Karel Gott, and opposite Gustáv Husák (*left*) at a reception held at Prague Castle, May 9, 1983. ČTK / Kruliš Jiří

East. Soon Abu Iyad's outfit started handing over reports about US activities and plans in the region. For example, it passed on a report on Secretary of State Alexander Haig's visit to Jordan and Saudi Arabia in April 1981; on a tour by President Ronald Reagan's special Middle East envoy, Philip C. Habib, and his meeting with the Lebanese and Syrian presidents; on Secretary of Defense Caspar Weinberger's 1982 visit to the Middle East; and on the latest agreement between Israel and the US.[4] These were all important events that Prague was eager to learn more about.

While the Czechoslovaks were often critical of the low-grade value of the information passed on by the PLO's security service, at times it did provide interesting details that, if true, enabled Prague to feel the pulse of US-Arab relations. Of particular interest was one report that detailed the April 1981 meeting between Haig and King Hussein of Jordan. According to Palestinian sources, it began with a heated exchange about the recently signed Camp David Accords—the peace treaty between Anwar Sadat's Egypt and Menachem Begin's Israel. Pressing the king to join the accords, a tempestuous Haig argued that Hussein must "either stand by the United States or stand against it—there was no other way for Jordan." While promising to reconsider his approach to Camp David,

Hussein took a swing at his archenemy up north—Hafez al-Assad's Syria. He told his American guest that "Kissinger's policy toward Syria was wrong as Assad stands with one foot in Washington, and with the other in Moscow." Hussein insisted that the US should in no way assist Assad's efforts to remain in power and "let him fall."[5] Prague was intrigued to hear about details of disputes between its key adversaries.

In addition to information exchange, joint operations targeting the United States were discussed from an early stage. Prague was particularly interested for its new liaison partners to help infiltrate US embassies in the Middle East— namely, in Lebanon, Jordan, Syria, Egypt, and somewhat ironically also in Israel. The Palestinian liaison, Abu Ayman, did not need much persuading and swiftly agreed. In fact, he told the Czechoslovaks that his boss, Abu Iyad, had recently discussed joint operations against the US embassy in Beirut with none other than the KGB. The Palestinians were keen to help but at the moment had limited access. Although Abu Ayman claimed that they had indeed had "their people" placed within the strategically important facility, they were all let go after the outbreak of the Lebanese Civil War when Washington downsized its mission in the increasingly dangerous metropolis. While they were working to reestablish their presence in the embassy, the Palestinians suggested they could, for now, at least assist "externally"—by surveilling US diplomats known to be CIA officers and purchasing classified documents from people who had direct contact with CIA officers stationed at the embassy. This, Abu Ayman reminisced, used to be possible in the early 1970s, hinting at the existence of a black market of such items.[6]

At a February 1982 meeting at the PLO headquarters in Beirut, Abu Ayman told his Czechoslovak counterpart that they were well on their way to infiltrating the US embassy. In fact, he confirmed that the PLO was able to "implant their agentura" in the highly secure facility. In the same breath, however, he cautioned that this was no quick win. It would take some time to bear fruit due to the intense security measures.[7] By April the Palestinians were still no closer to success. In fact, due to the worsening security situation in Beirut, the Americans continued to tighten their security measures: there was now 24-7 camera surveillance and increased physical protection, and the security perimeter around the embassy had also been expanded.[8] All this was making matters much more complicated for the alleged PLO agentura with access to the building.

Two months later, when Israeli tanks started rolling into Beirut, the Israeli invasion of Lebanon was underway. Reluctant to leave its strategic stronghold in the Levant, the PLO fought tooth and nail against the invasion and its local foes. Ultimately, by the end of summer 1982, Arafat and his men had to leave Beirut. Prague was sure that their effort to penetrate the US embassy via their Palestinian allies was over. In the fall, however, the First Directorate received an early Christmas present from its Beirut rezidentura: a list of US embassy employees in Arabic, including CIA employees, a complete 1981 phone directory, and a number of US-made recording devices, some of which included manuals.[9] Although this signaled great progress and, in fact, validated the PLO's vows to infiltrate the diplomatic mission, it was also clear that now that the PLO was pushed out from Lebanon, this was a success that would not be replicated.

Within the context of the Middle East, Israel topped the Soviet Bloc's list of key enemies. With regard to Israel, information exchange was firmly focused on high politics and military capability. Prague asked its Palestinian counterparts to deliver a comprehensive assessment of Israel's domestic political developments and an overview of its political, military, and security apparatuses and their capabilities. This was not a self-serving exercise: the StB wanted to understand the depth of Palestinian knowledge about the workings of its main adversary and hence better understand their liaison partner's capability in this regard.[10] Soon Abu Ayman started delivering reports on this area: on strategic agreements between the United States and Israel, on the Israeli Labor Party, and on internal issues within Israel's Ministry of Defense.[11] While this was no premium intelligence, the PLO's departments dedicated to collecting information about the Jewish state had expertise and linguistic capability unparalleled in the Soviet Bloc.

Israel and Zionism were so high up on the agenda that, in fact, the first active measures (*aktivní opatření*, or AO) operation discussed as part of the Prague-PLO liaison was one targeting Israel. In many ways this was to be a litmus test of the Palestinians' determination and skill with regard to running sensitive operations aimed at manipulating information to gain advantage or undermine their enemies.[12] In this case, Czechoslovakia's foreign intelligence was keen to design an active measure aimed at discrediting Zionism, the foundational ideology of the state of Israel. This was to be achieved by publishing a long-forgotten book. The StB had recently obtained a rare copy of an eighteenth-century, anti-Semitic, two-volume work called *Entdecktes Judentum* (Judaism unmasked), written in the early eighteenth century by Johann Andreas Eisenmenger. Using Jewish and Arab "ancient historical sources," the book claimed to have exposed the foundations of "Jewish aggressiveness," which was being echoed by modern-day Zionism, according to the First Directorate.[13]

This was just the argument that the Soviet Bloc and indeed some Palestinian circles were looking to make. The problem this active measure was designed to overcome was the issue of availability and distribution. Apart from rare copies, such as the one in the Vatican Library, original versions of the book were few and far between. The newer editions, the First Directorate complained, were missing key sections. Although they did admit that the book had its limits, Prague's intelligence officers were eager to revive it and reintroduce the racist publication to contemporary audiences. The plan was simple: the StB would acquire a copy of the original edition, translate it into English, and pass it on to the PLO, which would in turn have it translated into Arabic. Subsequently, the PLO would find a suitable Arab publisher. The StB was ready to put this plan into motion but first needed the PLO to commit to finding a Middle Eastern government that would publish the estimated twenty thousand copies and ensure worldwide distribution to the public, prestigious universities, and scientists.[14]

All this was to serve two purposes. On one hand, according to the StB, the operation would help unmask the historical roots of Zionism and contribute to exposing "the aggressive, genocidal, and anti-Arab politics of the State of Israel." On the other, it would help reinforce international support for the creation of an independent Palestinian state. All would have to be done in utmost secrecy, of course, as the First Directorate argued that if the Mossad got a wind of this operation, it would "ruthlessly pursue all avenues in order to hamper it."[15]

Although from today's vantage point the plan sounds overcomplicated, and even Prague's intelligence officers were unsure whether its ultimate impact would justify the effort and money that would have to go into it, they took it to the Palestinians.[16] It was now up to Abu Iyad and Yasser Arafat to approve the plan. While ultimately the PLO gave the go-ahead and Prague got down to work, this joint First Directorate–PLO active measure aimed at reigniting an old conspiracy theory never took off.[17] Although the Czechoslovaks repeatedly reminded the Palestinians of the venture, no progress was made. Their stalling was perhaps caused by the rather complicated nature of the plan itself or the limited capacity that the PLO had to run such operations at a time when it was dealing with much more pressing—even existential—matters.

The second active measure proposed by Prague in the early days of its alliance with the PLO was also aimed at undermining Israeli interests on an international scale. In this instance, Prague offered to provide the PLO with a list of addresses of "pro-Zionist" businesses and institutions based in Western Europe and the United States. As opposed to the previous active measure, its Palestinian counterparts "expressed immediate interest,"[18] and six months later the StB provided the detailed list to its partners. While Prague was happy to also include a list of companies in Switzerland and Austria, but there, they admitted, they only had a list of small businessmen and farmers. It was now the Palestinians' turn. They were to produce a so-called Black Book of such organizations. The First Directorate suggested that once this had been published, it would assist with distributing two hundred copies via its rezidenturas.[19] Operation Black, as it went down in history, however, also never took off. Although the PLO security service may have used the list of addresses for other purposes, it never published the Black Book, nor did it work jointly with the StB to discredit these businesses.[20] Arafat's men seemed to have little patience for drawn-out active measures that entailed extensive planning and lacked immediate effect. As we shall see, they were more inclined to propose high-impact operations that would make better use of their own skill set.

## EYES ON THE MIDDLE EAST

With Palestinians spread far and wide across the Middle East and North Africa, the PLO had a front-row seat to Middle Eastern affairs. Accordingly, it was happy to regularly brief Prague's diplomats and intelligence officers on key developments pertaining to their foes—the so-called reactionary Arab states closely aligned with Washington, including Jordan, Egypt, and Gulf states, plus Turkey.

The focus and scope of the information the PLO passed on to its Czechoslovak allies varied, with some reports zooming in on regional events, such as the Iran-Iraq War, or local alliances, such as the Turkish-Kurdish dynamic. Other reports examined discussions at multilateral forums, most crucially at Arab League summits, or firmly focused on more technical military issues, including Saudi possession of Airborne Warning and Control System aircraft.[21] Prague was also interested in intelligence on research and development in science and technology in Arab countries, especially the petrochemical industry.[22]

While reporting on key regional developments, the Palestinians exposed their own role in wider Middle Eastern politics. In October 1981 Egypt's president, Anwar Sadat, was gunned down by a group of extremists called Egyptian Islamic Jihad who were enraged by Egypt becoming the first Arab country to recognize and make peace with Israel. When Hosni Mubarak, a Soviet-trained air force officer, took over as president, he faced opposition from the country's nationalists. Supported by Libya and the PLO, the Egyptian nationalist movement was waiting to see whether the new president would continue to pursue the close alliance with the United States crafted by his predecessor. The nationalists were ready to exert pressure on Mubarak to change this course and, in a worst-case scenario, stage a coup. The PLO told its Czechoslovak counterparts that they were very much a part of this effort—training cadets of the Egyptian nationalist movement in Lebanon who would be used in Egypt if the time for intervention became ripe.[23] Such insight into regional affairs and possible power shifts intrigued Prague, which fostered close relations with Cairo and supplied its military with strategic weapons in the early decades of the Cold War. While Egypt later switched sides and aligned with the West, the Soviet Bloc continued to closely track developments in the strategically important nation in the hope of regaining lost influence.

The PLO also told its Central European liaison partners that the Iran-Iraq War put its organization under strain as it was being pushed into publicly taking

Cruel Intentions 119

ILLUSTRATION 5.2. Egyptian president Anwar Sadat being assassinated during a military parade marking his country's 1973 war with Israel. October 6, 1981. *ČTK / Profimedia*

sides. The PLO had a long-standing relationship with Iraq and had benefited from its long-term, albeit unsteady, support for the Palestinian movement. Since the fall of Mohammad Reza Pahlavi, the shah of Iran, in January 1979, the PLO had also managed to forge closer relations with the new Iranian regime led by the shah's longtime political rival, Ayatollah Ruhollah Khomeini, an ardent critic of the West. Things, however, went sour when the PLO tried to position itself as middleman in negotiations over US hostages in Tehran. Its efforts were reportedly rebuffed by the Iranian regime, which saw this as a PLO effort to gain formal recognition by the United States. Although PLO-Iranian relations later improved, they were soured again by Arafat's attempts at shuttle diplomacy between Tehran and Baghdad when the war broke out. Allegedly, Iran accused Arafat of being duplicitous and demanded his unequivocal support of Tehran and denunciation of Baghdad.[24] Such insight allowed Prague to better understand how the shifting political landscape in the Middle East impacted the PLO's standing in the region and relations with key states.

PLO reports were not solely about exchanging information and analysis; at times they were designed to deliver warning or request assistance. One such warning pertained to the increasingly erratic Libyan leader Muammar Qaddafi.

The former army communications officer ascended to power in 1969 after staging a coup against the Western-backed Idris monarchy. Upon seizing power, the British-educated Qaddafi ejected Western military forces from Libyan territory, nationalized the country's rich oil industry, which he used to fund vast social and health-care reform, and launched a crusade against imperialism and colonialism. As part of this effort, the self-appointed heir of Nasser and reviver of Arab power invested considerable assets in building his military strength and funding foreign revolutionaries.[25]

The Libyan leader's relationship with the PLO was a tempestuous affair. While Qaddafi detested the PLO chairman, likening him to Israel's conservative prime minister, Menachem Begin, Fatah also did not pull any punches, referring to the Libyan leader as "the knight of revolutionary phrases." Middle Eastern alliances were, however, notoriously fickle, and so was this one.[26] In 1981 the two sides temporarily aligned, and it was at this very moment, in October 1981, that the PLO approached Prague with a plea.

Ronald Reagan had recently been voted into the White House and Arafat's new ally, Qaddafi, was on his list of most notorious villains, not least due to his increasingly obvious links to terrorism. The PLO was concerned that the Americans were planning an offensive against the Libyan leader. Recently, the JSS had picked up signals from its agent network hinting at a possible US covert operation against him. These sources alleged that the CIA asked its agents based in Arab countries to provide information on Qaddafi detailing his daily routine, habits, transportation routes, family life, security regime, and protocol for meeting visitors. Furthermore, the Americans were increasingly interested in the mood of Libya's general population and military, in its economic situation, and in its relationship with the Soviet Union. All this, the PLO argued, suggested that Washington was considering ousting Qaddafi.[27]

Prague knew that this prospect worried the PLO, which had recently received significant military support from Libya. In fact, Arafat's men had asked the StB earlier that year to help maintain the Qaddafi regime in power.[28] Czechoslovakia was also not keen to see Qaddafi go. Although difficult to deal with, he was an important ally. In fact, Prague delivered military training to Libyan troops and sold its leader weapons, military equipment, and hundreds of tons of its prized explosive, Semtex.[29] Nevertheless, fending off potential US interventions was clearly above Czechoslovakia's abilities, especially without further, more concrete, and credible information about such plans.

This the PLO never delivered. Arguably, that was due to the rapid deterioration of its alliance with Libya. In fact, less than two years later, during one of his visits to Prague, JSS head Abu Iyad had very little nice to say about Qaddafi. Calling him "crazy," he told Prague of the Libyan leader's latest visit to Belgrade when he reportedly enthusiastically suggested that China, Iran, Libya, and Yugoslavia create a military pact alternative to the NATO and Warsaw Pact alliances. When his startled Yugoslav hosts rejected his proposal and reminded him of their country's membership in the Non-Aligned Movement, Qaddafi became furious and immediately ordered the return of a Libyan oil tanker that was en route to the Balkans.[30]

Further warnings about leadership challenges and potential coups d'état followed. In January 1983 the PLO told its Czechoslovak counterparts about Assad's efforts to decapitate the Palestinian leadership, albeit metaphorically. After a meeting with top PLO representatives, Assad requested a private meeting with the PLO's Abu Iyad and Faruq al-Qaddumi, pressing the idea that one of them should take over the PLO leadership from Arafat. According to the source, Abu Iyad immediately told the Syrian leader that this was a decision the Palestinian people would have to make. In a time when tensions between Arafat and Assad were running high, the latter was looking for ways to change the PLO leadership to his favor.[31]

Besides information exchange, by autumn 1982 Prague was looking at ways it could use the PLO to infiltrate key international Arab institutions and use it as a vehicle for its active measures. The First Directorate's eyes were sharply focused on the Arab League—the most prestigious platform representing Arab states—based in Cairo. Here, it hoped its Palestinian partners could identify a contact within the Arab League's headquarters who could be used to discreetly feed information into the organization's publications.[32] The Arab League clearly had contacts with prominent Western press agencies and media outlets that were off limits to Prague and its allies. The First Directorate may have been drawn to this scenario for two reasons: to exercise influence over the important Arab organization and push its own content toward the Western media.

The PLO was also eager to help Prague influence the Arab world. In the early days of the liaison, Abu Ayman bluntly told his counterparts in Prague that the PLO would be happy to pass on "various information and disinformation to the highest representatives of Arab nations." Simultaneously, he suggested that the PLO would help disseminate white, gray, and black propaganda via its own channels to the press as well as radio stations. It could also help distribute leaflets with Prague's content under the PLO's own label or that of other organizations. If they so wished, the PLO could also print its own newspaper with StB-written content. Finally, Abu Ayman promised to put together a list of all PLO news outlets and publications that it published in Arab countries as well as Western Europe.[33]

The PLO and the First Directorate also agreed to coordinate their efforts prior to and during high-level international conferences and meetings. The Palestinians suggested this, arguing that they would be happy to take a stance on international issues that would be beneficial to them both. They added that they would be happy to coordinate with Prague and defend their position at various Islamic/Arab conferences—for instance, on the issue of Afghanistan.[34] Prague reacted well to these Palestinian proposals, which effectively amounted to running joint active measures campaigns in a region of which the Palestinians had superior understanding.

## HUNTING TRAITORS

Traitors and defectors were perennial concerns for communist states. They were not only loathed for abandoning the cause and betraying socialist ideals, but their very presence and activity abroad was a constant reminder of their treachery. During Abu Iyad's pivotal trip to Prague in March 1981, a bold proposal addressing this sore point was thus born. At the high-level meeting with their Czechoslovak counterparts, JSS representatives put forward a set of daring proposals that entailed kidnapping and liquidating Prague's dissidents abroad. As part of Operation Pelikán[35]—one of the most controversial joint ventures discussed as part of the Prague-PLO alliance—the PLO was to target two of Czechoslovakia's most visible dissidents living in Western Europe.

In 1981 Jiří Pelikán was an Italian citizen serving as a member of the European Parliament for the Italian Socialist Party, publishing a periodical called *Listy* (Letters), and generally living a quiet life in his home a stone's throw from Rome's Pantheon. He was a permanent fixture of the city's many cafés and restaurants. His Italian years, however, were predated by the dramatic story of his rise and fall back in his homeland. Born in interwar Czechoslovakia, Pelikán became in 1939 a member of the Communist Party of Czechoslovakia and soon joined the resistance against the Nazi occupation. After the war, he rose to prominence within the ranks of the Soviet-backed International Union of Students, serving as its director. This was no low-profile job. Pelikán traveled abroad—a luxury afforded to only a select few—and met bright and determined youth from across the globe, including one Yasser Arafat, then a rising star of the Palestinian movement.[36]

In the 1960s, as the era of the Prague Spring began to unfold, Pelikán moved up the communist ladder even further, becoming a member of the parliament and ultimately serving as the head of state-run Czechoslovak Television—the only channel available to the nation's population. Accordingly, by the summer of 1968, when Warsaw Pact tanks rolled into Prague, Pelikán was a powerful political player and public persona. All was well with the regime as long as he followed the party line. In August 1968, however, he decided to cross this line by publicly criticizing the Soviet-led invasion and organizing resistance among Czechoslovak journalists. The crushing of the Prague Spring was a watershed moment for all supporters of Alexander Dubček's attempt at liberalizing the

ILLUSTRATION 5.3. Jiří Pelikán, as president of the International Union of Students (*right*), standing next to Soviet cosmonaut Yuri Gagarin at the organization's 1962 congress, held in Leningrad. *ČTK / Profimedia*

country' communist regime. For Pelikán, this meant being stripped of all public positions and his citizenship and leaving the country.[37]

Much to the Czechoslovak communist regime's anger, Pelikán did not opt for a quiet life in exile. After settling down in Rome, he secured a seat in the European Parliament and continued to play a prominent role in public discourse. Crucially, he set up *Listy*, which occasionally provided insider information from communist Czechoslovakia to the country's dispersed émigré community. Immediately after his defection, the StB in tandem with the KGB began closely monitoring Pelikán's activities.[38]

In 1975, six years after his forced exile from Czechoslovakia, the country's leadership resorted to extreme measures aimed to intimidate. Following the party's orders, the First Directorate devised a plan that saw two of its officers send a letter bomb to the prominent dissident. Pelikán found it suspicious from the moment the package arrived. For months, he had been receiving anonymous letters containing newspaper clips about victims of Italian terrorist attacks, which suggested the StB was angry about his activities. Therefore, after receiving a package, he was extra careful and opened it outside his apartment. Inside was a book he had not ordered. Curious, he opened the book; immediately a tall flame flashed out of it. Pelikán swiftly threw the book under a staircase, where it exploded. Although the bomb had not been designed to kill, it was most certainly aimed to intimidate and silence him prior to the 1975 Helsinki Conference, held to ease tensions between Cold War adversaries.[39] The attack was also a very real reminder of the fact that although Soviet Bloc defectors may have escaped, they were not necessarily safe in the West.

Six years following this letter bomb incident in the early months of the Prague-PLO liaison, Pelikán was yet again discussed within the walls of StB headquarters in Prague. In fact, at the March 1981 meeting held to calibrate the PLO's clandestine relationship with Prague, Abu Iyad discussed Pelikán with Minister of the Interior Obzina. The Palestinian strongman admitted to knowing the Czech dissident personally, probably through their mutual contact Arafat, who knew Pelikán from his days as the leader of the General Union of Palestinian Students. By the end of the meeting, it was clear to Obzina that the Palestinians would be willing to liquidate the prominent dissident.[40] While no final verdict was reached on this issue, the news of this proposal trickled down the StB hierarchy.

Three months later, Prague qualified its view on the daring proposal. The guardian of the Prague-PLO liaison, Deputy Minister Vladimír Hrušecký, instructed the First Directorate to follow up on this issue with its liaison partners and convey that Prague was, of course, still interested in an operation against Pelikán and in "liquidating his standing and influence." Nevertheless, while he requested that the PLO elaborate on whether it had specific ways of penetrating Pelikán's inner circle or even of getting direct access to him, he emphasized that Prague was "against terrorism."[41] Hrušecký's message could have been a way to find out if the Palestinians were serious and indeed capable of carrying out such a daring feat in the heart of Rome, in order to gain more clarity before discussing the daring operation further. It, however, also signaled to the JSS that while Prague was happy to intimidate and undermine the work of Czechoslovak dissidents, it was less eager to engage in controversial operations that could invite international blowback.

In September 1981, six months after the initial discussions, the Palestinians informed their Czechoslovak counterparts that their service was ready to go ahead with Operation Pelikán. The PLO, however, expected Prague to send an employee of the Ministry of the Interior to Beirut, where specificities of this high-risk operation could be discussed and refined face-to-face.[42] While the PLO was ready, Prague was stalling. In fact, a number of heated exchanges ensued in the background between the First Directorate's leadership and its subordinate departments crucial to this operation—the Active Measures Department (a.k.a. Department 36) and the Department for Emigration and Ideo-Diversion (a.k.a. Department 31). The StB's experts on active measures and exiles complained to the First Directorate's leadership about not being fully informed of the operation and only receiving secondhand information. Furthermore, the Active Measures Department was against the operation as such: "Having repeatedly consulted this issue with Department 31, much like during our negotiations in June 1981, we categorically reject terrorist operations. Considering that Pelikán is a well-known personality (member of the European Parliament, etc.) and that he has been engaged in an ideological struggle against us, this operation (liquidation) would attract too much attention and ultimately cause us harm."[43]

Clearly Prague was "getting cold feet" as it vividly remembered the backlash its communist ally Bulgaria endured when in 1978 its intelligence service assassinated one of Sofia's most recognizable dissidents living in London, Georgi Markov.[44] This was not the 1950s or 1960s when Czechoslovakia's communist regime dared to strike against its critics with the harshest of methods, carrying out at least two dozen kidnappings and a handful of assassinations.[45] Times they had changed, and such bold, miscalculated moves could cause a reaction that Prague could not countenance.[46] But despite having good reasons to stay away from such high-risk operations, Prague's Active Measures Department remarkably did not reject all of the PLO's suggestions.

Alongside Operation Pelikán, Yasser Arafat's men proposed a venture against another Czechoslovak dissident. Born in a small Czech town in 1933, Jan Tesař was a historian and essayist who, since his early twenties, had a rocky relationship with the Czechoslovak communist regime. In the late 1950s and early 1960s he was balancing between working for state-run research institutes and museums and stints as a freelance writer—all dependent on how out of favor he was with the communist regime at the time. In 1966, shortly before the Prague Spring, Tesař joined the Communist Party. Much like in Pelikán's case, his faith in the Czechoslovak regime quickly faded with the crushing of the Prague Spring. Although he resigned his party membership shortly afterward, unlike Pelikán he decided to stay in Czechoslovakia.[47]

During the 1970s he became a thorn in the regime's side. Subjected to arrests and incarcerations, he not only actively participated in antiregime activities and became a signatory of the famous Charter 77—an open petition published in 1977 calling for the Czechoslovak government to respect and defend the civil and human rights of its citizens—but also cofounded a forum designed to host regular meetings with Polish dissidents and ran the dissident magazine *Dialogy*. By 1980 Tesař had become too troublesome for the regime and was, like many others, forced into exile.[48] He soon settled in Paris, where he remained politically active.[49] Much like Pelikán's case, Tesař's political activism irritated Prague. It was here, in his new home, that the PLO was to strike on behalf of Prague.

A year into Tesař's exile, Abu Iyad and his men had begun their intelligence liaison with Prague. While discussing the assassination of Pelikán, they also exchanged ideas on the kidnapping of Jan Tesař. In their discussions with the PLO, the First Directorate made it clear that Tesař was a real problem. In fact, they regarded his activities abroad as "terrorist attacks" against Czechoslovakia—perhaps a good demonstration of how loosely Prague used the term, especially when it came to its own enemies. According to the PLO's plan, Tesař was to be kidnapped by its operatives and secretly incarcerated in one of the Palestinian camps in the Middle East. Unharmed and alive, he would be kept there for a "prolonged period of time."[50] This was a remarkably superficial plan considering the amount of risk such an operation would carry and the logistical acumen it would take to pull it off.

It was thus surprising that unlike with Operation Pelikán, the First Directorate was not immediately opposed to it. Somewhat naively, its Active Measures Department considered the option of having JSS kidnap Jan Tesař as "more appropriate"—without actually discussing what such long-term internment would entail or achieve. Although they were not ready to go ahead with it just yet, they agreed to "not protest" if the Palestinians insisted on the operation. Moreover, they also decided that if the PLO again raised the issue of liquidating Jiří Pelikán, they would instead sign off on a kidnapping similar to that proposed for Tesař.[51]

It is unclear why Prague's foreign intelligence felt compelled to consider these operations that they assessed as alarming and counterproductive. Perhaps it was to appease their bosses, who had initially expressed at least theoretical interest in this joint venture during high-level political talks with the powerful Abu Iyad. Or perhaps it was to follow an unofficial liaison etiquette aimed at not upsetting their Palestinian allies, who were clearly looking to demonstrate their relevance and reciprocate for the long-term security support provided by Prague. Or perhaps some in the First Directorate did, indeed, believe that kidnapping dissidents from Western Europe to the Middle East was an effective way to deal with irritating opponents.

While discussing the fate of the two dissidents, the PLO proposed a third operation: an attack on the headquarters of Radio Free Europe in Munich. The Communist Party apparatchiks at the helm of the Ministry of the Interior's International Relations Department cautiously suggested that to seriously consider the idea, they would require further information. Once the Palestinian suggestion landed on the desk of the Active Measures Department, however, the experienced operators rejected it out of hand.[52] The First Directorate's firm response may have been triggered by a recent attempt at the same target. Only a month earlier, the infamous Carlos Group had placed a bomb in the proximity of the Czechoslovak office at Radio Free Europe. Although we now know that this was an operation sponsored by the Nicolae Ceaușescu regime in Romania and that the Czechoslovak section had not been the intended target, the uproar that followed the botched operation likely underpinned Prague's cautious approach.[53]

Based on what we know today, all of the dramatic possibilities discussed with the PLO during the course of 1981 came to naught. Jiří Pelikán continued to live in Rome and saw the end of communism as well as his own political rehabilitation overseen by the first democratic Czechoslovak president, Václav Havel. In fact, in 1990 Pelikán became an adviser to Havel. Ultimately, Jan Tesař was also never subjected to incarceration in the Middle East. After the collapse of communism he, too, reconnected with his homeland and moved to Bratislava, where he continues to live at the time of writing.

## FALSE FLAGS AND TERRORIST NETWORKING

In 1981 on a balmy spring day in Beirut, Abu Ayman told his Czechoslovak counterpart, the seasoned StB operative Ján Kuruc, that the PLO was working on establishing relations with "progressive" organizations engaged in antigovernment operations mostly in Western Europe. Arafat's men were primarily interested in gaining information from these groups and exercising leverage over their activities. They wanted to gauge Prague's reaction to this plan and to discuss ways how these murky liaisons could either be a part of or benefit the broadly cast Prague-PLO alliance.[54]

Initially, Prague seemed to be eager to get involved, especially as this venture sounded like a promising opportunity to collect intelligence beyond the Iron Curtain. These groups often had good access to states, regions, and facilities that were off limits to Prague. Working together, they could perhaps force-multiply their information-collection abilities. One such organization was the Kurdistan Workers' Party (PKK). Over the years, the PLO had developed a close working relationship with the group characterized by financial and material assistance. Crucially, in 1981 it organized a forty-five-day special-operations training for ten PKK members. Abu Ayman was keen to discuss how the PLO's partners could be of benefit to the Soviet Bloc.[55] To highlight their potential utility, he explained that the PKK had branches located near a NATO radar installation close to Diyarbakir in Turkey—at the time an intelligence outpost for monitoring Soviet rocket testing at Kapustin Yar—and, most important, that the PKK had its own agentura among NATO employees. With Prague's technical support, Abu Ayman argued, the group could perhaps collect intelligence from these installations. While intrigued, the StB officer insisted that any such operation would have to be a false flag—apparently a Fatah operation without any hint of Czechoslovak involvement. Abu Ayman agreed to be the middleman but suggested that a closer liaison with the Kurds, as well as other antigovernment organizations in Greece, France, the United Kingdom, Italy, and Belgium, might be of benefit to Prague.[56]

Although these grandiose plans never materialized, the PLO also lobbied hard on behalf of two of its other—West German and Japanese—partner organizations. A month after his PKK pitch, Abu Ayman traveled to Prague where he outlined the PLO's relations with an alphabet soup of notorious Cold War

ILLUSTRATION 5.4. Fusako Shigenobu, featured in the Soviet Union's *Album of Terrorists*, issued in 1976 and shared with allies. ABS, f. HS SNB – I. S, reg. č. 20968

terrorist groups. Referring to them as "progressive," he told his Czechoslovak hosts that the PLO had fostered relations with the Revolutionary Cells and the Baader-Meinhof Gang in West Germany. Without providing much detail, the Palestinian highlighted their utility by telling his hosts that these organizations were able and willing to carry out operations across Western Europe.[57]

Abu Ayman, however, seemed most passionate about securing Prague's assistance for an obscure boutique terrorist franchise called the Japanese Red Army (JRA). In the summer of 1981, he relentlessly lobbied for Prague to embrace the terrorist outfit.[58] For years now, he told the Czechoslovaks, the PLO had collaborated with the JRA, which it considered to be "very determined and revolutionary people." Known for its role in the 1972 Lod Airport attack, the group was led by the charismatic Fusako Shigenobu and was now looking to expand. Recently the JRA had opened an office in Beirut and wanted to set up safe houses across the Soviet Bloc. Relentless, Abu Ayman presented the Czechoslovaks with JRA promotional material suggesting the Ministry of the Interior set up a meeting with the group's leadership.[59] Unpersuaded, Prague never followed up on this offer.

More than two years later, however, the JRA was back on Abu Ayman's agenda. In December 1983 the Palestinian resumed his lobbying efforts in favor of Fusako's outfit. At a meeting in Prague, he told his hosts that the PLO was a guarantor for a variety of groups that had settled down in Lebanon. Now that the Palestinian leadership had been ousted from there, however, some of these groups were also being forced to relocate. In a last-ditch effort to try to sell the JRA to Czechoslovakia, Abu Ayman asked the communist country to take in several members of the organization. The reply from a representative of the minister of the interior's office was reserved. While promising to inform his superiors about this suggestion, he signaled that the chances of approving such resettlement were low due to the Japanese organization's "politically sensitive nature."[60] This was Prague's code for deeming the Japanese group too controversial and unpredictable. Since its inception, it had made headlines for all the wrong reasons and was known for little else than its lethal terrorist campaigns. Crucially, the JRA was but a small fish in the sea populated by other groups that were much more readable and politically mature and could hence be considered as a worthy investment.

At this stage Prague also rebuffed the PLO's effort to facilitate a partnership between the StB and the Red Brigades. Suggesting Czechoslovakia assist the infamous Italian group, the PLO argued that this would enable Prague to make use of its "services." Referring to the Italian outfit as "terrorists," the Czechoslovaks unequivocally told their Palestinian partners that they "cannot and will not establish direct connections" with the Red Brigades or other groups of their ilk. Prague, however, stayed short of discouraging its Palestinian partners from aiding such controversial terrorists. Instead, and rather respectfully, it assured the PLO representatives that "the way the PLO JSS uses these movements for operations and its struggle against the imperialist enemy is their own business."[61]

Ultimately, Abu Ayman's attempts to pitch the PLO's partner organizations to Prague were futile. While acquiring information about their adversaries via false flag alliances—such as with the PKK—seemed an appealing prospect for Prague, they were cautious about which Cold War jackals they aligned with. In fact, based on available documents, they never followed up on Abu Ayman's suggestion to create an alliance with the West German, Japanese, or Italian Marxist terrorist organizations. Prague exercised considerable caution in this regard.

***

Prague's cooperation with the PLO in the realm of intelligence exchange, active measures, and terrorist networking was a strenuous one. The partners continually struggled to achieve a workable equilibrium with regard to intent and effort. Their seven-year-long clandestine relationship was characterized by a mismatch in expectations, objectives, and modi operandi. It never went beyond mere cruel intentions.

When it came to information exchange—the PLO's main contribution to this alliance—this left much to be desired. The First Directorate expressed clear interest in the intelligence supplied by the PLO. While Arafat's men vowed to provide information about the principal adversary, Middle Eastern states, and the security situation in the region, their reporting rarely went beyond what was available in Arab newspapers, and at times they were clearly being economical about how much to provide to their partners at a particular time. Prague expected cutting-edge insight into a world that the PLO knew better. It, however, received rationed low-grade intelligence at best.

The complex active measures aimed at discrediting the enemy, most chiefly Israel, also never took off. Although Prague came up with an elaborate plan to revive old anti-Semitic texts and distribute them across the Middle East, the PLO never embraced the operation. We are also not aware whether Arafat's men utilized extensive lists of alleged "pro-Zionist" companies and institutions, which were to be used for their discreditation.

While lukewarm about running joint disinformation and discreditation operations, the PLO seemed keener on some of the more daring international operations. To this end, it proposed three high-risk ventures—kidnappings, assassinations, and a bombing—aimed at some of Prague's most active dissidents in Western Europe. Although Prague's powerbrokers briefly considered these proposals, they received pushback from senior First Directorate officers responsible for this agenda who categorically rejected such acts, fearing blowback and condemnation. Despite drawing this line in the sand and ultimately refusing to subcontract assassinations to its liaison partner, Prague did consider other PLO suggestions—such as abduction and long-term incarceration of dissidents. Ultimately, however, neither Prague nor the PLO never seriously developed these plans, and hence the former refrained from using its controversial nonstate ally for high-risk covert measures.

Finally, Prague was unenthusiastic about engaging with fringe Marxist terrorists. While the JSS representatives were eager to consort with other Cold War jackals—be they Japanese, German, or Italian—Prague repeatedly refused these risky associations. Realizing that it would not be able to control the Palestinian organization and its liaisons with the era's most controversial nonstate actors, it politely declined their offers and looked the other way.

Much of this mismatch may have been caused by a clash of cultures and diverging strategic interests. Whereas Prague was a seasoned covert operator, with past experience of assassinations and kidnappings, by the 1980s it was acutely aware of the impact such operations might have on wider strategic and economic goals. The PLO, which came of age in a much different political and security climate, seemed more risk-prone when it came to dealing with traitors and other adversaries. Prague was acutely aware of this and hence regularly reiterated to Arafat's men that it would not partake in terrorist campaigns and discouraged them to this effect.

Overall, this was not a smooth operational alliance of well-suited trusted partners. While the Palestinians often overpromised and underdelivered, the Czechoslovaks were often forced to push back against controversial plans or requests that, if exposed, could besmirch their reputation or upset their strategic goals. Although Prague attempted to exercise control over JSS, which it saw as the more junior partner in this liaison arrangement, time and time again it found that the unpredictability of Middle Eastern politics, the volatile security situation in the region, and the mercurial nature of its liaison partner made this a Sisyphean effort.

## NOTES

1. Josef Vlček (Náč. OMS, Kancelář MV ČSSR), "Informace o přijetí delegace Sjednocené bezpečnostní složky Organizace pro osvobození Palestiny, vedené jejím předsedou Abu AJADEM ve dnech 9-13.3.1981 v ČSSR," ABS-90078.
2. Vlček.
3. Ján Kuruc (Bejrút-I.S), June 4, 1981, "Záznam zo schôdzky," ABS-12470/108.
4. Seman, "Záznam jednání s představiteli Sjednocené bezpečnostní služby OOP Abu AJMANem v Praze v dnech 9.-11. června 1981. Příloha 5," June 15, 1981, ABS-12470/108; Barbuš (Beirut, I.S), March 19, 1982, "Záznam zo schodzky," ABS-12470/108.
5. Barbuš.
6. Seman (I.S/47), December 30, 1981, "Jednání s představitelem SBS OOP ABU AJMANem (REZA)."
7. Barbuš (Bejrút-I.S), February 15, 1982, "Záznam zo schôdzky," ABS-12470/108.
8. Barbuš (Bejrút-I.S), April 26, 1982, "Záznam zo schôdzky," ABS-12470/108.
9. Due to suspended courier services, this material had been kept at the rezidentura in Beirut. Barbuš (Bejrút-I.S), October 14, 1982, "Záznam," ABS-12470/108.
10. Seman (I.S/47), December 30, 1981, "Jednání s představitelem SBS OOP ABU AJMANem (REZA)".
11. Seman (I.S/47), April 7, 1982, "Záznam o jednání se zástupcem SBS OOP REZOU 2.4. 14.00-15.30 na FMV," ABS-12470/108.
12. For more on active measures, see Koura and Kaňák, "Czechoslovak Foreign Intelligence Files," 450–81; and Daniela Richterova, Peter Rendek, and Radek Schovánek, "Covert Measures in Peace and War: The Czechoslovak Way," in *Covert Action: National Approaches to Unacknowledged Intervention*, ed. Magda Long, Rory Cormac, Genevieve Lester, Mark Stout, and Damien Van Puyvelde (Washington, DC: Georgetown University Press, forthcoming 2025).
13. Václav Stárek (Náč. I.S/36)–Ondrej Dovina (zástupca Náč.I.S), December 3, 1981, "Jednání s funkcionáři SBS-OOP, stanovisko odboru 36," ABS-90078; Ján Kuruc (I.S/47), May 21, 1982, "Záznam o jednaní so zástupcom SBS OOP REZOM dňa 19.mája 1982," ABS-12470/108; "Podklad pro jednání se SBS OOP v červnu 1981," n.d., ABS-12470/108.
14. Kuruc, "Záznam o jednaní so zástupcom"; "Podklad pro jednání se SBS OOP."

15. Kuruc, "Záznam o jednaní so zástupcom"; "Podklad pro jednání se SBS OOP."
16. Seman, "Záznam jednání s představiteli."
17. Václav Stárek (I.S/36), December 15, 1982, "Věc: Seznam adres prosionistických firem a institucí," ABS-12470/108.
18. Seman, "Záznam jednání s představiteli."
19. V. Stárek (36-I.S), "Věc: Seznam adres prosionistických firem a institucí," December 15, 1982, ABS-12470/108.
20. Ján Kuruc (I.S/47), May 21, 1982, "Záznam o jednaní so zástupcom SBS OOP REZOM dňa 19.mája 1982," ABS-12470/108.
21. Seman (I.S/47), "Jednání s představitelem SBS OOP."
22. Seman.
23. Barbuš (Bejrút-I.S), October 15, 1981, "Záznam zo stretnutia," ABS-12470/108.
24. Bílek (Bejrút-I.S), February 19, 1981, "Přijatá šifrovka," ABS-12470/106.
25. See more on what Western intelligence agencies knew of Qaddafi in the latter part of the Cold War in Aviva Guttmann, "Turning Oil into Blood: Western Intelligence, Libyan Covert Actions, and Palestinian Terrorism (1973–74)," *Journal of Strategic Studies* 45, nos. 6–7 (2022): 993–1020.
26. Yehudit Ronen, "Libya's Qadhafi and the Israeli-Palestinian Conflict, 1969–2002," *Middle Eastern Studies* 40, no. 1 (2004): 85–98.
27. Barbuš (Bejrút-I.S), October 15, 1981, "Záznam zo stretnutia," ABS-12470/108.
28. Seman, "Záznam jednání s představiteli."
29. More on Semtex in chapter 6.
30. J. Vlček (Náč. OMS, Kancelář MV ČSSR), March 17, 1983, "Informace o průbehu a výsledcích návštěvy delegace SBS OOP, vedené předsedou Abu Ayadem, v ČSSR ve dnech 7-10.3.1983," ABS-12470/108.
31. Berounský (Bejrút-I.S), January 21, 1983, "Záznam ze schůzky," ABS-12470/108.
32. Ján Kuruc (I.S/47), May 21, 1982, "Záznam o jednaní so zástupcom SBS OOP REZOM dňa 19.mája 1982," ABS-12470/108.
33. Seman, "Záznam jednání s představiteli."
34. Seman.
35. This operation was first revealed by investigative journalists Karel Vrána, Jakub Szántó, and Pavel Novotný in the Czech Television report "Československý ministr plánoval s arabskými teroristy atentát, který překazila až StB" [Czechoslovak minister planned an attack with Arab terrorists, which was ultimately stopped by the StB] on May 20, 2017.
36. Kate Connolly, "Jiri Pelikan: A Reform Communist of Czechoslovakia's Prague Spring; He Fought on from Italy and Became a Socialist MEP," *Guardian*, June 30, 1999.
37. Connolly.
38. See file ABS-12613.
39. The details of this StB operation are best detailed in Radek Schovánek, "Atentát na Pelikána," *Minulost.cz*, June 6, 2015, https://www.minulost.cz/cs/atentat-na-pelikana.
40. Vlček, "Informace o přijetí delegace"; Seman, "Záznam jednání s představiteli."
41. Seman, "Záznam jednání s představiteli."
42. Emil Hradecký (Náč. OMS, Kancelář MV ČSSR)–Karel Sochor (Náč.I.S), November 26, 1981, "Jednání s funkcionáři Sjednocené bezpečnostní složky OOP," ABS-90078.

43. Stárek-Dovina, "Jednání s funkcionáři SBS-OOP."
44. Christopher Nehring, "Umbrella or Pen? The Murder of Georgi Markov: New Facts and Old Questions," *Journal of Intelligence History* 16, no. 1 (2017): 47–58.
45. See an overview in Richterova, Rendek, and Schovánek, "Czechoslovak Way of Covert Measures."
46. While Prague's external sharp measures subsided in the 1970s and 1980s, primarily due to the signing of the Helsinki Accords, internally the regime continued to viciously persecute its opponents. The StB ran the infamous Operation Asanace, characterized by intimidation and physical violence aimed at forcing "enemies of the state" into emigration. "Tajné akce StB—Akce Asanace," Česká televize, 2008.
47. "Tesař, Jan," Courage: Connecting Collections, http://cultural-opposition.eu/registry/?lang=en&uri=http://courage.btk.mta.hu/courage/individual/n91011&type=people.
48. Also part of Operation Asanace. "Tajné akce StB—Akce Asanace."
49. "Tajné akce StB."
50. Stárek-Dovina, "Jednání s funkcionáři SBS-OOP."
51. Stárek-Dovina.
52. This was not the first time that the StB considered and rejected an attack against Radio Free Europe. A decade earlier, the First Directorate rejected a similar plan proposed by one of its agents who had infiltrated the US-funded broadcaster largely staffed by dissidents. Prokop Tomek, *"Objekt Alfa": Československé bezpečnostní složky proti Rádiu Svobodná Evropa* (Prague: Úřad dokumentace a vyšetřování zločinů komunismu, 2006).
53. Richard H. Cummings, *Cold War Radio: The Dangerous History of American Broadcasting in Europe, 1950–1989* (Jefferson, NC: McFarland, 2009), 92–145.
54. Ján Kuruc (Bejrút-I.S), June 3, 1981, "Záznam zo schôdzky," ABS-12470/108; Ján Kuruc (Bejrút-I.S), May 25, 1981, "Záznam zo schôdzky," ABS-12470/108.
55. Kuruc, May 25, 1981, "Záznam zo schôdzky." See also Stanley G. Zabetakis and John F. Peterson, "The Diyarbakir Radar," *Studies in Intelligence* 8, no. 4 (Fall 1964).
56. Kuruc, May 25, 1981, "Záznam zo schôdzky."
57. Seman, "Záznam jednání s představiteli."
58. Ján Kuruc (Bejrút-I.S), June 10, 1981, "Záznam zo schôdzky," ABS-12470/108.
59. Seman, "Záznam jednání s představiteli."
60. S. Brož, December 15, 1983, "Záznam z jednání s představiteli SBS OOP," ABS-12470/108.
61. Stárek-Dovina, "Jednání s funkcionáři SBS-OOP."

# 6

# A Very "Special" Relationship

In September 1985 the JSS's envoy in Prague, Beshara Traboulsi, sat down with representatives of one of Czechoslovakia's arms-exporting companies. It was not his first time purchasing weapons for the PLO, which he claimed would be used for the struggle against imperialism and Zionism in the Middle East. This time, however, he arrived with an unusual request—one hundred silencers to match 7.65mm pistols. This shocked the experienced Czechoslovak arms dealers, who understood that selling such closely controlled material would constitute a high-risk business transaction. To resolve this potentially explosive issue, the communist businessmen turned to the country's powerful StB. Czechoslovakia's security service soon delivered an unequivocal verdict: although admitting that the weapons trade always carried a certain level of risk, it thought its Palestinian partners had gone too far. Arguing that silencers were "not used in open conflict" but in fact predominantly employed in "terrorist operations," it put a stop to the deal.[1]

Acquiring arms and military equipment was key to the PLO. Armed struggle was in the organization's DNA and, particularly until Arafat's 1974 speech in the United Nations, guerrilla warfare against Israel was its main means of effecting a change. Unsurprisingly, then, arms and military equipment—euphemistically referred to by the Czechoslovaks as "special material and equipment"—were key items that the PLO and its factions sought to acquire via liaison with states. From the very beginning, this agenda played a leading role in its approaches toward the Soviet Bloc. As a prominent arms producer and dealer, Czechoslovakia was an attractive potential partner.[2]

Accordingly, throughout the life span of their alliance, Prague donated and, more often, sold special material to the Palestinian umbrella organization. This was, however, a complicated task often characterized by a mismatch in expectations, objectives, and modi operandi. Recognizing this, in the mid-1980s Prague was increasingly worried about the risks associated with these transactions—not least the potential reputational blowback in case its weapons were used in highly visible and controversial terrorist attacks, which were occasionally staged by various Palestinian factions. While its anxiety about potential reputational damage stopped Prague from selling certain arms to the PLO, its desire for profit also led the communist country to bend rules in a way that would enable it to sell arms to Arafat's men while maintaining deniability.

Overall, Prague's "special material" donations to its Palestinian partners were modest. Despite the country being one of the world's most prolific arms producers, records suggest that Czechoslovakia only ever donated firearms to the PLO on four occasions. In 1981, 1982, 1984, and 1988, Prague provided Arafat's men with over two hundred submachine guns and a hundred pistols worth about $40,000 in today's dollars.[3] In addition to this, as their relationship matured, the Ministry of the Interior gifted various spyware—including coding devices—to the Palestinian guerrillas worth about $30,000 today.[4] Arguably, this free-of-charge special material was donated to show solidarity with the Palestinian struggle in the Middle East as well as to help solidify the fragile security alliance between the unlikely partners.

While its donations to the PLO were relatively modest, Prague seemed happy to provide special material to the violent nonstate actors on a commercial basis. Throughout the 1980s Czechoslovakia sold Arafat's men a variety of weapons and, in one instance, a significant amount of explosives. Overall, Prague's arms-for-money venture with the controversial nonstate actor was a highly clandestine matter, which involved a number of state bodies and private entities.

The Palestinians used various channels to acquire Czechoslovak special material. One way they would approach Prague would be via a commercial route. As a world-renowned arms producer and exporter, communist Czechoslovakia sported a variety of state-owned arms-exporting companies housed at the Federal Ministry of Foreign Trade, such as the Main Technical Administration (Hlavní technická správa, or HTS), also known as Omnipol. While initially Omnipol was set up to export hunting and sports arms and civilian aircraft, gradually it became best known for its role in special material sales. Largely manned by military staff, the company handled and coordinated large deliveries of special material based on intergovernmental agreements. A separate state-owned export company, Merkuria, also played a key role in the PLO's special relationship with Prague. Initially focused on the import and export of a wide array of engineering consumer goods ranging from petroleum lamps to baby carriages, in the early 1970s it ventured into the more sinister business of selling weapons and pyrotechnics. Crucially, goods acquired from Merkuria were not subject to end-user certification, whereas for deals made with Omnipol this was mandatory.[5] This, as we shall see, would make Merkuria an important player in arms deals with the PLO.

Typically, especially in the early days, the Palestinians would use private Lebanese businessmen as middlemen for doing business with Prague's arms dealers.

**ILLUSTRATION 6.1.** An employee of a precision-engineering manufacturing plant in Uherský Brod assembling a Vz. 70 pistol, 1977. *ČTK / Nesvadba František*

By the early 1980s, however, when Prague-PLO intelligence liaison really took off, the PLO representatives visiting Prague for high-level discussions with the Ministry of the Interior would also hold direct talks with these state-owned commercial entities. By the mid-1980s, when the Prague-PLO intelligence liaison came to a halt after the Amman Accords, the JSS's thick-mustached representative based at the PLO Office in Prague, Beshara Traboulsi, would take over this agenda. He would hold meetings with Czechoslovakia's arms-exporting companies, strike deals, and discuss the details of weapons and military equipment transport. The most frequently used transportation route for commercial weapons exports to nonsocialist countries was via train to the Yugoslav port of Kardeljevo (today the Croat port of Ploče) or the Bulgarian seaside resort town of Varna located on the Black Sea. Here, the arms and matériel, which was covered by a special protection regime, was loaded onto ships and sailed to its final destination.[6]

The second channel the PLO used to approach Czechoslovakia for acquiring weapons was diplomatic. During meetings held with Prague's diplomats in the Middle East, Palestinian representatives would request such special support. These requests would be forwarded to the Foreign Ministry headquarters, which would in turn seek the approval of the Communist Party.[7] The third avenue used by Palestinians to acquire Czechoslovak weapons went straight to the top ranks of the Communist Party. Typically, PLO representatives or those of other factions would request weapons and military equipment during high-level meetings. In these tightly controlled operations, the party would supply small arms to their ideological nonstate friends from the Middle East.[8] From what we know, the PLO and Fatah mostly used the commercial and diplomatic route to acquire weapons from Prague. The third, Communist Party option was geared toward smaller entities with fewer resources and better communist credentials, such as the Lebanese and Jordanian communist parties or the more left-leaning Palestinian factions.

Although ultimately the Palestinians developed multiple avenues to negotiating and acquiring arms and matériel, from what we know Prague initially shied away from providing lethal support to the nonstate actors. This hesitation was underpinned by its concern about some of the Palestinian group's questionable ideological credentials as well as its occasional links to international terrorist campaigns.

## A SLOW START

One of the first recorded meetings between Czechoslovakia's arms dealers and the Palestinians took place in October 1970 in Amman, at the tail end of the Jordanian Civil War.[9] At the commercial department of the Czechoslovak embassy, a three-member group of Fatah representatives met unexpectedly high-caliber Czechoslovak arms dealers—the director general of Omnipol, Tomáš Mareček, who headed Czechoslovakia's main arms-dealing enterprise for seventeen years until his death in 1984, and his colleague August Morávek. During the meeting, the Palestinians confessed the obvious: their movement was in the midst of a crisis. The PFLP's daring hijacking operations had undermined the Palestinian movement's standing in Jordan and clearly led to its ousting from this key Arab state. The various groups within Fatah were now discussing next steps, weighing different strategies and tactics.[10]

According to the Palestinian delegation that met the Omnipol director, the key takeaway from the events in Jordan was that Fatah needed heavier military equipment—tanks and airplanes, no less. Although the Palestinians did

ILLUSTRATION 6.2. The Czechoslovak embassy in Amman, with a kebab shop, Hamburger Inn, attached to its premises, early 1970s. *ABS, f. I.S, reg. č. 12594/102*

not explicitly ask for such unprecedented support, their actual request was only slightly less ambitious: the Fatah representatives asked Prague to set up a production facility for various ammunition, with some suitable for Soviet-made Kalashnikovs. Furthermore, they were keen to acquire factory machinery for manufacturing explosives, primarily TNT—which was not originally a Soviet Bloc product. Finally, the delegation was also keen to get their hands on the equivalent of the new American- and British-made infrared search and track systems that started appearing in the early 1960s.[11]

To assure the Czechoslovak arms dealers that this was not an unrealistic request, the Palestinians confessed that they currently had offers for older and used ammunition-production equipment from Italy and Yugoslavia but no equivalent for Kalashnikov ammunition production. In a further effort to impress Czechoslovakia's top arms dealers, the Palestinians argued that money was no object and that they had full support of the Kuwaiti government as well as approval from the Syrian, Iraqi, and Jordanian governments to set up ammunition factories on their territory.[12]

The experienced Omnipol chiefs Mareček and Morávek were cautious and noncommittal about the Palestinians' ambitious request. Crucially, despite the delegation's effort to frame its message carefully, the Czechoslovaks were not persuaded about the Palestinians' claims to have smooth relations with Arab governments. They thought things were more complex and did not want potential conflicts to undermine Czechoslovak business interests in the region—especially a potential order from the Kuwaiti Ministry of Defense that Omnipol was eyeing at around the same time. Moreover, for any further conversations to progress with Fatah, political backing from both Prague and Moscow would be required. Finally, for such complex investment ventures to be put into place, other conditions and requirements would have to be met.[13]

Overall, Fatah's first approach to Prague's arms dealers was at best ambitious and at worst unrealistic. Although Mareček and Morávek attentively listened to and engaged with the Palestinians, at this time their stance toward cooperation with the PLO was cautious, much like that of Prague's party leaders and bureaucrats. Although their hesitation was arguably driven more by commercial than political or security interests, it would take many years before Prague would be ready to fully develop this line of collaboration.

\*\*\*

The year 1975, when Prague made its relations with the PLO official, also marked the first direct arms delivery to the PLO. Although details of the deal remain elusive, we do know that it was set in motion after Arafat's first official visit to Prague in May of that year, designed to cement the PLO's official partnership with Czechoslovakia. Shortly after the visit, Omnipol was to provide the PLO with at least limited military matériel. This was a crucial time for the PLO to better equip its forces. The Lebanese Civil War was in its early stages. Stakes were high, and the security situation in the region was rapidly deteriorating. Arafat was clearly eagerly awaiting the Czechoslovak contraband—so much so that when he accidently bumped into a Czechoslovak intelligence officer under diplomatic cover who was delivering photos from Arafat's recent visit to Prague to his secretary, the PLO chairman reportedly sat him down and impatiently inquired about "the ammunition issue." No doubt starstruck, the officer immediately telegraphed Prague to inquire about the delivery. By July Omnipol confirmed that it had, indeed, delivered "ammunition" to the PLO.[14]

Three years later, in 1978, there was a major shift in policy. Based on verbal consent by the International Department of the Czechoslovak Communist Party, the first official negotiations on weapons began. Prague's state-owned arms companies were now authorized to hold commercial meetings with the PLO and its factions. Shortly thereafter, Moscow intervened, instructing Prague to conduct such negotiations only with official PLO representatives.[15]

It would, however, take years for this cooperation to develop fully. From 1978 to 1981, all negotiations via this channel failed to bear fruit. They would typically follow one of several patterns: the Palestinians turned to Czechoslovakia, requesting a wide array of items. Subsequently, they were told which items of Czechoslovak production Prague could supply. Ultimately, however, the Palestinian side failed to react to such offers or reacted with such delay that further meetings were unproductive. Accordingly, Prague's decision to sell weapons to the PLO only fully materialized in the early 1980s. By 1981 the two sides finally made steps to make their special relationship work. This resulted in four donations and a number of weapon sales from Prague to the Palestinians at commercial prices.

## FULL SPEED AHEAD

A key turning point in this special relationship was Abu Iyad's pivotal March 1981 visit to Prague. During his negotiations with the Czechoslovak interior minister and other top officials, the JSS chief placed weapons high on the agenda. During the meeting, perhaps as a show of good faith toward Czechoslovakia's new liaison partner, the Ministry of the Interior promised the PLO that it would provide fifty Škorpion machine pistols, sixty-one submachine guns, and a hundred semiautomatic pistols.[16] Three months later, Abu Ayman, who became the linchpin of this liaison channel, told Prague the PLO wanted to obtain more weapons not only for the JSS but also for its partner organizations.[17] In less than a year, arms and other military equipment were being regularly discussed as part of this liaison channel. These were the Beirut years of the PLO. The organization was still staging attacks against Israel, the Lebanese Civil War was in full swing, and Palestinian factions were very much involved in this.

Accordingly, we know that in the first half of 1982, Abu Ayman held at least three separate meetings with the communist country's arms dealers. Although the negotiations were generally held in good spirits, Abu Ayman was dismayed by the prices offered. Expecting much larger discounts than the 2 or 3 percent offered, the Palestinian envoy pleaded with his liaison partners at the Ministry of the Interior to intervene and help the PLO drive the prices down. In fact, much like various Middle Eastern governments before them, the Palestinians complained bitterly about having to do such precarious business with strictly for-profit entities. In the Soviet Union as well as in the GDR, he argued, things were set up differently. Special material purchases were discussed directly with the interior ministries, which were much more accommodating to them.[18]

Abu Ayman was particularly flustered because this was no small-scale venture but instead a sizable deal reportedly worth $27.3 million in today's money.[19] It is not clear whether this impressive purchase ever went ahead. We do know, however, that around the outbreak of the June 1982 Israeli invasion of Lebanon, one particular deal did indeed materialize. During this point of crisis, Prague had supplied the PLO with one thousand Škorpion machine pistols, which were paid for in cash by the representative of the JSS in Prague.[20]

During the heavy fighting in the summer of 1982, other PLO factions followed suit requesting arms supplies. Unsure how to manage and assess these requests, the Czechoslovak Communist Party finally called a meeting of all key "special material" stakeholders to coordinate their efforts. Representatives of its powerful International Department met with their counterparts in the Federal Ministry of National Defense and the Federal Ministry of Foreign Trade to devise a plan. Overall, the Palestinian and Lebanese demands were considered quite small, which would enable the Defense Ministry to satisfy them with materiél held in its reserves and even utilize stock that had been written off as obsolete (e.g., certain submachine guns).[21]

Among requests from various actors embroiled in the civil war—the Lebanese Communist Party, George Habash's PFLP, and Nayef Hawatmeh's DFLP—were also those of Fatah. Arafat's men were keen to acquire fifteen hundred submachine guns, one hundred RPG-7s (including two thousand rounds of ammunition), two thousand anti-tank mines, and three thousand offensive and defensive grenades.[22] This meeting represented the first effort of Czechoslovakia's key stakeholders to meet and coordinate their efforts with respect to arms supplies to Middle Eastern nonstate actors. While we have no record of these requests being delivered, arguably they made Prague aware of what each group needed and informed Prague's 1984 donation to the Palestinians.

By the mid-1980s, key Czechoslovak stakeholders responsible for facilitating arms deals with the PLO were clearly working at full speed. By December 1984, a certain "Amin," standing in as Abu Iyad's deputy, flew to Prague to not only inform the Czechoslovak government about the ongoing crisis in the PLO but also to discuss "organizing the transportation of 4 tons of explosives from CSSR [Czechoslovak Socialist Republic]."[23] Although records do not specify the type of explosive, there are two likely hypotheses for what Prague supplied to their Palestinian partners.

According to the first hypothesis, Prague could have sold the PLO explosives that could be thought to originate in the West—TNT or another type. This would ensure the Czechoslovak government plausible deniability in case the Palestinians used the explosives in controversial terrorist attacks against their enemies. Second, it could have been a Czechoslovak-made explosive. Prague's most infamous export of this kind was Semtex—an easily employed plastic explosive developed in Czechoslovakia that is crucially difficult to detect. It was used in the Vietnam War, during the Troubles in Northern Ireland, and had most likely brought down Pan Am Flight 103 over Lockerbie, Scotland, in 1988. Semtex became popular among the Cold War jackals as well as among leaders such as Libya's Muammar Qaddafi, who allegedly bought hundreds of tons of it from Czechoslovakia's state-owned arms companies.[24]

The documentation of Amin's arrangement with the Czechoslovak government is the only record of a Prague-PLO explosives deal known to date, and we do not know the details of whether or how this sizable amount of contraband made it to the PLO. (For scale: it has been reported that Flight 103 was downed with just 1.5 kilograms of Semtex.[25]) We do, however, know more about other deals that followed as well as the hurdles that accompanied them.

On January 17, 1986, Beshara Traboulsi, the legalized JSS representative in Prague, met with Omnipol representatives. He was not there to negotiate but to discuss the modus operandi for transporting arms to the Middle East. Prague had pledged to supply the Palestinians with a hundred RPG-7s, thirty Vz. 26 light machine guns and Vz. 58 assault rifles, thirty Vz. 50 pistols, and a quantity of electric detonators as well as ammunition. The parties agreed that Omnipol would deliver the special material to the port of Rostock in East Germany, and from there the Palestinians would take care of shipping it by container ship to the Middle East. Once the container was loaded with the arms, the rest of the vessel was to be filled with furniture bought by Traboulsi to conceal the boxes of arms. To further disguise the consignment, worth today about $125,000,[26] the boxes would be sprayed in a different color than the usual military olive green. The Czechoslovak representatives emphasized to Traboulsi that Omnipol's logo must not feature on any of the accompanying documents.[27] For Prague, deniability was clearly key.

Internally, however, the deal was blessed by the Office of the Minister of the Interior, one of the stakeholders responsible for security and intelligence liaison with the Palestinians. The Soviets were also kept informed as a report about the transaction was passed on to "Mr. P," one of Moscow's intelligence advisers in Prague. Moreover, this was clearly not a onetime deal. As the meeting with Traboulsi was coming to an end, the Palestinian envoy assured the Omnipol representatives that soon the PLO would be making a further order of fifty pistols, five thousand 9mm Vz. 82 pistols, and a hundred Soviet RG-4 hand grenades. Suggesting the PLO would welcome a 10 percent discount for its next order, Traboulsi's attempt at haggling was quickly shut down by the experienced arms dealers.[28]

## RED LINES

Some orders were more controversial than others. On July 3, 1985, the JSS's Beshara Traboulsi signed a contract with Merkuria. This time it was not for the usual arms requested by Palestinian factions. The Palestinian security envoy paid for three Vz. 70 pistols with silencers. As Traboulsi was accompanied to all meetings by a representative of the Ministry of the Interior, who supported and recommended the request, Merkuria went ahead with the deal.[29]

Two months later, however, Traboulsi turned up again asking for one hundred such silencers to be delivered to match 7.65mm pistols. At this point, the Merkuria representatives were alarmed. They were fully aware that this would be a high-risk business transaction as it concerned rigorously regulated material. "It would not be a problem to establish the producer or the presumed supplier," Merkuaria argued. "In the event these weapons would be misused, this would damage Czechoslovakia in the foreign policy domain." When this report reached the StB, which was keeping a tight watch over the country's arms dealers, it concluded, "Business with special material always carries a certain level of risk. In this particular case, however, it concerns the export of material, which is not used in open conflict. On the contrary, in practice it is used predominantly for terrorist operations. In my opinion, the potential risks cannot be outweighed by any economic nor even political benefit."[30]

Prague knew that even the less controversial arms deals could provoke undue attention if uncovered. In the summer of 1986, the StB's directorate tasked with watching over the country's arms-exporting companies received some worrying news. In early 1986, off the Algerian shores, Italian military intelligence assisted by Israeli forces was reported to have used submarines to sink two small ships supposedly carrying Czechoslovak weapons for the PLO or one of its factions.[31] Not long before, on October 7, 1985, the PLO's faction the Palestinian Liberation Front, headed by Abu Abbas, had hijacked the Italian cruise ship MS *Achille Lauro* while anchored off Egypt and killed a Jewish American passenger. The sinkings were possibly Italian retaliation or an attempt to deter future attacks by the PLO on its territory or targets—or both.

Soon, worried that its arms shipments to the Palestinians could have been intercepted by the "imperialists," Prague launched an audit of its recent exports to the PLO. Senior Omnipol figures directing the country's main arms exports were questioned by the StB. None, however, seemed to have been aware of any problems with deliveries. Furthermore, Omnipol had not sold the PLO any weapons since mid-1985, arguably referring to their earlier sales of the three silencers. A similar review was conducted at the partner export company Merkuria. Its deputy director also denied supplying any such material to the PLO over the past two years. While it had been supplying weapons via a Lebanese middleman to the Middle East, he had not reported any problems linked to Czechoslovak shipments.[32]

Finally, the StB concluded that if the information on the incident was indeed true and the weapons were of Czechoslovak manufacture, then they must have been reexported to the PLO from a third country or party.[33] This episode highlighted the challenges linked to international arms export to Cold War jackals.

Apart from damage to its international reputation, Czechoslovakia also feared its security assistance to the Palestinians could be sabotaged by its powerful state enemies. Moreover, it now realized that reexports of their goods to controversial actors by third parties—such as Muammar Qaddafi's Libya—could also cause reputational damage and blowback.

Based on what we know, Prague first provided weapons directly to the PLO after it had established an official political and diplomatic partnership with the organization. While Czechoslovak arms companies sold significant amounts of weapons to the Palestinians for profit, throughout the lifetime of the alliance Prague also provided modest donations of arms and military matériel to the PLO. These donations were temporarily suspended during the Czechoslovak-PLO rift of the mid-1980s, with zero arms being provided free of charge from 1984 to 1988. Remarkably, however, commercial weapon deals seemed to have been undeterred by the Amman Accord fiasco and the rift between the PLO and its Soviet Bloc allies. When it came to arms sales, business trumped politics.

Overall, there were various parallel approaches to handling and indeed supplying the PLO with weapons and, in one documented case, explosives. In most instances Czechoslovakia's state-owned arms-exporting companies were used for this highly clandestine venture, but the Ministry of the Interior and the Ministry of National Defense also donated a limited number of military equipment from its reserves. While Prague did in most cases readily bend rules of international arms trade, it gradually drew clear red lines beyond which it was not willing to go.

## NOTES

1. J. Horák (XI.S), September 17, 1985, "Export speciálního materiálu z ČSSR použitelného k teroristickým akcím," ABS-3665/7.
2. Throughout the Cold War, Prague donated or sold vast amounts of weapons and military hardware to the third world, with Iraq, Syria, Egypt, and Libya topping its sales lists. This was a way for Moscow and Prague to strengthen strategic alliances in the region as well as to generate revenue and acquire much-needed hard currency. See more in Richterova, Pešta, and Telepneva, "Banking on Military Assistance"; Golani, "Historical Place"; Laron, "Logic Dictates"; and Pavel Žáček, "Military Intelligence from Libya and Terrorism," *Behind the Iron Curtain* 2 (2012).
3. The original sum was CZK 214,000. One-third of these weapons were modern and highly sought-after Czechoslovak Škorpion machine pistols, whereas two-thirds were decommissioned weapons used by the Czechoslovak army and security forces in the 1940s and 1950s.
4. The original sum was CZK 176,000. Private archive.
5. Vladimír Francev, *Československé zbraně ve světě: V míru i z.a války* (Prague: Grada, 2015), 145.

6. "INFORMACE," n.d. 1985, ABS-3665/7.
7. "Přehled styků s Organizací pro osvobození Palestiny ve speciální oblasti," n.d. 1983, NA, ÚV KSČ—1945–1989, Praha-GH, Ka 840.
8. "Přehled styků s Organizací."
9. See more on first Fatah approaches to Warsaw Pact arms companies in Przemysław Gasztold, "Warsaw and the Fedayeen: Wars in the Middle East, Secret Arms Deals and Polish Relations with the Palestine Liberation Organisation, 1967–1976," *Cold War History* 24 no. 2 (2024): 161–86.
10. "Ze zprávy s. Morávka ze služební cesty," November 14, 1970, ABS-12470/000.
11. "Ze zprávy s. Morávka."
12. "Ze zprávy s. Morávka."
13. "Ze zprávy s. Morávka."
14. Smíšek (Bejrút-I.S), Záznam, June 16, 1975, MZV, To-T-1975-79/Libanon, 115/117.
15. "Přehled styků s Organizací pro osvobození Palestiny ve speciální oblasti," n.d. 1983, NA, ÚV KSČ—1945–1989, Praha-GH, Ka 840.
16. Josef Vlček (Náč. OMS, Kancelář MV ČSSR), March 26, 1981, "Informace o přijetí delegace Sjednocené bezpečnostní složky."
17. Seman, "Záznam jednání s představitele Sjednocené bezpečnostní služby OOP Abu AJMANem v Praze v dnech 9.-11. června 1981. Příloha 4.," June 15, 1981, ABS-12470/108.
18. Seman (Prague), March 17, 1982, "REZA-záznam o jednání v Praze dne 12.2.1982," ABS-12470/108. For more on state experiences with purchasing weapons from Czechoslovakia, see Richterova, Pešta, and Telepneva, "Banking on Military Assistance."
19. The original sum was $9 million. Ján Kuruc (I.S/47), May 21, 1982, "Záznam o jednaní so zástupcom SBS OOP REZOM dňa 19.mája 1982," ABS-12470/108.
20. "Přehled styků s Organizací pro osvobození Palestiny ve speciální oblasti," n.d. 1983, NA, ÚV KSČ-1945–1989, Praha-GH, Ka 840.
21. Marián Kramár, August 18, 1982, "Záznam," NA-A ÚV KSČ—1945–1989, Praha-GH, 841.
22. Dvořák, August 16, 1982, "Záznam," NA-A ÚV KSČ—1945–1989, Praha-GH, 841.
23. Bílek (I.S/47), April 4, 1984, "Záznam pro NO. Věc: jednání s delegací SBS-OOP," ABS-12470/108.
24. Associated Press, "Bohumil Sole Dies," *Washington Post*, June 3, 1997.
25. Adam Goldman and Katie Benner, "U.S. Unseals Charges against New Suspect in 1988 Lockerbie Bombing," *New York Times*, December 21, 2020, https://www.nytimes.com/2020/12/21/us/politics/lockerbie-bombing-suspect.html?searchResultPosition=1.
26. The original sum was $46,761.
27. M. Sidoják (XI.S), February 6, 1986, B. Traboulsi, "Libanon a A.S.Ahnud, JLDR—jednání o nabídce speciálního materiálu pro PLO," ABS-3665/3; M. Sidoják (XI.S), March 6, 1986, "J.B. TRABOULSI, Libanon—doprava dodávky speciálniho materiálu pro jednotky OOP," ABS-3665/3.
28. Sidoják, March 6, 1986, "J.B. TRABOULSI, Libanon."
29. J. Horák (XI.S), September 17, 1985, "Export speciálního materiálu z ČSSR použitelného k teroristickým akcím," ABS-3665/7.
30. Horák.

31. "Informace o potopení lodí s nákladem zbraní československého původu," May 29, 1986, ABS-3665/7.
32. J. Horák (XI.S), June 10, 1986, "Záznam," ABS-3665/7.
33. M. Mikyska (XI.S), June 13, 1986, "Věc: Zaslání informace o provedeném šetření k prověrce poznatku o potopení lodí s nákladem čs. zbraní," ABS-3665/7.

# 7

# Training Palestinian Spies and Bodyguards

Security training was Prague's earliest and longest commitment to the PLO. The first phase of training began in 1980, not long after Abu Hisham first arrived in Prague to discuss security and intelligence collaboration on behalf of the PLO. Soon forty Palestinians were being trained on Czechoslovakia territory.[1] These early programs were, however, characterized by some dissonance. Crucially, at the very beginning the Palestinians were said to have requested what the Czechoslovaks termed "typical terrorist training." Such courses might have resembled the sabotage and guerrilla warfare tactics Prague taught to African revolutionaries in the 1950s and 1960s. This was the 1980s, however, and Czechoslovakia was less inclined to take risks, especially with a partner known to have a history of staging high-profile terrorist attacks. While Prague valued its Palestinian allies, it valued its international standing more and thus rejected this contentious request.[2]

Over the coming decade, however, Prague provided substantial training in security and intelligence to those who it hoped would become employees of a future Palestinian Ministry of the Interior. Although initially its education programs were not always up to standard, in the coming years Prague's training venture became more centralized and, eventually, also more professional. Crucially, in 1982 the Ministry of the Interior set up the Institute for Foreign Studies (Ústav zahraničního studia)—a clandestine facility designed to accelerate this highly sensitive enterprise—in Zastávka u Brna, a small, sleepy town in central Czechoslovakia.[3] The institute was secluded yet close to the large Antonín Zápotocký Military Academy located in the town of Brno, a well-equipped facility with years of experience in training the Czechoslovak socialist army.[4]

This acceleration of Prague's security and intelligence education for liaison partners was a long time coming. In the late 1960s Czechoslovakia suspended the multifarious training for third word cadets it had begun a decade earlier. This halt was caused by the profound political crisis Czechoslovakia found itself in after the violent suppression of the Prague Spring. Following the Soviet-led intervention of August 1968, the country's government descended into internal turmoil, which extended to the interior and defense ministries. In turn, this led to a halt in the country's foreign training programs. It took several years for Alexander Dubček's successor, Gustáv Husák, to remove reformers from positions of power and reestablish Czechoslovakia as a committed member of the Soviet Bloc—a period that became known as *normalizace* (normalization).[5] Once normalizace was complete, the Ministry of the Interior was ready to renew its security and intelligence assistance role in the third world.

The venture picked up in 1976, and by the early 1980s almost two hundred third world cadets had been trained at schools and facilities run by the Ministry of the Interior.[6] In 1982 Prague founded the Institute for Foreign Studies, by which it demonstrated its determination to reinstate itself as a global assistance provider. The clandestine facility was tasked with "training cadres of security services of socialist countries as well as of those nations that have managed to break away from imperialist domination and have embarked on the path to socialist development." During these heavily subsidized courses,[7] Prague aimed to show the cadets the "true face of imperialism led by the US" and thus influence the thinking of foreign students in a way that would "reassure them about the historical necessity of national liberation revolutions transforming to socialist revolutions."[8] According to Petr Schwarcz, who served as a lecturer at the institute, the ultimate goal was to instill the cadets with a positive attitude toward Czechoslovakia, to create so-called social capital, and to forge lasting connections between them and the communist state.[9]

In the closing decade of the Cold War, the Ministry of the Interior's Institute for Foreign Studies educated and trained a total of 1,092 students from across the developing world. The nature and intensity of their training was negotiated as a part of wider security agreements between third world governments and Czechoslovakia.[10] While the 121 Palestinians who completed various courses at the facility were the only nonstate actors trained there, they represented the institute's third most sizable population after Afghan and Ethiopian cadets.[11]

Overall, this was an impressive large-scale operation centered on two educational formats: a full four-year college course, completed by eighty-seven students, including four Palestinians,[12] and a variety of specialized short-term courses aimed at requalifying or further training experienced security personnel from selected third world countries. While some short-term courses focused on "state security"—surveillance, select technological training, and cryptography—others were designed to teach foreign intelligence or law enforcement.[13] Throughout its existence, the institute conducted sixty-five special courses geared toward the needs of their clients.[14] At any given time, there would be 120 to 250 cadets, with the vast majority enrolled in short-term courses.[15]

## TRAINING THE PLO

That the PLO was the only nonstate actor trained at the newly established Institute of Foreign Studies underscored its significance to the Soviet Bloc's third world agenda. After initial training in smaller, less-equipped facilities, this was an upgrade designed to make the Czechoslovak security assistance courses for their Palestinian liaison partners more efficient and ensure appropriate accreditation as well as their practical applicability.[16]

The Palestinians were particular about the type of training they received. In 1982, prior to the arrival of the institute's first cadets, the PLO's JSS representative in Prague, Beshara Traboulsi, urged its leadership to focus courses on practical subjects, not general theory, with an emphasis on teaching cryptography, secret writing, telephone tapping, and managing agent networks.[17] Overall, the Palestinian mission preferred short-term specialized courses, three to six months, to the full four-year college degree programs, which also entailed a preparatory year of Czech language training.[18] Unremarkably, the battle-ready PLO cadets also requested more firearms training, which the ministry readily facilitated.[19]

The Palestinians had a clear preference for state security–style courses, where trainees were taught military tactics, especially for search operations and the liquidation of armed hostile groups. As part of these courses, they were taught various counterterrorist strategies designed to repel attacks against government officials, self-defense, hand-to-hand combat, and target practice with an array of Czech-made arms.[20] Somewhat paradoxically, the Palestinians were taught the opposite of what they had initially demanded. Instead of "typical terrorist training," they were educated in sophisticated tradecraft and defensive skills that, the Czechoslovaks assumed, would be useful to the PLO once it became a state of its own. Prague was clearly investing in training the future spies and bodyguards responsible for keeping the top echelons of the PLO safe from the many threats they faced.

This particular educational track was also designed to hone other professional skills. The Palestinians were trained in the ins and outs of criminology, which included lessons in interrogation strategies, investigation, managing arrests, handling ballistics, and document analysis. This also included investigation of terrorist events. To improve the Palestinians' competence in counterintelligence, they were trained to spot, develop, recruit, and run agents; manage various subversive activities; and run operations to counter enemy penetration, disinformation, surveillance, and countersubversion.[21]

Prague designed this program largely as an exercise in understanding and eventually undermining methods employed by enemy services—various imperialist intelligence outfits—including their agent-acquisition and management

**ILLUSTRATION 7.1.** A rare photo of Beshara Traboulsi (*center*) seen shaking hands with an instructor at the Institute for Foreign Studies during the graduation ceremony of Palestinian cadets, December 18, 1987. *ABS, f. VŠ SNB, IVZ, k. 150, č. J. VŠK-0035/ZS-88*

practices, their surveillance modi operandi, and wiretapping and radio communication capabilities in the field. While the focus here was on the United States, West European states, and Japan, the institute, somewhat ironically, also taught the PLO the inner workings of one of the organization's principal backers—the People's Republic of China. This demonstrated the complexity of Cold War alliances.[22]

Finally, the Palestinian cadets also attended a variety of highly specialized courses. For instance, in August 1983 the StB designed a special class in cryptography aimed at using alphabet ciphers and encryption conversion tables attuned to both English and Arabic. During the two-month training, cadets came to understand different encryption systems, engaged in practical encryption exercises, and gained insight into key code-breaking techniques. Remarkably, due to the lack of appropriate teaching material, the lecturers used David Kahn's 1967 classic *The Codebreakers* as a core text for educating the cadets in the history of cryptography.[23]

Czechoslovakia's training program was in line with that of other Soviet Bloc countries. In fact, several Palestinians enrolled at the institute were known to have completed training in other communist countries, including the Soviet

Union, the GDR, and Romania.[24] In 1976 the KGB trained ten of Wadi Haddad's PFLP-EO's hit men at the Andropov Institute (at the time called the FCD Red Banner Institute), specializing in intelligence, counterterrorism, interrogation, surveillance, and sabotage. Further courses resembling the syllabus of the Czechoslovak institute's "state security track" training were run in 1977 and 1978. Here, however, they were also trained in the art of sabotage—a skill notably absent from the syllabus Prague designed for the PLO.[25] The GDR also provided military and intelligence training. Placed at eight East German military academies from 1972 to 1983, almost eight hundred Palestinians graduated from these programs.[26] Overall, GDR training was more focused on military operations than intelligence.

The last batch of Palestinian trainees enrolled at the institute for a ten-month course only ten days prior to the Velvet Revolution in 1989. Scheduled to stay in Czechoslovakia until August 1990, it remains unclear whether the Palestinians ever finished the course.[27] According to Petr Schwarcz, who taught at the institute until the fall of communism, "when the regime was crumbling, everyone was following these events closely, this was an era of great uncertainty for the cadets as well as the teachers."[28] The pathbreaking revolution effectively put an end to Prague's program of "saving" third world countries from "imperialist domination" and helping them "embark on a path to socialist development." From January 1990 no new cadets were taken on, and shortly thereafter Czechoslovakia—working hard to transform its own services onto a democratic footing—ceased its training of foreign security and intelligence officers.

## ARAFAT VERSUS LENIN

Overall, running these courses proved to be a taxing exercise. In fact, Prague was faced with many of the same challenges it had experienced while providing security assistance to African revolutionaries two decades earlier. Not all Palestinian cohorts sent to Czechoslovakia were found to be intellectually or practically able to cope with the curriculum at hand. Some groups were unhelpfully heterogeneous with regard to their previous education and experience. One particular group, enrolled in a course in secret writing, had to be provided with substitute introductory chemistry classes in order to master this ancient form of spycraft.[29] Another was remarkably diverse in its military skills, with some members achieving low standards in their shooting and showing an overall lack of physical fitness despite superficially good health. In fact, three members of this cohort were not recommended to engage in this particular specialization upon their return to the Middle East.[30]

Similar to the courses run in the 1960s by the Felix Dzerzhinsky Central School, modules on Marxism-Leninism were also a standard component of training at the institute. Despite repeated Palestinian requests to give preference to practical modules and exercises, these ideology-heavy modules managed to creep into each group's curriculum. Lectures on "ideological divergence" (the use of Zionism, nationalism, and anti-Sovietism by internal and foreign enemies); a module on "K. Marx, B. Engels, V. I. Lenin—the commanders and ideologues of the proletariat, the oppressed and exploited masses"; and others on the evolution of the international workers' movement and the history of the Communist Party of Czechoslovakia were all added to the course plan.[31] Cadets had to sit through long lectures on class struggle, critiques of anticommunism, and on the security policies of Marxist-Leninist states.[32] When their complaints mounted, Marxism-Leninism was removed from their curriculum, but it returned via a new module sneakily titled "Security Policy." This showed that although Prague was ready to alter some of its modules and trainings based on Palestinian demands, ideological education was not up for debate. This teaching, carefully designed to influence cadets' worldviews, made it into the curriculum one way or another.

The trainees were further indoctrinated with socialism in their spare time. In addition to ballet performances and classical music concerts, each group would visit socialist-themed exhibitions and commemoration sites, such as those dedicated to the communist antifascist struggle of World War II. They would be required to attend ad hoc political lectures on the foreign policy of the Communist Party of the Soviet Union, the Soviet struggle to maintain world peace, or the threat of US ballistic missiles in Europe. Moreover, other extracurricular activities were devised to strengthen the cadets' "socialist awareness," including a quiz titled "What Do You Know about the USSR?"[33] Finally, the Palestinians also actively participated in celebrations of the seventieth anniversary of the "Great October Socialist Revolution" by composing a celebratory "combat letter."[34]

Discipline, good behavior, and participation in extracurricular activities were strictly enforced. This proved to be particularly challenging, as most Palestinian cohorts typically included a handful of unruly cadets ready to challenge the institute's strict discipline. The Palestinians would frequently depart from the premises, arrive late, and miss classes. Moreover, some cadets were found to have engaged with "women of questionable reputation," with some spending today's equivalent of one or two thousand dollars on this activity.[35] By October 1984 four children had been fathered by Palestinian trainees in the vicinity of the institute.[36] The authorities also complained about the Palestinian officers' excessive smoking and in some cases alcohol abuse.[37]

In addition, the institute's authorities found the Palestinians to be argumentative. In class, they often engaged the lecturers in "testing" discussions and complained about the theoretical modules' lack of applicability. Outside of class, they were also known to cause trouble. While they engaged generously with the African and Cuban cadets, they were more reserved with other groups—for instance, generally keeping separate from the Vietnamese trainees.[38] Conflicts, both verbal and physical, were recorded, especially with the Afghan cohort. As the Czechoslovak authorities soon discovered, the Palestinians were themselves torn by infighting, caused by ongoing feuds between different PLO factions.[39]

The ideological diversity of Palestinian students frustrated the institute's personnel. When the first Palestinian group arrived in the institute in 1982, it became quickly apparent that they represented numerous ideologically disparate factions. On one end of the ideological spectrum were the Palestinians inspired by socialist ideas. Out of a total of fourteen, two cadets openly declared their allegiance to Marxism-Leninism, and another four claimed to be communist sympathizers. However, the Czechoslovak authorities had come to believe that the worldview of the communist sympathizers was "tainted" by anarchism, nationalism, and anti-Semitism. Furthermore, the Czechoslovak communists worried about the views of particular cadets on what they termed "individual terror"—the use of violence by individuals to achieve a political goal—finding them in conflict with Lenin's approach, which favored mass violence as a means of political change.[40]

In an effort to steer their Middle Eastern guests in the desired direction, the institute's staff distributed socialist and Marxist-Leninist literature—for example, presenting them with biographies and pictures of Lenin and Stalin. Such efforts to turn the institute's PLO population into "the right kind of cadets" at times resulted in unexpectedly grotesque episodes. In one particular case, the students engaged in a silent poster war, which saw the communist students display a picture of Lenin in their dormitory room, while the other Palestinians proudly pinned up pictures of PLO chairman Yasser Arafat. Although the cadets' adoration of Lenin undoubtedly pleased the Czechoslovaks, eventually they concluded with disappointment that this was superficial and that only one member of the group would ever qualify as a member of the Communist Party.[41]

At the other end of the ideological spectrum were what the Czechoslovaks referred to as "Ramadanists." These were three "openly Muslim" cadets, two of whom observed Ramadan throughout the training. The institute personnel soon realized that these were no friends of communism. In fact, the "Ramadanists" considered communist ideology harmful to the present stage of the Palestinian struggle. Although they considered socialist countries their allies, the staff believed the Muslims "misunderstood the deeper ideological, political and class context of this alliance." Furthermore, the group leader was the source of much criticism by the Czechoslovak personnel, as according to them he overemphasized in his speeches the fight against Zionism, imperialism, and the importance of international support for their struggle. While he did that,

Prague lamented that he forgot to praise the role of the USSR and other socialist countries and failed to make a clear link between Zionism and American imperialism.[42] The institute's leadership clearly had a rigid view of interpreting the world and expected the Palestinian cadets to conform to it.

This ideological diversity, which they termed "immaturity," had caught the Czechoslovaks by surprise. While they continued to propagate socialist ideology among foreign cadets, they accepted that many of the Palestinians could not be expected to shift their ideological and political thinking to the left due to their deeply rooted "archaic religious beliefs" and affinity toward pro-Western Arab states. To ensure greater political cohesion among PLO cadets in the future, the institute vowed to adopt a more selective recruitment strategy.[43]

## SURVEILLANCE AND RECRUITMENT

The Soviet occupation of Czechoslovakia in August 1968 changed the character of the Czechoslovak society for the next twenty years, imposing harsh ideological indoctrination and strict party discipline. The normalizace also had a profound effect on the country's intelligence apparatus. Decimated by defections and purges triggered by the Soviet invasion, in the latter half of the 1970s Prague's clandestine services looked for ways to renew their lost capabilities. The institute in Zastávka u Brna presented a unique opportunity for building a new agentura abroad, particularly in the third world. To this end, Prague's counterintelligence branch launched an operation aimed at both recruiting new spies among the cadet population and detecting possible penetration of the institute by Western intelligence services.

As part of what became known as Operation Harbor (Akce Přístav), all of the StB's key directorates—foreign, domestic, and military—helped assess the level of risk associated with the cadets.[44] They stationed their officers as undercover members of the institute's staff and tasked them with collecting information about the students as well as political developments in their home countries.[45] Reports on cadet profiles, conflicts between them, and any security issues linked to their presence in Czechoslovakia were at the top of their agenda. Crucially, the StB was interested in unmasking foreign intelligence penetration or any other "antisocialist" behavior demonstrated by the students. According to Schwarcz, who ran courses in Czechoslovakia as well as in Africa, the institute had to be cautious about incoming cadets as they feared some could have been recruited by adversarial services. Hence, foreign students were not exposed to state secrets but were provided with information as general as possible.[46]

In the autumn of 1986, when the StB found that an entire group of cadets from the Seychelles had previously been trained by the British in police and security tradecraft, this warranted extra caution about their loyalties to the

Soviet Bloc.[47] With respect to the Palestinians, the StB was particularly worried about Israeli penetration. This was a real concern, and no mere paranoia. All Palestinian armed groups—however moderate or extreme—were aware that Israel's security and intelligence services were working hard on infiltrating their ranks. The Israelis tended to recruit either Palestinian students in Europe or the occupied territories. After appropriate preparation and training, these clandestine doubles would be sent back to Europe or the Arab world to infiltrate Palestinian organizations and groups.[48] This concerned the institute, especially as the StB had virtually no background information on the incoming cadets. This problem only intensified when the StB found that two of the Palestinian cadets had previously been incarcerated in Israel. Furthermore, the StB was also aware that some cadets may have been sent on the course and tasked with counterintelligence by their own leaders or governments—to collect information about other cadets, lecturers, restricted and secret installations used by the school, or to pursue particular religious or ethnic agendas.[49]

The institute's staff rarely received much information about the incoming students. When it came to the Palestinian groups, their members traveled on passports from an array of Middle Eastern countries—Morocco, Yemen, Egypt, Jordan—and likely under fake names, which further complicated any vetting procedures. When they arrived at the institute, however, a number of measures were put in place that helped establish some facts about the student population. For example, the cadets' mail was regularly intercepted by the StB. (Remarkably, however, it did not always have appropriate language skills to translate this potentially interesting material.) Lecturers were debriefed about their students. Group leaders were accommodated in wiretapped dormitory rooms.[50] These measures contributed to a better understanding of whom the Czechoslovaks were training. Thanks to this set of surveillance measures, several Palestinian cadets were found to have been previously incarcerated for "antistate activities" in Lebanon and Jordan. Shrapnel wounds, bullet wounds, or other combat-related injuries found during compulsory medical examinations revealed that many had engaged in direct combat or had been injured during operations.[51] Medical intelligence is now a leading subdiscipline of which the Czechoslovaks were early practitioners.

The clandestine institute was also eager to tap into the minds of its foreign cadets. Accordingly, they were asked to write papers on topics of prime interest to the socialist regime. This was a fishing expedition as Prague was keen to learn what these often midlevel security and intelligence professionals or fighters knew about issues such as the intelligence services of the United States and other NATO member states, their operations against the third world or the Soviet Bloc, and their use of subversion, covert action, and other practices used to suppress national liberation movements.[52] On a regular basis lecturers

ILLUSTRATION 7.2. Muslah Owni Abdulla as a student at the Institute for Foreign Studies in the late 1980s. *ABS, f. VŠ SNB, IVZ, k. 158*

were also ordered to collect information from cadets on political, economic, and military issues from their home countries.[53] Arguably, Czechoslovakia pioneered programs of liaison-based collection that was perhaps paralleled by the United States in Latin America and has since been copied by other European countries. The United Kingdom's International Intelligence Director's Course at its Defence Intelligence and Security Centre is a notably successful example.

From the outset, the StB instructed its officers based at the institute to pay particular attention to Palestinian students. Although the StB did not know much about the men they were training, at times they did learn unsettling information about their pasts. In November 1987 Czechoslovak counterintelligence flagged the arrival of one Muslah Owni Abdulla, who was enrolled in a short-term course for state security specialists. The Palestinian operative was found to have taken part in the preparation of terrorist attacks in West Germany in 1972 and in Morocco one year later. This made the institute's leadership anxious and necessitated increased StB control during his stay. Soon the Czechoslovaks learned that in the early 1980s Abdulla, also known as "the Shaman" (Šaman), had fought for Fatah in Lebanon, Jordan, and on the Golan Heights. He had undergone special training in China and Pakistan and attended a four-month course in the GDR, focused on military training and "subversive activities." This was also not his first time at the Czechoslovak institute. Having completed a similar course at Zastávka u Brna in the past, Abdulla was now the leader of an incoming group of Palestinian cadets.[54]

Despite his questionable credentials, Abdulla was highly regarded by the institute's staff. Remarkably, while claiming to be illiterate and not taking any notes during the course, he was awarded a final grade of A, his lecturers commending his phenomenal memory.[55] This approach suggests that in the 1980s, although Prague was concerned and paid increased attention to cadets who had clearly overstepped the porous line between national liberation struggle and terrorism, they did not take steps to disassociate themselves from them but rather adopted a surveillance-based risk-management strategy of control.

Simultaneously, the institute represented fertile ground for the StB to spot and develop informants or agents among the cadets. If they were recruited, Prague hoped to use their services upon their return to their countries of origin or when they had secure employment in their own diplomatic or military missions abroad. Although assessments of individual cadets suggest that some were indeed considered suitable for recruitment,[56] recent scholarly assessments conclude that only a few of these efforts were genuinely successful.[57]

In 1987 the StB tried their luck with a certain Ahmad Mustafa Ahmed Mohammad, who first attended the institute in 1983 as part of a small international cohort of students enrolled for a four-year university program. Studying alongside cadets from Hungary, Guinea-Bissau, and South Yemen, Mohammad soon became one of the best students at the institute, completing a dissertation on the role of Palestinian national security in the struggle for self-determination. Apart from being a diligent student, Mohammad also built a life outside his studies. During his time in Czechoslovakia, he got married, fathered a son, kept close contact with the Palestinian diaspora, and enjoyed driving colorful, ostentatious sports cars.[58]

Mohammad first came onto the StB's radar in 1986. Three years into his university studies, the young Palestinian told one of his instructors that he knew of several Israeli Arabs studying at civilian universities in Czechoslovakia. This piqued the StB's interest. He might have information that could help the StB make sense of the complicated relationships and allegiances among Arab students studying in Czechoslovakia. To make sure he really had the adequate access and knowledge, the local StB office in Brno activated its local Arab agentura to find out more about Mohammad's background.[59]

Soon they gathered information about his international travel and contacts on Czechoslovak territory. In 1967, as a fourteen-year-old, Mohammad had been captured by the Israelis along with twenty of his family members. After a monthlong incarceration, he escaped to Lebanon and later Syria, where, as a seventeen-year-old, he joined one of Fatah's security services. Soon, he was running an undercover group in Kuwait and by 1975 had moved to South Yemen to serve as a junior diplomat at the PLO office. While based in Aden, Mohammad engaged in various operations across the globe—including an alleged countercoup in the Seychelle Islands. In 1982, during the pivotal Israeli invasion of Lebanon, the Palestinian was to have actively participated in what the StB termed "a secret war with the Mossad."[60]

Given his background, the StB was eager to exploit Mohammad's access to other Palestinian students, Lebanese interpreters, and the PLO office in Prague. Moreover, they wanted to get his insight into Israeli intelligence and any knowledge he might have about Palestinians with links to terrorism residing on Czechoslovak territory.[61] Accordingly, in April 1987 the StB first approached the Palestinian, asking him to shed light on the backgrounds of the growing Palestinian student community in Brno. Mohammad agreed. He detailed the student allegiances and assured the Czechoslovak security men that, at the moment, none of the Palestinian students studying in Brno was a member of the feared Abu Nidal Organization. This was a promising start.

By autumn the Palestinian was meeting his StB contact regularly, continuing to provide background on various foreign students enrolled at Czechoslovak universities. He also tipped off Prague's security service about an alleged Iranian drug-smuggling route that went to Europe via Turkey—allegedly used by Tehran to help finance its protracted war with Iraq. Mohammad was also key to StB understanding the role the PLO played in various Arab states and the Intifada as well as Israeli "terrorist operations" against Palestinian leadership. Overall, he provided the StB with tip-offs and reports on twenty-three issues, which enabled the service to attain a more sophisticated understanding of the Palestinians and Middle Eastern politics in general.

Although the StB found him a reliable and trustworthy source, they never attempted to recruit the well-informed Palestinian as an official agent. Instead, they classified Mohammad as a "candidate secret collaborator" (*kandidát tajné spolupráce*, or KTS)—a category ascribed to potential future collaborators and agents. Arguably, this was not a typical agent-handler relationship. In fact, Mohammad told his StB contact that he viewed their meetings as part of the PLO-Czechoslovak security alliance and was eager to engage in information exchange. It soon became clear that KTS Otakar, as the StB code-named him, was keen for the StB to also share information they collected from other sources about Middle Eastern students on Czechoslovak territory. He viewed his interactions with the StB as a quid pro quo affair. At one of their last meetings, he asked his StB contact for access to the mail of a certain Jordanian Palestinian who was suspected of collaborating with Israel.

Despite showing strong interest in this liaison, KTS Otakar had very clear boundaries. He refused to provide any information about employees of the PLO

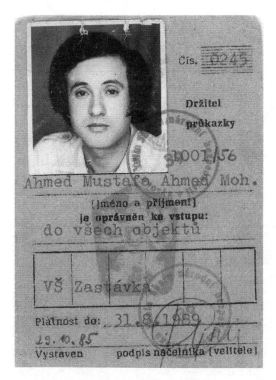

ILLUSTRATION 7.3. Ahmad Mustafa Ahmed Mohammad as a student at the Institute for Foreign Studies before he became Arafat's bodyguard in the first half of the 1990s. *ABS, f. VŠ SNB, IVZ, k. 164*

Office in Prague and deliberately made it seem that he was not in frequent contact with them. Moreover, he was also reluctant to provide information on other cadets studying at the institute.

After his graduation, Mohammad disappeared from the StB's radar. The institute never really developed a full list of alumni, which could enable them to track their whereabouts or reconnect with them. From time to time, however, former students did reappear. This was very much the case with the StB's most trusted Palestinian in the institute. Weeks before the communist regime's downfall, Yasser Arafat visited Prague for a round of official meetings. With him arrived a familiar figure—the imposing Ahmad Mustafa Ahmed Mohammad. Prague soon learned that he now occupied an important post—that of Arafat's head of personal security during foreign travel. He accompanied the heavily guarded Palestinian leader on official engagements in Yugoslavia and Japan and across the Middle East and Central Europe.[62] This was a prestigious job, and while the StB largely failed in its efforts to recruit Palestinian cadets as agents, seeing Mohammad occupy this prominent role must have given the institute staff a feeling of satisfaction. After all, from the first days of this training venture, Prague's goal was to turn its Palestinian cadets into spies or bodyguards, not terrorists.

***

Security and intelligence training was Prague's longest commitment to the PLO—possibly uninterrupted during the temporary freeze in Czechoslovak-Palestinian relations caused by the Amman Accord. In terms of training, the Palestinians enjoyed privileged support well beyond that received by any other third world nonstate actors in the latter part of the Cold War.

While the contents of its programs were largely tailored to Palestinian needs, Prague drew an early red line and refused to provide so-called terrorist training. From the outset, however, Palestinians were considered high-risk participants either due to potential links to terrorism or their unruly behavior while in training. In many ways these challenges were not unique to the PLO but echoed those Prague faced during all its clandestine Cold War trainings of third world revolutionaries. Security assistance proved to be a challenging exercise across the board.

## NOTES

1. In 1980 thirty Palestinians completed a six-month course, and in 1981 another ten completed a three-month course in the Czech towns of Slapy and Kabáty.
2. Jaromír Kolouch (I.S/36), June 8, 1981, "Záznam k jednání na OMS FMV dne 3.6.1981," ABS-12470/108; ÚZS VŠ SNB, February 28, 1984, "Návrh koncepce rozvoje zahraničního studia na VŠ SNB—zaslání k prostudování," ABS-f. Institut pro výchovu a vzdělávání FMV v Zastávce u Brna (hereafter IVZ), Ka 150.
3. This was set up within the country's College of the National Security Corps (Vysoká škola SNB), an institution run by the Ministry of the Interior.
4. Petr Dvořáček, "Ústav zahraničního studia Vysoké školy Sboru národní bezpečnosti a jeho role ve vzdělávacím systému ministerstva vnitra," *Marginalia Historica* 3, no. 2 (2012): 114–15.
5. Pavel Kolář and Michal Pullmann, *Co byla normalizace? Studie o pozdním socialismu* (Prague: NLN, ÚSTR, 2017).
6. Josef Friedrich (Náč. ÚZS), December 22, 1989, "Věc: Podklady k informaci pro I. Náměstka MV ČSSR-předložení," ABS-f. IVZ, Ka 150.
7. The institute spent an average of $30,000 (today $85,000) per university-level graduate and $3,360 (today $9,500) per six-month course graduate. Ústav zahraničního studia (hereafter ÚZS) VŠ SNB Zastávka u Brna, January 31, 1984, "Návrh koncepce rozvoje zahraničního studia na Vysoké škole SNB," ABS-f. IVZ, Ka 150.
8. ÚZS VŠ SNB, 31.1.1984, "Návrh koncepce rozvoje zahraničního studia na Vysoké škole SNB," ABS-f. IVZ, Ka 150.
9. Petr Schwarcz, interview by the author, September 7, 2015.
10. J. Friedrich (Náč. ÚZS VŠ SNB), October 14, 1987, "Věc: Vyhodnocení smluv mezi ČSSR a jednotlivými zeměmi, jejichž studentům je poskytováno vydělání na ÚZS," ABS-f. IVZ, Ka 152.
11. The full list of nations and organizations represented: Afghanistan (397), Angola (57), Ethiopia (123), Guinea-Bissau (40), Guinea-Conakry (10), South Yemen (21),

DRC (60), Mozambique (51), PLO (121), Vietnam (57), Cuba (70), Seychelles (5), North Korea (25), Nicaragua (33), and Cambodia (22). Friedrich, 116–17.
12. These full-time degree courses were stopped in 1985.
13. ÚZS VŠ SNB, n.d. 1986, "PLÁN SPOLUPRÁCE ÚZS s výkonnými součástmi FMV," ABS-f. IVZ, Ka 150.
14. J. Friedrich, December 22, 1989, "Věc: Podklady k informaci pro I. Náměstka MV ČSSR—předložení," ABS-f. IVZ, Ka 150.
15. Ludvík Přikryl (Náč. VŠ SNB)–Jaromír Obzina (Ministr vnitra), 1982, "Porada Ministra vnitra ČSSR s náměstky ministra vnitra ČSSR. K bodu: Návrh na zřízení Ústavu zahraničního studia Vysoké školy Sboru národní bezpečnosti," ABS-f. IVZ, Ka 150.
16. ÚZS VŠ SNB, February 28, 1984, "Návrh koncepce rozvoje zahraničního studia na VŠ SNB-zaslání k prostudování," ABS-f. IVZ, Ka 150.
17. ÚZS VŠ SNB.
18. ÚZS VŠ SNB, January 31, 1984, "Návrh koncepce rozvoje zahraničního studia na Vysoké škole SNB," ABS-f. IVZ, Ka 150.
19. J. Friedrich (ÚZS VŠ SNB)–Alojz Lorenc (I. Nám. MV ČSSR), January 7, 1988, "Vyhodnocení studijního pobytu palestinské skupiny 10/5 na ÚZS VŠ SNB," ABS-f. IVZ, Ka 150.
20. J. Friedrich (ÚZS VŠ SNB), July 11, 1989, "Věc: Hodnocení palestinských studentů- zaslání," ABS-f. IVZ, Ka 206.
21. Bohumil Štěpánek, April 21, 1983, "UČEBNÍ PLÁN pro 6 měsíční kurz P-2-StB," ABS-f. IVZ, Ka 157; ÚZS VŠ SNB, n.d. 1982, "Učební a tématické plány pro 6 měsíční kurz zahraničních studentů StB," ABS-f. IVZ, Ka 157.
22. ÚZS VŠ SNB, "Učební a tématické plány."
23. František Vydra (Náč. zvláštní správy FMV)–B. Štěpánek (Náč. ÚZS VŠ SNB), August 1, 1983, "Provedení kryptologického kursu," ABS-f. IVZ, Ka 157.
24. J. Friedrich (ÚZS VŠ SNB)–II.S-SNB, February 15, 1988, "MUSLEH AWNI ABDULA, skupina Palestinců-poznatky," ABS-f. IVZ, Ka 150.
25. Andrew and Mitrokhin, *World Was Going Our Way*, 255.
26. Jeffrey Herf, *Undeclared Wars with Israel: East Germany and the West German Far Left, 1967–1989* (New York: Cambridge University Press, 2016), 380–83.
27. J. Friedrich, December 22, 1989, "Věc: Podklady k informaci pro I. Náměstka MV ČSSR-předložení," ABS-f. IVZ, Ka 150.
28. Schwarcz, interview by the author, September 7, 2015.
29. Vratislav Podzemský (Náč. Technické správy FMV), October 14, 1987, "Věc: Proškolení skupiny palestinských studentů v problematice speciální chemie," ABS-f. IVZ, Ka 207.
30. "Vyhodnocení pobytu palestinské skupiny 10/6 na ÚZS VŠ SNB Zastávka u Brna," ABS-f. IVZ, Ka 208.
31. B. Štěpánek, April 21, 1983, "UČEBNÍ PLÁN pro 6 měsíční kurz P-2-StB"; ÚZS VŠ SNB, 1982, "Učební a tématické plány pro 6 měsíční kurz zahraničních studentů StB," ABS-f. IVZ, Ka 157.
32. B. Štěpánek (Náč. ÚZS VŠ SNB)–Melichar (Oddelení Mezinárodních Styků, FMV), December 5, 1983, "Věc: Učební plan studijní skupiny P4—předložení," ABS-f. IVZ, Ka 207.
33. Vladimír Vala (ped. Vedoucí P4, ÚZS VŠ SNB), "Hodnocení skupiny P-4," ABS-f. IVZ, Ka 207.

34. "Vyhodnocení pobytu palestinské skupiny 10/6 na ÚZS VŠ SNB Zastávka u Brna," ABS-f. IVZ, Ka 208.
35. Original sum of $400 to $700. V. Vala (ÚZS VŠ SNB), 1983, "Průběžné hodnocení skupiny P2," ABS-f. IVZ, Ka 158.
36. F. Sobocik (S-StB Brno), October 4, 1984, "OPERATIVNÍ SITUACE kontrarozvědné ochrany Ústavu zahraničního studia VŠ SNB v ZÁSTAVCE U BRNA," ABS-f. IVZ, Ka 150.
37. ÚZS VŠ SNB, August 9, 1982, "Věc: Vyhodnocení kurzu 'P'," ABS-f. IVZ, Ka 179.
38. V. Vala (ÚZS VŠ SNB), 1983, "Průběžné hodnocení skupiny P2," ABS-f. IVZ, Ka 158.
39. ÚZS VŠ SNB, August 9, 1982, "Věc: Vyhodnocení kurzu 'P'," ABS-f. IVZ, Ka 179.
40. ÚZS VŠ SNB. For more on Lenin's take on "individual terror," see Joan Witte, "Violence in Lenin's Thought and Practice: The Spark and the Conflagration," *Terrorism and Political Violence* 5, no. 3 (1993): 135–203.
41. ÚZS VŠ SNB.
42. ÚZS VŠ SNB.
43. ÚZS VŠ SNB.
44. Schwarcz, interview by the author, September 7, 2015.
45. Ludvík Přikryl (Náč. VŠ SNB)–Jaromír Obzina (Ministr vnitra), n.d. 1982, "Porada Ministra vnitra ČSSR s náměstky ministra vnitra ČSSR. K bodu: Návrh na zřízení Ústavu zahraničního studia Vysoké školy Sboru národní bezpečnosti," ABS-f. IVZ, Ka 150.
46. Schwarcz, interview by the author, September 7, 2015.
47. Karel Sochor (Náč. I.S), October 10, 1986, "Akce 'PŘÍSTAV'—součinnost," ABS-f. IVZ, Ka 150.
48. Seale, *Abu Nidal*, 7.
49. Seale, 7.
50. Vladimír Laucký (S-StB Brno), January 27, 1988, "SOUČINNOSTNÍ PLÁN kontrarozvědné ochrany Ústavu zahraničního studia VŠ SNB v Zástavce u Brna," ABS-f. IVZ, Ka 150.
51. J. Friedrich (ÚZS VŠ SNB)–II.S-SNB, February 15, 1988, "MUSLEH AWNI ABDULA, skupina palestinců-poznatky," ABS-f. IVZ, Ka 150.
52. K. Sochor (Náč.I.S-SNB), October 10, 1986, "Akce 'PŘÍSTAV'—součinnost," ABS-f. IVZ, Ka 150.
53. V. Laucký (S-StB Brno), January 27, 1988, "SOUČINNOSTNÍ PLÁN kontrarozvědné ochrany Ústavu zahraničního studia VŠ SNB v Zástavce u Brna," ABS-f. IVZ, Ka 150.
54. J. Friedrich (ÚZS VŠ SNB)–II.S-SNB, February 15, 1988, "MUSLEH AWNI ABDULA, skupina Palestinců-poznatky," ABS-f. IVZ, Ka 150.
55. Friedrich–II.S-SNB.
56. See the personal evaluations of Palestinian and Afghan students in ABS-f. IVZ, Ka 207-14.
57. Dvořáček, *Ústav zahraničního studia*, 121.
58. Over the years, only four Palestinians were enrolled in this four-year higher-education course.
59. V. Laucký (S-StB Brno)–J. Friedrich (ÚZS VŠ SNB), October 30, 1987, "Věc: Záznam ze součinnostního jednání," ABS-f. IVZ, Ka 150.

60. Laucký-Friedrich.
61. Laucký-Friedrich.
62. Miroslav Vychopeň (StB Brno), November 17, 1989, "Příslušníci bezpečnostních složek al-Fatahu, absolventi ÚZS VŠ SNB v Zastávce u Brna—poznatky o jejich pobytu v ČSSR," ABS-38165/12.

# 8

# Liaise, Watch, and Infiltrate

In parallel with its foreign intelligence and security liaison, Prague established another liaison channel with Arafat's men—a domestic one. The StB was hoping the PLO Office in Prague could assist its officers in keeping pace with the more radical Cold War jackals who recently began mysteriously appearing in Czechoslovakia. From 1979 onward, the StB met regularly with representatives of the office. This was, however, not an untroubled alliance. A mixture of problems plagued the StB's liaison with the office, including the mission's hypersensitivity to security threats, controversies surrounding the office and its representatives, internal rivalries, and their direct and indirect links to international terrorism. Accordingly, as Prague grew increasingly suspicious about its domestic liaison with the Palestinians, it took measures to monitor and infiltrate the highest echelons of the PLO Office to better understand the Palestinian representation it had helped create and finance.

## LIAISING WITH THE PLO OFFICE

The first steps toward intelligence liaison with the PLO Office in Prague were led by tactical concerns. In the summer of 1979 a number of groups and individuals, whom Prague referred to as "terrorists," were detected on Czechoslovak territory. These were none other than the notorious Carlos the Jackal, who just several years earlier kidnapped key OPEC oil ministers and shot three French policemen at point-blank range; Abu Daoud, who had become infamous for his role in the 1972 Munich Olympics massacre; and members of the Abu Nidal Organization, known for targeting Jewish and moderate Palestinian targets with equal wrath. The StB was concerned about their arrival on Czechoslovak territory and needed help. With little expertise in issues of international terrorism, it reached out to its Palestinian partners based in Prague. Hence, three years after the establishment of the PLO Office in Prague, the StB's Second Directorate—in charge of the country's domestic security—first sat down with Atif Abu Bakr, the PLO representative, with the intention of "exchanging information."

From the outset, it was clear each party arrived at the meeting with different expectations and objectives. Predictably perhaps, Abu Bakr took advantage of the meeting to make a case for introducing permanent protection for his residence and the PLO Office and further permits to carry arms—reminding the StB of assassinations of PLO representatives in 1978 and other violent clashes such as those initiated by Iraqis in Bulgaria, Moscow, Yugoslavia, and Romania. He also gave the StB a lecture on the dangers posed by the Iraqi embassy and its intelligence staff, arguing that "the Iraqi regime uses Prague as the headquarters for its activities, which it carries out in other European countries. The Iraqis have eighteen intelligence agents in Czechoslovakia, who conduct intelligence operations under cover names and fake passports," he told the StB at their first meeting.[1]

Patiently listening, the StB waited for the right moment to inquire about the enigmatic figures who had recently shown interest in the Czechoslovak capital. Eventually Abu Bakr provided them with what they came for. The PLO diplomat confirmed to the StB that Carlos had in fact visited Czechoslovakia a number of times and enjoyed close contacts with the Iraqi embassy in Prague. Although the PLO representative claimed not to know Carlos personally, he told the Czechoslovak counterintelligence officers that Carlos had a "positive relationship with the Palestinians and members of the Palestinian resistance movement." As Carlos often visited Beirut, Abu Bakr suggested the JSS could provide further information on his relationship with the PLO.[2]

The PLO office head did not stop there. He admitted to the StB that he knew Abu Nidal, former head of Fatah in Baghdad, who later left the PLO to create his own extremist terrorist organization under Iraq's sponsorship, which was now viciously targeting the PLO leadership across the globe. He also provided the Czechoslovaks with information about Abu Daoud, the Munich massacre's mastermind. While informing the StB about the senior terrorist's whereabouts, Abu Bakr also defended his friend of fifteen years and argued that Abu Daoud was now trying to distance himself from terrorism. But if Abu Daoud were to mount attacks, Abu Bakr tried to calm the StB, he would do so only in capitalist countries. Moreover, the PLO representative told the StB that Abu Nidal, Carlos, and Abu Daoud had all cooperated with each other at different times and each had a hotline to Saddam Hussein.[3]

This first step toward intelligence exchange with the PLO was promising, but Prague remained cautious about Abu Bakr and his proposition to create a regular and close liaison with the Czechoslovak Ministry of the Interior on the issue of international terrorism and so-called hostile individuals. They suspected that Abu Bakr was not showing his full hand.

In fact, it took Prague several months before the top echelons of the Ministry of the Interior gave the green light for establishing an official intelligence exchange channel with the PLO Office. Their consent came with major caveats—reflecting the country's cautiousness toward its controversial partner. "From our end," the Office of the Deputy Minister of the Interior argued, "this mutual exchange of political and security, as well as some intelligence information, needs to be carried out only in respect to selected security issues and only in those cases, when a potential leak of such information to another country would not have negative effects on us." At this early stage, the PLO clearly did not have the StB's full trust. Furthermore, the security chiefs insisted that its officers only use this particular channel for acquiring intelligence "that would otherwise be difficult for the CSSR to access."[4] It was to primarily serve to inform the StB about Middle Eastern persons or groups that could pose a potential threat to the communist country or attack other targets on its territory, be they Western embassies or Middle Eastern dissidents.

This domestic liaison channel was being set up at around the same time Abu Hisham came to Prague to first discuss international intelligence liaison between the PLO's JSS and the communist country's Ministry of the Interior. As we know, this largely international liaison was designed to cover a wide portfolio of topics and ranged from information exchange to joint operations, arms sales, and training. In contrast with this, the domestic channel set up between Prague's Second Directorate and the PLO Office in Prague was very narrow and cautious. Although Prague never openly stated the reasons for its reserved approach to this liaison channel, arguably this was underpinned by eroded trust that already existed between the PLO Office and the StB.

For years now, Prague's security men felt that the head of the PLO Office was exaggerating security threats and his own importance in order to secure privileges for himself and his staff. Although they knew Abu Bakr and his associates would jump at any opportunity to prove their importance to Prague's security service, the StB was aware that he might want to use this channel to sidetrack his rivals. This would, most likely, affect the credibility of any information that would be supplied via this liaison. Moreover, the StB worried that the Palestinians might request information that could become target intelligence. Information could not be wholly trusted in the hands of a controversial ally with a violent past. Finally, this approach could also have been caused by the more cautious and controlling nature usually ascribed to domestic security services—most notably those of nondemocratic states.

The liaison agreement was never written down. In fact, we know that Prague took extra caution not to commit the rules of the liaison to paper, advising that "the rest of the orders will be given to you personally by the first deputy minister of the interior." Nevertheless, in hindsight, the StB's first meeting with Abu Bakr represented the start of an informal security relationship between the Ministry of the Interior and the PLO Office in Prague. Their irregular meetings, largely initiated by the Palestinian side, were held either at the ministry, the PLO Office, or one of the two safe houses allocated for this purpose.[5]

## THE ATIF ABU BAKR ERA

From 1975, when it was first decided that the PLO would open its office in Czechoslovakia, the StB was aware the mission would constitute a security risk. Prague feared that by establishing the PLO Office "adversarial special services might want to use this situation and conduct operations that might have negative consequences for the host country." Moreover, they were acutely aware of the intense inter-Arab animosities—especially those between Iraq and the PLO—and the fact that "there are a number of embassies in Prague that do not view the PLO positively."[6] Clearly fearing that the office could become the target of an attack, the StB deployed a number of its counterintelligence departments to monitor as well as watch over the new Palestinian mission.[7]

In 1978 the PLO leadership was hit by a coordinated assassination campaign across Europe, the Middle East, and Asia. In January the PLO representative in London, Said Hammami, a moderate advocating coexistence with Israel, was shot dead in Mayfair.[8] In June Ali Yassin, the PLO head of mission in Kuwait, was also assassinated. Less than two months later, in August 1978, the PLO representative in Paris, Ezzedine Qalaq, was shot at point-blank range at least a dozen times, and his aide, Hammat Adnan, died in a hospital after being hit by a grenade.[9] The ANO, a breakaway franchise of the PLO with close ties to Iraq, was believed to have staged the attacks in an effort to punish moderate Palestinians.[10] This wave of violence raised red flags at all PLO missions around the world.

At this time, the PLO Office was headed by Atif Abu Bakr, who first arrived in Prague in 1976 and remained in place until November 1983. Peter P., who taught the PLO representative Russian and after the fall of communism rose to become one of the country's top intelligence officers specializing in terrorism, found him to be an intellectual and a talented poet.[11] Others, however, remembered him as being quite cold, keeping his distance from the Czechoslovak representatives he was set to work with.[12]

Abu Bakr was, however, also a relentless criticizer of all things that clashed with his own worldview. A self-proclaimed member of the leftist wing of the Fatah, he became a vocal critic of Iraq, which was directly supporting the ANO's assassination campaign against Palestinian moderates.[13] His confrontational style and vocal criticism of top Iraqi officials who arguably gave the green light for financing the assassination campaign only added insult to injury.

Five days after the Paris attack, in August 1978, the PLO Office in Prague first requested increased protection, fearing that copycat attacks could be staged

ILLUSTRATION 8.1. Abu Bakr, the head of the PLO Office in Prague in the 1970s. ABS, f. Správa sledování SNB–svazky (SL), a.č. SL-11 MV

against its employees.[14] The office felt exceptionally vulnerable as its deputy head was the brother of the slain PLO representative in Paris, Ezzedine Qalaq. The PLO had other reasons to worry about its mission's security. It claimed that only days earlier three armed men had broken into the PLO Office in Sofia and that on the morning of August 8 an unidentified Arab person tried to break into the PLO Office in Prague. In a matter of days, Czechoslovak authorities provided the PLO mission with round-the-clock protection.[15]

Nevertheless, this did not fully reassure the Palestinians stationed in Prague. After they changed all the locks of the office and practically ceased activities there for over a month, in mid-September 1978 two Palestinian bodyguards arrived at the PLO mission.[16] This made Prague sit up sharply. It protested against having possibly armed Palestinian commandos, which it knew nothing about, on its territory.[17] In addition to this practical concern, the regime's paranoia also kicked in. Always on the lookout for "foreign agents," the StB argued that the duo had possibly come to Czechoslovakia for ulterior "intelligence purposes."[18]

Finally, two months after their arrival in Prague and following much back-and-forth between Czechoslovak authorities and the PLO, a compromise was found. Prague was doubtful that the security men were sanctioned by Arafat but eventually accepted the narrative presented by Abu Bakr that such "protectors" were in fact sent to a number of states to shield the PLO Office personnel "from extremists." Admitting that a terrorist attack in socialist countries was unlikely, Abu Bakr nevertheless insisted that it could not be completely ruled out as there was a steady inflow of Arab students and tourists into Czechoslovakia, which would make such attack possible. Underlining that he was serious in his concerns, the PLO representative asked for other members of the office and his wife to be granted permission to carry arms, arguing that Syrian and Iraqi diplomats stationed in Prague also had weapons brought over via diplomatic bags. Although the StB and Communist Party representatives were not entirely sure whether Abu Bakr was genuinely worried about his security or whether he wanted to use this situation to increase his status in Czechoslovakia, they finally gave in. The StB suggested a combined model of protection to be adopted with one Palestinian and one Czechoslovak security officer stationed at the PLO mission.[19]

The StB's liaison with the PLO Office during the Abu Bakr era was cautious, and its content was varied. During some meetings, Abu Bakr shared his analysis of the PLO's alliances with Middle Eastern states. At other times, he warned the StB of alleged security threats. On July 16, 1980, Abu Bakr informed the StB of a thirty-member group of "Arab terrorists"—Palestinians and Iraqi and Sudanese nationals—who had arrived in Vienna on a mission to attack Egyptian diplomatic posts in Austria and West Germany. The PLO representative suggested that these terrorists, allegedly led by the Iraqis, might also direct their attacks against socialist states and most prominently Czechoslovakia, which was known to harbor the largest number of Arab communists and progressive forces. Alarmed, the StB took preventative security measures: its officers were instructed to collect further details on the operation, interrogate Czechoslovak nationals who had previous contact with terrorists such as Carlos, debrief its key agents tasked with monitoring terrorists, and alert relevant authorities to monitor all incoming Arab nationals.[20]

When an attack never materialized, Abu Bakr's tips on potential terrorist threats lost credibility. It seems that gradually the StB came to terms with the fact that Abu Bakr's reporting was often based on hearsay and left the StB with a large amount of information of dubious quality. The best-case scenario was that the relatively high-profile PLO representative was growing increasingly paranoid at a time of intense Palestinian infighting. The worst was that he was intentionally feeding his liaison partners disinformation. For Abu Bakr, this was clearly a transactional relationship. The Palestinian did not volunteer information without wanting something in return—for example, increased protection of PLO facilities in Prague.[21]

Abu Bakr's interaction with the StB during his tenure showed that Czechoslovakia clearly had an appetite for more information on international terrorism. Especially from the mid-1970s onward, the country felt increasingly vulnerable—predominantly because it was becoming a favorite destination for Cold War jackals. Nevertheless, they found Abu Bakr to be an unhelpful and potentially deceitful ally. Unsurprisingly, then, when in 1983 he left his post in Prague, the StB was hopeful its future Palestinian counterpart would be a more serious liaison partner.

Their hopes were crushed not long after his replacement arrived. While Abu Bakr's successor was a familiar face and an important player from Abu Iyad's inner circle, his reign over the PLO Office in Prague was characterized by a taste for political revenge and worsening relations with the host country caused by suspected links to terrorism.

## THE ABU HISHAM ERA

Abu Hisham, who set up the Prague-PLO intelligence and security liaison back in 1979, took over as head of the PLO Office in March 1984. Born in 1945 in Gaza as Samir Abdul Fattah, in the 1970s he rose quickly through Fatah's security ranks. The seasoned officer was alleged to have been engaged in a number of covert operations, including a 1974 assassination attempt against King Hussein of Jordan, for which he was allegedly incarcerated in Morocco. Although habitually a security professional, in the early 1980s he crossed the often blurred line between intelligence and diplomacy, first becoming the PLO's official representative in Bulgaria and moving on to the post in Czechoslovakia. According to Ivan Voleš, who was Abu Hisham's main diplomatic contact in Prague, this role seemed to come naturally to him as the PLO envoy was "very much a politician and a manipulator."[22]

Prague was aware of his background as a covert operator but did not have much wiggle room to reject him. This was because, prior to Abu Hisham, the PLO nominated two other envoys who were not approved by Prague, for suspected links to terrorism.[23] Although he was not much to their liking as Prague knew of his security career and likely involvement in acts of terror, it reluctantly approved his nomination. Arguably, it opted for this compromise in an effort to avoid unsettling what was at this point an established political alliance. Nevertheless, although Abu Hisham was ultimately given agrément, he was unequivocally told that Prague did not want him to engage in any "terrorist-related activities on Czechoslovak territory."[24]

The new head of Prague's PLO Office did not make a good first impression. Much to the irritation of the StB's Second Directorate—in charge of domestic security and the liaison channel with the PLO Office—Abu Hisham seemed as hypersensitive to security threats as his predecessor. He would thus follow where Abu Bakr left off—requesting that the PLO Office be relocated to a villa due to security concerns and making other such demands. By this time, Prague had become somewhat better at assessing which threats were real and had little patience with unwarranted pleas for increased security. Accordingly, from his first months in office, Abu Hisham's behavior irritated Czechoslovak Communist Party representatives and diplomats who found him to be something of a prima donna. Things escalated so quickly that in the first year of his mission the

ILLUSTRATION 8.2. The only publicly available photo of Abu Hisham (*second from left*), seen observing a meeting between President Husák and PLO chairman Arafat in 1989. *ČTK / Kalina Michal*

stakeholders essentially agreed that if he had any reservations about his security, "he should choose another country where he would feel safe."[25]

At his first meeting at the Ministry of Foreign Affairs, the new representative continued to make a bad impression. Meeting the country's top Middle Eastern diplomats, the Palestinian envoy protested about the nature of a recent upgrade of the PLO Office. In February 1983 Prague had changed the status of the PLO representation in Prague to a diplomatic mission. From this point on, the head of the representation was accredited by the Ministry of Foreign Affairs. This shift followed similar upgrades by Moscow, Sofia, Budapest, and East Berlin and signaled a sharp improvement in Prague-PLO relations.[26] Abu Hisham, however, considered Prague's upgrade insufficient and proposed a new framework agreement to the startled Czechoslovak diplomats for whom this first meeting was supposed to be a courtesy call. This thoroughly annoyed Prague, and it took a year for Abu Hisham and the Ministry of Foreign Affairs to mend their fences. "As the Palestinian issue is subject to a coordinated approach among socialist countries," the Foreign Ministry recommended that "apologies of the Extraordinary Representative be taken into account."[27]

While strategic objectives made the diplomats forgive the eccentric Palestinian envoy, the Ministry of the Interior clearly did not consider him a suitable partner. Accordingly, it refused to deal with Abu Hisham and instead liaised with Beshara Traboulsi, the designated JSS representative at the mission who later attempted to purchase a hundred silencers from Prague's arms dealers. However, liaison with Traboulsi closely resembled that with his previous boss. Much like the intellectual poet Abu Bakr, Traboulsi told the StB fantastic tales of planned terror attacks, collusion, and deception, and overall was found to exaggerate alleged security threats against the PLO mission.[28]

Each time, it took months and considerable effort for the StB to verify these claims. Ultimately, they found no evidence to substantiate Traboulsi's warnings and were forced to conclude that their Palestinian partners at the PLO Office in Prague were providing them with "information that has in many cases been significantly distorted and unreliable." They had several explanations for this. Their Palestinian liaison partner was likely doing this to find out to what extent the StB had penetrated the PLO mission in Prague and how much it knew about their contacts. Or perhaps it was to better understand how thorough StB was in vetting Palestinian students and cadets trained at the Institute for Foreign Studies.[29]

Abu Hisham, aware of Traboulsi's continuous cooperation with the StB, was clearly irritated by his subordinate's close relations with these authorities. He thus prohibited him from passing any information to their Czechoslovak counterparts without his consent. If Traboulsi was to activate his liaison channel with the StB in the future, he was to first seek Abu Hisham's consent on whether this information would be handed over and, if so, to what extent. Effectively feeling left out and facing increasing fragmentation within the PLO, the PLO Office head constrained his own organization's intelligence liaison with the communist country.[30]

From his earliest moments as the PLO envoy, Abu Hisham struggled to persuade Prague to accept him as a partner. The country's diplomats adopted the "forgive but don't forget" mantra following his initial problematic start in the office. However, the Ministry of the Interior never actively sought liaison with the powerful Palestinian who had been sent to Prague to strengthen Yasser Arafat's alliance with the important communist ally.[31] Abu Hisham's status as an outsider may have been accelerated by a general decline in Prague's relationship with the PLO, triggered by the latter's 1983 rift with Syria and subsequent short-lived alliance with King Hussein.

Nevertheless, there were more serious concerns about Abu Hisham that undoubtedly contributed to this and occupied the suspicious minds of Prague's diplomats and spies. The PLO representative seem to be a central figure in Palestinian infighting, which had been plaguing the organization since mid-1983. Amid the confrontation with Israel, a number of senior PLO military officers based in Lebanon's Beqaa Valley, led by Col. Abu Musa, had declared an armed revolt against Arafat, who was at the time in exile in Tunis.[32] This clash spilled over into the Palestinian communities living and working in Europe, including the Soviet Bloc.

Crucially, in November 1984 the StB learned of Abu Hisham's possible role in what Prague referred to as a "Palestinian terrorist operation." A Palestinian diplomat and an Abu Musa loyalist serving in Poland, Talib Hamud Amr, was to have been subjected to a fake arrest by the PLO's JSS, kidnapped, and taken to Tunis, then the seat of the organization's leadership. Fearing that Amr might face capital punishment in Tunis at the hands of Arafat supporters, his faction friends intervened with Prague. After all, the kidnapped man was married to a Czechoslovak citizen, and according to the source the whole operation was orchestrated by none other than Abu Hisham. To add further pressure to his plea, the source told the Ministry of the Interior that similar purges were likely to occur across other socialist countries, including Czechoslovakia, and that these would trigger further violence.[33]

According to Polish security files, Amr had been arrested for aggravated assault of a local taxi driver, who nearly died after the Palestinian beat him in Warsaw's Novotel Hotel. Suspecting the assailant of being an ANO sympathizer, the PLO as well as the Polish government was keen to withdraw Amr from Warsaw. When the PLO delegation tasked with escorting him to Tunis arrived at the Okęcie Airport, a crowd of ANO supporters gathered there to stop the expulsion. While reluctant to get drawn in to inter-Palestinian affairs, the Poles had had enough and wanted Amr gone. Accordingly, they helped escort the Palestinian and the PLO delegation to a plane and facilitated his expulsion from Warsaw. Based on available documents, Arafat was indeed waiting for the unruly PLO member upon his arrival in Tunis, but Amr was not—as his supporters feared—sentenced to death.[34]

Much like their Polish colleagues, the StB was eager to stay away from Palestinian infighting. It thus never acted on this request and refrained from appealing on Amr's behalf. This episode, however, added another red flag next to Abu Hisham's name, as he was allegedly implicated in the affair. It also showed that Prague and other host states were being increasingly drawn into Palestinian infighting and, at times, even pressured into taking a stance at times of crisis.

Overall, intelligence liaison with the PLO Office in Prague did not fulfill its main purpose. Initially the StB's domestic branch was given approval to liaise with the Palestinians in Prague predominantly on issues of terrorism. This cooperation, however, bore little fruit for the communist country, which was increasingly worried about unsolicited visits by Cold War jackals. In fact, the liaison proved to be burdensome for the StB, which found itself inundated by frequent but rarely credible warnings by PLO envoys. What is more, during the reign of Abu Hisham, who served in Czechoslovakia until the early 1990s, it became clear to Prague that he was a potentially dangerous figure who needed to be kept under close watch. Accordingly, to compensate for this dysfunctional liaison channel and find out more about the PLO mission, the StB created a web of informants who supplied it with information not only on the Palestinian movement and the PLO Office in Prague but also on the feared jackals.

## SPYING ON THE PALESTINIANS

On September 26, 1978, secret collaborator "Mušír" met his StB handlers for the first time at the popular Café Astra in downtown Prague. The Palestinian had worked at the PLO Office in Prague since its establishment and was now effectively the deputy to Abu Bakr, the PLO representative. During the meeting, held in a friendly atmosphere, Mušír agreed to collaborate with the StB. The new recruit urged the StB that this collaboration had to remain confidential. Aware of the sensitivities, his future handlers asked their new asset to choose his cover name and provided him an emergency contact number. They agreed that the Café Astra was a good place for further meetings.[35]

During the Cold War, Czechoslovakia was the geographical and, in many ways, cultural and intellectual center of the socialist world. As the headquarters of various prominent international organizations—including the Soviet-dominated International Union of Students, the Federation of Journalists, and the theoretical and ideological magazine *Issues of Peace and Socialism*—the country attracted elite third world communists from around the globe, many of whom had escaped their homelands due to political persecution. Moreover, since the 1950s, dissident communities from the Middle East had found refuge in Central Europe. To Prague, first came the hard-line communists fleeing Iran, followed by Syrian and Iraqi communist elites forced into exile after the Ba'athist coups in their respective homelands.[36] Over the years, thousands of Arab students also chose Czechoslovakia for their university studies, not least due to Prague's generous scholarship programs directed at third world students. Finally, Czechoslovakia was also a popular destination, with tens of thousands of Arabs annually visiting the country's tourist sites and spas. Many within this ecosystem were Palestinian—journalists, students, tourists, communists, diplomats, or businessmen. Being a police state, Czechoslovakia worked hard to monitor and penetrate this subculture of Middle Eastern nationals, with a particular interest in employees of Middle Eastern diplomatic missions and university students.

Agent networks were crucial in the story of Prague's liaison with the PLO. Within this context, the StB created an agentura, tasked to report on various issues, objects, or persons of interest. Collaborators could be recruited within four different categories—agent (*agent*, or A), confidential contact (*důvěrný styk*, or DS), ideological collaborator (*ideový spolupracovník*, or IS), or confidant (*důvěrník*, or D)—depending on their motivation, value, or willingness to cooperate.[37] Each category warranted a different approach. In some instances secret collaborators were wittingly cooperating with the StB. In others they were recruited under a false flag, with diplomatic and trade covers being among the most frequent.

During the closing decades of the Cold War, the StB created a wide network of Arab and Palestinian assets from within this ecosystem. These agents were predominantly tasked with helping Prague gain insight into the most intimate matters pertaining to the PLO, its office and later diplomatic mission in Prague, and the underworld of international terrorism. Crucially, the StB managed to recruit key representatives at the PLO Office who would report back to the secret police. They told their StB handlers stories of embezzlement, ties to terrorists, and neglect of key duties by PLO representatives in Prague. They became a crucial substitute for the dysfunctional domestic liaison channel the StB tried to set up with the PLO Office in the late 1970s. This was key to Prague's surveillance of its unpredictable Palestinian liaison partner as well as of international terrorists who descended on Prague in the second half of the 1970s.

Mušír was among the StB's top spies in the PLO Office. He provided the StB with firsthand information on the PLO Office and its personnel, with a special focus on the controversial PLO representative, Abu Bakr. His deputy, Mušír, had a front-row seat to Abu Bakr's dealings in Prague, and what he saw, he did not like. For years, he told the StB about undue use of PLO funds for Abu Bakr's personal medical expenditures. This was obvious embezzlement, argued the StB collaborator, as the PLO Head was effectively stealing this money from Palestinian students, who were meant to be its primary recipients. Prague was also repeatedly told about how Fatah students were given clear preference for what aid Abu Bakr did distribute, at the expense of those associated with other factions. This misuse of power and privilege caused discord among the employees of the PLO Office as well as the wider Palestinian community living in Czechoslovakia.[38]

Mušír was also crucial to providing the StB with information on international terrorists, citing dates of their arrival in Prague, cover names, and details of the fake passports of such people as Abu Daoud and Atif Bseiso, the latter alleged to be Abu Daoud's accomplice in planning the 1972 Munich Olympics massacre. Furthermore, he provided the StB with insight into the world of Palestinian students living in Prague and their affiliations with the different Palestinian factions—some of which were still engaged in acts of terror. Finally, he was vital to understanding some of the strategic shifts within the PLO that the liaison channel failed to reveal. This was particularly important in respect to the PLO-Iraq conflict, which the StB was increasingly worried about.[39]

The StB's informants were also at work during Abu Hisham's reign as the head of the PLO Office in Prague. Much like his predecessor, he was suspected of financial machinations. The StB knew that his previous tenure in Bulgaria was problematic—Prague was informed that during his time there he had engaged in a multimillion business of forging US dollars—which were to be printed in Tunisia, Yemen, Sudan, and Lebanon and exported to other countries, including Iraq and Czechoslovakia.[40] Moreover, in the mid-1980s, some members of the diaspora accused Abu Hisham of terrorizing PLO dissidents and organizing operations against them across the Soviet Bloc.[41]

Another key informant during this period was none other than Beshara Traboulsi, the representative of the PLO's JSS in Prague—code-named Kámoš (Buddy). With access to privileged information, Traboulsi provided the StB with some of the most intriguing insights into the mind of the PLO and its leader, Yasser Arafat. During his visit to Prague in 1988, Chairman Arafat was "clearly disgruntled," Traboulsi told the StB, because he was not welcomed upon his arrival by the general secretary of the Czechoslovak Communist Party, Miloš Jakeš, and greeted with appropriate military honors.[42]

Furthermore, the StB learned that Kámoš was planning a campaign to discredit his boss, the unpopular PLO Office head Abu Hisham—who was said to be engaged in multiple love affairs with Czechoslovak women. Together with another Palestinian, also on the StB's payroll, Traboulsi devised a preliminary plan. They would hire Czechoslovak prostitutes to record their romantic encounters with the PLO boss in Prague. Traboulsi would secure a silent camera suited for the task. There is no way Abu Hisham would notice, argued the security specialist, as he was severely nearsighted and "cannot see beyond two meters." If and when they managed to acquire this documentation of Abu Hisham's amorous activities, they planned to pass it to PLO intelligence chief Abu Iyad, who would then make sure that Arafat got rid of him. The StB was intrigued by this entrapment plan and tasked its other spies within the community with overseeing the development of this saga.[43]

The plan never delivered: Abu Hisham remained in his post, and Traboulsi's relationship with the PLO Office head deteriorated further. In the autumn of 1988, the PLO's security representative was in fact fired by Abu Hisham, who accused his subordinate of being an StB snitch. Somewhat ironically, Abu Hisham delegated Traboulsi's delicate security agenda to his deputy. This was none other than the reliable and enthusiastic StB asset Mušír.[44] The PLO chief could not escape the glare of StB spies on the inside.

Arguably, by the late 1980s the PLO Office in Prague was encircled by StB spies who constantly reported on the details of Abu Hisham's life and work. To complement their human intelligence assets, the StB eventually also deployed its SIGINT capabilities, continually wiretapping the PLO Office.[45] In May 1986 it also conducted a special technical search of its premises. Disguised as a team of technicians who came to install a security system the PLO had requested from the Ministry of the Interior, the StB carefully searched the premises and found a trove of internal PLO documents as well as records on Central Intelligence Agency (CIA), Bundesnachrichtendienst (BND), SIS, and Italian foreign intelligence activities in the Middle East with a special focus on the PLO.[46]

\*\*\*

Throughout the 1980s, the StB was increasingly aware that some of the PLO representatives it was dealing with fostered close connections with groups and individuals whom Prague considered terrorists and that they were not entirely genuine in their dealings with Czechoslovak authorities. Prague thus swiftly adopted a new approach—a different tool from its Swiss Army Knife that was the StB. As an alternative to this malfunctioning domestic liaison, the StB recruited key PLO personnel who provided insight into the life of the PLO Office and its representatives. Recruiting such high-ranking PLO personnel stationed in Prague was, overall, a remarkable achievement for a service that had little experience with countering or monitoring nonstate actors. Soon it paid off when these high-ranking PLO spies began to provide Prague with information key to countering radical Palestinian groups that started descending on Prague.

## NOTES

1. Václav Šubrt (Head of X.S/3), August 24, 1979, "Záznam," ABS-19324/1.
2. Šubrt.
3. Šubrt.
4. Dezider Hronec (Kancelár sekr. NMV ČSSR)–Karel Vrba (Náč.II.S-SNB), November 15, 1979, ABS-1932/1.
5. Hronec-Vrba.
6. "Vyjádření MPO/1 k návrhu materiálu pro vládu ČSSR, týkajícímu se kanceláře OOP," August 22, 1975, A-MZV, To-T-1975-79/Palestina, 128/111.
7. Václav Stárek (Náč.X.S)–J. Hrbáček (Náč.II.S), February 12, 1976, ABS-19324/2; Vláda ČSSR, April 29, 1976, "Usnesení předsednictva vlády Československé socialistické republiky," NA-A ÚPV-ČSSR/ČSFR, 88/1976.
8. "P.L.O. Official Is Slain in London," *New York Times*, January 5, 1978.
9. Jonathan Kandell, "2 P.L.O. Men in Paris Slain in Arab Feud," *New York Times*, August 4, 1978.
10. J. Kandell, "2 Suspects in Killing of Paris P.L.O. Officials Said to Admit Belonging to Group Tied to Iraq," *New York Times*, August 5, 1978.
11. Peter P., interview by the author, September 4, 2015.
12. Josef Krejčí, interview by the author, September 16, 2015.

13. Informant Said, May 14, 1979, "Kancelář OOP v Praze-současná situace ve složení pracovníků," ABS-19324/3; J. Marek (MZV), November 10, 1983, "Ukončení mise představitele OOP v ČSSR," ABS-19324/4.
14. M. Lagron, August 8, 1978, "Informace," ABS-19324/2.
15. Václav Pokorný (X.S-SNB), August 8, 1978, "Záznam," ABS-19324/2; M. Allari (Kancelář OOP)–ČSSR Výbor solidarity, August 8, 1978, ABS-19324/2.
16. V. Pokorný (X.S), September 22, 1978, "Jednání s pracovníkem Organizace pro osvobození Palestiny za účelem ochrany objektu-zpráva," ABS-19324/2.
17. V. Stárek (Náč.X.S)–Ján Hanuliak (I. Nám. MV ČSSR), September 23, 1978, ABS-19324/2.
18. Informant Jasin, November 2, 1978, "Allari Mohamed Ali, pracovník Organizace pro osvobození Palestiny /OOP/ v ČSSR, návštěva Palestince ze zahraničí-záznam," ABS-19324/2.
19. V. Pokorný (X.S), November 13, 1978, "Jednání operativ. pracovníka 3. odboru X.S-FMV s vedoucím Organizace pro osvobození Palestiny /OOP/-záznam," ABS-19324/2.
20. Jan Větrovec (II.S/5), July 17, 1980, "Záznam," ABS-16987/3.
21. J. Větrovec (II.S/5), December 4, 1980, "Informace-akce "ORIENT," sv.č. 16987," ABS-16987/3.
22. Ivan Voleš, interview by the author, August 28, 2017.
23. These were Abdul Rahman Abu Jabar, former head of the PLO Office in Jordan, and head Nimer Hammad, who actually moved to Prague in December 1983—after a posting as PLO Office head in Italy—hoping Czechoslovak authorities would approve his appointment. Czechoslovakia, however, refused to provide accreditation to Hammad. Officially the Ministry of Foreign Affairs stated that he "could not guarantee the successful development of bilateral relations." At the time of writing, he is serving as an adviser to Palestinian National Authority president Mahmoud Abbas. Milan Belica (MZV, 8.t.o.), March 19, 1984, ABS-19324/4).
24. Belica.
25. Jiří Jíra (II.S/5), May 14, 1984, "Záznam," ABS-19324/4.
26. Vláda ČSSR, February 24, 1983, "Usnesení vlády Československé socialistické republiky," NA-A ÚPV-ČSSR/ČSFR, 40/1983.
27. J. Martínek, June 25, 1984, "Střetnutí na Ministersvu zahraničních věcí," ABS-16987/4.
28. Karel Fiřt (Náč.II.S)–Zdeněk Němec (Náč.XIV.S), February 19, 1985, "Věc: Seznam objektů určených ke kontrole-zaslání," ABS-16987/5; E. Hradecký (Náč. OMS FMV)–K. Fiřt (Náč.II.S), January 3, 1985, "Věc: Palestinští teroristé-informace," ABS-16987/5.
29. K. Fiřt (Náč.II.S)–OMS FMV, April 23, 1985, ABS-16987/5.
30. Informant Mušír, April 5, 1987, "Bechara Traboulsi, představitel Sjednocené bezpečnostní služby OOP při kanceláři OOP v Praze—pokyn ředitele kanceláře ABU HISHAMA omezující výkon jeho funkce," ABS-16987/7.
31. Informant Marek, June 14, 1988, "KTS MAREK—vytěžení ze schůzky," ABS-16987/8.
32. For more on the rebellion led by Abu Musa, see Sayigh, *Armed Struggle*, 561–73.
33. "K připravovaným teroristickým akcím Palestinců v některých socialistických zemích," n.d., ABS-38165/2.
34. Amr features in Polish security service documents as "Amer Taleb." For more on the story, see Gasztold-Seń, *Zabójcze układy*, 179–82.

35. Informant Mušír, January 8, 1980, "ABU BAKER Atef, vedouci zastoupení Organizace pro osvobození Palestiny /OOP/ v ČSSR, sdělení o jednání s pracovníky MV ČSSR a jeho proirácká orientace-zpráva," ABS-16987/3; Informant Mušír, March 13, 1981, "ABU BAKER Atef, vedoucí Organizace pro osvobození Palestiny, činnost a styky s palestinskými představiteli—zpráva," ABS-16987/3.
36. Peter P., interview by the author, September 4, 2015.
37. For categories of First Directorate collaborators, see Koura and Kaňák, "Czechoslovak Foreign Intelligence Files."
38. Koura and Kaňák.
39. Informant Mušír, October 2, 1978, "Jednání s KTS "ALI" k situaci na OOP a mezi zahraničnými student—zpráva," ABS-16987/2.
40. Informant Mušír, May 29, 1984, "ABU HISHAM, nový řiditel kanceláře OOP v Praze-poznatky k osobě," ABS-19324/4; informant Mušír, February 8, 1985, "Abu Hisham, ředitel kanceláře OOP v Praze-poznatky k osobě," ABS-19324/5.
41. "Abu Hisham, ředitel kanceláře."
42. Milan Beluský (II.S/5), July 13, 1988, "Záznam ze schůzky se stykem 'KÁMOŠ,'" ABS-16987/8; Informant Hatem, June 12, 1988, "Abu Hisham—ved. dipl. mise OOP v Praze, snaha o jeho kompromitaci-zpráva," ABS-16987/8.
43. Informant Hatem, June 12, 1988, "Abu Hisham."
44. Informant Honza, October 4, 1988, "TRABOULSI Bechara-poznatek," ABS-19324/5.
45. K. Vrba (Náč.II.S)–B. Carda (Náč. S-SNB hl.m. Prahy a Středočeského kraje), December 13, 1984, "Věc: Součinnost v realizaci ZTÚ OBRAZ," ABS-19324/5.
46. V. Sýkora (II.S), May 16, 1986, "Záznam," ABS-19324/6.

# 9

# Countering PLO Extremists

Although shortly after 1974 when Arafat embraced diplomacy Prague set up a political (and later a security and intelligence) partnership with the PLO, it was under no illusion that its liaison partner had severed all ties to terrorism. The country's diplomats and security officers were well aware that there were fringe groups and individuals in the Fatah and PLO ranks who either had a rich history of conducting terrorist attacks or were still actively using terror as a tactic. Prague was particularly worried about two types of violence: infighting between various PLO factions, which could result in kidnappings or assassinations, and attacks mostly against foreign diplomats and missions based in Czechoslovakia. Gradually, through its agentura placed within the Palestinian and wider Arab diaspora as well as thanks to listening in on its liaison partner's communications, the StB started getting a better idea about which jackals were coming to Czechoslovakia. And what its counterterrorism officers saw worried them.

Accordingly, in the 1980s the communist country—in parallel with its liaison with the PLO—started taking incremental steps to counter Palestinian fringe groups and individuals as they arrived. Although it never prosecuted, incarcerated, or extradited any of the jackals, by 1982 it had detained and ultimately ousted members of some of Fatah's most feared fringe groups with known links to terrorism. Chief among them were those connected to the short-lived yet infamous Black September enterprise, best known for the terrorist operation it orchestrated during the 1972 Olympic Games in Munich.

## "A PALESTINIAN STATE OF MIND"

On November 28, 1971, Jordan's prime minister, Wasfi al-Tal, was on a state visit to Egypt. Returning to the Sheraton Cairo Hotel after attending the Arab League summit, al-Tal was gunned down by two Palestinians. His very public assassination marked the arrival of a new organization in the international terrorist milieu: Black September.

This amorphous and fluid network of operatives was mainly focused on two targets—Jordan and Israel. Unlike all other Palestinian organizations, however,

Black September never attempted to stage guerrilla or military operations on Israeli soil or the occupied territories. Throughout its brief existence, from 1971 to 1973, it was entirely committed to conducting terrorist and sabotage-style attacks, staging dozens, mostly in Western Europe. After its inaugural assassination of the Jordanian prime minister, other attacks followed, each adding new enemies to Black September's list.

The versatile network of operators that it was, the Black September employed varied methods of terror. It was said to have sent letter bombs, hijacked planes, and engaged in some old-school sabotage by blowing up oil storage facilities and refineries in Rotterdam and Trieste. Nevertheless, its most notorious attack was the Munich Olympics massacre of September 5–6, 1972, when eight Black September commandos killed two Israeli Olympic team members and took nine more hostage. Twenty hours into the drama, during a botched West German attempt to free the hostages at a local airport, all the Israelis, five members of the Black September commando unit, and one West German policeman were dead.[1] The terrorist attack, which went down in history as the Cold War's 9/11, made governments left and right of the Iron Curtain sit up and start taking terrorism seriously. Soon states in the West, and later also in the East, developed national counterterrorism policies and practices, set up special units trained to neutralize terrorists, and started engaging in international discussions on hostage taking.[2]

The organization Black September had grown out of frustration caused by the Jordanian Civil War of 1970, which had led to the ousting of the PLO and its factions from Jordan, effectively putting an end to their ability to stage attacks against Israel. After the forced exodus, there were two schools of thought within Fatah: those who were keen for the faction to go fully underground, reject coexistence with Arab regimes, and aim to topple the Jordanian regime; and those who were more inclined to follow the official policy of Fatah aimed at a more moderate policy. While those who joined the Black September effort subscribed to the first school of thought, their frustration was further fueled by a more pragmatic reason. It saw other factions—such as George Habash's PFLP—become increasingly visible thanks to high-profile terrorist attacks aimed at international targets. There was an element of competition.[3]

Although no direct command-control relationship between Arafat and the new terrorist outfit was ever firmly established, it is widely believed that Black September was a label some Fatah members used for their international terrorist operations.[4] There was close overlap between the two organizations with regard to their membership. Key figures associated with the outfit also came from Fatah ranks. Abu Iyad, chief of PLO security and the godfather of the liaison channel with Prague, was one of them. Although his role in Black September continues to be a matter of debate, his public defense of its numerous operations earned him the label of the spiritual father and mastermind of its flagship attacks.[5] Abu Daoud, a former Fatah commander, whose association with the group became somewhat more transparent over the years, became one of Black September's best-known commanders.

While there was clear overlap, the organization's affiliation with Fatah was kept deliberately vague. There were, however, rare moments when these links were illuminated to the public. In 1973, when Abu Daoud was arrested in Jordan during a botched Black September attempt to overthrow King Hussein, the tall Palestinian in thick-rimmed glasses told the world during an awkward televised press conference that the outfit was deliberately kept separate from Fatah to afford the official Palestinian faction plausible deniability.[6] Effectively, the goal of the organization was for there to be no organization—it was to operate in the shadows. As Abu Iyad later admitted, "there was not an organization. There was a cause, Black September. It was a Palestinian state of mind."[7]

Although the bread crumbs did indeed lead back to Fatah, some argued that Black September was not Arafat's creation but quite the opposite—a mutiny against the PLO chairman and the old ways of Fatah leadership, which seemed to be taking the Palestinians further from, not closer to, their desired goal of liberation and independence. In fact, Patrick Seale, one of Britain's most respected journalists and narrators of Middle Eastern affairs, argues that Black September commandos were made of "angry, vengeful guerrillas, graduates of the same camps, often friends or relatives bound together by common loyalties and common hatreds" and that these complicated micronetworks "were not easily reined in."[8]

Initially the StB was as much in the dark when it came to Black September as the next intelligence service. And the little that it did know, it was piecing together from Arab newspapers and its Middle Eastern agentura. But soon it was starting to get a better picture of what the organization was about. It was increasingly clear to Prague's spies what Black September rules were: to operate completely underground, without any political pressure or structure to be accountable to, and definitely no dependence on Arab regimes. A secret committee was assigned to recruit and train new cadres, which according to rough estimates numbered anywhere between 150 and 500. Committed to strict secrecy, they were compartmentalized into small, isolated cells. Members were stationed in cities mostly across the Middle East and Europe.[9]

Although throughout the 1970s Czechoslovak spies paid attention to incoming reports about the mercurial Black September, its operations and targets seemed miles away. While occasionally the StB received unverified reports of suspected Black September members passing through Czechoslovak territory, none of this caused major concern. This, however, all changed with the arrival of one of the most recognizable figures of the infamous covert network in Prague.

It would not only test the limits of Prague's patience with its PLO allies and the robustness of its surveillance architecture but also see Prague take one of its first resolute steps against an international terrorist residing on its territory.

## "A DECENT PERSON"

In the summer of 1978, when the StB found that Abu Daoud, the commander of the Munich Olympics massacre, had checked into the same hotel in Prague as the International Olympic Committee, it knew that it could no longer sit back and passively observe Black September. Petrified of bloodshed on its territory, Prague needed to find out more: What was his business in Prague? Was he linked to the friendly PLO or to the renegade and widely feared Carlos Group? Had he visited Prague before? And, most crucially, was it a mere coincidence that he had arrived in Prague just as the International Olympic Committee was holding its annual meeting there?

This potentially lethal mix of hotel guests rang alarm bells for the StB. Suspecting the worst and knowing little of his intentions, in the following months the StB activated its networks of spies—mostly Arab diplomats and students living in Prague. It also ordered the further recruitment of assets working at the PLO Office in Prague.[10] Any future Abu Daoud visits to the country were to be immediately reported to the leadership of the Ministry of the Interior, the First Directorate (which could help collect further intelligence from foreign assets), and "Mr. P," the KGB adviser to the Ministry of the Interior. Abu Daoud was to be put under close physical surveillance—followed everywhere, his phone calls tapped and mail intercepted. Czechoslovakia wanted to have the Black September commander under close control.[11]

The man the StB was now deployed to track was a seasoned security operator. Born in 1937 in Jerusalem as Mohammad Daoud Oudeh, Abu Daoud achieved iconic status among the Cold War terrorist elite thanks to his role in the Munich Olympics terrorist plot. The typically mild-mannered and self-deprecating high-school teacher turned lawyer turned guerrilla commander and terrorist was first introduced to the world of armed struggle in 1968, when he was recruited for a security and intelligence course in Cairo by Ali Hassan Salameh, the infamous Red Prince. Graduating at the top of his class, Abu Daoud quickly rose through the ranks of the PLO's security establishment, designing its intelligence branch, commanding thousands of Fatah troops mounting attacks on Israel from Jordan, and after the 1970 PLO expulsion relocating to Lebanon.

While the PLO was licking its wounds after its banishment from Jordan, Abu Daoud joined the more shadowy struggle against Israel. Soon he became a central figure in Black September, responsible for many of its attacks. Hand-picking the attackers, arranging logistics, transporting arms and grenades,

ILLUSTRATION 9.1. Abu Daoud in front of the Orloj, Prague's astronomical clock, May 24, 1982. *ABS, f. Správa sledování SNB–SL, a.č. SL-5698 MV*

surveilling the Olympic village, and allegedly helping the last attacker jump over the security fence minutes before the attack made him the central figure in Black September's most notorious operation, which unfolded before the eyes of almost a billion viewers worldwide.[12]

Despite his prominent role in a multitude of Black September operations, Abu Daoud was never caught. Thanks to a mixture of luck and backing by various Middle Eastern governments, he managed to artfully evade imprisonment and multiple attempts at assassination. In February 1973, following a failed attempt to storm the Jordanian parliament and overthrow the king, he was sentenced to death and subjected to two mock executions. As a result of pressure from key Arab leaders, shortly before the breakout of the Yom Kippur War, he was given amnesty and released from prison.[13] Three years later, in January 1977, the Palestinian again found himself in police custody. To attend the funeral of an assassinated colleague, Abu Daoud had traveled to Paris under a fake Iraqi identity and as part of an official delegation. During his visit, Israel and West Germany filed extradition requests—hoping to put on trial the man responsible for the Munich murders. In a matter of weeks, thanks to Iraqi intervention, Abu Daoud was again a free man.[14]

Finally, we also know that the Palestinian survived the Mossad's Operation Wrath of God, an assassination campaign triggered by the Munich terrorist attack targeting PLO and Black September representatives. Following the massacre, which saw Jews killed on German soil—a sobering echo of the Holocaust—the Israeli government decided to act. Under the leadership of Golda Meir, a decisive, no-nonsense American-bred former labor leader, Israeli intelligence launched its campaign of assassinations and sabotage aimed at decimating the Palestinian leadership scattered around the world. The operation saw bombs set off and lethal shots fired by Mossad officers and agents in Paris, Rome, Lisbon, and Madrid. While dozens of Palestinians were killed as part of this operation, which lasted almost two decades, it left lingering questions about whether all of those who met their maker via the Mossad's hidden hand were indeed connected to terrorism and the Munich massacre, the key impetus for the operation.[15] Moreover, it made operatives such as Abu Daoud consistently look over their shoulders and remain vigilant.

In the latter half of 1977, fearing further arrests and assassination attempts in the West, the tall, battle-hardened Palestinian began visiting the Soviet Bloc, known for its close relations with his official employers, Fatah and the PLO. From 1978 to 1982, Czechoslovakia was one of his favorite destinations east of the Iron Curtain. Traveling undercover and employing numerous identities and diplomatic passports, Abu Daoud made it difficult for the StB to keep up with his movements. While Prague's spies soon became better at detecting his arrivals, when he emerged in Czechoslovakia for the second time in August 1978 the StB was still puzzled about the reasons for his visits. Was he traveling in his official Fatah capacity, or was he there for some other kind of murky business? Did the Communist Party know? When entering Czechoslovakia, Abu Daoud stated he was traveling for a meeting at the Central Committee of the National Front—a body set up by the Communist Party to control all political activity. A prompt investigation demonstrated this to be a lie. None of the Czechoslovak power hubs knew of Abu Daoud's sudden and mysterious arrival in Prague. At a remarkably early stage, Czechoslovakia's decisionmakers resolved that they had no wish for the controversial terrorist to be on their territory, stating, "Employees of the CC NF [Central Committee of the National Front] have no interest in meeting with ABU DAOUD or in having him visit the CSSR."[16]

The PLO mission's approach to Abu Daoud was schizophrenic. On one hand, the PLO Office's head, Abu Bakr, was clearly friendly with the Black

September commander—regularly meeting him in Prague and helping arrange logistics during his stay. When asked about Abu Daoud by the StB, the PLO representative said that the two had been friends for fifteen years. Abu Bakr tried to reassure the StB that Abu Daoud was not a threat to the Soviet Bloc, adding that he had "lately distanced himself from terrorist activities." Moreover, "if he were to organize some terrorist operation himself, this would be directed toward capitalist states."[17] Abu Bakr was Abu Daoud's most ardent defender in Prague.

On the other hand, the role of the deputy head of the PLO Office, who would later become the StB asset code-named Mušír, was somewhat more Machiavellian. While designated by his boss to chaperone and drive Abu Daoud around Prague, he supplied the StB with details of the Palestinian's program throughout a number of his visits. Mušír was a loyal source with excellent access.[18] This shows that the PLO mission, plagued with internal rivalries, often lacked a coordinated approach to such controversial partners. Determined by political loyalties or personal ties, some members of the Palestinian representation would advocate a benevolent approach by the Czechoslovak authorities to such known terrorists as Abu Daoud. Others, including Mušír, would assist the StB or the relevant Communist Party bodies in tracking them down and monitoring their stay on Czechoslovak soil.

It was, however, not only the Czechoslovak authorities who were concerned about the Black September commander arriving in Prague. According to the StB's Syrian contact "Salim," Abu Daoud came to Czechoslovakia on the invitation of the Iraqi embassy, which was financing his stay. Salim also told the StB that "a number of people who are aware of his stay in CSSR are nervous about his presence." "This includes the employees of the PLO Office in Prague," he maintained, "although their meeting with DAOUD seemed friendly."[19] The reasons underpinning this anxiety were plentiful. Following Abu Daoud's arrest and controversial release by the French authorities less than six months earlier, riots broke out in Israel. US president-elect Jimmy Carter denounced Paris's decision to release the terror-tainted Palestinian.[20] Association with him had become toxic. Moreover, at this stage Abu Daoud was a harsh critic of Yasser Arafat, calling the PLO chairman "a dictator and traitor," accusing him of a style of politics that was subservient to imperialist countries and reactionary Arab regimes.

Gradually it became apparent that Abu Daoud was in Czechoslovakia for business as well as pleasure. In addition to meeting PLO colleagues stationed in Prague, the Palestinian also reunited there with an old friend. This was none other than Atif Bseiso, Abu Daoud's accomplice in the Munich murders, who later became the PLO's intelligence envoy in Western Europe.[21] During his time in Czechoslovakia, Abu Daoud also paid a visit to his colleague and later fierce Arafat opponent, PLO commander Abu Musa, who was recovering in the Czech spa town of Mariánské Lázně from a Syrian assassination attempt.[22] Overall, during his various visits, Abu Daoud mostly met with Middle Eastern diplomats, military attachés, and intelligence officers based in Prague. He was also seen in the company of Arab students studying in country and a number of arms dealers, the latter habitués of the Czech capital. Clearly used to doing business in public, Abu Daoud met most of his contacts in Prague's numerous cafés. StB informants reported on these encounters in much detail—noting that at these meetings, the Palestinian and his acquaintances were "capable of drinking impressive amounts [of coffee] within relatively short time."[23]

In August 1979, during a clandestine rendezvous of several prominent Cold War terrorists in Prague, Abu Daoud also took coffee and breakfast with the most notorious terrorist of the time—Carlos the Jackal. Although not much is known about the content of their encounter, surveillance reports suggest this was not a mere courtesy call. The men met to conduct business. After their early morning meeting at the five-star Hotel Intercontinental, where both of them were staying, Carlos took out his safe deposit box at the reception desk and was joined in his room by Abu Daoud. When they reemerged in the hotel lobby, the Palestinian handed Carlos an envelope. Subsequently, he rushed to the reception desk to send a telex.[24] The contents of the envelope remain unknown.

Despite his notoriety, not all meetings the Black September commander held in the country were discreet. In May 1982 Abu Daoud got drunk with the Iraqi intelligence envoy to Czechoslovakia. Shortly before three in the morning, the Palestinian staggered out of the Intercontinental, hands in pockets, and later leaned against a car, reeking of alcohol. The StB reported, "The manner in which he moved suggested that he was in a very drunken state." Overall, the StB surveillance teams observed that Abu Daoud was in general not particularly keen to keep a low profile, reporting that "in the hotel, DAOUD greets everyone who is of Arab descent."[25]

If not accompanied by his East German girlfriend, Abu Daoud also used his visits to Prague for other amorous relations. According to StB reports, Daoud liked to surround himself with women of "questionable reputation" whom he either picked up in the hotel or "[brought] in from the outside."[26] In an effort to recruit these women as assets who could provide valuable information about the Palestinian, the StB ran background checks on them. While it remains unclear whether any actually became StB informants, we do know that when the StB's Bulgarian partner service asked it to "expressly send any compromising material" on Abu Daoud, it readily shared its knowledge of Abu Daoud's love escapades.[27]

The real purpose of Daoud's visits and meetings in Prague remains the subject of speculation. The Czechoslovak capital may have served as a place for

ILLUSTRATION 9.2. Abu Daoud on Pařížská Street in Prague, November 9, 1982, with, the StB believed, a prostitute, less than twenty-four hours before being forced to leave Czechoslovakia. *ABS, f. Správa sledování SNB–SL, a.č. SL-5698 MV*

planning further attacks. It could have been a stopover on an arms-trafficking route stretching from the Middle East to Western Europe—a business Abu Daoud was intimately familiar with. Or the Palestinian could have been sent to Prague by the PLO to check up on the myriad splinter groups and smaller terrorist organizations associated with the Palestinian cause, including the Carlos Group. It is also possible, however, that he came to the Czechoslovak capital simply to enjoy some down time and relax in a country that he thought was unlikely to pursue him for his terrorist crimes. If so, his hopes of finding a haven in Prague would soon be crushed.

In 1982, during Abu Daoud's eighth visit to Prague, the StB decided to act. After having patiently surveilled the Palestinian during his multiple stays in Czechoslovakia (a phase termed here as "watch and wait") and unsuccessfully attempted to block him from reentering the country by adding his cover identities on its persona non grata list (an approach referred to here as "block and prevent"), Prague knew it had to further escalate its approach. It thus moved to what would become its signature strategy reserved only for the most feared of the jackals—that of "trick and oust." Although it remains unclear what triggered the decision, we now know that on November 8, 1982, through an Iraqi intermediary, the StB sent a clear message to the Palestinian that "in the interest of his own safety," he should urgently leave Czechoslovak territory and not engage in "any activities or contacts" until his departure.[28] When Abu Daoud failed to comply, he was picked up in the Hotel Intercontinental by the StB and taken in for questioning. While he was in custody, Prague's watchers searched his room to gather further clues about his business in Prague.[29]

During the four-hour ordeal, the tension in the interrogation room was palpable. The Palestinian tried to appease his captors by expressing his sympathy for all socialist countries, adding that he came to Prague to relax because he felt safe there. He also tried to distance himself from some of the most problematic of his associations. Perhaps slowly realizing that the StB was carefully tracing his whereabouts and knew of his contacts with Carlos, the battle-hardened Abu Daoud told the StB that the Venezuelan was nothing but a "hotel bum with whom he does not want to have anything to do." He also, however, expressed his outrage at the StB's sudden and daring move—threatening to cause a diplomatic scandal. Moreover, he made it clear to the StB men that they had little power over his movements, boasting, "At this very moment, I have four different Arab passports in my luggage." However, the StB was adamant. Abu Daoud was ordered to leave Czechoslovakia and stay in the Hotel Intercontinental until his departure on the next day.[30]

As a precaution, the StB escorted Abu Daoud to his hotel and stationed an all-night guard at the entrance. When he tried to slip out of the hotel shortly after midnight, the infamous terrorist was ordered back inside by a Czechoslovak counterintelligence officer. Locked in a golden cage for the night, the Palestinian was furious, "I am beginning to believe that political persecution is a part of life in Czechoslovakia," Abu Daoud complained to a member of the hotel staff who was also on the StB's payroll during an elevator ride up to his luxurious room. "I will never come back to Czechoslovakia," he fumed, "and I will also tell all my friends and acquaintances to look for another state to operate in. I am a decent person, and I have never experienced such treatment anywhere in the world." At daybreak on November 10, escorted by two StB officers, the Munich Olympics massacre commander left Czechoslovakia for good.[31]

Although it remains unclear what exactly triggered his expulsion, the ousting of Abu Daoud from Czechoslovakia seems to have been linked to the Politburo's concern about the increasing concentration of Cold War jackals on Czechoslovak territory. Crucially, Prague was aware of the deadly rivalry among the various factions and groups that descended on Central Europe and that Abu Daoud was a contentious figure. A year prior to his ousting from Czechoslovakia, he had been shot at six times in the Viktoria Café in Warsaw.[32] Although he survived that attack, it was clear to the Politburo and StB that Abu Daoud was a persistent target for Israel as well as his Palestinian rivals. Eager to prevent violence erupting on its territory, Prague vowed not to let the controversial Palestinian freely roam the streets of its capital again. If he were to visit Czechoslovakia again, the StB was ready to oust him. In fact, from this point on, Prague would give the same treatment to others it deemed potential threats.

## FORCE 17

Force 17 was an amorphous organization perhaps best described as a special operations unit of Fatah, the main PLO faction. Throughout its lifespan, Force 17—according to one theory named after the telephone extension of Fatah's Beirut headquarters, and another alleging its cryptic alias it derived from its address—became one of the PLO's more recognizable and longest-standing security outfits. Arguably, its creation as PLO chairman Yasser Arafat's own security element was motivated by his perpetual fear that Abu Iyad or Abu Jihad, two of the strongest men in the PLO, each of whom sported his own military or security organization, could easily depose him.

Force 17 was initially set up in Lebanon as Arafat's bodyguard unit by the young and ambitious Ali Hassan Salameh, also known as "the Red Prince," whose goal was to turn it into a professional intelligence organization.[33] By the late 1970s, Force 17 had grown in size and significance. Although in 1979 Ali Hassan Salameh was assassinated in Beirut as part of Israel's infamous Operation Wrath of God—revenge for his alleged role in the Munich Olympics massacre—Force 17 survived its founder. By the mid-1980s, it sported two subunits: one directly responsible for Arafat's protection and the other tasked with running international covert operations. It was headed by two men, Abu Hula and Col. Mahmoud al-Natour, a.k.a. Colonel al-Hawari. Unlike with the effectively leaderless Black September, Force 17 answered directly to Arafat.[34]

In the closing decade of the Cold War, Force 17 members were suspected of, and indeed some were clearly incriminated in, staging terrorist attacks. On September 25, 1985, a Force 17 commando unit stormed a yacht moored in Larnaca, Cyprus, and proceeded to murder three Israelis. The PLO tried to justify the operation by alleging that the Israelis were Mossad agents spying on the PLO's "sea bridge" to Lebanon. In a typically strong counterterror reaction, in less than a week Israel retaliated by bombing the PLO headquarters near Tunis, killing seventy-three Palestinians and Tunisians.[35] In July 1987 Arafat's unit was rumored to have been responsible for the murder of the Palestinian political cartoonist Naji al-Ali in London. The artist was to have infuriated the PLO chairman by depicting him with a woman, despite Arafat always claiming to have been married to the revolution.[36]

Force 17 was also intimately engaged in Palestinian infighting. In fact, in 1986 Prague learned from Lebanese sources that Force 17 was Fatah's key

ILLUSTRATION 9.3. Gunmen surround the blasted car of PLO security chief Ali Hassan Salameh (the Red Prince) on January 22, 1979, in Beirut. Salameh and seven other persons were killed and several wounded in the Israeli-orchestrated attack. *ČTK / AP / As Safir*

instrument in fighting the Abu Nidal Organization—a breakaway faction of the PLO determined to stage violent attacks against more moderate Palestinians and seeking to depose Arafat. After the ANO carried out a series of attacks against Arafat supporters, Force 17 retaliated and in April 1986 staged several terrorist attacks in northern Syria—detonating timed explosive devices on public transportation, allegedly costing more than a hundred lives.[37] This signaled to the StB that Force 17 was not a peripheral player but instead a force its opponents had to reckon with.

Although these conflicts seemed too far away for Prague to worry, the StB soon received information suggesting that similar vendetta attacks could take place in Czechoslovakia. Prague therefore decided to keep a close watch on any incoming Force 17 representatives. In mid-August 1986, its fears materialized when a Force 17 representative going by the name of Ahmed Jawad arrived in town, allegedly to recruit new members for the unit's European special operations section led by al-Hawari. The so-called Hawari branch was to be mostly tasked with politically motivated assassinations and terrorist attacks, such as the one carried out earlier in the year in northern Syria.[38]

While in Prague, Jawad attempted to recruit a certain Jousef, a thirty-year-old Palestinian living there. The recruiter's pitch was indeed generous. If Jousef joined the highly secretive, dangerous subunit of Force 17, he would be paid as a sort of signing bonus the back pay of a Fatah member dating to 1981, which would effectively amount to $32,000 today.[39] Going forward, he would receive today's equivalent of $1,600 per month.[40] But from that point onward, Jousef would have to show unlimited loyalty and follow strict protocol: secrecy, limiting contact only to approved persons, absolutely no contact with Syrians, restricted movement, and so on. There was only one punishment for indiscipline or failure to complete tasks—liquidation. Jawad also told the potential recruit that he would have to swear an oath of allegiance to Force 17 on the blood of a fallen Palestinian fighter. To prove he was serious about the unit's rituals, Jawad showed him a piece of cloth stained with dried blood. This did little to persuade Jousef, who did not hide his hesitation about taking on such a risky job. While Jawad tried to alleviate his concerns by promising more money or studies in any country of his choice, Jousef asked for three days to make up his mind. Ultimately, Jousef refused the offer and found a way out of what seemed an incredibly risky, perhaps literally dead-end job.[41]

Much to its concern, the StB soon learned that Jawad had in fact rented a flat and settled down in Prague. He sustained his life there also thanks to the generous support of the head of the PLO Office, Abu Hisham.[42] Arguably, in addition to his main mission aimed at building a network of collaborators, Jawad sustained close contact with envoys of one of the PLO's most powerful adversaries—Hafez al-Assad's Syria. During his time in Prague, he kept in close contact with Syrian security representatives, including the Syrian rezident serving under cover of second secretary, Col. Ragheb Hamdun. To the Syrians, Jawad was an important intelligence contact thanks to his operational role within Force 17 and links to key Palestinian security strongmen, including Abu Iyad. Liaison with him also had broader political significance. As Syrian relations with Fatah left much to be desired, Jawad—thanks to his direct links to Arafat—could help make relations better or at least alleviate further deterioration.[43]

While in Prague, bold Force 17 member Jawad made no effort to live a clandestine life. He connected with several Czech women with whom he frequented fancy restaurants in the hotels Intercontinental and Panorama. When his Syrian friend Colonel Hamdun challenged this ostentatious behavior, Jawad dismissed his concerns, arguing that such liaisons were not self-serving and could be used for future Force 17 operations. Previously, Jawad boasted, he had used the services of a certain Polish woman to great effect during "an operation in Cyprus." The StB was not surprised because it had been well informed of his amorous relations established during his stay in the GDR several months before. There, in addition to consorting with various women, Jawad fueled conflict between Palestinian representatives, which—the StB's sources reported—almost ended in a shootout. Ultimately, the all-powerful Abu Iyad had to step in to prevent hostilities from breaking out.[44]

Prague was unhappy about having this volatile individual on its soil, even more so as Jawad was recruiting Czechoslovak nationals or permanent residents for what could only be described as terrorist activity. Accordingly, Prague decided to use its diplomats to send a clear message to their Syrian and Palestinian partners. In early November, it was the job of the head of the Middle Eastern Department—one of the best Arabists of his generation, Ivan Voleš—to explain to his Syrian and Palestinian counterparts that Prague was aware of their associations with Jawad and that it was not happy about this shady business. Voleš, who led many such uncomfortable meetings, first summoned the Syrian chargé d'affaires. Cutting to the chase, he told his visitor he was aware of Syrian links to a Force 17 member, Ahmad Jawad, who had settled down in Prague and was now attempting to recruit Palestinian students there. It was clear that he had participated in terrorist attacks across Europe—Greece, Cyprus, West Germany, and Malta. Not beating around the bush, Voleš reminded his Syrian colleague that such conduct was against Czechoslovakia's interests and that the Syrian embassy should stay away from activities that were contrary to good diplomatic behavior. To appease Voleš, the Syrian diplomat assured him that Damascus was not planning any terrorist attacks in Czechoslovakia and that dealings with Jawad were strictly a personal initiative of one of his staff members.[45]

On the same day, Voleš summoned another Middle Eastern envoy to Černinský Palace, the impressive seat of the Ministry of Foreign Affairs. This was none other than Abu Hisham, the head of the Palestinian Office. Voleš, whose relations with the Palestinian left much to be desired, was direct. He told Abu Hisham what Prague knew about Ahmad Jawad and his links to the Syrians. Opting for a soft approach, Voleš made no demands but asked for help in preventing violence. Abu Hisham, however, chose a path of resistance—challenging Voleš's conclusions about the alleged Force 17 member. But soon the Palestinian calmed down and assured his host that the Palestinians only ever saw Prague as a place of political dialogue—alluding to the many times Palestinian factions did indeed meet in the Czechoslovak capital to attempt reconciliation—and would not misuse the country's generosity to pursue more controversial activities. Accordingly, Abu Hisham told Voleš that he had instructed the PLO headquarters not to give any intelligence tasks to the employee at the PLO Office responsible for security issues.[46] A seasoned diplomat, Voleš could hardly believe this. Having seen Beshara Traboulsi's fingerprints all over PLO liaison and training, he knew this was simply an effort by Abu Hisham to dodge a diplomatic bullet.

A little over a month later, shortly before Christmas, the StB's Second Directorate learned why Abu Hisham was so quick to disassociate himself from Ahmad Jawad. According to an StB informant, the PLO Office head used to be a member of Force 17. During this time, Abu Hisham was said to have participated in the group's covert operations and had allegedly killed some of the unit's targets. This all made sense to the StB and explained why Abu Hisham supported Jawad during his stay in Prague and, indeed, at times referred to him as "our person."[47] Prague now knew it could not trust Abu Hisham to help them get rid of Jawad. Accordingly, it escalated its approach from "watch and wait" to "block and prevent"—adding all six of his cover identities on its persona non grata list.[48]

This, however, failed to prevent other Force 17 representatives from visiting Prague, and in 1988 Prague snapped. Its patient and passive approach was clearly not paying off. Members of Force 17 with terrorist track records were frivolously arriving in Czechoslovakia on fake documents, carefree about their visa status, and arrogantly relying on the PLO Office for cover. Prague was pushed over the edge by a certain Fuad Fallah. At first, not much set Fallah apart from the other Arab visitors to Prague: He had close ties to the PLO Office, spent most of his time in the company of other Arab nationals, and found a Czech girlfriend. Soon, however, the StB learned from a trusted source that shortly before his arrival to Prague in early 1988, Fallah had been part of a Force 17 duo that orchestrated a terrorist attack in Cyprus against a Palestinian with alleged links to the Mossad. This was enough for Prague to act and escalate from block and prevent to trick and oust.[49]

Helpfully, during Fallah's almost three-month stay, both his visa and his Lebanese passport had run out. The StB used this as a pretext to take a bold step and confront him in his girlfriend's flat. The StB was, however, not one to confront terrorist suspects head-on. Hence, its officers pretended this was a regular police check on a visitor in the flat. When Fallah presented them with his expired documentation, the officers were left with no other choice—they wanted him to believe—but to arrest the foreigner. In order for their ruse to result in a successful ousting, however, the StB had to exert pressure on Abu Hisham, who was the official guarantor of Fallah's stay in Czechoslovakia, not to extend the controversial visitor's stay. The Palestinian envoy soon gave in and put Fallah on a flight to Tripoli with a homeless passport issued by the PLO.[50]

\*\*\*

Prague's approach to the PLO's most radical offshoots—Black September and Force 17—whose representatives descended on Czechoslovak territory in the closing decades of the Cold War, evolved over time. It was first characterized by a subtle watch-and-wait strategy largely made up of surveillance via agent networks. Gradually, however, the country exercised more pressure by engaging its top diplomats to make it known to the terrorists' Arab hosts that they were not welcome. Once this proved to be an insufficient deterrent, the country opted for a block-and-prevent approach, designed to preempt returns by controversial PLO associates. When this failed, in select high-profile or particularly worrying cases, Prague adopted even bolder trick-and-oust countermeasures, which saw suspicious Force 17 associates or villainous figures such as Abu Daoud arrested under false pretext and driven from its territory.

Overall, Prague engaged with the PLO in various ways, and the StB was key to this multitrack approach. First, the StB's domestic and foreign directorates were used to foster a long-term security liaison with Arafat's men, dominated by information exchange, training, and weapon supplies. Second, they were deployed to alleviate some of its concerns about the controversial nonstate actor by monitoring and infiltrating the Palestinian organization, which it did with much success. Third, to prevent violence erupting on its territory and avoid reputational damage, in extreme cases Prague diplomats and spies were tasked with steps directed at preventing, countering, or even ousting some of the more radical elements attached to its liaison partner.

## NOTES

1. For a most thorough account of the Munich attack as well as its aftermath, see Reeve, *One Day in September*; and Klein, *Protiúder*.
2. Blumenau, *United Nations and Terrorism*.
3. "K současným problémům palestinského hnutí (část 3.)," November 9, 1972, ABS-12470/000.
4. Although some claim that Arafat was aware and did bless Black September operations, most Arafat and PLO scholars agree that he did not exercise direct control over their operations. See Chamberlin, *Global Offensive*, 191.
5. Seale, *Abu Nidal*, 84–85.
6. "Synd 27/03/73 Interview Guerilla Leader Abu Daoud on Black September," AP Archive, March 27, 1973, https://www.youtube.com/watch?v=MF4AYcS337w.
7. Abu Iyad quoted in Reeve, *One Day in September*, 35. For excellent chapters on Black September, see Peter Taylor, *States of Terror: Democracy and Political Violence* (London: BBC Books, 1993).
8. Seale, *Abu Nidal*, 84–85.
9. "K současným problémům palestinského hnutí (část 3.)," November 9, 1972, ABS-12470/000.
10. Václav Pokorný (X.S/3), July 8, 1977, "ABU DAÚD, Palestinec hlavní organizátor teroristické akce proti izraelským sportovcům na Letních olympijských hrách v Mnichově 1972, návštěva v ČSSR-zpráva," ABS-18227.
11. V. Pokorný (X.S/3), August 21, 1978, "ABU DAUD—představitel palestinského hnutí odporu-návštěva v ČSSR," ABS-18227; II.S, August 23, 1978, "Představitel palestinského hnutí odporu na návštěvě v ČSSR," ABS-HFSB, a.č. H-720/II.
12. For more on Abu Daoud, see Seale, *Abu Nidal*; Reeve, *One Day in September*; Taylor, *States of Terror*; Thomas Scheuer, "Ich brachte die Waffen nach München," *Focus*, no. 24 (June 14, 1999), http://www.focus.de/politik/deutschland/deutschland-ich-brachte-die-waffen-nach-muenchen_aid_177704.html; and Thomas Scheuer, "Jedenfalls lebe ich noch," *Focus*, no. 4 (January 23, 2006), http://www.focus.de/politik/deutschland/olympia-72-jedenfalls-lebe-ich-noch_aid_214369.html.

13. Seale, *Abu Nidal*, 89–90.
14. Christopher Dobson and Ronald Payne, *Terror! The West Fights Back* (London: Macmillan, 1982), 14. Abu Daoud's release caused an uproar and demonstrations in Israel. Protest letters from Jewish groups and associations were also sent to the British Foreign and Commonwealth Office, asking that the matter be taken to the European Court of Human Rights. See TNA, FCO 93/1137.
15. For more on the operation, see Reeve, *One Day in September*; and Klein, *Protiúder*.
16. Václav Stárek (Náč.X.S)—OMS FMV ČSSR, September 4, 1978, "ABU DAUD, pobyt v ČSSR-sdělení pro přátele MStB NDR, ABS-18227.
17. Václav Šubrt (Náč.X.S/3), August 24, 1979, "Záznam," ABS-18227.
18. V. Pokorný (X.S/3), August 24, 1978, "Záznam," ABS-18227.
19. Informant Salim, August 27, 1979, "ABU DAUD, Palestinec-organizátor teroristické akce Palestinců v Mnichově—turistický pobyt v ČSSR," ABS-18227.
20. "Israelis, Carter Denounce French Release of Arab," *Washington Post*, January 13, 1977.
21. A. Chmelíček (Náč.II.S/6)–7-II.S, October 14, 1980, "Předání poznatku," ABS-HFSB, a.č. H-720/IV.
22. V. Pokorný (X.S/3), August 13, 1978, "ABU DAUD, palestinský terorista, příjezd do ČSSR-zpráva," ABS-18227.
23. Informant Kníže, June 1, 1982, "KHALED AL JENDI-syrský st. přísl. -zpráva do akce RAK; SIRKIS Fareed—jemenský st. přísl.," ABS-24751.
24. "Akce BAK-sledování," August 22, 1979, ABS-SL 454 MV.
25. "Akce BAK-sledování," May 17, 1982, ABS-SL 5698 MV.
26. Informant Válek, November 9, 1982, "MAHDI TARIK Sharik, liban.st.prísl.—zpráva do akce RAK," ABS-24751.
27. Emil Hradecký (Náč. OMS MV ČSSR)–KarelVrba (Náč. II.S), December 13, 1982, "Věc: Mahdi Tarik Shakir—informace k č.j.: OS-002096/6-82," ABS-24751.
28. Milan Solnický (Náč.II.S/6), November 9, 1982, "INFORMACE," ABS-24751.
29. M. Solnický (Náč.II.S/6), November 16, 1982, "INFORMACE," ABS-24751.
30. Solnický.
31. Informant Klasek, August 29, 1979, "Arabští teroristé-poznatky k pobytu v ČSSR, styky a politické názory," ABS-19324/1; "Akce BAK-sledování," November 9–10, 1982, ABS-SL-5698 MV.
32. See more in file "RAK," ABS-24751.
33. See more on Salameh in Bird, *Good Spy*; Taylor, *States of Terror*; and Michael Bar-Zohar and Eitan Haber, *The Quest for the Red Prince* (London: Weidenfeld & Nicolson, 1983).
34. F. Hnídek, September 9, 1986, "'AHMED,' představitel palestinské bezpečnostní složky, skupiny 17, zabývající se zvláštními operacemi-zájem o získávání čsl. občanů a budování pozic v ČSSR," ABS-19324/6.
35. Sayigh, *Armed Struggle*, 585–86.
36. Sayigh, 603. Arafat did eventually get married three years later to Suha Arafat.
37. "K některým aspektům činnosti 'jednotky 17' na území ČSSR," n.d., ABS-38165/12.
38. F. Hnídek, September 9, 1986, "'AHMED,' představitel palestinské bezpečnostní složky, skupiny 17, zabývající se zvláštními operacemi-zájem o získávání čsl. občanů a budování pozic v ČSSR," ABS-19324/6.
39. Original sum of $10,000.
40. Original sum of $500.

41. Hnídek, September 9, 1986, "'AHMED."
42. F. Hnídek, December 18, 1986, "ABU HICHAM, ředitel kanceláře OOP v Praze- vztah k bezpečnostní skupině 17 Al Fatah," ABS-24113/14.
43. Hnídek.
44. F. Hnídek, September 9, 1986, "'AHMED,' představitel palestinské bezpečnostní složky, skupiny 17, zabývající se zvláštními operacemi-zájem o získávání čsl. Občanů a budování pozic v ČSSR," ABS-19324/6.
45. Zídek and Sieber, *Československo a Blízky východ*, 254.
46. P. Sviták (8.t.o., MZV), November 5, 1986, "Záznam o návštěvě."
47. Hnídek, December 18, 1986, "ABU HICHAM."
48. II.S/5, "Informace," January 1987, ABS-38160/001.
49. Jiří Jíra, April 27, 1988, "Příkaz: k umístnění do cely předběžného zadržení a zajištění MSVB Praha," ABS-19324/8; Procházka, October 26, 1988, "Vyhodnocení," ABS-19324/8.
50. Procházka, "Vyhodnocení."

# PART III
# THE REJECTIONISTS

# 10

# Keeping Things Semiofficial

In June 1974 top Palestinian leaders met in the oppressive heat of Cairo for the annual session of the Palestinian National Council, the PLO's legislative body. While these meetings were often marked by disagreements and public rows, this one would make history. After a heated debate, the council accepted a Fatah-sponsored plan that became known as the Ten Point Program. Although the document did call for the liberation of occupied Palestinian territory and certainly placed emphasis on the use of armed struggle, it also left room for territorial compromises and, most important, diplomacy. This infuriated the more militant and mostly left-leaning factions of the PLO that saw armed struggle as their bread and butter. In a show of defiance against Arafat and Fatah, they left the PLO and set up what became known as the Rejectionist Front. While never a truly unified entity, the front was a mercurial conglomerate of various Palestinian factions that were deeply antagonistic to any rapprochement to Israel. Some factions later made amends with Arafat and rejoined the PLO, only to leave again in protest of other policies the PLO chairman adopted.[1]

The Soviet Bloc was somewhat torn in its approach to key Rejectionist factions. On one hand, Moscow and Prague wanted the Palestinians to remain united and hence were not keen to establish official relations with separate Palestinian factions and blocs that challenged Arafat's authority. Moreover, some Rejectionist factions were intimately linked to Cold War terrorism. Crucially, the Rejectionist Front's most dominant faction—the Popular Front for the Liberation of Palestine, led by George Habash—had pioneered the Cold War wave of international terrorism with a series of high-profile hijackings culminating in the spectacular Skyjack Sunday, which led to Jordan's catastrophic civil war. These were all reasons to stay away. On the other hand, however, the Soviet Bloc also had good reasons to engage with some of the Rejectionist factions. Crucially, key Rejectionists were ideologically closer to the communists east of the Iron Curtain than the volatile Arafat, constantly eyeing Western support. In fact, Habash and the leader of the second-largest Rejectionist outfit, Nayef Hawatmeh of the Democratic Front for the Liberation of Palestine, were ardent Marxists.

Accordingly, Czechoslovakia, much like its Soviet Bloc allies, had to find a sophisticated way to engage with these factions. It opted for a middle-way approach. Although Prague did ultimately develop high-level dialogue with Habash's PFLP and Hawatmeh's DFLP, this was all confined to Communist Party contacts. Unlike Arafat, Rejectionist leaders never dined with the Czechoslovak president or were officially welcomed at the Ministry of Foreign Affairs. The two key Rejectionist factions also never developed the kind of security and intelligence partnership with Czechoslovakia that Fatah and the PLO enjoyed. Prague did not want to aggravate its relationship with Arafat by according the same status to the factions, which persistently challenged his authority. It was also wary of setting up a close alliance with the godfathers of modern international terrorism.

While Prague's liaison with the Rejectionists very much differed from that it struck with Arafat, there were also some notable commonalities. Much like in the case of Fatah, Czechoslovakia harbored an inherent mistrust of the controversial Rejectionist factions and sought to influence them from within. Accordingly, while it engaged in a cautious liaison with them via the Communist Party, Prague also used the StB to surveil, infiltrate, manipulate, and, in extreme cases, to oust the more radical elements associated with the Rejectionist Front.

## "THE MADMAN OF THE PALESTINIAN LEFT"

The PFLP led by George Habash was one of the most powerful Palestinian factions, following Arafat's Fatah. Although it emerged as a distinct faction after the 1967 Arab-Israeli War, the roots of Habash's political activism and armed struggle went all the way back to the 1950s. As a medical student at the American University of Beirut, Habash was one of the founding fathers of the Arab Nationalist Movement (ANM). After the Six-Day War, the ANM merged with two other groups, creating the PFLP, which soon became a key faction within the PLO. Inspired by Marxist-Leninist ideology, Habash's faction saw the struggle against Israel as part of a wider battle against Western imperialism, embodied by reactionary Arab regimes. By the late 1960s, it had set up a headquarters in its key supporter state—Syria—and managed training camps in Jordan.

Before long, the PFLP became an internationally recognized brand. In July 1968 a PFLP squad infamously hijacked an El Al flight from Rome to Tel Aviv—setting off the Cold War wave of international terrorism. In the following years the PFLP would deploy terrorist attacks against Israeli, Western European, and US targets—taking the Palestinian struggle onto the global stage. Most notably, in September 1970 it staged the largest coordinated terrorist attack in the modern history of terrorism, Skyjack Sunday.[2] This operation, in which Habash defied the authority of Jordan's King Hussein by turning his territory into the

ILLUSTRATION 10.1. George Habash in Beirut on December 17, 1973, urging Palestinians to boycott a projected Arab-Israeli peace conference to be held in Geneva. ČTK / AP

scene of a hijacking drama and confronted Western states—including the United States, the United Kingdom, West Germany, and Switzerland—had a dual effect on the PFLP. It instantly increased its popularity among young Palestinians, who rushed to join the faction's ranks and made it an internationally known force. It also made potential allies more hesitant about associating with Habash and his men.

This was very much the mood in Prague throughout the 1970s. By staging Skyjack Sunday, the PFLP tipped the already irritated Jordanian king over the edge and triggered a civil war that resulted in the ousting of the Palestinian guerrillas from his country. A month into the confrontation, Prague's diplomats were increasingly concerned about these developments. Although Jordan was notably a pro-Western state, Prague was not eager to see the unruly Palestinian guerrillas dethrone the king. Czechoslovak diplomats warned that if the PLO were to take over Jordan, the situation would be "uncontrollable and potentially threatening to national liberation efforts," resulting in "further destabilization of the region."[3] They also found that predominantly in the United States, the hijacking of planes by "Palestinian partisans" put the entire Palestinian movement if not the entire Arab world in a bad light and further pushed US public opinion toward Israel.[4] Overall, Prague thought that the terrorist operations of the PFLP and DFLP had "hurt the liberation struggle of Palestinians" and had in fact been used as an excuse by "Jordanian reactionary circles and imperialists to attempt the liquidation of the Palestinian Resistance Movement." Simultaneously, however, Prague conceded that these "radical operations" had also found support among a segment of Palestinian partisans as well as "the masses."[5]

Despite these reservations, several years later Prague gave the PFLP a chance. On September 12, 1972, somewhat ironically less than a week after the Munich Olympics massacre, the PFLP leader Habash met with Czechoslovakia's Solidarity Committee, the front organization set up by the Communist Party for dealing with third world national liberation movements and nonruling communist parties. During this private visit to Prague, where he was accompanied by his family, Habash tried to persuade the Czechoslovaks that he was a changed man—eager to explain the "mistakes and shortcomings" that had occurred during the PFLP's "struggle against imperialism," code for its campaign of hijackings and terrorist attacks against civilians. Arguing that after the 1967 defeat Arab states had abandoned the Palestinian cause, Habash told his hosts that as a reaction to this the PFLP had "mobilized all its forces" and fully embraced the only effective form of resistance: armed struggle against Israel.[6]

Having explained why the PFLP had embraced terrorist tactics, Habash told the Czechoslovak representatives that those were the old ways. At a recent summit, the group had gone through a process of self-reflection and decided to "abandon all forms of struggle, which isolate it from the masses and which weaken their relations with the international revolutionary movement." Perhaps sensing Prague's skepticism, the PFLP leader repeatedly admitted to having made serious mistakes, emphasizing that although it was not easy for him to put an end to these "activities," he now "personally" disapproved of operations such as "the one at the Olympics."[7]

Habash, however, did not travel to Prague solely to explain himself. This was a trip primarily aimed at establishing collaboration. The PFLP leader wanted to run this by Czechoslovak diplomats in Prague. In terms of material support, he asked Czechoslovakia to train "PFLP cadres" and to accept Abu Bassam Sharif, a prominent member of the PFLP's politburo, who urgently needed medical treatment for wounds inflicted when an Israeli letter bomb exploded in his face. As such cases were quite common, lamented Habash, he asked his hosts to donate an explosives detector to prevent similar setbacks in the future.⁸

Prague appreciated Habash's new take on the Palestinian struggle, noting that it was clearly influenced by the recent talks he had attended in Moscow. Nevertheless, it remained skeptical about his euphemistic and lukewarm denunciation of terrorism. Less than two years prior to this meeting, during the height of the PFLP's hijacking campaign, Prague had little good to say about the man in charge of Arafat's biggest rival faction. To the country's diplomats, Habash was the most radical Palestinian leader, "ready to unleash a third world war," moaned Prague, "if it would help destroy Israel." They also knew he had few fans among the Middle Eastern political elite, with Egyptian president Gamel Abdel Nasser and Libyan leader Muammar Qaddafi allegedly nicknaming Habash "the madman of the Palestinian Left."⁹

After some deliberation, the Foreign Ministry advised its diplomats in Beirut to, for now, refrain from fostering regular contacts with Habash. Prague's cautious approach to the PFLP was primarily fueled by the fact that despite denouncing terrorism at the March 1972 Beirut summit, the group continued to orchestrate terrorist acts. Worryingly, only two months after the summit, in cooperation with the Japanese Red Army, the PFLP staged a kamikaze-style attack at Lod Airport in Israel. In Prague's eyes, "this operation was entirely meaningless," resulting in the deaths of twenty-six innocent people and seventy wounded. Hence, when Habash assured the Czechoslovak diplomats that "he personally condemns" terrorist attacks, his hosts viewed this with much skepticism. Prague was also mindful that the PFLP statute still called for the liquidation of Israel. In addition to this, in the early 1970s Prague was wary that support for PFLP per se might upset the PLO and Fatah as well as contribute to further fragmentation of the Palestinian movement.¹⁰

Despite Prague's inclination to keep "the madman of the Palestinian Left" at arm's length, Habash did not stay away. In 1973 and 1974 the PFLP leader paid numerous visits to the Czechoslovak embassy in Beirut. During these sessions it was clear that Habash's politics were set in stone. He came across as a vehement defender of the armed struggle and as a strict opponent of all peace efforts, be it the "Geneva track," the "US avenue," or any bilateral peace treaties agreed on by Israel and individual Arab states.¹¹ In 1975, during one such meeting, Habash again tried to win the diplomats over by highlighting that the Soviet Bloc countries were collectively his "number one ally." While noting that now his faction and the Soviet Bloc were in the same "anti-imperialist camp and fighting the same enemy," he also lamented that this was not clearly understood throughout the socialist world and that his efforts to create close relations with the bloc had, thus far, been rebuffed.¹²

While complimenting his hosts, Habash also did not miss an opportunity to highlight a key issue of disagreement: the PFLP was not only looking to remove the consequences of the Israeli "aggression" of 1967, hinting at the occupation of Palestinian territories by Israel that followed the Six-Day War, but also events dating all the way back to 1948. To Habash, who had allegedly been forced out of his family home with his parents and marched for three days until they reached Arab armies, the 1948 war that symbolized independence to the Israelis was very much not only a national but also a personal "Nakba"—displacement of the Palestinians. Habash thought it had been a mistake for the Soviet Union to recognize the State of Israel.[13]

Although Prague clearly did not feel the same way about Habash and his faction, they kept in contact with the Palestinian strongman throughout the late 1970s. Meeting him in war-torn Beirut was, however, increasingly difficult. In April 1977, when he met the new Czechoslovak ambassador to Lebanon in the office of *Al-Hadaf*, a weekly Palestinian political and cultural magazine, the meeting was somewhat rushed. Arguing that it was unsafe for the leader of the PFLP to stay in one sector of the dangerous city for too long, it lasted all of twenty minutes. This was enough time, however, for Habash to make it clear to the incoming envoy that if Arafat were to join Egyptian president Anwar Sadat in his peace efforts with Israel, he would set up his own Palestinian umbrella organization.[14] This was a hard education for the ambassador, who would endure many similar meetings with the warring Palestinian factions competing for Soviet Bloc support.

## THE DEMOCRATIC MARXIST

Throughout the 1970s, other ideologically friendly Rejectionist factions shopped around for support of the Soviet Bloc. The DFLP,[15] which had broken off from Habash's PFLP in 1969, was one such group. The sizable group of defectors from Habash's faction rallied around the unashamedly Marxist Nayef Hawatmeh, born in Jordan in 1938, who first became politically active alongside Habash in the ANM. In comparison to the PFLP, Hawatmeh's new faction was more focused on political propaganda among students and intellectuals than in armed struggle.

Prague's diplomats and Communist Party representatives first met DFLP representatives in May 1970. Hosted by the Communist Party's powerful International Department, the DFLP representatives sought to establish strong links with Prague and, crucially, purchase "special material" for their troops. To highlight their Marxist-Leninist credentials, the DFLP representatives emphasized their close relations with communist parties in Jordan, Syria, and Iraq. Thus far, they pointed out, the Soviets and East Germans had promised to provide

ILLUSTRATION 10.2. Nayef Hawatmeh (*right*) sitting next to Yasser Arafat and Kamal Nasser, a PLO spokesman, during a press conference in Amman, June 1970. ČTK / AP / *Anonymous*

funding and military and medical training. Simultaneously, and somewhat predictably, the DFLP representatives used the meeting to criticize their partners and competitors within the PLO—citing the reactionary elements within the most dominant organization, Fatah. Although the meeting was held in a friendly atmosphere, it was far from a game changer in the group's relationship with Prague.[16]

In fact, until the late 1970s, it seems that the DFLP struggled to secure another meeting in Prague and to create any direct links with the communist state. Although the faction's representatives were frequent visitors to Czechoslovak embassies in the Middle East and, at times, visited Prague as part of Arafat's official delegations, progress was slow, and the DFLP had to work hard to persuade Prague that it was a partner worthy of its recognition and support.[17]

In early 1971 Nayef Hawatmeh approached the Czechoslovak embassy in Damascus. Early in the meeting, the leftist Palestinian leader tried to ingratiate himself with his hosts by underlining that during the Prague Spring, the DFLP had "expressed public support for the socialist forces in Czechoslovakia" and was pleased that socialism had prevailed. Although Prague considered the group's methods and goals "extreme," it also considered it an "undoubtedly progressive force." Accordingly, the Czechoslovak ambassador went the extra mile to ask for support, pleading with his bosses, "Our Soviet friends here [in Damascus], who supply the PLO with significant assistance, as well as our comrades from the leadership of the Syrian Communist Party are of the opinion that we could and should indeed provide some level of assistance." This, he added, could be in the form of military assistance and training, medical treatment of fighters, support for publishing activities, or establishing direct liaison between the DFLP and the Czechoslovak Communist Party.[18]

Arguably, Prague was stalling and relying on the PLO to redistribute aid to the various factions of the Palestinian movement. The Rejectionists, however, often provided feedback that suggested that this was not the case. In fact, the DFLP persistently complained to Czechoslovak diplomats in Beirut about problems with redistribution of supplies within the PLO. Assistance from Soviet Bloc countries provided to the PLO never reached the DFLP, Czechoslovak envoys in Beirut were told. The DFLP chose to express its concerns about this problem to Prague's diplomats in Lebanon because the representative of DFLP traveling to Prague with Arafat would not be able to make this request because "in Prague they want to present a unified stance under the PLO umbrella and not go into internal conflicts, which continue to exist."[19] This showed Prague that to the PLO factions, the Beirut liaison with Czechoslovakia presented a much more genuine channel.

By the summer of 1977, when DFLP representatives managed to arrange a meeting with the Czechoslovak ambassador in Beirut amid the civil war, it was clear Prague still had not adopted a more active stance. The DFLP envoy was visibly frustrated by the country's unchanged posture, arguing that the DFLP now had direct contact with and were receiving assistance from the Soviet, Cuban, and Bulgarian communist parties. In fact, Hawatmeh was at this very moment in Moscow on a working visit. They did, however, admit that Czechoslovakia was not the only Soviet Bloc member stalling. In late 1976, the DFLP envoys told their hosts, they were meant to establish direct contact with the leadership of the GDR's communist party, but due to Arafat's negative stance toward such contacts, Hawatmeh's visit to East Berlin was indefinitely postponed. Although they emphasized their recognition of Arafat as the leader of the Palestinian liberation movement, they—as members of a Marxist-Leninist party—also believed that they had the right and, in fact, the duty to foster official contact with representatives of communist parties.[20]

At around the same time, the DFLP was knocking on the doors of other Czechoslovak embassies across the Middle East, trying to arrange an official invitation for Hawatmeh to meet Communist Party representatives in Prague. Czechoslovakia's former ambassador to Damascus and later foreign deputy minister for the developing world, Dušan Ulčák, recalls the ad hoc nature of these visits. "People like George Habash and Hawatmeh would come by unannounced, when they were passing by the embassy they would stop by for an impromptu lunch—these were mostly social occasions mixed with political chat." After one such request, the Czechoslovak ambassador to Damascus sought the advice of his Soviet counterpart. Even before he reported the request to Prague, he asked the Soviet diplomat about Moscow's take on the DFLP. He learned that alongside official relations with the PLO Moscow was in fact fostering bilateral relations with the DFLP and providing the faction with moderate support consisting of some stipends and medicine but that the Soviets did not consider this in any way substitute to their channel with Arafat.[21]

## THE THAW

Although in the 1970s, Prague resisted fostering direct political liaison with the two factions, Habash and Hawatmeh continued to request support from Prague's envoys across the Middle East. Czechoslovakia's embassies in Beirut, Damascus, and Aden were regularly visited by representatives of various Palestinian factions asking for assistance. Meeting with Palestinian representatives was very much a part of their portfolio. The task of these diplomats was to build an active relationship, which would enable them to better navigate and understand Palestinian issues, internal Arab politics, and issues pertinent to the Palestinian-Israeli conflict. Moreover, Prague was also keen to use its envoys to influence or perhaps even control these unruly groups who were in need of its support. As Ivan Voleš, Prague's key Middle Eastern diplomat of the late Cold War era, recalled his interaction during his time as Prague's ambassador in Aden, "all Palestinian factions were there. Al-Fatah, PFLP, DFLP all had their envoys there who sort of 'stuck onto' the socialist diplomats, offering their services and information and, simultaneously, trying to find a way to travel to the Soviet Bloc, arrange stipends, medical treatments for their fighters or secure military material." This was a mutually beneficial relationship: the Palestinians could show they were being active, and the diplomats gained good contacts and intelligence from the local environment.[22]

At the same time, however, there was often a dissonance between what the Palestinians wanted and what Prague was willing to provide. At times Czechoslovakia's envoys in the Middle East were under pressure from the many Palestinian factions to commence or accelerate Prague's assistance to them. This was, however, hard because throughout the 1970s the Ministry of Foreign Affairs was clearly stalling when it came to providing support to the Rejectionists. In one such case, this infuriated the Czechoslovak envoys stationed in Beirut, who let their dissatisfaction be known to their bosses that to maintain this active relationship and be able to influence these persons and their organizations the embassy urgently needs the MFA (Ministry of Foreign Affairs) and other relevant CSSR institutions to swiftly respond to some of our reports and requests relevant to the Palestinian issue and to hopefully give them a green light. This will mostly concern meetings with official Palestinian representatives where they request medical care, stipends, [and] material support, and this would also relate to positively responding to requests made via unofficial means by the PFLP and the DFLP, which are equally important to the Palestinian cause as Fatah but do not get as much attention from us (e.g., also when it comes to manning PLO offices abroad).[23]

Prague's diplomats in the region argued in favor of fostering these parallel relations with the PLO's individual factions because this was a model also adopted by partner embassies in Lebanon, most important that of the Soviet Union.[24] By contrast, during his 1975 visit in Prague, Arafat urged Czechoslovakia to communicate only with the official PLO representation in Beirut. He argued that other Palestinian leaders and organizations associated with the PLO were not authorized to communicate directly with Czechoslovakia without his consent.[25] Although this clearly showed Prague that divisions between factions were integral to the DNA of the Palestinian movement, it did not keep the country's diplomats and Communist Party cadres from engaging in parallel unofficial liaison with the smaller Palestinian factions.

Significantly, Prague's foreign intelligence agreed that this was in fact the best approach. In 1978 it argued that semiofficial relations with the PFLP and DFLP best reflected the opportunities for Moscow and other Soviet Bloc states. The ideal way forward, according to Prague's spies, would be to continue to follow developments within the PLO and—in addition to official relations with the umbrella organization—to "maintain semiofficial relations with leading representatives of the PFLP and DFLP, continue to meet delegations from these organizations, gain an overview of their political efforts, and influence them during political discussions via political and material support as well as strengthen their Marxist approach to dealing with the Palestinian question." While Prague's foreign intelligence was committed to the same goals as the country's diplomats and Communist Party representatives, it was also aware that Czechoslovakia and the Soviet Bloc could not just sit back and watch while their ideological allies within the PLO were being bullied by the dominant faction.

Hence, the StB's First Directorate suggested a more activist approach to these semiofficial relations—one that would use political and material support to influence Rejectionist thinking and actions. Moreover, Prague's spies bluntly stated, "We need to count on the fact that we will be able to use these active relations with progressive representatives of the PLO to nations of the socialist community politics in the ME [Middle East] whether these representatives remain in Arab states or whether they manage to return to Palestine."[26] This very much echoed Prague's 1960s approach to various African national liberation movements. Connections—official, semiofficial, or clandestine—were a long-term strategy to make friends in faraway yet strategically important regions.

By the late 1970s, however, Prague had changed course, placing a stronger emphasis on its relations with these left-wing organizations. In fact, 1979 was a breakthrough year for Czechoslovak-Rejectionist relations. In September, when they rejoined the PLO Executive Committee, George Habash and Nayef Hawatmeh finally received their long-awaited invitations to Prague and, throughout the closing decade of the Cold War, frequently visited for political talks, prolonged medical care, and spa treatments, which would entail meeting the Communist Party elite.[27]

The first one to rush to Prague was Hawatmeh. While meeting Communist Party strongman Vasiľ Biľak, the DFLP leader made a good impression, especially by emphasizing that the complex political environment in the Middle East had to be seen through a Marxist-Leninist lens. There was, however, also some hesitation as Hawatmeh seemed to have tried to position himself as somewhat of an arbiter of the Palestinian resistance movement and Arab communists. In fact, he seemed to see himself as the future leader of a unified Communist Party of Palestine. This approach was not welcomed by representatives of the various communist parties in Arab countries or Prague's "friends" in Moscow. Furthermore, he let his grandiosity show when it came to assistance requests. His hosts considered his appeals for support "unrealistic" and, in fact, even more demanding than those made by the much larger PLO. Crucially, Prague noted that they were well beyond its means.[28]

Gradually, however, the DFLP leader learned how to ingratiate himself with his Czechoslovak hosts. As the key manager of meetings between Palestinian factions and Communist Party officials, Josef Krejčí observed the various leaders' communication strategies. While he found Habash to be quite pleasant and seemingly genuine, Hawatmeh came across as a bit of wise guy or a cunning fox. During meetings, his replies seemed calculated—designed to be exactly what the Czechoslovaks wanted to hear. For instance, during one such meeting he pledged that when the DFLP liberated Palestine, it would be a leftist state. Although this was clearly unrealistic, Krejčí recalls Biľak liking it.[29]

*** 

In December 1980 George Habash arrived in Czechoslovakia. This was, however, no typical short-term bilateral visit. While based in Damascus, Habash had suffered a stroke and was in urgent need of medical attention. As part of the warming of relations between Prague and his PFLP, the communist country agreed to host the Palestinian strongman for extended specialist treatment at one of its top facilities in the famous spa town of Karlovy Vary. During his top-secret stay in the communist country, which lasted several months, Habash conducted business and strengthened ties with the Czechoslovak Party and government elite, including the powerful party secretary, Vasiľ Biľak.[30] According to Josef Krejčí, who got to know Habash well during his time as chair of the Solidarity Committee, the fact that Czechoslovak doctors helped save his life was a formative experience for the PFLP leader, who thereafter developed a soft spot for the communist nation.[31]

This feeling soon became mutual. By 1983 Czechoslovakia's top Communist Party leadership recognized that the formerly "extremist" PFLP, once known as one of the "main organizers of terrorist operations," was now a "constructive player within the PLO." The DFLP was also seen as a "progressive leftist Palestinian organization" with allegiance to Marxism-Leninism and recognized for its rejection of terrorism.[32] This was a hard-won acceptance, and throughout the 1980s both Rejectionist leaders took full advantage of Prague's welcoming approach. They each visited the Central European state a handful of times, mostly for short bilateral meetings or medical treatment. In the last years of the Cold War, they also frequently traveled to Prague to attend conferences and summits, some of which were aimed at achieving peace and unity with the Palestinian umbrella organization.

Although their leftist ideological credentials were undoubtedly appealing to Prague, its increasingly warm approach to the Rejectionists was arguably also led by other factors. Semiformal relations with Habash and Hawatmeh pursued in parallel with the PLO enabled the communist country to gain further insight into Middle Eastern political developments as well as into the Palestinian movement as such. Moreover, the two leftist factions deserved its support because they—so Prague thought—balanced out the more right-wing elements within the Palestinian milieu, which were susceptible to influences from reactionary Arab nations, most prominently Saudi Arabia.[33] In fact, thanks to this overt semiofficial liaison with the DFLP, Prague learned about Arafat's plans to sign the controversial Amman Accord with King Hussein, which again fractured PLO unity and led to the temporary suspension of the Prague-PLO liaison.[34] Gradually, the Rejectionists were proving their strategic value.

## SECURITY ASSISTANCE AND TRAINING

As in the case of Arafat's men, security assistance dominated the Rejectionists' agenda from the very beginning. Prague, however, opted for a cautious approach. It refrained from providing Habash and Hawatmeh with special assistance until it set up semiofficial relations with both factions at the end of the 1970s. Once Prague warmed to them politically, it provided the Rejectionists with moderate security support, which, however, never reached the intensity or scope of that provided to Fatah.

Habash's and Hawatmeh's men were first trained in Czechoslovakia in the autumn of 1980 as part of a multifaction group of thirty Palestinians at a security course in Slapy. This was the first such course ever run for the Palestinians and was negotiated by Abu Hisham a year earlier when Prague launched its security liaison with Fatah.[35] As we know, Prague refused Abu Hisham's controversial request for so-called terrorist training but gave the green light for training Fatah, PFLP, and DFLP cadets in security and intelligence tradecraft.[36] This was a significant step for the Rejectionists, who had by then courted Prague for over a decade.

Several years later, the two factions were also provided with a moderate amount of much-needed weapons. Prague decided to arm Habash's and Hawatmeh's men during the dramatic summer of 1982, when Israel invaded Lebanon and heavy fighting broke out.[37] In mid-August the Communist Party of Czechoslovakia gathered key "special material" stakeholders to coordinate their efforts and help accommodate requests of various groups and factions that had arisen since the start of hostilities. Here, among others, they discussed the PFLP's requests for hundreds of RPG-7s and submachine guns and thousands of rounds of ammunition. The DFLP was also hoping that the Czechoslovaks would equip its ranks with over a thousand Kalashnikovs, Škorpion machine pistols, and RPG-7s.[38] In addition to special materiel, they requested an urgent supply of midrange radio transmitters, which would enable the spread of ideological propaganda in support of the Palestinians across Arab states.[39] Although records do not detail the delivery of these items of choice, Prague's consideration of gifting special material to the Rejectionists represented a step change in its attitude.

As their political relations matured, Prague developed off-the-books ways of providing the Rejectionists with weapons. While they never developed direct relations with the country's many state-owned arms companies, the Communist Party found a side door via which it provided arms to ideologically close nonstate allies. This side door was the Office of the Secretary of the Communist Party. At these high-level meetings, various Middle Eastern communist parties, George Habash's PFLP, and Nayef Hawatmeh's DFLP requested small arms for their ranks. According to Maroš K., who worked in the powerful International Department of the Communist Party from 1980 to 1990, it was all very simple: "I listened to their demands during the meeting. Then I wrote up a short report and gave it to my boss [head of the International Department] to sign. Then he sent it directly to Biľak, who signed off on it, and that was that." After this express decision-making process, party employees would assist in purchasing

ILLUSTRATION 10.3. As first secretary of the Communist Party of Czechoslovakia, Vasiľ Biľak, a tailor born in a small Slovak town, got to see the world, be it while selling weapons to ideologically allied groups or riding camels in East Asia. Seen here in Mongolia, with the minister of foreign affairs, Lubomír Štrougal, behind him, June 1, 1973. *ČTK / Mevald Karel*

the requested light weapons. Maroš K. recalls one particular arms-shopping trip he was sent on by the party with a representative of the Lebanese Communist Party:

> We went to Pařížská Street where there was a large arms shop, and we bought, if I remember correctly, one hundred handguns. Naturally, this had

to be signed off by Biľak. At the shop we told them what we wanted. They made a few phone calls. We went to the back office where they placed the weapons into suitcases, and then we took them to the aircraft. The pilots were informed about the contents, and they naturally didn't want to fly with it. They resisted, arguing that they cannot transport such things.... But eventually they did take off with the weapons.[40]

Such requests for arms required consultation with Moscow. Whether these deals went ahead or not was determined by the importance of each group and whether its request was realistic. Moreover, Moscow's advice was sought when the various partners wanted something out of the ordinary. For instance, when Nayef Hawatmeh's DFLP requested larger-scale military supplies that included vehicles, Maroš K. recalled that "in this particular case Biľak himself had to call Moscow to get their blessing."[41]

Although they shared ideological DNA, Czechoslovakia was much more careful about forging ties with Palestinian Marxists than it was about allying with Arafat. Their radical solutions to the gladiatorial Israeli-Palestinian conflict, history of use of terrorism, and erratic political behavior prompted the communist country to stay away from top-level dialogue until the late 1970s. Once Prague did let them in, it forged semiofficial relations facilitated by the Czechoslovak Communist Party, characterized by limited security assistance—small-scale training and one-off supplies of small weapons.

Czechoslovakia's persistent rejection of official relations throughout the 1970s, however, did not mean that Prague wholly ignored these important Palestinian factions. In fact, throughout the decade, when Prague's diplomats kept Habash and Hawatmeh at arm's length politically, the StB worked hard to recruit sources within Rejectionist ranks. These assets, Czechoslovak spies hoped, would provide insight into the minds and plans of these ideologically close but behaviorally controversial nonstate actors.

## NOTES

1. Sayigh, *Armed Struggle*, 342–45.
2. Dobson and Payne, *Terrorists*, 233; Naftali, *Blind Spot*, 41–48.
3. J. Černý (MZV), September 22, 1970, "Informace pro všechny čs. ZÚ o situaci v Jordánsku," A-MZV, T-1970-74/8.t.o., Ka 1.
4. I. Rohaľ (ZÚ Washington), September 30, 1970, "Věc: Poznámky k vývoji na Středním východě," A-MZV, T-1970-74/8.t.o., Ka 1.
5. B. Pištora (MZV, 8.t.o.), November 27, 1970, "Palestinské hnutí odporu," A-MZV, T-1970-74/8.t.o., Ka 1.
6. V. Šťastný (ČS Výboru solidarity)–V. Jízdný (MZV, 8.t.o.), September 28, 1972, "Informace o přijetí předsedy Lidové fronty pro osvobození Palestiny (PFLP) dr. G. Habaše na čs. Výboru solidarity," A-MZV, T-1970-74/Itálie, Izrael, Japonsko, Ka 3, 114/111.

7. Šťastný-Jízdný.
8. Šťastný-Jízdný.
9. B. Pištora (MZV, 8.t.o.), November 27, 1970, "Palestinské hnutí odporu," A-MZV, T-1970-74/8.t.o., Ka 1.
10. Tajovský (MZV, 8.t.o.), January 5, 1973, "K informaci o přijetí předsedy PFLP G. Habáše na čs. výboru solidarity," A-MZV, T-1970-74/Itálie, Izrael, Japonsko, Ka 3, 114/111.
11. J. Brožovský (MZV, 8. t.o.), May 10, 1976, "Věc: mimořádná politická zpráva 'Organizace palestinského osvobozeneckého hnutí,'" A-MZV, T-1975-79/Libanon, 115/311.
12. V. Jílek (Bejrút-I.S), August 4, 1975, "Rozhovor generálního tajemníka FPLP dr. G. Habáše se s.Brožovským a s.Jílkem dne 31.7.75," ABS-12470/101.
13. Jílek.
14. A-MZV, To-T-1975-79/Libanon, 115/117.
15. Earlier called the People's Democratic Front for the Liberation of Palestine (PDFLP).
16. Korselt (MZV, 8.t.o.), May 4, 1970, "Záznam o jednání s představiteli Lidové demokratické fronty pro osvobození Palestiny," A-MZV, T-1970-74/8.t.o., Ka 1.
17. Velvyslanec ČSSR v Damašku—MZV, 8.t.o., February 15, 1971, "Věc: návštěva vůdce FDPLP Nayefa Hawatmeh na ZÚ," A-MZV, T-1970-74/Sýrie, Ka 1, 116/111.
18. Velvyslanec ČSSR v Damašku.
19. V. Smíšek (FMZV), May 3, 1975, A-MZV, To-T-1975-79/Libanon, 115/117.
20. V. Žák, June 16, 1977, "Čs. Velvyslanec dr. V. Žák, člen PÚV FDLP Dr. Issam Haddad (Yeid Alawi)," A-MZV, To-T-1975-79/Libanon, 115/117.
21. Dušan Ulčák, interview by the author, September 8, 2015; "Věc: Zájem FDLP o vyslání delegace do ČSSR," October 23, 1978, A-MZV, TO-T, 1975-79/Sýrie, Ka 1, 116/112.
22. Ivan Voleš, interview by the author, September 2, 2015.
23. Velvyslanec ČSSR v Bejrútu—MZV (8.t.o.), February 10, 1978, "Věc: Palestinské záležitosti— hodnocení," A-MZV, To-T-1975-79/Libanon, 115/111.
24. Velvyslanec ČSSR v Bejrútu.
25. Bernášek (FMV), May 5, 1975, A-MZV, To-T-1975-79/Palestina, 128/112.
26. I.S/47, May 11, 1978, "Podklady pro SIR: Současný stav a perspektivy řešení palestinské otaázky," ABS-12470/011.
27. "Základní údaje o palestinském hnutí odporu /PHO/. Podklady k návštěvě," March 25, 1983, A ÚV KSČ, f. GH, OOP, Ka 840.
28. Zajíček (8 t.o.), October 23, 1979, "Delegace DFOP v ČSSR," A-MZV, To-T-1975-79/Palestina, 128/112.
29. Josef Krejčí, interview by the author, September 16, 2015.
30. Zídek and Sieber, *Československo a Blízký východ*, 239.
31. Krejčí, September 16, 2015.
32. "Základní údaje o palestinském hnutí odporu /PHO/. Podklady k návštěvě," March 25, 1983, A ÚV KSČ, f. GH, OOP, Ka 840.
33. "Materiály k oficielní přátelské návštěvě Jásira Arafáta v ČSSR. Styky ČSSR–OOP," n.d. 1983, NA-A ÚV KSČ-1945-1989, Praha-GH, Ka 840.
34. Jízdný, April 14, 1983, "Z informace genseka DFOP Hawatmy k palestinsko-jordánskému jednání v Ammánu," NA-A ÚV KSČ, f. GH Ka 841-9079.
35. J. Závada (Náč.I.S/47)–E. Hradecký (Náč. OMS), November 11, 1980, "Věc: Bezpečnostní kurs členů OOP-poznatky," ABS-12470/108.

36. J. Kolouch (I.S/36), June 8, 1981, "Záznam k jednání na OMS FMV dne 3.6.1981," ABS-12470/108.
37. Zídek and Sieber, *Československo s Blízky východ*, 245, 247.
38. Dvořák, August 16, 1982, "Záznam," NA-A ÚV KSČ-1945-1989, f. GH, Ka 841.
39. M. Kramár, August 18, 1982, "Záznam," NA-A ÚV KSČ-1945-1989, f. GH, Ka 841.
40. Maroš K., interview by the author, January 8, 2018.
41. Maroš K., January 8, 2018.

## 11

## In the Gray Zone

During the blistering heat of the summer of 1972, sitting in his downtown Beirut office, a twenty-nine-year-old Palestinian opened an inconspicuous package. In it he found what looked like a copy of the memoirs of his great hero, Che Guevara, the "nowhere man." In seconds, the book exploded in his hands. While the Palestinian survived the mail-bomb attack, he was left with four missing fingers, a disfigured face, partially blind, and deaf. Remarkably, the attack did not derail his career in the PFLP. In the 1970s, despite his father's desperate pleas to stay away from armed struggle, he rose up the ranks of George Habash's organization and, in the latter part of the 1970s, became a key point of contact for Prague's spies based in the battle-scarred city of Beirut. This was, however, no traditional intelligence liaison or an agent-handler relationship. Instead, it was an awkward and ruleless affair that situated the increasingly powerful Palestinian somewhere in the gray zone between intelligence asset and partner.

Bassam Abu Sharif was no ordinary foot soldier. Born in the ancient city of Jerusalem, he grew up in a middle-class Palestinian family in Jordan and graduated from the American University of Beirut. A devout Marxist and "Guevarista," he joined the PFLP shortly after the Six-Day War of 1967. During the height of the group's international terrorist campaign and its most daring operation, Skyjack Sunday, he stood resolutely at Habash's side. Soon, he became the editor of the PFLP's political and cultural weekly *Al-Hadaf*, a member of the PFLP's politburo, and shortly prior to the assassination attempt became its spokesperson.[1] His rise to prominence was the likely impetus for the attack that left him permanently disfigured, allegedly orchestrated by Israel's Mossad as retaliation for the May 1972 Lod Airport massacre carried out for the PFLP by its loyal allies in the Japanese Red Army.[2]

While throughout the 1970s Prague resisted direct political dialogue and contact with the Rejectionists, it did not want to stay entirely in the dark. George Habash and Nayef Hawatmeh were key players within the Palestinian movement, and their actions—political or violent—had profound impact on Palestinian unity as well as how the entire movement was perceived abroad. What is more, they were of a similar ideological bent as Prague—a characteristic that the communist country did not share with Arafat's faction. Accordingly, in the 1970s Czechoslovakia's foreign intelligence branch, the First Directorate, sought to establish contacts with the two factions to gain insight into Palestinian political developments, attempt to exercise control over their politics, and use these well-placed sources to pursue Soviet Bloc goals in the Middle East.

In April 1974, two years after the assassination attempt on the PFLP spokesman's life, Prague's spies based at the Beirut rezidentura struck up a relationship with Bassam Abu Sharif designed to achieve all these goals. Over the next six years, these case officers regularly met Abu Sharif—the man Habash promoted and the Israelis sought to kill. This was, however, no straightforward intelligence liaison or a classic agent-handler relationship. It was something in between.

## THIS IS THE BEGINNING OF A BEAUTIFUL FRIENDSHIP

The relationship developed organically. In 1974 Bassam Abu Sharif was settled into his job as PFLP spokesman. Besides serving as the editor of *Al-Hadaf*, he was the deputy head of the Union of Palestinian Journalists. Meeting foreign diplomats and envoys was a part of his portfolio to promote and explain PFLP politics, arrange foreign visits for PFLP leadership, and request material and other support. Czechoslovak spies were also not based in Beirut to merely watch and wait. They were deployed to develop contacts with key political figures, extract information, and ideally recruit them for their service. Moreover, their job was to conduct active measures aimed at weakening the West and promoting Soviet Bloc policies.[3] Meeting Lebanese and Palestinian politicians was a way to achieve these demanding goals.

Abu Sharif was an ideal target for Prague. His editorial job at *Al-Hadaf* and his extensive contacts in political and journalistic circles made him useful for spreading active measures or propaganda across the Arab world. Accordingly, during their first meeting, Abu Sharif and the StB's case officer in Beirut assigned to the task, Jiří Brožovský (code-named Bílek[4]), agreed that the PFLP would publish Czechoslovak-made materials in *Al-Hadaf* for their English-language bulletin. This was music to the ears of the First Directorate's propaganda wizards, who were keen to insert anti-imperialist propaganda into newspapers across the third world. Others in the First Directorate, however, considered this an important step toward something bigger: contact with Abu Sharif would enable them to penetrate the PLO. At this time, the Palestinian umbrella organization was still a relatively unknown entity to Prague as it would take another two years for Czechoslovakia to establish official relations with Yasser Arafat.[5] Having people on the inside was important—whichever faction they might be aligned with.

Abu Sharif was, however, no altruist. He jump-started PFLP's relations with Soviet Bloc states to give the faction the gravitas that Habash and his spokesman believed it deserved. Moreover, from the outset it was clear that the young, heavily scarred, and impaired Palestinian was seeking medical treatment for his injuries. At the time, Czechoslovakia was known for its superior health care system and generous medical assistance programs for partners from across the third world. Accordingly, when Abu Sharif first met Brožovský in 1974, the prospect of medical treatment was very much on the agenda.[6] The Czechoslovak envoy also saw this as an access point to this important potential asset and hence immediately made a case to Prague for securing his treatment. Providing medical care for the wounded Abu Sharif, Brožovský reasoned, would not only be the right thing to do on humanitarian grounds but would also be of political importance, having a direct impact on Czechoslovak prestige.[7]

Soon their regular meetings developed into a friendship and settled into a rhythm. Within six months of meeting him, Brožovský reported back to Prague that his relationship with the Palestinian was such that he could just pop by the *Al-Hadaf* editorial office at any time and discuss various political issues with him. It was clear that Abu Sharif was also warming up to the Czechoslovak "diplomat" because he started confiding in him, seeking his advice on the PFLP's potential exit from the PLO. Over the next six years, Czechoslovak case officers regularly met the PFLP spokesman either in his *Al-Hadaf* office or in a restaurant. During such long conversations, they discussed geopolitics and regional developments as well as intra-Palestinian relations.

They were often joined by Abu Sharif's friends and colleagues, who passed by or came to see him for a meeting. Quba Taysir, who also developed a close relationship with the Czechoslovaks and was in fact classified as an agent by the StB,[8] would often join these conversations. Here the prominent Palestinians would gradually open up to the Czechoslovak envoys. In June 1975, when *Daily Star*, an English-language newspaper in Lebanon distributed across the Middle East, published an article titled "The Terrorist Mind: The Secrets of Black September," which discussed Abu Sharif's role in his organization's terrorist operations and his approach to political violence, the PFLP strongman dismissed the damning piece, saying it was mostly a "fabrication." In the same breath, however, he confessed that its publication brought back fears of another attack on his life. To avoid a possible knee-jerk reaction to the *Daily Star* piece by the Israelis, he told the Czechoslovak envoy that he was sleeping at a different location every night and was, in fact, planning to go lie low for several weeks in Prague.[9]

Nevertheless, this relationship was not all chats and dinners. From the outset, Abu Sharif was Prague's main vehicle for planting propaganda in the Palestinian press. In October 1974 Brožovský asked him to publish an article written by Prague's First Directorate on Middle Eastern issues (Active Measure Car).

**ILLUSTRATION 11.1.** Abu Bassam Sharif (*left*) arriving at a reception organized in honor of the departing Iraqi ambassador in Beirut, sometime in the 1970s. *ABS, f. I.S, r.č. 12470/302*

As this was their first joint active measure, Brožovský exhorted Abu Sharif not to tell anyone that the article had been written in Czechoslovakia and emphasized that he could contribute today's equivalent of approximately $250 to the *Al-Hadaf* editorial office for each published piece. Abu Sharif acknowledged this gesture, but the two never spoke of it again.[10]

After laying the ground rules, Brožovský asked Abu Sharif for further assistance—planting an article on US politics and mercenary training in Saudi Arabia (Active Measure Bidet).[11] Showing Brožovský who was in charge, Abu Sharif did not merely copy-and-paste such planted texts. In most cases he agreed to publish them only after further PFLP editing. A month later, after adding additional sections about CIA operations, Active Measure Bidet was included in the newspaper's next issue.[12] In the spring of 1975, Abu Sharif delivered yet again, publishing another Czechoslovak-made article (Active Measure Manon). In the same issue, the PFLP newspaper also published a two-page overview of the Czechoslovak economy designed to promote the country's communist economic model.[13] Later in the year, he published another piece—this time in French about US-Saudi relations (Active Measure Náboj). Although Abu Sharif did not ask for rewards, the case officer gave him today's equivalent of $250, arguing that this was a contribution from him personally as he was now basically a subscriber to the PFLP publication—a thinly veiled attempt to disguise the bribe as a friendly gesture.[14] Overall, during the first two years of their collaboration, Abu Sharif assisted in placing four articles in various PFLP publications. He was now key to Czechoslovakia's active measures enterprise in the Palestinian press.[15]

As the relationship progressed, it expanded into further areas of collaboration. Abu Sharif briefed Brožovský and his successors on political developments across the Middle East or provided insight into PLO politics—including details on contacts between the PLO and the United States. Furthermore, he provided insight into the ongoing Lebanese Civil War and visits by prominent Western politicians to Beirut. Finally, he reported on contacts with their liaison partners—most interestingly with their backers in Beijing.[16] Prague was keen to get local insight on such meetings because Beijing was Moscow's chief rival in the third world and for influence over the Palestinian movement. As in the case of other sources, this was no high-grade intelligence. Nevertheless, Prague found Abu Sharif's briefings useful and complementary to what it gathered via other sources or collection means.

Abu Sharif's collaboration with the Czechoslovaks did not seem to be led by financial gain. He never requested financial rewards, and Prague envoys never officially suggested compensation for his assistance with active measures.[17] He did, however, gradually start making other requests. In the summer of 1974 he told the Czechoslovak envoy—perhaps in the hope that he would be able to endorse this effort—that the PFLP would be sending to Prague an official request for weapon supplies.[18] Although Brožovský patiently listened, there is no evidence he took steps to assist the PFLP in acquiring weapons from Czechoslovakia. Over the course of their relationship, Abu Sharif would make further requests of Prague, most of which were deemed too demanding or risky and were eventually ignored or disregarded by headquarters.

The Palestinian, however, also requested less controversial support. In November 1974 Abu Sharif asked the Czechoslovak envoy for a year's worth of newsprint—approximately 150 tons—to continue publishing *Al-Hadaf*. Although it was clear to Brožovský that this request was important to continuing the relationship he had been cultivating with the editor of the Palestinian newspaper and for planting further active measures in the publication, he did not seem to get much response from Prague.[19] Other requests aimed at helping

Abu Sharif with sustaining and distributing the newspaper followed. In 1975, to circulate *Al-Hadaf* in Jordan where it was banned, Abu Sharif asked his Czechoslovak contact if the embassy could help transport fifteen copies to the Czechoslovak embassy in Jordan where his PFLP contacts would pick them up. Prague considered this operation "too sensitive" and, eager not to upset relations with Jordan, decided not to help with the request.[20] It was increasingly apparent that while the First Directorate was eager to foster contacts in various Palestinian factions, it was willing to invest and risk very little to sustain them.

This cautiousness was also at play when Abu Sharif asked for some personal favors. In June 1975, while planning a brief visit to Prague, the avid gun collector asked Brožovský to help him acquire a Czechoslovak-made Škorpion machine pistol, which he had been longing for. Realizing the risks of Habash's right-hand man sporting a Škorpion donated by Prague, Brožovský was noncommittal, emphasizing that it might be difficult to deliver the weapon to the Middle East. It is likely that he did not want Abu Sharif to be showing off the iconic Czechoslovak weapon. He knew that he was heavily armed, always carrying a revolver, which he usually strategically placed in front of him on his desk during meetings, and there was always a Kalashnikov leaning in the corner of his office.[21]

Although it is unclear whether Abu Sharif ever got his Škorpion, we know that Brožovský wanted to get at least something done for the Palestinian who occupied the gray zone between asset and partner. Accordingly, in late 1975 the Beirut-based case officer requested a more generic 7.65mm pistol for the PFLP strongman, arguing that gifting Czechoslovak-made guns should not be a problem as these were relatively commonplace in Lebanon.[22] Unlike many of the other requests that fell on deaf ears, by January 1976, very much to Abu Sharif's delight, he had received a brand-new pistol from his Czechoslovak contact.[23]

Although productive, the early years of Abu Sharif's contact with Czechoslovak envoys were also tainted by complications and disagreements. Prague was not always pleased about the content published in *Al-Hadaf*. In January 1975 Brožovský rebuked Abu Sharif for publishing a piece that criticized Arafat's PLO, alleging that PLO representatives met Zionists in the Czechoslovak capital. Surprised by Brožovský's blunt confrontation, Abu Sharif seemed uneasy and quickly changed the subject, leaving the issue unresolved.[24] There were other articles that made Brožovský's blood boil. The Central European country did not appreciate the PFLP's open criticism of its alliance with the PLO, which was often discussed on *Al-Hadaf*'s pages.[25] Brožovský was clearly hoping that his increasingly close relationship with Abu Sharif would guarantee more measured coverage of the PFLP's Palestinian partners. The *Al-Hadaf* editor quickly dispelled these efforts to control his newspaper's reporting.

Other political disagreements also surfaced during their meetings. With regard to the future of the Middle East, Prague found PFLP politics too bellicose, once having to tell Abu Sharif that Czechoslovakia was not in favor of war in the region "unlike the whole of the PFLP leadership."[26] Prague was also acutely aware of the PFLP's close connection with China—one of the Soviet Bloc's key rivals. Worries about the PFLP's loyalties were amplified when Brožovský saw Chinese diplomats or journalists frequent Abu Sharif's office.[27] This exposed the harsh reality of liaising with nonstate actors who were keen to secure support from whoever was willing to give it.

## COURTING PRAGUE

Despite these cracks in their relationship, Abu Sharif clearly saw this unofficial contact as a possible avenue to official recognition. While the Czechoslovak envoys asked Habash's spokesman to be patient about looking to expand the PFLP's collaboration with Czechoslovakia, Abu Sharif was undeterred.[28] During the latter part of the 1970s, he traveled to Prague multiple times with the aim of jump-starting official relations. Despite this enthusiasm, he would find most of these visits disappointing affairs.

Abu Sharif's first attempt to court Czechoslovakia came only two months after Arafat's first official visit to the Central European nation. Although he met representatives of the Solidarity Committee, he returned to Beirut disappointed. Abu Sharif not only thought the meeting was on too low a level but found it frustrating that he was not given a platform to explain PFLP politics and prepare the ground for future relations. His disappointment was further exacerbated by the fact that for three years now there had been no progress with regard to securing his medical treatment.[29]

Brožovský empathized with the disheartened Palestinian. Although he understood that political recognition and setting up official relations with the PFLP were well above his pay grade, he thought Prague could have done more to secure Abu Sharif's medical treatment, his main motivation for liaison. In fact, Prague's coldness and persistent rejection of Abu Sharif's requests was undermining Brožovský's efforts in Beirut and the relationship he had built with the Palestinian. Accordingly, the intelligence officer repeatedly pressed Prague on this issue, even soliciting the support of the Czechoslovak ambassador.[30] Time and time again, however, his requests were answered with empty promises or flatly denied. Admittedly, securing medical treatment for such a high-risk patient was no simple task. Approval had to be given by the highest ranks of the Czechoslovak Communist Party.[31] Gradually, however, it became clear that the party was stalling primarily for a political reason: it was wary of the PFLP's questionable political loyalties to China. Additionally, some of the Communist Party members just did not like Habash and his associates.[32]

In early 1976 Abu Sharif's frustration with Prague's foot-dragging reached a peak. He told Brožovský that he was now trying to secure medical treatment via a different route—the International Association of Journalists. Abu Sharif's shift in strategy worked. After years of stalling, he had found a side door to securing medical treatment in the communist country. In mid-1976 he finally received permission for medical treatment in Prague—not as the PFLP spokesperson but rather as member of the International Association of Journalists.[33] Upon learning about Abu Sharif's impending trip to Prague, the country's foreign intelligence wasted no time and began devising a plan of how to use this visit to its advantage.

While helping Abu Sharif arrange his long-awaited trip, the StB planned for his official recruitment. They wanted to take him from the gray zone and officially put him on their payroll. During his stay in Prague, the country's foreign intelligence was also going to push Abu Sharif on several issues. It was keen to emphasize that he should be more careful about telling others, including his secretary, that he was publishing articles written by his Czechoslovak contacts. They also wanted to find out if the PFLP had any information about two unnamed employees of the US embassy who were currently being held in detention. As Abu Sharif was planning to stay in Prague for some time, this plan was considered attainable.[34]

In May Abu Sharif finally arrived in Czechoslovakia, where he would be treated at the Vinohrady Hospital. This was no quick fix. After his initial plastic surgery, Abu Sharif would have to return six months later for additional treatment. While undergoing the procedures, Abu Sharif also had his mind set on other business—securing special assistance from Prague. Although thus far direct sales to the PFLP had stalled unlike others from the GDR, Poland, and the USSR, his optimism at brokering such a direct deal was fueled by Prague's recent indirect sale of weapons to the PFLP. The recent transaction had been arranged via one of Qaddafi's middlemen, who paid for the controversial merchandise and arranged transport via Libya. Despite Prague's clear attempts to keep any association with the PFLP under the radar, Abu Sharif was set on persuading his hosts that his Palestinian faction was an outfit worthy of collaboration.[35]

Overall, the trip did not deliver on most accounts. Although Abu Sharif was satisfied with the medical treatment he received in Prague, he seemed to have achieved little in the way of PFLP's recognition or supplies of special materiél. Similarly, Prague seemed not to have gone ahead with Abu Sharif's recruitment or benefited from his stay in other ways. Perhaps without progress in recognition, the First Directorate had little to offer to Abu Sharif for his services. Despite this lack of progress, however, the StB was set on continuing its relationship with the PFLP spokesman. The person trusted to do this was none

ORGANISATION INTERNATIONALE DES JOURNALISTES
INTERNATIONAL ORGANIZATION OF JOURNALISTS
МЕЖДУНАРОДНАЯ ОРГАНИЗАЦИЯ ЖУРНАЛИСТОВ
ORGANIZACION INTERNACIONAL DE PERIODISTAS

Mr. Bassam Abu Sharif,
Secretary
for International Relations,
Union of Palestine
Writers and Journalists,
P.O. Box 3075,
B e i r u t
Lebanon

Prague, February 11th 1976

Dear Friend and Colleague,

The Directing body of the Czechoslovak Union of Journalists and the I.O.J. Secretariat General have a pleasure of inviting you to the medical treatment, eventually to the recovery stay in one of the Czechoslovak sanatoriums. Doing that, Czechoslovakia, its journalists and the I.O.J. Secretariat General appreciate your personal contribution to the fight of Palestinian people and your merits in the development of the brotherly relations especially to the journalists organizations of the socialist countries within the frame of your activities as a secretary for international relations. We do hope that after having consulted this invitation with the Directing body of your Union, you will accept it and inform us as soon as possible, when we can await you and Mrs. Sharif in Czechoslovakia. (We suggest to solve all technical questions by cable or in correspondence.)

In the meantime, we wish you much of a success and good health.

With friendly regards,

Czechoslovak Union
of Journalists
Zdeněk Hořeni,
President
Marcel Nolč,
Secretary General

I.O.J. Secretariat General
Jiří Kubka,
Secretary General
Helmut Brauer,
Secretary

Note:
Should you be in need of a special medical treatment, kindly let us have your medical statement three weeks before your departure at least, so that we may prepare for you the corresponding medical treatment.

ILLUSTRATION 11.2. Abu Bassam Sharif's letter of acceptance for medical treatment in Prague. *ABS, f. I.S, r.č. 12470/302* other than Ján Kuruc, the case officer who would become the main point of contact for the PLO's Abu Ayman in 1980s. In early 1977 Kuruc was sent to Beirut and became Abu Sharif's key point of contact.

Following his return from Prague, the Palestinian continued to push for Prague's recognition of the PFLP. A way forward, he thought, would be a high-level visit. Accordingly, in October 1977 George Habash traveled for his first business trip to Prague. This, however, turned out to be a fiasco. Habash felt he was treated by Czechoslovak communists as a second-class citizen—provided with inadequate accommodation and received at a very low level. His remarks also allegedly fell on deaf ears, failing to generate further discussion. Abu Sharif was furious and at his next meeting with Kuruc told the startled case officer that if Prague chose to be entirely pro-Fatah, this would eventually turn against it. The PFLP spokesman was ready to unleash a very public campaign against Czechoslovakia in the Arab press. In this tense atmosphere, Kuruc judged it wiser to swiftly conclude the meeting and get out of Abu Sharif's way.[36]

His rushed exit reflected Kuruc's own frustration with Prague's approach to the PFLP. Prague's tendency to ignore the Rejectionist factions was, much like during his predecessor's posting, complicating his own mission in Lebanon. Accordingly, in his report to Prague he bluntly laid out the state of affairs:

> The persistent unwillingness of Cs. [Czechoslovak] bodies, especially the employees of the office of the Cs. Solidarity Committee toward fostering contacts and cooperation with other Palestinian representatives other than the official PLO representatives (i.e., al-Fatah) does not have a positive impact on our work here, be it the official line of work of the Embassy, as well as when it comes to the objectives of the *rezidentura*, which wants to continue to use its contacts within the PFLP and DFLP to acquire information and to carry out various AOs [*aktivní opatření*: active measures]. If as a directorate we will not be able to impact this issue from the top in Prague, then we can expect that the representatives of these organizations, which are undoubtedly progressive and led by Marxist leaders, will not cooperate with us to the extent we would expect them to. This problem has been present throughout my entire stay in Beirut.[37]

Despite empathizing with Abu Sharif, Kuruc was also ready to push back against his persistent complaints. When they next met for lunch on Beirut's fashionable Hamra Street, the Czechoslovak case officer offered the Palestinian some unsolicited advice on how to improve the PFLP's reputation and standing. While not stating explicitly that its legacy of terrorism was a problem for Prague, he suggested that the PFLP should use the media to dissociate its brand from terrorism. Furthermore, Kuruc advised that Habash's outfit should drop the "Rejectionist Front" label, which made it look like a faction that fundamentally rejects everything. The Palestinian struggle would never get anywhere without unity.[38]

But in 1978 things started deteriorating in Beirut, the security situation going from bad to worse. In January an explosion shook *Al-Hadaf*'s office while Abu Sharif was hosting a group of Czechoslovak and Soviet journalists. Although Habash had left five minutes prior to the explosion and there were no fatalities, the multiple injuries and severe destruction underscored the deteriorating security situation in the city.[39] In March Wadi Haddad, one of the PFLP's most notorious associates and author of its most daring terrorist operations (and later the leader of PFLP–External Operations), died of what appeared to be a rapid case of leukemia. Abu Sharif was put in charge of organizing his memorial at the Beirut Arab University, which would attract top Palestinian dignitaries. He was also busy accompanying Habash on important excursions to Cuba and the GDR. Abu Sharif had all but disappeared from the StB's radar.[40]

This made Prague impatient. In August 1978 it ordered its rezidentura in Beirut to either intensify collaboration with Abu Sharif so he could be reclassified as a "confidential contact"—the First Directorate's second-highest collaborator rank—or exclude him from Czechoslovakia's agentura in Beirut.[41] Although Kuruc tried to bring Abu Sharif back in by asking him to continue publishing articles prepared by the Czechoslovaks, the PFLP spokesman did not comply. In fact, other PFLP sources seemed more promising at this time, especially Quba Taysir, who promised to publish Czechoslovak materials in a new English-language PFLP publication.[42] In mid-1979 the Beirut rezidentura started questioning its approach. As its agentura in the PFLP expanded, it wondered whether it was feasible to have four informants in one organization, as this created overlapping tasks and crossing of information.[43]

A year later, in the autumn of 1979, Habash and Abu Sharif finally traveled to Prague for an official visit. Although the optimism brought about by the change in Prague's direction seemed to have temporarily made Abu Sharif keener about collaborating with Kuruc, this enthusiasm did not endure. Shortly after the trip, StB case officers based in Beirut suggested to Abu Sharif that he collaborate with the embassy on a "broader basis." Although details are scarce, it seems this invitation to reinvigorate the relationship with the Palestinian did not succeed.[44] In the coming months, Abu Sharif persistently avoided the Czechoslovaks. This, coupled with the fact that Prague now had semiofficial relations with the PFLP's highest echelons, including George Habash, dealt the final blow to this now frail gray zone liaison. Accordingly, in March 1980, after six years, the StB's contact with Abu Sharif was ceased. He was now to be liaised with via official channels—most crucially via the Communist Party's Solidarity Committee that the Palestinian so very much loathed.[45]

\*\*\*

From 1974 to 1980, Prague ran a gray zone liaison relationship with George Habash's right-hand man. Despite Bassam Abu Sharif's best efforts, his contact with the Czechoslovak spies stationed at the Beirut rezidentura never matured into a full-scale intelligence liaison bearing the hallmarks of those developed with the PLO in the last decade of the Cold War. And despite the Czechoslovak case officers' best efforts, their contact with Abu Sharif never turned into the formal "agent" or "agent spotter" role they envisioned for the PFLP spokesman, which would have enabled them to penetrate the PFLP further, exercise control, and task the well-connected Palestinian. As a result, they were stuck in a gray zone without clear rules, hierarchies, and goals. Although this arrangement did deliver for a while, resulting in information and assistance, with active measures being exchanged for promises of medical treatment, future recognition, and occasional gifts, by the late 1970s it had started to fold.

This was probably due to a combination of factors, which included Prague's reluctance to create a full-fledged liaison with the PFLP spokesman, the increasing prospect of semiofficial relations replacing this clandestine channel, and perhaps even thanks to Abu Sharif's own change of heart. The high-profile PFLP spokesman, alive at the time of writing, gradually started distancing himself from Rejectionist politics. In the early 1980s he became more skeptical of armed struggle and gravitated toward the mainstream Fatah. Accordingly, in 1981 he was removed from the PFLP's politburo, and by 1987 he had been expelled from the faction altogether. Later, as Arafat's adviser, he would finally get the reception in Prague he so longed for. And, after the end of the Cold War, the once fierce advocate of armed struggle became central to some of the peace efforts aimed at achieving a two-state solution.

## NOTES

1. See more in Abu Sharif and Mahnaimi, *Best of Enemies*.
2. P. G. Steinhoff, "Portrait of a Terrorist: An Interview with Kozo Okamoto," *Asian Survey* 16, no. 9 (1976): 830–45.
3. In true communist bureaucratic fashion, case officers stationed abroad had to annually design at least two active measures.
4. See "Bílek" Brožovský's personal file, ABS-2474/30.
5. Bílek (Bejrút-I.S), April 24, 1974, "Záznam ze schůzky," ABS-12470/302.

6. Bílek (Bejrút-I.S).
7. Bílek (Bejrút-I.S), October 8, 1974, "BASSAM—záznam," ABS-12470/302.
8. The file of Agent Tabako (later Targo) remains classified.
9. Bílek (Bejrút-I.S), June 6, 1975, "Záznam ze schůzky," ABS-12470/302.
10. The original sum in Lebanese pounds/lira was LL/LBP 100. All sums in LBP were converted into USD first and subsequently adjusted to inflation in 2022 USD. Whenever the year was unclear, the average exchange rate over the relevant period and the mid-point inflation index was used. The source for USD/LBP conversion rate was the Banque du Liban (https://www.bdl.gov.lb/statistics/table.php?name=t5282usd). The source for the Consumer Price Index used in the inflation adjustment was the Minneapolis Fed (https://www.minneapolisfed.org/about-us/monetary-policy/inflation-calculator/consumer-price-index-1913-).Bílek(Bejrút-I.S), October 8, 1974, "BASSAM—záznam," ABS-12470/302.
11. Bílek (Bejrút-I.S), February 13, 1975, "Záznam ze schůzky," ABS-12470/302.
12. Bílek (Bejrút-I.S), March 9, 1975, "Záznam ze schůzky," ABS-12470/302.
13. Bílek (Bejrút-I.S), April 8, 1975, "Záznam ze schůzky," ABS-12470/302.
14. Original sum 100 LBP. Bílek (Bejrút-I.S), June 20, 1975, "Záznam ze schůzky," ABS-12470/302.
15. Bílek (Bejrút-I.S), October 8, 1974, "BASSAM—záznam," ABS-12470/302.
16. Ratiborský (I.S/47), October 10, 1975, "AT BASSAM—vyhodnocení spolupráce za období duben 1974—srpen 1975," ABS-12470/302.
17. Bílek (Bejrút-I.S), January 31, 1975, "Záznam ze schůzky," ABS-12470/302; Bílek (Bejrút-I.S), April 8, 1975, "Záznam ze schůzky," ABS-12470/302.
18. Bílek (Bejrút-I.S), August 25, 1974, "BASSAM—záznam o styku," ABS-12470/302.
19. Bílek (Bejrút-I.S), November 28, 1974, "BASSAM—záznam o styku," ABS-12470/302.
20. Bílek (Bejrút-I.S), February 13, 1975, "Záznam ze schůzky," ABS-12470/302.
21. Bílek (Bejrút-I.S), June 20, 1975, "Záznam ze schůzky," ABS-12470/302.
22. K. Kotek (47-I.S), October 21, 1975, "AT BASSAM—zakoupení pistole 7,65mm," ABS-12470/302.
23. Bílek (Bejrút-I.S), January 27, 1976, "BASSAM—záznam," ABS-12470/302.
24. Bílek (Bejrút-I.S), January 31, 1975, "Záznam ze schůzky," ABS-12470/302.
25. Bílek (Bejrút-I.S), May 13, 1975, "Záznam ze schůzky," ABS-12470/302.
26. Bílek (Bejrút-I.S), February 13, 1975, "Záznam ze schůzky," ABS-12470/302.
27. Bílek (Bejrút-I.S), June 20, 1975, "Záznam ze schůzky," ABS-12470/302.
28. Bílek (Bejrút-I.S), October 8, 1974, "BASSAM—záznam," ABS-12470/302.
29. Bílek (Bejrút-I.S), August 2, 1975, "BASSAM—záznam," ABS-12470/302.
30. Bílek (Bejrút-I.S), December 11, 1974, "BASSAM—léčení v ČSSR," ABS-12470/302.
31. Bílek (Bejrút-I.S), October 29, 1974, "BASSAM," ABS-12470/302.
32. Bílek (Bejrút-I.S), May 13, 1975, "Záznam ze schůzky," ABS-12470/302.
33. Bílek (Bejrút-I.S), April 2, 1976, "Záznam ze schůzky," ABS-12470/302.
34. Bílek (Bejrút-I.S), May 13, 1976, "Záznam ze schůzky," ABS-12470/302.
35. Seman (I.S/47), June 2, 1976, "AT BASSAM," ABS-12470/302.
36. Bílek (Bejrút-I.S), September 10, 1977, "Záznam ze schůzky," ABS-12470/302.
37. Bílek (Bejrút-I.S).
38. Bílek (Bejrút-I.S), November 8, 1977, "Záznam ze schůzky," ABS-12470/302.
39. Bílek (Bejrút-I.S), January 17, 1978, "Přijatá šifrovka," ABS-12470/302.
40. Bílek (Bejrút-I.S), March 13, 1978, "Záznam ze schůzky," ABS-12470/302.
41. "AT BASSAM," 10.8.1978, ABS-12470/302.

42. Lieskovský (Bejrút-I.S), March 5, 1979, "Záznam zo schôdzky," ABS-12470/302.
43. Lieskovský (Bejrút-I.S), June 5, 1979, "Záznam zo schôdzky," ABS-12470/302.
44. Mináč (Bejrút-I.S), December 17, 1979, "Záznam zo schôdzky," ABS-12470/302.
45. Mináč (Bejrút-I.S), March 18, 1980, "AT BASSAM–návrh na další postup," ABS-12470/302.

# 12

# Countering the Rejectionists

In the early 1980s, Prague's relations with the Rejectionist factions were gaining momentum. In the closing decade of the Cold War, Czechoslovakia, in tandem with its Soviet Bloc allies, set up semiofficial relations with the leftist Palestinian factions. Arguably, this was a strategic decision led by the Soviet Bloc's desire to maintain Palestinian unity, as in the late 1970s both leftist factions had rejoined the PLO, as well as by the Rejectionists' close relations with Prague's key ally in the region, Syria. This, however, did not mean that Prague now automatically and blindly trusted these factions. Crucially, it remained worried about associates of George Habash's PFLP, which had infamously triggered the Cold War wave of international terrorism and became one of the most prolific users of terrorist tactics in the late 1960s and early 1970s. Accordingly, as its relations with the PFLP matured, Prague remained vigilant and monitored (and at times countered) the activities of its most extreme elements.

## WADI HADDAD'S DISCIPLES

In the summer of 1978, Bassam Abu Sharif organized a grandiose and very public gathering at the Beirut Arab University. Held in the increasingly dangerous city, the event brought together an unusually illustrious group of Palestinian representatives, including the PFLP's George Habash and Fatah's enigmatic Abu Iyad. This was, however, no happy occasion. They were gathered to pay their respects to Wadi Haddad, who had died several months earlier, apparently of cancer, in an East German hospital. The man they had come to celebrate was not one to seek the limelight or speak for the Palestinian movement. He operated from the shadows.

Wadi Haddad was born in 1927 in Safed, the highest city in Galilee. As a young man during the 1948 Arab-Israeli War, he had been forced to flee to Lebanon. After completing his medical degree at the American University of Beirut alongside George Habash, the two left for Jordan to set up a medical clinic and worked for the United Nations Relief and Works Agency for Palestine Refugees in the Near East. Alongside their medical work, however, they soon became fierce political activists and cofounded the Arab Nationalist Movement. After the devastating defeat of Arab armies in the Six-Day War in 1967, Habash and Haddad transformed the Palestinian wing of the ANM into the PFLP. As we know, by the late 1960s, the PFLP became one of the largest factions operating under the PLO umbrella. It was also the first Palestinian organization to use international terrorism as a political strategy—characterized by spectacular aircraft hijackings.

Wadi Haddad became the central figure of the PFLP's hijacking operations. In fact, in the late 1960s and early 1970s, he became one of the most feared Palestinian activists-cum-operators. From a base in Jordan, he orchestrated the 1968 hijacking of the El Al flight from Rome to Tel Aviv that inaugurated the Cold War–era terrorism. His other projects were much more spectacular and had profound political impact. Crucially, he was the mastermind behind the September 1970 Skyjack Sunday, which saw three planes blown up in the Jordanian desert and triggered a protracted international hostage drama. Haddad's penchant for high-profile terrorist attacks was not, however, welcome by all in the PFLP. Accordingly, the PFLP cofounder soon became isolated within the faction and moved on to create his own offshoot organization, the aforementioned PFLP for the Liberation of Palestine–External Operations.[1]

Setting up his own outfit enabled Haddad to continue staging international terrorist campaigns. In the subsequent years, he undertook high-profile hijackings and hostage operations. In 1975 he joined forces with a certain flamboyant Venezuelan known as Carlos, who helped Haddad orchestrate the 1975 OPEC raid. A year later, under Haddad's direction, a joint Palestinian-German terrorist squad hijacked an Air France airliner with 248 passengers to Entebbe, Uganda. These events not only generated public attention and outrage but also won Haddad powerful enemies.

Chief among his adversaries was Israel, which, after the 1972 Munich massacre, orchestrated dozens of vendetta assassinations against prominent Palestinian figures. Haddad was on the top of Israel's hit list and, despite his shadowy nature and strict operational security, ultimately did not manage to evade the wrath of the Mossad. While in March 1978 he seemed to have died of what appeared to be a rapid case of leukemia, years later it transpired that Haddad's death had been all but natural. He was in fact killed by the Mossad, which had injected a toxin into his toothpaste.[2]

Although Haddad went down quietly, he left behind an army of zealots committed to continuing his work. Without a leader, however, the terrorist outfit split into two. One branch settled down in Baghdad, closely allied itself with Saddam Hussein's regime, and began devising operations against Syria and Iran. The other, led by a certain Abu Salim and his deputy, Zakki Hillo, operated in other Arab countries and set up bases in South Yemen, Algeria, Libya, and

Yugoslavia. Abu Salim's group, made up of approximately twenty-five members, allegedly inherited much of the wealth accumulated during Haddad's lifetime via airplane-hijacking campaigns, estimated to be around $60 million in today's money.[3] As opposed to the 1970s, when their group's founder presided over the PFLP-EO, Abu Salim's men were now primarily working for Arab regimes and their security services. In addition to terrorist attacks and covert operations, the groups was allegedly engaged in all manner of other machinations, including financial blackmail and extortion.[4]

In November 1984 Abu Salim, Wadi Haddad's most powerful disciple, appeared in Prague's luxurious Hotel Intercontinental. The country's domestic security branch was caught off guard. Abu Salim and his two-man entourage had sneaked into Czechoslovakia with Yemeni diplomatic passports issued on fake names. The StB learned of their presence in Prague only thanks to a trusted agent run by the country's foreign intelligence branch. The StB was very much aware of Haddad's legacy and referred to him unambiguously as a representative of a "Palestinian terrorist organization."[5] They, however, knew little about his men, who had now descended on the Czechoslovak capital. Accordingly, to find out more about their business there, the StB's domestic security first activated its watch-and-wait approach—putting the trio under tight surveillance and activating its agentura.[6]

Although the StB never found out the real reason why Abu Salim's group visited Prague, it was not keen on having Wadi Haddad's associates on Czechoslovak territory. Several months after their visit, the StB's Fourteenth Department—a short-lived bureaucratic effort by the StB to address the issue of terrorism—took subtle measures to prevent the men from returning. It activated its prevent-and-block approach, which saw the Yemeni pseudonyms used by Haddad's men added to the Unwanted Persons Index (Index nežádoucích osob, or INO)—the country's persona non grata list—for the next five years. The StB argued that this was necessary because the unwelcome guests were suspected of organizing terrorist activities on its territory.[7]

Prague clearly feared these men and the violence that might erupt as a result of their presence. Several months prior to Abu Salim's visit to Prague, his deputy was shot on the sunny streets of Madrid by a Mossad hitman riding as a passenger on a motorcycle.[8] Although Zakki Hillo survived, he was badly injured and in need of urgent medical care. In March 1985 a prominent Lebanese arms dealer, a distant relative of the infamous Syrian arms dealer Monzer al-Kassar, arrived in Prague on a reconnaissance mission. He was not there to strike an arms deal but to explore options for medical treatment of his dear friend Hillo. Although after the near-fatal attack in Madrid the Waddi Haddad disciple was able to get some much-needed medical attention in a Polish military hospital and was now in stable condition, Hillo still could not walk and hence took the advice of his Polish doctors to secure rehabilitation treatment in Czechoslovakia.[9]

This information caught the eye of the heads of the foreign and domestic intelligence branches of the StB. Remarkably, however, they seemed to have decided not to actively obstruct Hillo's several-month-long rehabilitation visit in Czechoslovakia. Instead of agitating Haddad's men, whom the StB knew little about, the spy chiefs were keen to reverse back to the well-tested watch-and-wait approach. Karel Sochor, head of the country's foreign intelligence branch, explained when he wrote to his counterpart in the Second Directorate, "In the event that ZAKKI's medical treatment in CSSR takes place, we have the possibility to monitor his stay via a secret collaborator."[10] Accordingly, they relaxed and patiently watched as other friends of Hillo's attempted to arrange medical care for the wounded Palestinian. At this stage, Prague did not consider this a high-risk visit.

Soon, however, things took a turn. In early 1983 the StB learned that Hillo's main rivals—members of Wadi Haddad's faction loyal to the Baghdad branch—had secured visas for Czechoslovakia under false Yemeni identities. Prague knew that these were dangerous men. In 1976 they had allegedly attempted to shoot down an El Al aircraft over Nairobi.[11] The operation ended up in utter failure. Not only was the attack not successful but the operatives were arrested and sentenced to a ten-year prison sentence in Israel. Shortly before their sentence ran out, they were released as part of a 1985 prisoner swap between Israel and Amal, a Lebanese Shia militia. What is more, they were allegedly set on assassinating Hillo's wife—a former member of the German Baader-Meinhof terrorist group—who was to have participated in the Nairobi attack but escaped Israeli incarceration.[12] This all confirmed the StB's now growing conviction that preventing Wadi Haddad's associates from residing on Czechoslovak territory was paramount to preventing clashes between the warring camps.

Soon, the StB domestic branch was given a chance to demonstrate this conviction in practice. Shortly before the Christmas of 1986, it was alerted by its agentura in the Hotel Intercontinental that a certain Nabil Wahbi Hussein and his wife had checked into room 513. This set off alarm bells across the StB's domestic directorate because this name was on a list of potential cover names for Hillo's friends. Without much hesitation, the StB decided to escalate from "block" to "oust." Accordingly, they sent one of its officers to the downtown hotel to carry out the uncomfortable, and potentially dangerous, job of expelling the terrorist. When he arrived at the hotel at nine thirty in the morning, Hussein was still asleep. Admittedly, being woken up made it all the more difficult for the Palestinian to accept the news. The StB officer opted for a soft approach, telling him that it would be in the interest of his own safety to leave Czechoslovak territory on the next possible flight. Although Hussein at first resisted the news, arguing that he and his wife were in Prague to simply do some Christmas shopping, he soon realized that the StB envoy was not there to negotiate. Visibly upset by the intervention, much like Abu Daoud several years earlier, Hussein vowed never to return to Czechoslovakia.[13]

\*\*\*

Similarly to the PLO, Prague adopted a multitrack approach toward the Rejectionists. First, in the 1970s it sought to infiltrate the organization by striking what turned out to be a gray zone liaison with one of the PFLP's top representatives in Beirut. Second, toward the end of the decade, when the Rejectionists briefly rejoined the PLO, it created semiofficial relations with both key Rejectionist factions, which also encompassed moderate security assistance. Third, in an effort to prevent Palestinian infighting and violence erupting on its territory, it took steps to counter extreme spin-off groups that traced their origins back to Wadi Haddad, one of the founders of the PFLP. During the closing decade of the Cold War, the Czechoslovak government gradually developed various strategies to deal with such extremists. These would become exceptionally useful when the most high-profile of the Cold War jackals started descending on Prague.

## NOTES

1. Sayigh, *Armed Struggle*, 344.
2. Bergman, *Rise and Kill First*, chap. 13.
3. The original sum was $10 million to $12 million.
4. Jan Skořepa (Náč.I.S/17), November 23, 1984, "Věc: K pobytu představitele palestinské teroristické organizace v Praze," ABS-H-721/10; "Poznatky k extremistické organizaci Wadího CHADDÁDA," 1986, ABS-38165/2.
5. J. Skořepa (Náč.I.S/17), November 20, 1984, "Věc: K pobytu představitele palestinské teroristické organizace v Praze," ABS-H-721/10.
6. Ivo Juska (Zást.Náč.II.S/6), November 22, 1984, "INFORMACE," ABS-H-721/10.
7. Zdeněk Neměc, January 16, 1985, "NÁVRH na zařazení do indexu nežádoucích osob na dobu 5-ti let," ABS-24113/5.
8. Bergman, *Rise and Kill First*, 278.
9. Karel Sochor (Náč.I.S)–Karel Fiřt (Náč.II.S), March 25, 1985, "Věc: Libanonský příslušník W.H. NABIL–zpráva," ABS-24613/10.
10. Sochor-Fiřt.
11. "Israel Concedes It Holds 2 Germans in Terror Plot," *New York Times*, March 21, 1977, https://www.nytimes.com/1977/03/31/archives/israel-concedes-it-holds-2-germans-in-terror-plot.html.
12. "Snahy o obnovení činnosti organizace dr. Wádího Chaddáda," n.d. 1986, ABS-38165/2.
13. Josef Dynžík, "Záznam," February 12, 1986, ABS-38165/12.

# PART IV
# LES ENFANTS TERRIBLES

# 13

# "My Name Is 'Carlos,' and I Am a Good Person"

In early February 1979 a confident, well-built, and impeccably dressed foreigner arrived at a Czechoslovak–East German border crossing. A routine search through his luggage revealed a cache of suspicious items: large sums of money in different currencies, a collection of passports issued for different identities, and an array of photographs and telephone numbers. Unsettled by these findings, the East German border guards denied the enigmatic traveler entry into the communist state.

Much to their surprise, only several hours later, the same man was back at the border. This time, however, he presented the bewildered border officers with a passport issued under a different name. His undeniable resemblance to the suspicious foreigner from earlier in the day prompted the diligent border guards to turn him away yet again. Refusing to accept this reality, the traveler made one last-ditch attempt to win them over. He quickly scribbled something on a piece of paper and passed it to the uniformed men. The note, written in English, read, "My name is 'Carlos,' and I am a good person." Unfazed by the persistent man's repeated attempts to cross the heavily guarded border, the East German guards again turned him away. This triggered a heavy barrage of curses and threats by the "good person," who told the diligent border guards that they were making "a grave mistake."[1]

Although it seemed that after his second attempt the relentless man had finally given up, several days later, he was back at the very same border crossing. This time, however, he was armed with a South Yemeni diplomatic passport. Disarmed by his diplomatic immunity, the border guards finally let him through into East Germany.[2]

In the late 1970s Carlos the Jackal, who took the mantle from Wadi Haddad as the world's most notorious terrorist, was set on creating a new home in the Soviet Bloc. For almost a decade, he had vacationed and held meetings in Sofia, Bucharest, Belgrade, and East Berlin. Crucially, for several years he set up a temporary base in the Hungarian capital, Budapest. Prague was on his list of top destinations within the Soviet Bloc. Although he never settled there, Carlos and his group considered the Czechoslovak capital "just the right place to meet

239

and organize." In fact, Carlos visited Prague up to ten times—meeting with his associates and potential partners and mingling with Middle Eastern diplomats, spies, and terrorists.[3]

Unlike with the PLO and the Rejectionists, however, Prague never struck any kind of alliance with Carlos. From his first visit in 1978, it considered him a threat and a reputational hazard. Accordingly, the StB activated a number of the tools it had developed as part of its Swiss Army Knife approach to deal with the dangerous terrorist and his associates.

## BECOMING CARLOS

By the time he began courting the Soviet Bloc, Carlos the Jackal was a well-known figure in the world of international terrorism. In fact, by attacking high-profile targets in Britain and France (some Jews, including Israelis) as well as Iranian and Arab targets elsewhere for over a decade, he became the enfant terrible of late Cold War terrorism. The self-proclaimed Marxist revolutionary turned hired gun made the intelligence services of the democratic world look "inept and ridiculous."[4] In fact, in 1976 West Germany offered today's equivalent of $100,000 for information leading to his arrest, and by 1982 Carlos topped the assassination list of French president François Mitterrand.[5]

Born Ilich Ramírez Sánchez in Venezuela, Carlos began his terrorist career in the early 1970s when he joined the ranks of Wadi Haddad's PFLP-EO. In 1968 this son of a rich Marxist lawyer was studying at Patrice Lumumba University in Moscow. Failing academically and refusing to abide by the institution's strict discipline, Carlos was expelled in 1970 due to "anti-Soviet provocation and indiscipline." Soon afterward, he began searching for a raison d'être.[6]

Although a Venezuelan, through his friendship with Palestinian students at the Patrice Lumumba University, Carlos developed an interest in the Palestinian cause—so much so that after being expelled he traveled to Beirut to volunteer to fight for the Palestinians. There he met PFLP spokesman and StB "gray zone" contact Bassam Abu Sharif, who—intrigued by the young man's "explosive intelligence" and "a chameleon-like nature"—recruited him for the cause and famously chose his nom de guerre. The apprentice revolutionary spent the first stage of his career at the PFLP's training camps in Jordan, where he briefly joined the Palestinian guerrillas in their war against the Jordanian king.[7]

By 1971 Carlos had relocated to Europe and soon began working full-time for the group's European branch, immersing himself in the world of false documents and safe houses. By 1973 he had become the group's hit man. Carlos's first solo operation took place in the heart of London. On the evening of December 30, 1973, the stocky Venezuelan turned up at the house of Joseph Edward Sieff, the chairman of the retailer Marks & Spencer, in the heart of the upscale

ILLUSTRATION 13.1. Photos of young Carlos, who often wore disguises to match the multiple identities he needed to cross international boundaries and avoid arrest. ABS, f. H, a.č. H-720/2

neighborhood of St John's Wood. After knocking on the door, the twenty-four-year-old aspiring terrorist forced a butler at gunpoint to take him to Sieff. Meeting his target in the upstairs bathroom, Carlos shot the honorary vice president of the British Zionist Federation and recent host to right-wing Israeli prime minister Menachem Begin in the face. Remarkably, the Jewish businessman's life was saved by an unusually resilient set of front teeth and the fact that Carlos was unable to deliver a second shot due to a jammed gun. Carlos's biographer John Follain suggests that this failure to kill his target was a "disappointing baptism." Nevertheless, as the terrorist apprentice later admitted, "it was at this time that the real Carlos was born."[8]

Carlos's early years as Haddad's hit man in Europe were characterized by further failures. The unsuccessful attack on Sieff was followed by a botched attack on a branch of the Israeli Bank Hapoalim in London and two off-target RPG attacks at Orly Airport in Paris in January 1975.[9] In the summer of that year, France's then domestic intelligence agency, Direction de la surveillance du territoire (DST), received a tip-off from a well-off informant, Michel Moukharbal, who happened to be the middleman between Carlos and his Palestinian bosses. This was a hard-won confession. It took the DST five days and multiple threats to break the reluctant Christian Lebanese and make him share details about a certain contact he had in Paris, who allegedly served as Haddad's assassin in Western Europe. On June 27 he directed the DST to a studio apartment in the Latin Quarter where the hit man's girlfriend lived. Perhaps she would know more about her partner's whereabouts? Although skeptical about Moukharbal's tip, the responsible DST commissioner, Jean Herranz, got into an unmarked vehicle with the Lebanese source and two inspectors and headed in the direction of 9 Rue Toullier.[10]

At first, Commissioner Herranz approached the building and walked upstairs to the apartment accompanied by one of the inspectors, leaving the other to keep watch on Moukharbal in the car. In the apartment, he found a party underway—whiskey-filled glasses, a young woman playing the cuatro, and a jumpy, intoxicated Venezuelan man. When the latter refused to admit any connection to Moukharbal, the DST decided to bring the Lebanese informant up to the apartment. The moment the exhausted Lebanese informant entered the apartment to confirm whether the Venezuelan was indeed his hit man, things took a sudden turn. Shortly after Moukharbal pointed his shaking finger at the increasingly irritated Venezuelan—acknowledging their connection—bullets started flying through the miniscule apartment. The drunken Carlos, armed with a long-barreled Czechoslovak-made gun capable of firing eight bullets a second, shot Moukharbal and the two inspectors dead and severely wounded Herranz. The apartment that only minutes ago emanated soothing Latin American music was now the scene of a massacre. This deadly shooting spree was a humiliating affair for the DST and propelled Carlos to the top of France's enemy list.[11]

While aware that he was now being intensely pursued by French and other Western agencies, Carlos did not lie low for long. Six months later, Carlos and his PFLP-EO associates staged his largest operation yet. In December 1975 they raided the OPEC ministers' meeting in Vienna—killing three and kidnapping a number of prominent targets. Although Carlos and his colleagues managed to escape Vienna with some of their most prominent targets—the Saudi Arabian and Iranian oil ministers—Carlos failed to kill the kidnapped men in the name of the Palestinian cause as instructed by his PFLP-EO boss, Wadi Haddad. Instead, he allegedly chose to cash in a multimillion-dollar check for their release. This disobedience of Haddad's orders led to Carlos's ousting from the radical organization.[12] Ironically, what was to become Carlos's most notorious operation also proved fatal to his association with Wadi Haddad.

This unequivocal rejection forced Carlos to go solo. By March 1978 he had set up his own terrorist outfit, officially called the Arm of the Arab Revolution.[13] To establish new partnerships and perhaps even find a permanent home, the so-called Carlos Group began traveling across the Middle East and the Soviet Bloc.

## THE COMPANY YOU KEEP

By the time Carlos started visiting Prague, he had created a close circle of collaborators. During his travels through the Soviet Bloc, Carlos was accompanied by his closest associates, most notably his West German deputy and head of operations, Johannes Weinrich; Kamal al-Issawi, a Palestinian formerly of the Syrian intelligence service and later the PFLP;[14] and Magdalena Kopp, also known as "Lilly," Carlos's West German girlfriend, later wife, and mother to his daughter Rosa. Kopp served as the group's secretary and occasional document forger.[15]

This close-knit group of terrorists came to the baroque Czechoslovak capital for both relaxation and work. When they were not shopping for expensive perfumes, alcohol, and cigarettes, they were busy meeting friends and fostering alliances. Meetings held by the Carlos Group in Czechoslovakia can be divided into three categories: Middle Eastern diplomats and spies mostly stationed in Prague, fellow terrorists, and arms dealers drawn to Prague's arms industry.

Fraternizing with diplomats and intelligence officers was key to Carlos's terrorist infrastructure. He mostly sought the company of Iraqi, South Yemeni, and later Syrian diplomats as well as employees of the PLO Office in Prague. With ambitious terrorist plans yet without a permanent home, the group needed the support of state actors. Crucially, to survive in illegality and move across international borders, members of the group adopted various identities, which required a steady inflow of new travel documents. Among the most popular were Iraqi, Kuwaiti, Lebanese, and Syrian passports. By 1980 Carlos and his group were reported to have obtained genuine Syrian diplomatic passports issued by the Syrian Ministry of Foreign Affairs.[16] The group was also likely to acquire documents indirectly, through Palestinian contacts. According to a former South Yemeni deputy minister of the interior, Aden had lost track of how many passports it handed out to "the Palestinians," who then passed them on to various terrorist groups.[17]

Foreign diplomats and spies based in Prague were key to Carlos's venture in various other ways. During his trips there, they provided safe houses where the terrorists held clandestine meetings with prospective and existing partners. Embassies, such as that of Iraq, staffed by Saddam Hussein's family members, often enabled the Carlos Group to use their diplomatic vehicles to move around the cobblestone streets of Prague.[18]

These were not exclusively work relations. Carlos was wined and dined by Middle Eastern diplomats in their residences and repaid the favor by hosting them for meals in restaurants across the city. These meetings illuminate Carlos's ever-changing alliances with Arab regimes. When the group's members first arrived in Czechoslovakia, they were closely associated with the Iraqi regime and its envoys in Prague. Less than six months later, however, around the time

ILLUSTRATION 13.2. A hidden-camera photo of Carlos and Magdalena Kopp, his German girlfriend and later wife, while walking through the old town of Prague. August 8, 1979. *ABS-SL 454*

Saddam Hussein achieved power, Carlos became vocally anti-Iraqi and shifted his allegiance to Syria. In August 1979, during an evening spent with his Syrian friends in the Hotel Intercontinental's bar, Carlos expressed his disgust at Iraq's policy toward Iraqi communists and boasted that he had recently been arrested in Iraq and detained for twenty-four hours.[19]

In addition to diplomats and intelligence officers, Carlos used his time in Czechoslovakia to create or strengthen existing ties with other Cold War jackals. The StB was closely monitoring these ties and suspected that Carlos fostered relations with the Italian Red Brigades and Prima Linea terrorist organizations, the Basque nationalists Euskadi Ta Askatasuna (ETA), the Provisional Irish Republican Army (PIRA), as well as the Red Army Faction and members of the Armenian Secret Army for the Liberation of Armenia.[20] Carlos's meetings with fellow terrorists were carefully planned, exploiting Prague's relative openness to foreigners.

One of Carlos's most intriguing terrorist associations occurred in the autumn of 1978. When he first set foot in Prague, Carlos met a mysterious young Palestinian woman, known to the StB as Rihab al-Qasim. In her visa application to the Czechoslovak embassy in Baghdad, Rihab had asserted that she was an Iraqi student.[21] She was, however, neither a student nor an Iraqi. "Al-Qasim" was Souhaila Andrawes, the only surviving hijacker of one of the most high-profile terrorist episodes of the late Cold War, in Prague to seek medical treatment of injuries incurred during the operation.

On October 13, 1977, together with three PFLP-EO accomplices, Andrawes had hijacked to Mogadishu, Somalia, a Lufthansa Boeing 737 flying from Spain to West Germany with eighty-six passengers on board. Hostages remembered Andrawes as "a fury, screaming at them continuously, with grenades held ready in her hands, the pins linked to the rings on her fingers by a thin cord."[22] At the end of the five-day hijacking drama, Andrawes's accomplices were shot dead with the assistance of a British Special Air Service team flown to Mogadishu to help West German commandos assault the plane. Andrawes miraculously survived, although incurring severe injuries to her chest and knee. Sentenced to twenty years in a Somali prison, she was quietly released on medical grounds a year later and secretly transported to Iraq, presumably by Iraqi operatives.[23]

It was this jewel of Palestinian violent resistance that Carlos was trusted to escort during parts of her clandestine five-month rehabilitation in Czechoslovakia.[24] Andrawes was a protégée of the Iraqi ambassador to Czechoslovakia, Anwar al-Hadithi. It was thanks to his intervention that the young Palestinian woman had been admitted for treatment of her knee, shin, and chest wounds to an orthopedic clinic in Prague. Agent Oskar, the ambassador's close friend but also an StB informant, helped secure this. In January 1979 Andrawes underwent a second leg operation aimed at removing a bullet.[25] Although undercover and on "friendly territory," she was under constant protection and frequently interacted with various members of the Carlos Group. Keeping cover was a constant worry. While in the hospital, Andrawes told fellow patients she had incurred her injuries in Beirut when she accidentally stepped on a cluster bomb.[26] Although it is unclear whether the doctors knew about her true identity, during her stay Andrawes's mother, Carlos, and his associates hosted the doctor in charge of her recovery at Hotel Intercontinental.[27]

In addition to serving as the protector of the surviving Mogadishu hijacker, Carlos met other key figures of the terrorist underground in Czechoslovakia's capital. Later that year, in August, he met Black September commander and architect of the Munich Olympic Village massacre Abu Daoud. Although by then Daoud had suffered demotion within the PLO, he was still connected to some of its key players, including Abu Iyad, the head of the PLO's intelligence. To this day, it remains unclear what the purpose of their Prague meeting was. Although StB's agents in the Hotel Intercontinental eagerly observed the duo while they took breakfast together in the hotel's snack bar, the seasoned terrorists were cautious enough not to discuss their business in public.[28] The StB eventually suspected Abu Daoud of providing explosives and weapons to the Carlos Group.[29]

While in Prague, the gang spent significant time with international arms dealers. Arguably, by the late 1970s, in addition to staging international terrorist attacks, arms dealing had become the Carlos Group's bread and butter. With their multiple identities and diplomatic travel documents, the group's members could move across international boundaries with relative ease. This made them just the right kind of people to deliver arms to prospective clients. Although details of their business arrangements remain few, we do know that Carlos met numerous arms dealers in Prague. An important contact was John Nolan, who remained active in the African arms trade until the mid-2010s. While the StB believed that Nolan was "Carlos's man" in the PIRA, the more likely explanation is that he was involved in the group's weapons-dealing enterprise.[30]

Arms seemed to have been the glue that held together yet another one of Carlos's long-standing alliances—that with a Syrian arms dealer and fierce opponent of the Assad regime. Ousted from his home country, Sarkis Fareed Sarkis was now living in exile in Paris, heading a murky enterprise called Trans World Enterprises. In the closing decade of the Cold War, Sarkis visited Prague dozens of times, typically to meet Czechoslovak state–owned arms companies. He brokered deals for numerous states, including for hundreds of tanks and armored personnel carriers, which were to be delivered to Saddam Hussein's army. Observing their meetings via its agent network, the StB suspected Sarkis was a member of the Carlos Group. Accordingly, the Syrian was put under close StB surveillance.[31]

This revealed not only the depth of Carlos's engagement in the arms trade but also the lengths that arms dealers will go to secure deals, at times with improbable partners. In the mid-1980s Sarkis became the majority owner of an American arms-importing company, Bauska, based in Montana. Thanks to his extensive contacts with Czechoslovak arms dealers, he managed a great feat—to break what was effectively a US embargo on some Czechoslovak-made sports weapons with a sale of two hundred thousand pistols to the US military. In a further effort to open the US market to Czechoslovak weapons, Sarkis planned to bribe several US congressmen and members of the Reagan administration. To this end, he had one of Czechoslovakia's oldest arms-producing companies, CZ, manufacture for Bauska an exclusive model of its CZ 75 pistol. One was allegedly gifted to none other than President Reagan to encourage completely lifting the embargo.[32]

While the StB never got to the bottom of Sarkis's real identity, his biography and appearance are remarkably similar to those of one of the Cold War's most notorious private arms dealers, Sarkis Soghanalian—dubbed "the Merchant of Death." The short, stocky Armenian Lebanese, who at the height of his career was estimated to have made an annual profit of over $12 million, was involved in some of the twentieth century's most vicious conflicts, including those in Lebanon, Nicaragua, and Angola as well as the Iran-Iraq War. In addition to striking deals amounting to more than $1.5 billion with Saddam Hussein during his eight-year war against Iran, Soghanalian also supplied Exocet missiles to Argentina, which were later used in the Falklands War to sink HMS *Sheffield*. Despite numerous indictments by the US government, Soghanalian managed to avoid lengthy prison sentences for wire fraud and violations of UN sanctions by allegedly providing Washington valuable intelligence on his clients. Apart from fostering close relationships with American politicians, including former president George H. W. Bush, Soghanalian reportedly also had close ties with Iraq's Saddam Hussein, Nicaragua's Anastasio Somoza Debayle, and the Armenian Apostolic Church. The high-flying arms czar died in 2011 at the age of eighty-two in his Miami home, broke and abandoned by his powerful allies.[33]

Although clearly Prague did not understand the full significance of Carlos's business partnerships, it gradually started worrying about his associations with Middle Eastern diplomats, spies, terrorists, and arms dealers—so much so that after it initially patiently watched Carlos and his associates from a distance, it soon started viewing him as a real threat. It began to adopt a more activist approach to his terrorist enterprise.

## CARLOS AS A THREAT

In the early 1980s Carlos grew increasingly ambitious. He was set on creating a multinational organization that would wage war against a no lesser set of evils than "imperialism, fascism, Zionism, colonialism." To achieve these widely cast goals, Carlos was not only accumulating the necessary arsenal and technical equipment but also working hard to poach members of other terrorist groups for his own enterprise. In addition, he was looking to move his operations to Africa by placing "his people" in various governments there and using them to either take power or expand his enterprise across the continent.[34]

At the same time, he remained committed to perpetrating high-profile terrorist attacks. Some were carried out in the name of friendly governments. In 1981 his outfit bombed the Radio Free Europe offices in Munich on behalf of Romanian intelligence. Although Carlos's people ended up bombing the wrong part of the office—the Czechoslovak section instead of the Romanian one—these old-style attacks helped maintain his legacy as the Cold War's arch-terrorist. At the same time, his group continued to launch high-profile attacks for its own causes. Crucially, in the early 1980s these were primarily aimed at France as a form of retribution for the incarceration of two Carlos Group members, one of whom was Carlos's partner, the loyal Magdalena Kopp.[35]

Carlos, however, also remained committed to top-level assassinations. One of his group's long-term operational goals was to assassinate the Egyptian president, Anwar Sadat. In preparation, a member of the group surveilled the president's residence in Cairo and developed a number of scenarios that, if put into place, would have represented a tactical shift in Cold War terrorism. These included a plan to bomb Sadat's residence by air or carry out a "kamikaze-style" assassination. In 1982 Carlos was allegedly also planning to assassinate PLO chairman Yasser Arafat. The Syria-sanctioned operation was to be a revenge killing for Arafat's alleged betrayal of the Palestinian cause. Soon afterward, the Carlos Group also considered an Iraqi request to liquidate the US ambassador to Cairo.[36]

In the early 1980s, in addition to leading increasingly erratic operations, Carlos also forged close alliances with some of the world's most eccentric statesmen. Along with short-lived partnerships with the regimes of Saddam Hussein and Hafez al-Assad, Carlos forged a pact with Muammar Qaddafi of Libya. Although a tempestuous affair, this alliance was a quid pro quo arrangement designed to benefit both parties. Qaddafi provided Carlos with much-needed cash and weapons. To reciprocate, the Carlos Group vowed to liquidate the Libyan leader's opponents living abroad. The group was said to have received a list of no fewer than five hundred targets.[37] This was a prime example of the Cold War international terrorist as a naked opportunist.

In addition to these daring operations and alliances, the Carlos Group worked hard to expand its arms-dealing enterprise. According to intelligence assessments passed on by Hungarian counterparts, it set up a central weapons depot in South Yemen, close to Aden. Allegedly, since 1978, the group used this facility to store weapons, explosives, and matériel acquired from Syria, Libya, and other partner states. Many of these weapons were then passed on to partner groups, such as the resistance fronts against North Yemen, or sent to other locations in Europe where Carlos and his entourage spent time, including Budapest and Berlin. The cache close to Aden was no small hideaway: the Hungarian state security service—III Main Group Directorate of the Ministry of the Interior, which comprised the country's civilian intelligence services—estimated that Carlos had accumulated hundreds of grenades, RPG launchers, sniper rifles, and Browning pistols. To aid in their transfer, the group had also acquired its own equipment for forging passports. By the 1980s, in important ways, Carlos's organization resembled the workings of a real intelligence service.[38]

***

Carlos's increasingly daring missions and rising terrorist profile worried Prague. Although the terrorist repeatedly claimed that he would refrain from conducting terrorist activity on Soviet Bloc territory, the StB did not believe him and considered Carlos a threat from the outset. Prague was not principally concerned about Carlos attacking Czechoslovak targets—this would be a counterproductive move even by Carlos's standards. What the StB did worry about, however, was his proclivity for attacking Western or "imperialist" targets—so much so that in March 1979 the StB argued that "it cannot be ruled out that . . . members of this terrorist group are planning to carry out operations on the territory of socialist countries against pro-American and pro-Israeli elements."[39] Czechoslovakia found itself in a paradoxical situation: worried about protecting the diplomatic personnel and infrastructure of some of its fiercest enemies.

Another reason why Prague considered the Jackal a threat was his infamous temper. Czechoslovakia, much like its other Soviet Bloc allies, often boasted about how safe the country was in comparison to Western states, many of which were plagued by terrorism, mass protests, and arguably much higher crime rates. To sustain its orderly image, Prague was eager to avoid any outbreak of violence on its territory. Carlos's temper represented a threat to the image. During most of his stays, agents reported how agitated he could get if he did not get what he wanted. At times, he put his temper on full display. In the summer of 1979, after the terrorist had accidently locked himself out of his hotel room, a very public drama ensued. Unable to get back into his room, the furious Carlos set out to find the hotel director, stalking through the hallways of the packed Hotel Intercontinental with a large revolver in his hand.[40] Such high-risk behavior conducted in Prague's most luxurious hotel with notable foreign clientele made the StB increasingly uncomfortable.

Carlos's bad temper and increasingly ambitious operations also represented a potential threat to Czechoslovakia's international reputation. On one hand, Prague did not want to be seen as a supporter of international terrorism—a narrative increasingly propagated by the Reagan administration. On the other, as a country heavily dependent on the foreign arms trade, which required good working relations with ideological allies and foes, Prague was reluctant to alienate potential business partners by appearing to be in bed with the top Cold War terrorists who targeted them.

Accordingly, on March 20, 1979, five months after Carlos's first visit to Prague, the StB sought high-level political guidance from the leadership of the Ministry of the Interior and the Communist Party on how to address the increasing inflow of suspected terrorists to Prague. This was a sensitive area, and the StB visibly pushed decisions upward, arguing that "it is in their remit to decide on what steps need to be taken."[41]

We now know that communist Prague adopted a gradual three-step approach to Carlos and his group: watch and wait, block and prevent, and trick and oust. In the autumn of 1978, when he first set foot on Czechoslovak territory, the StB took out a well-tested tool out of their Swiss Army Knife arsenal—the watch-and-wait approach, aimed at closely monitoring and better understanding the notorious terrorist and his associates. The StB found Carlos difficult to control, arrogant, and unprofessional, describing him as "very self-confident and stuck up; often not abiding by the laws of cover, maintaining contacts with unreliable and unscreened persons."[42]

During its various visits, the Carlos Group was also closely watched by a vast pool of informants—mostly Arab nationals studying or working in Czechoslovakia and with good contacts with Middle Eastern embassies in Prague. Several informants—including "Filip"—were key to the StB's effort to monitor the group. Filip first met Carlos in August 1979 through a mutual Syrian friend visiting Prague, the group's logistics contact in Berlin, Ahmed Saleh al-Hamdani. Although Carlos introduced himself as "Salim," Filip immediately recognized the infamous terrorist. Shortly thereafter, al-Hamdani gave the StB informant a quick briefing on his new acquaintance: "Latin American, progressive, Marxist, revolutionary, lived in Iraq for a while, nowadays in the GDR." After they first met, Filip spent practically every day with Carlos and his right-hand man Johannes Weinrich during their three-week visit to Prague that August. Despite the language barrier, the StB informant still managed to report back details of Carlos's life and his views of the Arab world as well as the Soviet Bloc.[43]

StB agents employed in hotels across Prague were critical to the watch-and-wait phase. They regularly informed their handlers about suspicious foreigners arriving in Prague. During their frequent visits, the riverside Hotel Intercontinental near the Old Town area served as the group's home away from home as well as its business headquarters. During one of Carlos's sojourns there, a hotel informant observed that Carlos left his room only occasionally, clearly anxious about leaving it unattended. The StB also learned that the Carlos Group had its own security team monitoring the hotel for people who expressed "undue interest" in its boss.[44] Although the StB was keeping a low profile, a life on the run had taught the Carlos entourage whom to trust and when to remain vigilant.

StB surveillance allowed a glimpse into the mind of Carlos, and what it saw it did not like. Although Carlos came across as a "progressive individual in agreement with the politics of socialist states," it considered his liaisons with other terrorists and "Iraqi special services" a threat to Czechoslovakia's political interests.[45] Hence, in the spring of 1979, after it received guidance from the Ministry of the Interior and the Communist Party, the StB launched the second phase of its approach to Carlos and adopted measures aimed to block and prevent Carlos from entering Czechoslovakia.[46] By the end of the year, all aliases of Carlos and his closest associates were placed on the INO for a period of ten years.[47] A month later all Czech diplomatic missions abroad received a list of

ILLUSTRATION 13.3. Carlos in front of an advertisement for the movie *The Sting*, Prague, 1979. This photograph shows that even StB surveillance officers had a sense of humor. *ABS-SL 454*

persons—including Carlos, Weinrich, al-Issawi, and other known associates—who featured on the INO but were also thought likely to travel under multiple cover names.[48]

Shortly afterward, Prague effectively declared Carlos persona non grata, adding that "any further stays of Carlos in the CSSR have been banned by relevant Czechoslovak authorities."[49] We know the precise moment when Carlos realized he was not welcome. At 10:45 a.m. on September 7, 1979, he and his now wife, Magdalena Kopp, arrived at the Consular Department of the Czechoslovak embassy in Sofia to pick up their visas for yet another trip to Prague. Kopp was told she was "not allowed to visit CSSR." The couple was dumbfounded. After a feigned phone call to Prague, the consul told Carlos firmly that he also was denied entry into Czechoslovakia. The Venezuelan turned visibly nervous and, with "the corners of his mouth twitching," inquired about the reasons for this decision. When the consul told him this was outside his authority, the terrorist couple left to request visas from another Soviet Bloc state. Anxious about the reaction of these seasoned terrorists, exceptional security measures remained in place at the Czechoslovak embassy in Sofia until Carlos and Kopp left Bulgaria.[50]

At this stage, Prague also started using diplomatic channels to send a clear signal to Carlos and his associates from the Middle Eastern milieu that he was not welcome there. In August 1979, over a span of several days, Czech diplomats met the chargé d'affaires of the People's Democratic Republic of Yemen and the Iraqi ambassador, A. S. Qadir al-Hadithi.[51] During this meeting, the Czechoslovak diplomats openly stated that Carlos was preparing terrorist operations on Czechoslovak soil. Although the Iraqi ambassador first defended Carlos as a vigorous fighter for the Palestinian cause, he finally suggested that Prague simply oust Carlos if they did not want him on their territory. The Czechoslovak diplomats emphasized that this was only a friendly reminder that there could be "unwanted complications for the Iraqi Embassy" were Carlos, for instance, to use Iraqi diplomatic vehicles in one of his operations.[52]

## LIAISING AGAINST CARLOS

As Carlos was increasingly viewed as a threat, Prague liaised with partner services to find out more about his whereabouts and activities. Their meetings were also aimed at devising the best way to deal with the terrorists and coordinate security measures. Liaison was key to the first two phases of Prague's approach. Arguably, the Carlos Group was the pilot case for Central European cooperation as well as wider conversations on counterterrorism among Soviet Bloc allies.

In mid-1979 the communist allies started sharing assessments of the Carlos Group as well as their respective approaches to this dangerous organization. In July the Czechoslovak StB informed the East German Stasi that "a decision has been made not to grant CARLOS entry visa to the CSSR and appropriate measures were taken to this end." To help put this policy into practice, the StB asked the Stasi to share all information relevant to Carlos and his contacts and to inform it in the event the terrorist would plan to visit Czechoslovakia.[53] This was the start of an information exchange channel on Carlos—largely between the GDR, Hungary, and Czechoslovakia—that soon accelerated.

This was probably caused by Carlos's visibly increased sense of comfort on socialist territory. When, in August, he decided on Prague as a location to hold what was effectively a mini terrorist summit—bringing together over a dozen partners and accomplices—urgent calls were made between the concerned capitals. Information on associates traveling from East Berlin and Budapest poured into the StB headquarters via the newly established liaison channels.[54] As Carlos's partners were arriving in Prague, the Stasi urgently requested the first of what would become regular high-level liaison meetings.[55]

A day after the summit began, a Stasi delegation arrived in Prague. While its meeting with the StB's counterintelligence branch facilitated a detailed exchange of information, it also revealed major divergences in the approach of the two countries toward Carlos. The Czechoslovaks explained that soon after Carlos began visiting Prague in October 1978, he was denied access because Prague thought he "could be used to compromise one of the states of the socialist community." The Stasi offered a more benign view of Carlos and his group, emphasizing that he was not planning any "operations" against Czechoslovakia or other socialist countries, which the Stasi had verified through its contacts in the PLO.

But the Czechoslovak representatives were not convinced by the Stasi's optimism. They observed, "On the one hand, our friends from the GDR do not believe that CARLOS would undertake any operations against the CSSR. On the other hand, however, they admire his activities and the energy he had put into things, which are against our interests." Overall, much to the StB's surprise, the East German comrades insisted that Carlos "is not an enemy, but he could rather be considered a friend." Although the Stasi seemed to have accepted ruefully that Carlos would not be permitted a long-term stay in Czechoslovakia, it argued that "he could be granted short-term permits from time to time. This way, at least we will be informed about him and his group and can exchange information between ourselves—including the Hungarian Peoples' Republic, which is also closely concerned with this issue."[56]

Although the StB officers had left the meeting painfully conscious of the differences between them and the Stasi on Carlos, they agreed to continue in this cooperation because, despite strategic differences, East German tip-offs were tactically important for Prague. On numerous occasions, the Stasi informed the StB about developments related to the Carlos Group. For instance, in February 1980 the East Germans told their Czechoslovak counterparts that Johannes Weinrich had been detained at a Berlin airport as he had attempted to illegally import weapons and ammunition.[57]

In the summer of 1979 Prague established a similar operative liaison channel with the Hungarian state security service. Although until this point Hungary silently tolerated Carlos's stay on its territory, its government now shared the StB's circumspection about Carlos, and thereafter the two parties cooperated on "operational control" of his group and considered this arrangement mutually advantageous.[58] On the same page, Budapest shared important information with Prague about the group. Crucially, it highlighted the ideological discrepancies in Carlos's relationship to the East. While Carlos was perpetuating the myth that the Soviet Union and its partner states were his close allies, he was also being excessively critical, arguing that "socialist countries are lying to us and using us." This critique extended all the way to Moscow, which Carlos condemned for its invasion of Afghanistan. He also denounced the GDR and attributed the growing discontent with the regime in Poland to the weakness of the socialist system overall.[59]

The Hungarians also confirmed Prague's earlier suspicions about Carlos's alliance with Romania. Thanks to having access to Carlos's long-term residence in Budapest, the Hungarian state security service had unprecedented access to Carlos Group documents. These revealed that Bucharest had provided the terrorists with a hit list of Western-based dissidents who had annoyed the regime of Nicolae Ceaușescu to the point that it sought their liquidation. Carlos knew his price and was not afraid to claim it—allegedly asking the Romanian intelligence service to provide his team with passports from Western European states, weapons, and explosives as well as training on Romanian soil.[60] While digging through the group's documentation, the Hungarians also revealed links between the West German members of Carlos's enterprise—Magdalena Kopp and Johannes Weinrich—and Stasi collaborators. These were to help the group book hotels and flights and provide a special document that would enable Carlos's confidants to travel duty-free in and out of East Germany.[61]

Although Carlos reportedly felt good and safe in Hungary, at the start of the last decade of the Cold War the country's security services wanted him out. By late 1980 Hungarian security reported that its "operative monitoring" was now more focused on devising a strategy—synchronized with "friendly nations"—to curtail the activities of his group on the territory of socialist states and on how to push it out.[62] As the stakes for having the Carlos Group on its territory became too high for Hungary, it argued that the matter should be discussed and decided on by general secretaries of the national communist parties: "The Carlos Group is not an exclusively Hungarian problem but that of all friendly socialist states." Hence, in order to halt the group's activities, Budapest called for a joint approach that would lower the risk of retaliation to a minimum. Sworn to strict secrecy, both sides agreed to communicate all issues concerning Carlos "immediately and directly."[63]

Soon East Germany was also on board. By October 1980 Prague, East Berlin, and Budapest were on the same page with regard to their approach to Carlos. They recognized that his strategic and operational goals posed a potential political and national security risk to these socialist states. His alliances with his client states made him unpredictable, and his associations with numerous arms dealers and terrorists added to this toxicity. All three states agreed to keep the secretaries of their respective communist parties regularly informed about the Carlos organization. Putting an end to Carlos's operations in Central Europe was now their common goal.[64]

Yet the means of doing this were varied. Whereas Budapest and Prague sought to prevent the Carlos Group from entering their territories and to basically "push them off of their territory," the GDR's approach was less ostentatious. East Berlin wanted to maintain contacts with the group in order to stay informed, exert influence, and prevent undue influence by "antisocialist forces." Accordingly, it would continue to allow Carlos to either transit or plan short-term stays in East Germany as well as transport weapons that they would have reported to GDR authorities.[65] The approaches were different, but the objectives were the same.

In April 1981 this alliance shifted from words to actions. At a key meeting in Prague between Hungarian and Czechoslovak state security counterparts, two issues were given top priority: Carlos's growing partnership with Romania and specific measures to be taken against the Carlos Group. Romania, an increasingly eccentric and aggressive member of the Soviet Bloc, was now supplying the group with arms and passports, together with training. Reciprocating with enthusiasm and determined to prove its credentials, the group carried out an attack against Romanian dissidents in France and Germany using explosives. Moreover, on Romanian orders, Carlos conducted the aforementioned high-profile attack on Radio Free Europe. The Hungarian state security service claimed that the Radio Free Europe "success" had boosted the group's confidence and that they were now planning an attack on Egypt's president Anwar Sadat on Libya's orders.[66]

The authorities in Budapest were also increasingly alarmed by Carlos's unhinged behavior on their territory. In April 1981 at an opening of a casino for foreigners in Budapest, Carlos put his infamous wrath on full display. Attending the high-profile event with Johannes Weinrich and three other associates, he instigated a very public brawl, which had to be broken up by Hungarian state security service officers. Moreover, at around the same time, the group expressed interest in renting a tourist restaurant outside Budapest, intending to turn it into a training camp, complete with a shooting range. Carlos's increasingly eccentric behavior was disconcerting to Hungary, which was keen to keep his stay on their territory a secret.[67]

Deniability was, however, increasingly difficult to maintain. In the same year, West German authorities arrested a Swiss national, Georgio Bellini, alias "Roberto," of a Carlos-affiliated Swiss terrorist organization. Because this group cooperated closely with Carlos and took part in some of his operations, the Hungarians were concerned that his potential testimony "might throw an unfavorable light on the socialist countries," and hence "it is obvious that under these conditions Carlos's stay on the territory of the socialist countries is becoming dangerous." Emphasizing that there were now no disagreements among socialist countries regarding concrete and decisive counterterrorist measures, implying the GDR was also on board, the Hungarian Ministry of the Interior said it would proceed to permanently push the Carlos Group off its territory.[68]

ILLUSTRATION 13.4. Carlos (*right*) with his head of European operations, Kamal al-Issawi (*left*), at Prague Airport in the late 1970s, captured by an StB undercover camera. ABS-SL 454 MV

Crucially, by March 1981, the Stasi had also significantly altered its view of the Venezuelan terrorist. In the light of Carlos's recent behavior, East Berlin was now in favor of Hungary taking measures against the group. As a result, Carlos could no longer move freely on the territory of the GDR and was put under strict supervision. In fact, so eager were the East Germans to see Carlos leave Europe that they were reported to have discussed with their Cuban friends the possibility of relocating the group to a Latin American country to work with the liberation organizations of the region.[69]

The Hungarian authorities now decided that enough was enough. They took two weeks to solve "the problem of the Carlos Group" and then informed their Czechoslovak counterparts that they planned to summon Carlos to their offices and ask him and his group to leave Hungary, citing activities that ran counter to their policies. Moreover, it was to be made clear to him that his presence in any socialist country was undesirable. However, in an effort to prevent protest or perhaps even retaliation from Soviet allies such as Libya and Syria, which had links with the Carlos Group, Hungary ultimately opted for a milder solution than the one it had originally envisioned: while it told Carlos he was no longer allowed to reside on its territory, it allowed transit rights or short-term stays for him and his associates. The security officials were nervous about their impending mission, adding, "We do not know how Carlos will react to these measures. He is enjoying his stay in Hungary."[70] Ultimately, the plan worked. But it took another year for Carlos to finally close his base in Hungary and move to Romania.[71] By late 1982, these liaison channels—originally set up to deal with Carlos—were being deployed against a wide range of people on a shared terrorist list.[72]

Moscow did not seem to be engaged in Central European efforts to liaise against Carlos. Unlike with regard to the PLO, where Czechoslovakia clearly followed Moscow's lead in political as well as security policy toward Arafat's men, the Soviet Union did not seem to be regularly involved in decision-making about Carlos's future in Central Europe. While from the mid-1970s the Venezuelan clearly featured on all of the Soviets' major terrorist lists, there were no regular consultations or briefs suggesting a joint approach coming from Moscow.[73] Although occasionally it shared tactical information on the group's members who were intercepted entering Soviet territory, such news was rare.[74] According to Vladimír Nergl, a former StB officer who worked on the Carlos case, "the Soviets didn't want him there, so they [the Soviet Bloc] were tossing him around like a hot potato. . . . When we asked for advice on what to do with him, the Soviet advisers were nowhere to be found."[75]

While Moscow was not sharing or giving much guidance to the more junior Soviet Bloc services, the KGB did want to stay informed about Carlos's whereabouts and asked its Soviet Bloc allies to keep it up to date about "activities of extremist terrorist organizations, so that we can take these into consideration when it comes to our practical work."[76] KGB advisers stationed in capitals across the Soviet Bloc were also regularly informed about terrorist threats the national services were increasingly encountering.

Primarily due to the reputational hazard Carlos represented should his presence in the Soviet Bloc be exposed, the bilateral liaison channels gradually turned into a web of alliances aimed at pushing the Carlos Group out of communist territory altogether. This transformation was accelerated by connections between Carlos and countries such as Romania and Libya, whose own activities the bloc considered no less wild and dangerous during the 1980s. Indeed, the fact that Romania and Libya continued to work with Carlos seemed to denote them as a rogue axis.

## OUSTING CARLOS

By 1983 the StB thought the presence of the Carlos Group on Czechoslovak territory was history. It had been almost two years since one of its members arrived in Prague. Accordingly, in March 1983 the StB archived its operational file on Carlos set up to monitor his group.[77] This, however, proved to be premature. Throughout the first half of the 1980s, the group's members and associates continued to use Czechoslovakia for business.[78] Crucially, Kamal al-Issawi, Carlos's head of operations in Europe and also known as Abu Hakam, remained a serious problem for the StB in the early 1980s.[79]

In August 1985, despite the Stasi's warning to the StB, al-Issawi entered Czechoslovakia on a Yemeni diplomatic passport.[80] On the evening of August 19, 1985, the StB knocked on his hotel room door. After a brief search, the tall Palestinian with a thick mustache was taken away for questioning. Although clearly distressed by the StB's unexpected move, he eventually gave in and admitted to being a representative of the Carlos Group, lamenting that this association had recently caused him problems in Hungary and the GDR as well as capitalist countries. Conceding that Carlos's relations with these two countries were now under a strain, al-Issawi was now looking for a new safe harbor for the group. For this purpose he was eyeing Prague, where he was looking to rent or buy a house; purchase cars, arms, and blank travel documents, including diplomatic passports; and arrange permission for long-term stays for the Carlos Group on Czechoslovak territory.

The StB was stunned as the agitated Palestinian went on to present a case for the Carlos Group. Its primary aim, he resumed, was to use terrorist tactics against Zionism, imperialism, and reactionary Arab governments. In addition to terrorism, he also told the StB that the group specialized in the illegal arms trade. Although arms dealing was tricky between the East and the West, al-Issawi boasted that it had already managed to transport tons of military equipment. During a lengthy exchange, the StB made it abundantly clear to al-Issawi that his group's goals were in stark contrast with Prague's Marxist-Leninist ideology and that "our society considers terror an utterly foreign concept." Although the Palestinian pleaded that good relations with Czechoslovakia were important to his group, this was to no avail. Carlos's close associate was unequivocally told to leave Czechoslovakia as soon as possible. The next day he was escorted to the airport and put on a flight to Warsaw.[81] Immediately after his departure, al-Issawi was put on a permanent blocking list, with the instructions "Report arrival. Cancel visa. Do not let into the CSSR, even if carrying a diplomatic passport."[82] Prague was serious about keeping Carlos's associates out, and it wanted the border police to be on the same page.

Following al-Issawi's expulsion, the StB remained on high alert with regard to the Carlos Group. Fearing further visits of his accomplices or retaliation for Prague's newfound unequivocal stance toward the group, it kept the eyes and ears of its agentura wide open. For almost a year, it seemed that Carlos had heard Prague loud and clear—that he was not welcome on Czechoslovak territory.

On June 10, 1986, however, the StB's hopes were shattered when one Walid Wattar unexpectedly turned up in Prague with two associates—all traveling on

Syrian diplomatic passports and one of them heavily pregnant.[83] Although at first the trio raised no suspicions, a day after they entered Czechoslovak territory Hungarian authorities informed the Czechoslovak Ministry of the Interior that Wattar was none other than Carlos the Jackal. He had arrived in Prague with his pregnant wife, Magdalena Kopp, and his most loyal associate, Johannes Weinrich—with the alleged goal of Kopp giving birth in Prague. At the time, Czechoslovakia was known for its superior medical facilities. Carlos witnessed this firsthand years earlier when he chaperoned the Mogadishu hijacker Souhaila Andrawes during her five-month-long medical treatment in a Prague hospital.[84]

By day two of their visit, the StB finally caught up with the terrorists. Surprisingly, while Carlos was aware of Prague's hostile attitude, he did not attempt to stay out of the public eye. The trio took a casual late-night walk through Old Town, stopping by some of the city's landmarks, including the world-renowned astronomical clock, the Prague Orloj. If the terrorists felt relaxed during their visit to Prague, the StB officers assigned to monitor the terrorists were anything but. In fact, by this time the StB was on high alert. Upon learning of the terrorists' arrival, it deployed its newly established antiterrorist unit to protect the US embassy, alerted its agents discreetly placed in hotels and diplomatic missions, and put the group under physical and technical surveillance. Remarkably, it also ensured a pyrotechnician was on standby—acutely aware of Carlos's bad temper and proclivity to violence when put under pressure. The StB was anxiously tracking their moves until a political decision was made.[85]

By June 13, three days into their stay, key Czechoslovak powerbrokers gave the green light to oust the three terrorists. Prague could now graduate to its trick-and-oust approach. The trio's expulsion was to be achieved by a mixture of measures and interventions. In the morning Carlos was lured to the Hotel Intercontinental reception desk by a hotel employee, a trusted StB agent. While pretending to conduct a routine check of "Wattar's" passport, the agent noted that his visa would expire the next day. This set Carlos on a series of attempts to extend his visa, which included a rushed visit to the Ministry of Foreign Affairs. By noon, after a series of rejections, it was clear to the terrorists that none of the Czechoslovak authorities responsible for visas would extend his stay.[86]

While the terrorists were locked in their hotel room considering their next steps, the Czechoslovaks upped the ante. Earlier that morning, two high-ranking powerbrokers—the Czechoslovak deputy minister of the interior and the head of the Second Directorate—turned up at the door of the PLO Office in Prague. This was no courtesy call. They were there to officially ask the controversial Palestinian representative, Abu Hisham, to assist in pushing Carlos and the others out. Obliging, Abu Hisham was soon on the phone with the

Venezuelan terrorist, asking him to immediately leave Czechoslovak territory. Carlos was, however, in no mood to compromise. Ignoring the Palestinian representative's plea, he made a last-ditch attempt to secure the appropriate documentation. Agitated and armed, together with Weinrich, Carlos rushed to the Syrian embassy. After all, they all traveled on Syrian diplomatic passports, so how could Damascus refuse to help? Unbeknown to the terrorists, however, earlier in the day the Syrians had been discreetly asked by the Czechoslovak Ministry of Foreign Affairs not to extend the terrorists' visa.[87] Carlos was now pushed into a corner with the walls slowly closing in on him.

Shortly after noon, the empty-handed terrorists returned to the Intercontinental. Upon their arrival, Carlos and his associate hastily transferred the contents of their hotel safe deposit boxes into their briefcases—Weinrich visibly nervous, his hands shaking—settled their hotel bills, and retreated to their room.[88] The drama was, however, far from over. To contain Carlos's fury, which he displayed repeatedly throughout the day—including angrily telling hotel staff that, if necessary, "he will shoot first"—the StB sent two of its men to the terrorists' hotel room. Undercover, pretending to be Ministry of Foreign Affairs protocolists, the duo calmly explained that the foreigners' lives were in danger and that it would be best to leave Czechoslovakia immediately. Carlos flatly refused their diplomatic suggestion and broke into a frenzy—lecturing them about his ideological credentials, boasting about his powerful allies, accusing his closest circle of treachery, and the bewildered undercover officers of being sent there to provoke him. He was particularly furious about Abu Hisham's treacherous betrayal—vowing to liquidate him.[89]

With no sign of Carlos giving in to this concerted effort aimed at pushing him out, the relentless StB officers put into motion an old plan devised to trick him into leaving their territory. They informed the terrorists that "agents of the French special services" have been sent to liquidate them. This shifted the mood in the room, and soon afterward the terrorists agreed to leave the country. This was not a shot in the dark but a carefully curated scenario designed to play into Carlos's deepest fears. By 1986 he topped France's most wanted list. In fact, President François Mitterrand had told the head of his country's Directorate-General for External Security, "I authorize you to kill only Carlos and Abu Nidal."[90] The StB also knew that Carlos had previously gone underground when he was informed about a suspected French assassination attempt on his life on Syrian territory.[91] This time around, they were hoping he would do the same.

The StB's ruse ultimately worked. In a matter of minutes, the terrorists were ready to depart. Hopeful that its tale about French intelligence would work, the StB delayed a flight scheduled to leave for Moscow. The Czechoslovaks were eager to get the trio on that plane with a one-way ticket. They were, however, not ready to take chances and had an armed escort ready to facilitate Carlos's departure from Prague Airport. Soon, the terrorists packed their belongings and, before the eyes of the Czechoslovak officers, retrieved a new set of passports from a closed envelope and weapons for the journey—the five-months-pregnant Magdalena Kopp attaching a pistol belt to her maternity trousers. Entering the airport's transit zone via its staff entrance, three StB officers escorted Carlos and his associates to the runway and watched them board the plane for Moscow. By four thirty in the afternoon, the terrorists were safely in their seats, buckled up, and ready to leave the anxious Czechoslovak capital.[92]

At this point, Prague knew it had no other option but to push Carlos out. The eyes of the West were sharply looking at the Soviet Bloc's equivocal approach to terrorists. In mid-1984, the US deputy assistant secretary responsible for Eastern Europe and the Soviet Union, Mark Palmer, had summoned the ambassadors of key Soviet Bloc states. Without beating around the bush, he told them that Washington was aware that the likes of Carlos the Jackal were "protected" by these countries. They were not to expect any improvement in relations between the East and the United States unless such support was abandoned.[93] John Wiant, a former senior intelligence officer who served widely in the US intelligence community, remembered Palmer's meeting with the East Europeans: "Yes, Carlos had become both a focus on specific terrorism and a symbol of a possible nexus between him and the nihilistic terror groups in Germany." Washington was clearly worried not only about links between Soviet Bloc states and Cold War jackals but also alliances between various terrorist groups that enabled them to force multiply.[94]

Gradually other Western states began showing increased interest in tracking terrorists who passed or resided on Soviet Bloc territory. In November 1986, several months after Carlos's last visit to Prague, French intelligence interrogated one of his close allies, Sarkis, the veteran arms dealer, inquiring about how much the StB was aware of transits and meetings of Cold War jackals on Czechoslovak territory.[95] Czechoslovakia's reputation was on the line.

After his exceptionally tense June 1986 exit from Prague, Carlos never returned to Czechoslovakia. He spent the last decade of his life as a free man moving from one country to the other but with more and more former allies turning against him. Much like a hot potato—or a released grenade—Carlos was being tossed around. No state or leader wanted him on their territory.[96]

Remarkably, however, postcommunist Czechoslovakia was given a second chance to assist in his downfall. The StB's post-communist successor, the Office for Foreign Relations and Information of the Federal Ministry of the Interior, remained on high alert, monitoring developments linked to the group and keeping tabs on suspected accomplices in Czechoslovakia. Arguably, shortly after the fall of the Iron Curtain, the newly democratic country contributed to Carlos's identification and arrest by providing the StB's French counterparts, the DST, with surveillance photographs made by Czechoslovak services during his last stay in Prague. Arguably also, thanks to them, in 1994 DST officers, in collaboration with other Western intelligence services, finally caught up with Carlos in Sudan—and this time he did not slip away.[97]

In April 1994 French intelligence captured Carlos at a vulnerable moment in Khartoum, his last hideout. Soon he was put on trial for murdering French nationals. Jean-Louis Bruguière, a judge known for investigating Carlos's most vicious attacks committed in Paris, was tasked with the trial of the decade. He recalled receiving the phone call about Carlos's arrest: "It was a surprise. A very good surprise." Over the next several years, Bruguière interrogated Carlos fifty-five times. The Venezuelan tried to manipulate the judge during their extensive sessions, switching between aggression and flattery and trying to bond with him over Cuban cigars. Behind bars, however, Carlos's charm did not work. Bruguière built up his case based on thousands of documents from former Soviet Bloc countries, and in 1997 a French jury put Carlos the Jackal behind bars for life.[98]

# NOTES

1. Jiří Jíra (Náč.II.S/5), March 20, 1979, "INFORMACE o pobytu palestínských teroristů na území ČSSR," ABS-19324/1; "INFORMACE o pobytu palestínských teroristů na území ČSSR," n.d. 1979, ABS-19324/1; J. Jíra (Náč.II.S/5), August 17, 1979, "ZPRÁVA o jednání mezi delegacemi MStB NDR a II.Správy SNB v Praze uskutočněné ve dnech 16.–17.8.1979," ABS-19324/1.
2. Jíra, August 17, 1979, "ZPRÁVA o jednání mezi."
3. Bokr (rezidentúra Sofia, I.S), October 9, 1979, ABS-16987.
4. Follain, *Jackal*, 100.
5. The original sum was $20,000. "Weekly Situation Report on International Terrorism," September 7, 1976, National Archives and Records Administration, CREST: 25-Year Program Archive, https://www.cia.gov/readingroom/collection/crest-25-year-program-archive; Follain, *Jackal*, 162–63.
6. Follain, 13–14, 17–18.
7. Abu Sharīf and Mahnaimi, *Best of Enemies*, 69–72, 78–79, 89.
8. Follain, *Jackal*, xvii–xviii, 40–41; Smith, *Carlos*, 101–5.
9. Christopher Andrew, *The Defence of the Realm: The Authorized History of MI5* (London: Penguin, 2009), 617–18.
10. Follain, *Jackal*, 56–76.
11. Follain, 56–76.
12. Smith, *Carlos*; Abu Sharīf and Mahnaimi, *Best of Enemies*, 69–89; Follain, *Jackal*.
13. It also appears under various other names, including the Organization of Armed Struggle and the Arm of World Revolution.

14. Zdeněk Němec (Náč.XIV.S)–Ján Kováč (I.Nám.MV ČSSR), August 20, 1985, "Akce "CARLOS"–Informace," ABS-24113/4.
15. J. Jíra (Náč.II.S/5)–3-X.S, October 25, 1979, "Informace o činnosti arabských teroristů na území ČSSR—zaslání," ABS-19324/1.
16. Náč. OMS–Karel Vrba (Náč.II.S), March 4, 1980, "Skupina kolem CARLOSE–informace z NDR," ABS-19324/1; J. Jíra (Náč.II.S/5)–X.S/3, October 25, 1979, "Informace o činnosti arabských teroristů na uzemí CSSR-zaslání," ABS-19324/1.
17. J. Jíra (Náč.II.S/5), May 8, 1980, "INFORMACE—styky ministerstva vnitra JLDR s teroristickou skupinou 'RUCE SVETOVÉ REVOLUCE,'" ABS-19324/1.
18. On one occasion, StB surveillance also saw them in a Syrian diplomatic vehicle. Jaroslav Hrbáček (Náč.II.S), August 8, 1979, "INFORMACE o pobytu palestínských teroristů na území CSSR," ABS-16987; "INFORMACE o činnosti arabských teroristů v CSSR," n.d., ABS-16987; J. Jíra (Náč.II.S/5), March 20, 1979, "INFORMACE o pobytu palestínských teroristů na území ČSSR," ABS-19324/I.
19. Informant Filip, August 29, 1979, "Arabští teroristé-poznatky k pobytu v ČSSR, styky a politické názory," ABS-19324/1.
20. J. Jíra (Náč.II.S/5), August 17, 1979, "ZPRÁVA o jednání mezi delegacemi MStB NDR a II.Správy SNB v Praze uskutočněné ve dnech 16.8.–17.8.1979," ABS-19324/1.
21. V. Sýkora (II.S/5), November 28, 1978, "ZÁZNAM—o pobytu arabských teroristů v Praze," ABS16987/1
22. Follain, *Jackal*, 110–11.
23. "Hanseatisches Oberlandesgericht Urteil im Names des Forlkes in der Strafsache Gegen Souhaila Sami Andrawes Sayeh," November 27, 1996, private source, 9. For further information on the Landshut crisis, see Blumenau, *United Nations and Terrorism*, 74–86; and T. Geiger, "'Landshut' in Mogadischu," 413–56.
24. J. Jíra (Náč.II.S/5), March 20, 1979, "INFORMACE o pobytu palestínských teroristů na území CSSR," ABS-19324/1.
25. Informant Martin—II.S/5, November 27, 1978, "Podezření z pobytu arabských teroristů v CSSR–informace," ABS-16987; J. Jíra (Náč.II.S/5), March 20, 1979, "INFORMACE o pobytu palestínských teroristů na území CSSR," ABS-19324/1; Informant Oskar–II.S/5, November 27, 1978, "Príslušníci teroristické organizace-poznatky," ABS-16987; J. Hrbáček (Náč.II.S)–II.S/5, January 11, 1979, "INFORMACE o pobytu arabských teroristů v CSSR," ABS-16987.
26. Ivan Stubna (Náč.II.S/5), May 6, 1979, "ZÁZNAM o provedeném zpravodajském pohovoru," ABS-16987.
27. Sládečko (XVI.S), October 10, 1985, "Vyhodnocení materiálů RUCE SVĚTOVÉ REVOLUCE postoupených 6. odborem II.S SNB v září 1985," ABS-38160/4. At the time of writing, Andrawes lives in Oslo, Norway, with her family.
28. "Akce BAK-sledování," August 22, 1979, ABS-SL 454 MV.
29. Václav Subrt (Náč. X.S/3), August 24, 1979, "Záznam," ABS-19324/1.
30. Náč. OMS MV ČSSR–K. Vrba (Náč.II.S), March 10, 1980, "Mezinárodní teroristická organizace-sdělení," ABS-19324/1.
31. Miroslav Mikyska (Náč.XI/2)–(II.S/6), January 14, 1986, "Věc: Informace k osobě SARKIS FAREED SARKIS, nar. 28.12.1939," ABS-38160/4.
32. Mikyska.
33. Lauren Harper, "The Merchant of Death's Account Book," National Security Archive, February 23, 2015, https://nsarchive2.gwu.edu/NSAEBB/NSAEBB502/;

Michael Gillard, "Sarkis Soghanalian Obituary: World's Largest Private Arms Dealer for More Than Two Decades," *Guardian*, November 14, 2011, https://www.theguardian.com/world/2011/nov/14/sarkis-soghanalian-obituary.

34. József Varga (Ministerstvo vnitra III/II. Náč. 8. odboru), October 9, 1980, "Věc: 'C-79' kr. jméno případu. Vyhodnocení," ABS-38160/4. This report was sent to the StB by its Hungarian counterpart in charge of monitoring the Carlos Group. See more on the Hungarian approach to international terrorism in Balázs Orbán-Schwarzkopf, "Hungarian State Security and International Terrorism in the 1980s," in Hänni, Riegler, and Gasztold, *Terrorism in the Cold War*, vol. 1, 123–42.
35. Varga, October 9, 1980, "Věc."
36. Varga.
37. Varga.
38. Varga.
39. II.S, March 28, 1979, "Informace o pobytu palestínských teroristů na území ČSSR," ABS-16987.
40. "Akce BAK-sledování," August 24, 1979, ABS-SL 454 MV.
41. J. Jíra (Náč.II.S/5), March 20, 1979, "INFORMACE o pobytu palestínských teroristů na území ČSSR," ABS-19324/1.
42. J. Jíra (Náč.II.S/5), August 17, 1979, "ZPRÁVA o jednání mezi delegacemi MStB NDR a II.Správy SNB v Praze uskutočněné ve dnech 16.8.-17.8.1979," ABS-19324/1.
43. Informant Filip, August 29, 1979, "Arabští teroristé-poznatky k pobytu v ČSSR, styky a politické názory," ABS-19324/1.
44. "FAVAZ Ahmed-zpráva do akce BAK," August 24, 1979, ABS-16987.
45. "INFORMACE o činnosti arabských teroristů v ČSSR," n.d., ABS-16987.
46. J. Jíra (Náč.II.S/5), March 20, 1979, "INFORMACE o pobytu palestínských teroristů na území ČSSR," ABS-19324/1.
47. J. Jíra, May 3, 1979, "Návrh na zařazení do INO," ABS-19324/9; J. Jíra (Náč. II.S/5)—2/S[práva] p[asů a] v[íz]-SNB, August 21, 1979, "Návrh na zařazení do INO," ABS-19324/9.
48. J. Jíra, n.d., "Záznam," ABS-19324/1.
49. II.S., n.d. 1980, "INFORMACE o činnosti arabských teroristů v ČSSR," ABS-19324/1.
50. "Sofie," September 7, 1979, ABS-16987.
51. "Střetnutí mezi představiteli Ministerstva zahraničných věci ČSSR a chargé d'affairem JLDR s. A.Y.Mansour," August 10, 1979, ABS-16987; J. Jíra (Náč.II.S.5), August 10, 1979, "INFORMACE k pobytu člena arabské teroristické organizace v ČSSR," ABS-16987.
52. "Střetnutí mezi představiteli Ministerstva zahraničných věci ČSSR a velvyslancem Irácké republiky A.A.Kadir Al Hadithi," August 10, 1979, ABS-16987.
53. J. Hrbáček (Náč.II.S)—OMS MV ČSSR, July 27, 1979, "ADIL FAWAZ AHMED-dožádání pro přátelé z MfS," ABS-16987/1.
54. This liaison was carried out via the International Relations Department of the Ministry of the Interior, which would then pass information to the Second Directorate.
55. Josef Vlček (Zástupce náčelníka sekretariátu FMV)–J. Hrbáček (Náč.II.S), August 6, 1979, "CARLOS"—dožádaní z NDR, 16987/1; J. Jíra (Náč.II.S.5), August 8, 1979, "Informace," ABS-16987/1.
56. J. Jíra (Náč.II.S/5), August 17, 1979, "ZPRÁVA o jednání mezi delegacemi MStB NDR a II.Správy SNB v Praze uskutočněné ve dnech 16.–17.8.1979," ABS-19324/1.

57. V. Sýkora (II.S/5), February 19, 1980, "Záznam do akce BAK, č.sv.16987," ABS-19324/1.
58. Emil Hradecký (Náč. OMS MV ČSSR)–KarelVrba (Náč.II.S), September 8, 1980, "Mezinárodní teroristická organizace-sdělení," ABS-19324/1.
59. Varga, October 9, 1980, "Věc."
60. Varga.
61. Varga.
62. E. Hradecký (Náč. OMS MV ČSSR)–K.Vrba (Náč.II.S), September 8, 1980, "Mezinárodní teroristická organizace-sdělení," ABS-19324/1.
63. Hradecký.
64. Varga, October 9, 1980, "Věc."
65. Varga.
66. Milan Solnický (Zást.Náč.II.S/6), April 25, 1981, "Mezinárodní terorizmus zápis z porady s představitelem MV MLR s. plk. Wargou," ABS-19324/1.
67. Sládečko (XVI.S), October 10, 1985, "Vyhodnocení materiálů RUCE SVĚTOVÉ REVOLUCE postoupených 6.odborem II.S SNB v září 1985," ABS-38160/4.
68. Sládečko.
69. Sládečko.
70. Sládečko.
71. E. Hradecký (Náč. OMS MV ČSSR)–K. Vrba (Náč.II.S), May 19, 1981, "CARLOS—sdělení MV MLR," ABS-19324/1.
72. E. Hradecký (Náč. OMS MV ČSSR)–Z. Němec (Náč. XIV.S), August 5, 1982, "Akce "CARLOS"—návrh na schůzku s orgány MStB NDR," ABS-24113/4.
73. Jean-Louis Bruguière, interview by the author, June 2, 2016.
74. E. Hradecký (Náč. OMS MV ČSSR)–K. Vrba (Náč.II.S), January 5, 1982, ABS-HFSB, a.č. H-720/7.
75. Vladimír Nergl, interview by the author, January 9, 2018.
76. K. Vrba (Náč.II.S), February 20, 1980, ABS-16987/1.
77. J. Bouma (Náč.II.S/5), March 28, 1983, "Návrh na uložení spisu PO 'BAK' sv.č.16987," ABS-16987.
78. Informant Martin, March 11, 1982, ABS-19324/1; "Příjezd a odjezd osoby, který je na SPV SNB veden v seznamu teroristů," July 30, 1984, ABS-24113/4; Milan Beluský, May 16, 1985, ABS-24113/4.
79. Zdeněk Peterka (Náč.I.S/17)—Kancelář Náč. II.S, May 24, 1982, "Informace k teroristovi CARLOSovi," ABS-19324/1.
80. II.S/6, August 16, 1985, "Záznam ze součinnostní porady do akce 'CARLOS,'" ABS-24113/4.
81. Vladimír Nergl (Náč.II.S/6), August 20, 1985, "ZÁZNAM o provedení ZTÚ ANALÝZA v akci CARLOS čís.sv.24613," ABS-24113/4; Němec (Náč.XIV.S)–Ján Kováč (Zást. Ministra vnitra ČSSR), August 20, 1985, ABS-24113/4; V. Nergl, August 21, 1985, "Záznam o opatření v akci CARLOS čís.sv.24613," ABS-24113/4; Němec–Odbor pro mezinárodní styky kanceláře MV ČSSR, August 20, 1985, "OBADI AHMED Saleh—informace pro přátele MV PLR," ABS-24113/4.
82. Vítězslav Kába (Zást. Náč. XIV.S), August 19, 1985, "Žádost o blokaci," ABS-24113/4.; Sládečko (XIV.S), August 22, 1985, "Akce 'CARLOS'—záznam," ABS-24113/4.
83. V. Nergl–IV.S/5, June 12, 1986, "Akce 'TURISTA'—žádost o agenturní obsazení v hotelu," ABS-24113/4; J. Jíra (Náč.II.S/5), June 16, 1986, "Stanovisko k informaci ze dne 16.6.1986 č.j. N/V-603/86," ABS-24113/4.

84. Nergl, interview by the author, January 9, 2018.
85. K. Fiřt (Náč.II.S)–OMV Kancelář MV ČSSR, July 7, 1986, "CARLOS informace pro přátele z MV MLR," ABS-24113/4; IV.S, June 18, 1986, "SVODKA SLEDOVÁNÍ objekta TURISTA + 2 společníci," ABS-24113/4; K. Fiřt (Náč.II.S), June 17, 1986, "Informace," ABS-38160/4.
86. Karel Veverka (1.odd. 5 odbor), June 17, 1986, "Agent MÁLEK: WATTAR Walid, sýr. st. prísl.—zpráva do akcie CARLOS," ABS-38160/4.
87. Veverka; K. Fiřt (Náč.II.S), June 17, 1986, "Informace," ABS-38160/4.
88. Fiřt, June 17, 1986, "Informace"; IV.S, June 18, 1986, "SVODKA SLEDOVÁNÍ objekta TURISTA + 2 společníci," ABS-24113/4.
89. Fiřt, June 17, 1986, "Informace."
90. Fiřt; Follain, *Jackal*, 158, 163.
91. "Věc: Poznatky ke skupině CARLOS a ABU NIDAL—předání," January 23, 1984, ABS-38160/4.
92. Fiřt, June 17, 1986, "Informace"; M. Pitra a V.Wallis (II.S), June 16, 1986, "Záznam z kontaktu vízových cizinců ve věci příjezdu vedoucího teroristické organizace 'Ruce světové revoluce'—Carlos," ABS-38160/4.
93. Follain, *Jackal*, 182–83.
94. Jon Wiant, interview by the author, February 24, 2017.
95. Karel Sochor (Náč.I.S)–K. Fiřt (Náč.II.S), November 13, 1986, "Věc: K zájmu francouzských bezpečnostních složek o problematiku terorismu v návaznosti na ČSSR," ABS-38160/4.
96. Follain, *Jackal*, 195–215.
97. Peter P., interview by the author, September 4, 2015.
98. Jean-Louis Bruguière, interview by the author, September 22, 2022.

# 14

# Abu Nidal, the "Apostle of Palestinian Violence"

Abu Nidal was the founder of the Cold War's most far-ranging and lethal Palestinian terrorist organization. Although he kept a much lower public profile than the boisterous Carlos the Jackal, during the 1970s and 1980s the Abu Nidal Organization (ANO), also known as Fatah–Revolutionary Council, reportedly carried out hundreds of murders. Although Carlos's boutique terrorist franchise did indeed murder dozens of innocents, Abu Nidal killed on an unprecedented scale. He deployed his wrath at citizens of so-called imperialist and Zionist nations—most notably Americans, Europeans, and Israelis—but he also turned against Palestinian and Arab moderates. External enemies died in spectacular terrorist incidents staged across twenty countries.[1] Members of his own organization whom he suspected of treachery were tortured, shot, and buried, often in mass graves.

In terms of his personality and image, he was also no Ilich Ramírez Sánchez. Unlike the flamboyant and combustible Venezuelan fashionista with a penchant for luxury goods, women, alcohol, and the occasional gamble, Abu Nidal preferred a more ascetic lifestyle. Of nondescript appearance and deteriorating health, the Palestinian usually sported shabby zip-up jackets and old trousers. In everyday life, he reportedly shied away from the obvious luxuries and vices—apart from developing a nasty whiskey-drinking habit at a later age, which fueled his paranoia, fear, and fury. During the height of his terrorist career and his more sober days, Abu Nidal earned the reputation of a hardworking, clear-thinking, disciplined operator capable of building not only a prolific secretive terrorist franchise but also a business empire that turned him into one of the wealthiest of the Cold War jackals.[2]

Running a terrorist venture for over two decades, Abu Nidal became the most lethal of Middle Eastern terrorists. According to some estimates, his attacks and retributions resulted in nine hundred deaths.[3] Unsurprisingly, then, prominent watchers and hunters of Cold War jackals considered him the most wicked terrorist of the 1980s. His biographer Patrick Seale dubbed Abu Nidal "the apostle of Palestinian violence."[4] Jean-Louis Bruguière, who investigated numerous Abu Nidal cases, found him to be much more dangerous than

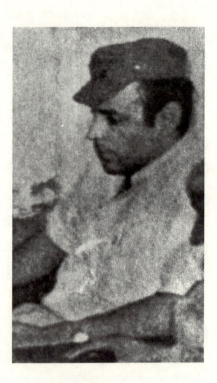

**ILLUSTRATION 14.1.** A rare photo of Abu Nidal released by the Israel Defense Forces in 1976. ČTK / AP / Israeli Army

Carlos the Jackal—the man Bruguière helped put behind bars.[5] Oliver North, a Reagan-era National Security Council staffer who dealt with counterterrorism and is best known for his role in the Iran-Contra affair, famously testified that "Abu Nidal makes the infamous terrorist Carlos look like a Boy Scout."[6]

## FROM RADICAL TO TERRORIST

Abu Nidal was born in 1937 as Sabri al-Banna in Jaffa, an ancient Arab port on the Mediterranean in Mandatory Palestine. He was the son of a wealthy orange grove owner and his second wife, a Syrian Alawite, who first met her husband as a sixteen-year-old servant in his second home in the Syrian coastal mountains. Although coming of age with eleven half-siblings was no easy upbringing, the first years of al-Banna's life were spent in the comfort of a middle-class home. His world was, however, turned upside down by two pivotal events: the loss of his father at a young age followed by the expulsion of his mother from the paternal home and the 1948 war between the Jews and Arabs of Palestine, which resulted in the establishment of the State of Israel and the forced expulsion of hundreds of thousands of Palestinians.[7] After having the family fortune confiscated by Israeli forces and spending close to a year living in a tent among other

Palestinian refugees in Gaza, al-Banna's family relocated to the city of Nablus in the West Bank, then under Jordanian rule.[8]

Amid this personal and geopolitical turmoil, the young al-Banna soon dropped out of school. The next years of his life spent under Jordanian rule were marked by poverty and a series of short-term blue-collar jobs but also attempts to catch up on his education. Although he never succeeded in acquiring further formal schooling, it was at this time that the young Palestinian first came across pamphlets of the semiunderground Jordanian Ba'ath Party, which, at the time, called for a greater voice for the Palestinians living in Jordan. By the age of eighteen, al-Banna became a full member of the political party. His radical political schooling had begun.[9]

His stint with the Ba'athists was short-lived. He parted with them in the mid-1950s as the party was plunging into political turmoil, and soon after he moved to Riyadh, Saudi Arabia, in search of a better life. This brief encounter with radical Middle Eastern politics, however, left an indelible mark on the young man's political consciousness—so much so that by the end of the decade he had set up a small faction of his own, pompously called the Palestinian Secret Organization, aimed at liberating Palestine via armed struggle. This was indeed a fertile era for Palestinian resistance, with myriad groups springing up across the Middle East, most famously Fatah, which Yasser Arafat set up in Kuwait in the late 1950s.[10]

Until the age of thirty, al-Banna went about his life running his electrician's shop in Riyadh by day and dreaming of Palestinian armed struggle by night. In June 1967 his life took a turn. Israel's preemptive blitz against its Arab neighbors resulted in an unprecedented expansion of the majority-Jewish state. Within six days, Prime Minister Levi Eshkol ruled over what was formerly Egypt's Sinai Peninsula and Gaza Strip, Syria's Golan Heights, and Jordan's West Bank and East Jerusalem. The humiliating Arab defeat was a wake-up call for those Palestinians who had hoped these powerful states would help them win their homeland back. Disillusioned and angry, many joined the armed struggle for the liberation of Palestine.[11]

Al-Banna was one of them. After being expelled from Saudi Arabia for political agitation, he moved with his four-member family to the then mecca of Palestinian resistance—Amman, Jordan. Soon he was running a business that effectively served as a contact point and front company for Arafat's increasingly popular Fatah. Becoming "the bureaucrat of armed struggle" gained him some powerful friends, among them the head of Fatah's intelligence branch, one Abu Iyad, as well as Abu Daoud, who became infamous for his engagement in the Black September enterprise.[12]

By 1969 al-Banna had adopted the nom de guerre Abu Nidal, meaning "Father of the Struggle," and started officially working for Fatah. He did not get down into the trenches with the other guerrillas but became one of the group's diplomats. Following a brief inaugural mission to Sudan, beginning in 1970 Abu Nidal was Fatah's envoy at a key post—Baghdad.[13] He was sent there as the PLO was sensing an impending showdown with King Hussein of Jordan, who was running out of patience with the unruly guerrillas staging attacks on Israel from his territory. Abu Nidal's job was to lobby on Fatah's behalf to ensure Iraqi support for the guerrillas in the event of a clash with Jordanian forces. When the confrontation ultimately came, however, Baghdad stood by King Hussein's side, watching him win a civil war that led to the humiliating expulsion of PLO fighters from the Hashemite Kingdom.[14]

It was at this time that Abu Nidal started parting with Fatah. Shortly after the civil war, he publicly scolded Arafat's men for agreeing to a cease-fire with the king and accused them of being cowards. Simultaneously, he began to part with his friend and mentor Abu Iyad, attributing much of the defeat to him. For some, it was clear that Abu Nidal had gone native, echoing Baghdad's criticism of the Palestinian movement and betraying its cause. For now, however, Fatah refrained from expelling him from the movement. It was better to keep the radicals in and not further provoke the Iraqis at a time when Fatah was at its most vulnerable.[15]

While Abu Nidal was allowed to go about his official duties as the Fatah envoy in Baghdad, he became further radicalized. In the early 1970s, when many of Arafat's men went rogue and carried out vicious terrorist attacks under the Black September banner, Abu Nidal was captivated by the methods they adopted. He was, however, not allowed to participate in these delicate and highly secretive operations. According to Seale, the increasingly temperamental and drink-prone bureaucrat resented being left out of what seemed to him as the ultimate form of armed struggle. It was at this time that he started plotting a revolt against Arafat and treading his own path to terrorism.[16]

Abu Nidal staged his inaugural terrorist attack while still serving as Fatah's envoy in Iraq. The pretext for his entry into the terrorist world was a death sentence imposed by Jordan on his longtime friend and fellow Fatah radical Abu Daoud. In the summer of 1973, the tall, battle-hardened Abu Daoud attempted to overthrow King Hussein, but his network was arrested before any shots were fired. This prompted Abu Nidal to act. On September 5, 1973, five Palestinians took over the Saudi embassy in Paris, taking thirteen people hostage and threatening to blow up the building unless Abu Daoud and his coconspirators were released from jail. Soon, the assailants boarded a plane with hostages and proceeded to zigzag between various Middle Eastern capitals hoping to get their demands met. After three days spent in the air or on airport runways, they finally surrendered to Kuwaiti authorities.[17]

Fatah's 1974 decision to pivot from armed struggle to diplomacy sealed Abu Nidal's divorce from the faction. As we know, Arafat's announcement of this shift had a profound impact on the PLO, splitting the already volatile organization into numerous factions. This was also the very moment Abu Nidal decided to fly solo. An ardent supporter of armed struggle, he refused to follow Arafat's direction and continued to build his new terrorist enterprise, which would vehemently reject the trajectory chosen by Fatah. Unlike the other Rejectionist factions—George Habash's PFLP in particular—Abu Nidal's splinter group never sought a real political alternative. To him, armed struggle was the main way of achieving the ultimate political goal—freedom for Palestine. Accordingly, the ANO's bread and butter was to be violence and terror. For this treachery, Fatah allegedly gave Abu Nidal a death sentence in absentia. However, it never carried the brutal punishment out so as not to invite the wrath of his state sponsors.[18]

In its embryonic phase, the ANO was sponsored by President Ahmed Hassan al-Bakr's Iraq, which also harbored disdain for Arafat. In fact, Baghdad diverted all the support and funds it previously gave to Fatah to Abu Nidal's new venture. Thanks to this, the ANO inherited a training camp west of the capital, a farm dedicated to growing food for the organization's members, a vast cache of passports, foreign scholarships, a monthly stipend amounting to today's equivalent of $1,100,000 per month,[19] and Chinese weapons allegedly worth $105 million today,[20] as well as means of propaganda—a radio station and a newspaper. He also managed to make friends in the Iraqi intelligence and security apparatus and thus enjoyed their protection. Most important, Abu Nidal became the gatekeeper for all things Palestinian in Iraq. All matters pertinent to the cause had to go through him.[21] As far as setting up organizations goes, Abu Nidal could not have hoped for more. From the very beginning he had it all—political backing, the infrastructure to pursue and promote his cause, and security.

All he needed next were capable and, above all, loyal members. Abu Nidal's defiance of Arafat won him popularity among many Fatah members who thought the kaffiyeh-wearing PLO leader's turn to diplomacy was an act of treachery. The organization recruited from the most vulnerable: refugee camp–bound Palestinians, Lebanese youngsters who came of age during the civil war, and Palestinian students based abroad.[22] Abu Nidal was particularly interested in recruiting young, ambitious men looking to do their bit for the Palestinian cause. In return, he promised them money, education, the thrill of a career in a clandestine organization, and support for their often poverty-stricken families.[23] According to rough estimates, by 1986 the ANO franchise had three hundred members. In the coming years, the number was to almost double.[24]

In many ways, the ANO was run like an intelligence service. At the recruitment phase, the prospective members were made to write their autobiography, including a detailed account of their family, friendships, and romantic relations. Much like in totalitarian security organizations, this document was to serve as the backbone of each cadet's file against which all future information could be compared. Strict compartmentalization and information control was enforced, and members were known to each other only by code names. They were first tested by being given small jobs, such as surveillance of members of rival organizations. The more loyal and capable they seemed, the more responsibility they were given.[25]

In important ways, however, the organization resembled less a spy agency and more a cult. Members were subjected to systematic indoctrination—lectures on the virtues of the ANO, on the importance of armed struggle for Palestinian liberation, and the evils of the PLO and its leaders. Indoctrinated members had to give up all common "vices"—alcohol, drugs, cigarettes, women—and sign up for an ascetic lifestyle. Public "self-criticism sessions" were a commonplace way to make members confess to breaking or bending ANO rules. If any such events occurred, the offenders would suggest their own punishment. In an ultimate show of loyalty toward to the organization, new members were forced to sign their own death warrant in the event they were eventually found to have undue political or intelligence connections. Those designated as traitors would be caught, interrogated, tortured, and eventually killed.[26]

Abu Nidal's penchant for violence also came through via his prolific terrorist campaigns. From the early days of his terrorist franchise, he carried out high-profile attacks across continents—in places as far and wide as Italy, France, Austria, Greece, Turkey, Romania, Thailand, India, Pakistan, Kuwait, Lebanon, and Sudan. His disciples opted for varied demonstrations of violence, which included killing sprees at airports, hotels, synagogues, and Jewish-owned coffee shops and restaurants, most famously the 1982 attack on the Chez Jo Goldenberg restaurant in Paris, which resulted in the death of six and many more injured. He also staged dozens of assassinations typically aimed at American, British, Palestinian, Saudi, or Israeli envoys, most notably the attempt to murder Israel's ambassador to London, Shlomo Argov, which formed the pretext for the 1982 Israeli invasion of Lebanon. His group also staged several high-profile hijackings of boats and airplanes, the best-known being the November 1985 hijacking of an Egyptian airliner to Malta, which resulted in the death of dozens.[27]

Toward the end of the 1970s, Abu Nidal's terrorist empire faced a number of challenges. With the death of Iraqi president al-Bakr, his principal backer, Abu Nidal lost his staunchest supporter. Although the ambitious new leader, Saddam Hussein, did not part ways with Abu Nidal immediately and, in fact, used his outfit as a proxy during the early years of the protracted Iran-Iraq War, their bond was not the same. At around the same time, Abu Nidal's organization suffered a split, and, to top it off, his health grew increasingly frail after a heart attack. As a result, he became more reclusive and paranoid. The organization ceased most of its activities.[28]

Remarkably, however, the ANO reemerged in the early 1980s. Abu Nidal found a new, albeit much more controlling and less generous sponsor in Syria. Hafez al-Assad, who allegedly blessed the union between his intelligence service and the terrorist group, was keen to deploy the ANO against the Muslim Brotherhood—fierce challengers of his authoritarian rule. Soon the parties made their alliance official and set up a joint committee designed to coordinate their information gathering and exchange.[29] While under Assad's protective shield, the ANO also began venturing out to Central Europe.

There were various reasons for why Nidalists were attracted to the Soviet Bloc. As opposed to Middle Eastern states, the region was viewed as a secure place of residence. It also represented a good base for trading arms, and, according to Seale, by being in Central Europe Nidalists could challenge the PLO, which had created close relations with many Soviet Bloc states during the 1970s.[30] For some years, Abu Nidal and his family settled down in Poland. He also set up a company there as well as in the GDR.[31] While initially Czechoslovakia did not feature prominently on the list of destinations of ANO members, in the last years of the Cold War Abu Nidal's key lieutenants turned their gaze toward Prague.

## TRACKING THE THREAT

Throughout the 1980s, the Czechoslovak government considered Abu Nidal its top international terrorist challenge. His organization first appeared on the StB's radar in 1978, when Abu Nidal put his commitment to murdering moderate Palestinians on full display by killing three key Fatah envoys in the West. As host to a sizable Palestinian population, the Czechoslovak government became disconcerted. Furthermore, Prague's domestic security apparatus also worried about the terrorist organization's increasing efforts to recruit Palestinian students on its territory. The StB feared that if more students signed up for membership in this aggressive organization, inter-Palestinian violence and even assassinations might spill over onto Czechoslovak territory.[32]

Accordingly, in the late 1970s the StB turned to the then head of the PLO Office in Prague, Atif Abu Bakr, who—they hoped—would have the best overview of Abu Nidal's terrorist plans because Abu Bakr's mother faction, Fatah, was the ANO's number-one enemy. While the Palestinian envoy promised to keep the security officers informed about potential visits of ANO members to Czechoslovakia, there was something off about his behavior.[33] Soon the StB's hunch was confirmed when it began receiving intelligence from its sources in the PLO Office suggesting that Atif Abu Bakr was, in fact, an ANO supporter. A key source argued that he "sympathizes with the activities of Palestinian extremists ABU DAUD and ABU NIDAL." These reports were supported by Abu Bakr's open criticism of his own boss, Yasser Arafat, and his subscription to the *Palestinian Revolution*, the ANO's weekly newspaper, delivered directly to the PLO Office. This was the first time the StB realized that Arafat's envoy in Prague could be playing a double game and nurturing a secret affinity toward more extremist Palestinian factions. They asked their agentura in the PLO Office to keep him under close watch.[34]

While doing so, they looked elsewhere for more reliable information. One of their go-to agents was Beshara Traboulsi, the longtime Fatah security envoy at the PLO Office. His reports signaled what Prague feared most—a potential spillover of inter-Palestinian violence onto Czechoslovak territory. By 1983 Abu Nidal had shifted his allegiance from Baghdad to Damascus. In the context of the recent PLO-Syrian rift, this was not good news for the PLO. In fact, Traboulsi rang the alarm bells multiple times, requesting better protection. He worried that Nidalists living in Czechoslovakia might be used by the Syrians to carry out attacks against his mission. Although the StB knew that warnings by the PLO Office were often disingenuous and, at times, designed to direct the StB against the office's opponents, hearing the name "Abu Nidal" made the StB sit up and take notice. Accordingly, these threats were further investigated, passed up to the minister of the interior, and the PLO mission was provided with enhanced protection.[35]

To better understand the extent of the ANO's operations in Central Europe, the StB liaised with partners services. Having cut their counterterrorism liaison teeth on the Carlos Group, Soviet Bloc states were now regularly exchanging updates and threat assessments on ANO members. Some of the partner reporting echoed worries of the PLO Office in Prague. In February 1983 the StB received news of an ANO commando unit arriving in Prague, its twenty-five members supposedly tasked with assassinating Arafat during his upcoming visit to Czechoslovakia. The StB's domestic counterterrorism departments launched a frantic search for the alleged assailants, compiling lists of Arab nationals who had recently entered the country, liaising with the border police, searching suspected safe houses, and requesting further information from partner services.[36] Although they found no further indication that the threat was real, it signaled more of what was to come.

Partner services continued to warn the StB of potential outbreaks of inter-Palestinian violence on their territory. In 1985, shortly after Arafat signed the controversial Amman Accord with King Hussein, Prague received further worrying news. The StB's Bulgarian counterparts suggested that the new head of the PLO Office in Prague, Abu Hisham, was Abu Nidal's next target.[37] If this were true, Abu Hisham could join a growing list of PLO representatives who were eventually killed by Abu Nidal affiliates across, mostly, Western Europe.

Abu Nidal famously detested Arafat's Fatah faction and envoys, allegedly once noting, "The PLO? A bunch of traitors penetrated by a few patriots."[38] Due to his long-term association with Fatah's security enterprise, Abu Hisham would have been the perfect target for sending a signal to Arafat as well as undermining Fatah's security capability in Central Europe.

When this threat also failed to materialize, the StB concluded that such attacks were unlikely to take place on Czechoslovak territory.[39] Yet it could not just stop watching this dangerous jackal and ignore signals hinting at his activity on its territory. The organization's terrorist wrath was showing no signs of abating. Throughout the 1980s Abu Nidal remained one of the most active players in the terrorist orbit. Even if Prague considered itself an improbable target, it was acutely aware of numerous ANO threats against foreign diplomatic missions—for example, the US embassy—on its territory.[40] Moreover, by the mid-1980s even Moscow seemed concerned, asking Prague to take appropriate measures to prevent ANO operations in Europe.[41] And so the StB continued to patiently monitor and investigate all signals pertaining to the Nidalists.

## ATTEMPTS AT LIAISON

Just as they were getting increasingly jaded by a regular stream of suspected Abu Nidal threats that never quite materialized, the StB received some breaking news. Atif Abu Bakr, the former head of the PLO mission in Prague, who hated Arafat and had a subscription to Abu Nidal's weekly newspaper, had defected from Fatah to none other than Abu Nidal—the prophet of Palestinian violence. Although alliances within the Palestinian factions had always been rather murky and mercurial, this was a high-level defection worthy of notice. The ANO had been killing off Arafat's envoys for years, and now one of them decided to join its ranks.

Soon the StB got more insight into his defection. While Abu Bakr had joined the most notorious terrorist organization of its time, he was not a proponent of the violent terrorist operations Abu Nidal was most famous for. In fact, he was appointed to be the organization's spokesperson, to lead its Political Directorate and help Abu Nidal shake off the label of "terrorist."[42] This was no easy feat as Abu Nidal had made violence inherent to his brand. His new spin doctor would have to work hard to change his image. In the years to come, however, the StB noticed that Abu Bakr became increasingly successful in promoting the outfit as a political, rather than a terrorist, organization. In fact, he made the notoriously people-shy Abu Nidal speak to international journalists. Out of the five interviews Abu Nidal gave in his lifetime, three were arranged under Abu Bakr's watch.[43]

An important part of this rebranding exercise was an effort to foster contacts with Central European governments and intelligence services, many of which Abu Bakr knew so well from his seven years of service in Prague and Budapest. Soon the StB learned that it was very much on his radar: Abu Bakr desired an unofficial intelligence liaison channel with Prague's security enterprise, which would also entail a joint business venture, for which Abu Nidal had allegedly put aside today's equivalent of $12.4 million.[44] In the long run, the Nidalists were keen to operate from—or even set up a headquarters and buy a house on—Czechoslovak territory. At the same time, Prague was learning that the ANO had made similar approaches to other Soviet Bloc governments, including those of Bulgaria, Hungary, the GDR, and the Soviet Union.[45]

However financially tempting, these approaches made Prague anxious. The StB was well aware of the ANO's menacing reputation and of the fact that it was in close contact with some of the world's most notorious terrorist outfits.[46] Hence, when in the mid-1980s, Abu Bakr started sending envoys to Prague with the intent of creating a liaison with the StB, the organization put up its defenses.

It first drew up the bridge in the summer of 1986. In August that year, a mysterious foreigner, Nassri Riafaat, arrived at Ruzyně Airport, on the outskirts of Prague. When he handed his passport to border control, the system started blinking red—the domestic security service had flagged him as persona non grata due to his membership in the ANO. He was not to be allowed into the country. Riafaat did not take this rejection lightly and remained adamant that his visa authorized entry. Soon the border police officers learned why he so much wanted to enter the country: he had been sent there on a mission to deliver an important message. Although cagey at first, he told the assembled StB officers that he had been sent by Abu Bakr to contact Czechoslovak government officials.[47]

While the StB did not let the ANO member into the country, it opted for an awkward compromise—enabling Riafaat to fulfill his mission at the airport. To facilitate this, the StB located one of the officials, an employee of the office of the minister of the interior, and asked him to come and meet the suspected terrorist in the airport's transit section. During the meeting, Riafaat delivered Abu Bakr's message sealed in an envelope. For hours afterward, the Palestinian hung around the airport and made phone calls. While waiting for his flight out of Prague, he was under close StB surveillance. The nervous security men also called in a pyrotechnics expert to inspect Riafaat's bag. His organization had detonated explosives at over a dozen airports—they were not taking any chances.[48]

Although ultimately harmless, this incident indicated that Abu Bakr was adamant about creating a liaison channel with the country that he used to call home. He may have sent Riafaat to reconnect with his old contacts in the Czechoslovak government. Since the late 1970s, the interior minister's international office had been the main liaison partner for the PLO diplomats and spies. Abu Bakr would have crossed paths with employees of the office on numerous occasions. If he was going to get any attention from the Czechoslovak authorities for his new employer, he would have to use these old, trusted contacts.

While Riafaat's apparent attempt to revamp Abu Bakr's network in Czechoslovakia did not launch, a half a year later Abu Nidal's spokesperson sent another envoy to Prague—his deputy in charge of international relations, Walid Chalid. This time the ANO representative managed to speak to the StB's foreign branch, the First Directorate. Authorized by Abu Bakr, he expressed interest in collaborating in political, economic, and security matters, especially when it came to exchanging information about adversarial intelligence services and international terrorist groups. If Prague showed interest, the group was ready to send over its experts to discuss further details. While on Czechoslovak territory, the envoy emphasized that it was not the ANO's intent to in any way harm the country's interests. In fact, Abu Nidal, the representative said, had given a strict order not to carry out any operations on Czechoslovak territory because, thus far, Prague had served as a safe place where Palestinian factions could meet and talk. He did not want to upset this mutual understanding.[49]

Prague seemed to have left all of Abu Bakr's advances unrequited. Despite his multiple attempts to rekindle his ties with the Czechoslovak communist regime, Prague did not take up the opportunity to create an alliance with Abu Nidal's enterprise. It was, however, keen to keep the ANO on its radar—to watch these dangerous Cold War jackals in an effort to better understand their future plans. In the spring of 1988 Prague got the chance to do just that: to get a glimpse into the inner workings of Abu Nidal's empire and its operations in Czechoslovakia.

## PRAGUE'S MEN IN THE ANO

On a hot day in April 1988, a Palestinian man in his early thirties got off a plane in the Libyan capital. Upon arrival, he was hastily escorted from the runway and driven to an apartment in a seaside residential area. Here he met none other than the ANO's Atif Abu Bakr. As they sat down for lunch, the functionary quizzed his guest about the PLO Office in Prague, its leadership, and its standing within the Palestinian diaspora. Questions soon turned into thinly veiled threats. As the Palestinian was told to write up a detailed account of his life, Abu Bakr warned him that any deception or lie would be discovered because the ANO knew all about him from their sources in Prague. The visitor's initiation into the ANO had begun.[50]

Three days later, the ANO hopeful finished writing up his detailed autobiography. He was told to sign a loyalty pledge that bound him to absolute secrecy about the organization he had just signed up to serve. He was to tell no one, including his wife, that he had joined ANO ranks and that collaboration with other factions or intelligence services was punishable by death. After he signed the menacing document, he was again asked to put pen to paper and write up situation reports about the workings of the PLO Office and the Palestinian diaspora in Czechoslovakia. The next day, Abu Bakr returned to interrogate the fresh recruit about his links to Arab diplomats and intelligence officers based in Prague as well as the StB. Abu Nidal's right-hand man wanted to make sure that the new recruit was a tabula rasa and not a plant. The young Palestinian denied all such associations.[51]

After four days of interrogation and confessions, he officially became a Nidalist. It was now time to task the new recruit. Abu Bakr took this upon himself: the new member was to return to Czechoslovakia and stay under the radar by avoiding any activities that could jeopardize his stay there. He was to be vigilant, avoid alcohol, womanizing, and any illegal activities, especially the sale of foreign currencies or restricted products, in which many Palestinians there were engaged. He was given a cover name and promised a monthly stipend of today's equivalent of $500.[52]

He was then given a detailed list of assignments. Crucially, the new ANO member was to surveil Palestinian students enrolled at Czechoslovak universities. As part of this effort, his job was to compile target profiles: family background, political affiliation, potential links to the Mossad and Arab security services, and future plans, including whether they were set to return to the occupied territories. Furthermore, he was to collect information about the PLO Office in Prague, now led by Abu Hisham. His new handlers were interested in acquiring a list of all its employees, their addresses and foreign contacts, and an overview of all official visits by Palestinian dignitaries, especially Abu Nidal's former mentor and head of Fatah security, Abu Iyad. Finally, they wanted more insight into the workings of Arab security and intelligence services in Czechoslovakia, especially their contacts with the Palestinian diaspora.[53]

In addition to surveillance and intelligence collection, the young Palestinian's job was to assist in disseminating ANO propaganda. He was to identify Arabs working for prestigious international organizations based in Prague—especially the International Union of Students, the World Federation of Trade Unions, and the magazine *Issues of Peace and Socialism*—and send them ANO statements on key developments, most recently the Israeli assassination of Abu Jihad in Tunisia. He was also tasked with developing a network of contacts—either Palestinian students or members of the Israeli Communist Party—who were planning to return to the occupied territories or Israel proper. All reports were to be sent to a personal address in Tripoli. To ensure security, he was to purchase a small safe.[54]

Within a week, the young Palestinian had been admitted into one of the most vicious Middle Eastern terrorist organizations. With his tasking complete, he was sent back to Prague to start his assignment. Instead of that, however, he headed to an StB safe house code-named Faust—a menacing reference to the main character in Goethe's timeless play about a man who sells his soul to the devil for eternal youth.[55] Although the young Palestinian had just signed up to serve Abu Nidal, his soul was firmly in the hands of the StB—the organization that sent him to infiltrate the ANO. Here, the young man, code-named Jirka by the StB, provided his handlers with a long debrief of his trip to Libya and the key ANO representatives he met there. He detailed their daily routines, provided addresses and descriptions of security arrangements in ANO offices and residences in and around the capital, cover names of key members, and information about their standing within the organization.[56]

The StB was thrilled to have penetrated the most notorious terrorist organization of its time. By planting Jirka within its ranks, Prague hoped to be able to monitor and perhaps manipulate the organizations' activities on its territory. In fact, StB had been so keen to infiltrate the ANO that three months later it authorized another one of its Palestinian agents, code-named Denis, to establish relations with the terrorist group and travel for an initiation meeting to Tripoli. Much like Jirka, Denis was subjected to several days of vetting and an interrogation by Abu Bakr. At the end of this ordeal, he was accepted as a member and given a set of tasks that complemented Jirka's operational goals: in addition to helping monitor the Arab diaspora and distributing Abu Nidal propaganda, Denis was to also keep an eye out for individuals or organizations that collaborate with or represent the United States or Israel and monitor Czechoslovakia's relationships with key Middle Eastern states. Both recruits were to adhere to strict secrecy and operational security and only engage with Abu Nidal representatives bearing a handwritten authorization from Abu Bakr.[57]

The two new recruits were instructed to work as a team. Their first months as plants in the ANO were characterized by caution by all parties involved. Jirka and Denis collected information about their targets and distributed a handful of ANO propaganda materials but aimed to keep a low profile. Arguably, the terrorist organization was also using these first months to give small tasks to their new assets to test their capacity, performance, and loyalty. The StB was also cautious. It understood that the ANO was keen to infiltrate its ranks. Aware of how fickle alliances in the terrorist underworld could be, it kept both of its plants under close watch.[58]

Gradually, the StB's worries eased as both agents kept it regularly informed about the activities they were conducting under the ANO banner. In addition to surveillance, collection, and propaganda, they were soon told to also serve as spotters of potential new ANO recruits. In the summer of 1988 they were tasked with recruiting a PLO Office employee who had expressed interest in switching sides.[59] If successful, this would be a great feat for Abu Bakr—infiltrating his former office, which was now run by one of his greatest nemeses. The PLO Office employee, however, soon backed out. Paralyzed by his fear of his current boss, Abu Hisham, who had made him promise absolute loyalty to Arafat, the young man refused to officially commit to the ANO. He was, however, open to remaining "friends" with Jirka and would "tell him whatever he wanted to know." Jirka was dissatisfied with this solution and suggested entrapping the hesitant Palestinian by giving him a financial reward and asking him to sign for the receipt of the ANO money. This would give the duo enough kompromat to force him into collaboration.[60]

While going about their ANO business, both assets were in regular contact with the StB and shared detailed information about their assignments. They shared copies of reports they sent back to Tripoli, some of which provided details of the Palestinian diaspora, activities of Syrian political exiles, overviews of activities of prominent arms dealers, and lists of Arabs based in Czechoslovakia suspected of links to various intelligence organizations. They also kept the StB updated about their contacts with various ANO representatives coming and going to Central Europe.[61] Prague was riding high. It now had a front-row seat to the workings of the ANO on its territory.

Soon after this promising start, however, things deteriorated quickly. Several months after being recruited, the two Abu Nidal operatives lost contact with Abu Bakr. Autumn 1988 was a tumultuous period for the organization as some of its key representatives defected from the organization. They left Abu Nidal and went straight to his archnemesis, Yasser Arafat.[62] During this time the entire Palestinian movement seemed to be in a crisis. In mid-November, at the meeting of the Palestinian National Council in Algiers, Arafat proclaimed the establishment of the State of Palestine, which angered his political opponents, including Abu Nidal. In early December, the First Intifada kicked off. This represented a challenge for all Palestinian groups, each trying to figure out how to engage with this unprecedented public discontent.

On December 12, 1988, ANO headquarters finally contacted its two men in Prague. Abu Bakr's nephew and fellow Nidalista Kifah Abu Bakr met Jirka and Denis at the Soviet Cultural Center, where he updated his assets on the recent turmoil in the Palestinian movement, stressing that the ANO disagreed with the way Arafat had declared an independent Palestinian state. When he asked them about their tasks, both assets revealed that they had ceased their activities because there had been no instruction from ANO headquarters. Kifah encouraged the duo to continue working toward the objectives they had been tasked with back in Tripoli. He also promised more guidance and money.[63]

The next day, the ANO emissary lived up to his promises. At a meeting in his room at the Hotel Paris, Kifah gave Jirka today's equivalent of $3,000 for his growing network of operatives.[64] Jirka was to split the sum fairly with Denis and the elusive young PLO Office employee who had initially been reluctant to collaborate with the terrorist organization but was recently coerced by Kifah into the game. As the ringleader, Jirka was given several additional tasks: to meet both members of his network at least once a week and task the PLO Office asset with producing regular situation reports. The ANO envoy was particularly interested in the current head of the office and the comings and goings of Force 17 members and members of the Israeli Communist Party, many of whom he suspected worked for the Mossad. Jirka and his team were also encouraged to make new contacts among Palestinian students outside of Prague. The ANO was keen to spread its influence beyond the capital.[65]

## BIG TALK IN A SAFE HOUSE

While the StB was closely watching how ANO representatives were rekindling their relationship with the boutique agent network in Czechoslovakia, a top representative decided to come out of the shadows and visit Prague. It was none other than the head of the organization's Political Section and the ANO's spokesperson—Atif Abu Bakr.

Although the StB was confident that Abu Bakr would not engage in violence on its territory, it understood the risks of having a high-ranking ANO representative visit Prague. He was a polarizing force, and violence among the warring Palestinian groups could erupt at any point. Hence, upon learning of his arrival in Prague, the StB swiftly tracked down the address of the safe house Abu Bakr and his men settled down in. Simultaneously, a decision was made to closely watch this Cold War jackal by intercepting his landline and tasking the relevant agentura to report back on his movements. Furthermore, perhaps boosted by their previous experience of expelling Abu Daoud, Carlos, and others, the StB decided to set up a meeting with the mercurial Palestinian to find out the reason for his arrival, to understand the ANO's intentions with regard to Czechoslovakia and the Soviet Bloc, and finally to refine its intelligence analysis of the current situation in the Middle East. Based on this, a decision on further measures would be taken.[66]

At midday on December 13, 1988, a week after Abu Bakr arrived in Prague, the StB met him face-to-face on Loretánské Square. Over the next two days, the security men held long discussions with the ANO envoy, first in a restaurant at the edge of Prague and then in an StB safe house. At this clandestine location, Abu Bakr opened up to the StB men whom he had met many a times during his half-decade role as the PLO head in Prague. Abu Bakr explained he had arrived in Prague on a South Yemeni diplomatic passport, under the cover name Muqbel Salem Ahmed. Somewhat apologetically, he explained to the StB that traveling incognito was a necessary security measure for prominent members

**ILLUSTRATION 14.2.** Abu Bakr (*left*) with his security escort in Prague, December 1988. *ABS, sb. OB, r.č. OBŽ-38165/6 MV*

of his outfit. He also informed them that immediately after his arrival in Prague, he had initiated contact with an employee of the International Department of the Communist Party and informed him about where he was staying in the city. This was none other than Maroš K., who worked closely with Vasiľ Biľak and helped transport weapons to the Middle East via a diplomatic pouch.[67] The message was loud and clear: Abu Bakr was playing nice. He had arrived in Prague as a friend, not a foe.

Unaccustomed to terrorists announcing their arrival to Prague, the StB was puzzled and inquired why Abu Bakr had contacted them. The Palestinian said that he had instigated the meeting to clarify the reasons for his Prague visit, explain his role in the ANO, and illuminate the group's activities and current political goals. He told the somewhat surprised StB officers that it was in his utmost interest to make sure that socialist states "correctly understood" that the ANO was no longer a terrorist organization "to the extent that it is depicted by Western representatives and media." It has become a political organization dedicated to resolving the Palestinian issue, he argued, by seeking to create a Palestinian state.[68]

Abu Nidal as a person and leader was also misunderstood, maintained Abu Bakr. In fact, the leader of the terrorist group was "a progressive" forced out of the

PLO in 1974 as he was sentenced to death in absentia by a tribunal set up by none other than Yasser Arafat. Maintaining that Abu Nidal was a leftist, Abu Bakr argued that Arafat's wrath was driven by a struggle for power and dislike of Abu Nidal's progressiveness. Consequently, Abu Nidal had been forced into illegality and exile, creating his own "revolutionary and left-wing" organization that would form a counterweight to the right-wing Fatah. Abu Bakr also told the StB that in fact Arafat was the first to use terror and assassinations against him, therefore forcing Abu Nidal to adopt similar tactics as a matter of retaliation. This was, he conceded, a tactical error on the part of Abu Nidal, admitting that his boss could have used other forms of struggle. Furthermore, Abu Bakr argued that many of the attacks attributed to his current employer had in fact been carried out by other groups—for instance, those loyal to Ahmed Jibril, the leader of a nationalistic PFLP splinter group called the Popular Front for the Liberation of Palestine–General Command, or Force 17, Arafat's elite group of security men and fighters. In fact, Abu Nidal was a victim of Arafat's campaign to discredit him.[69]

In a further attempt to win StB sympathy, Abu Bakr argued that after he joined the ANO in 1985, it had gradually transformed into a political entity. He brought in new members and changed the organizational structure in ways that made the formerly clandestine organization incorporate an official, public-facing element. In fact, in 1986 the PLO and ANO engaged in a cautious rapprochement, with the first meeting of Abu Bakr with Arafat's number two, Abu Jihad, in Libya being facilitated by Muammar Qaddafi. In 1987, for the first time in thirteen years, Abu Nidal himself met with Arafat, his longtime archnemesis, in Algiers. Although initially promising, after further violence by Fatah and the subsequent assassination of one of Arafat's closest associates—Abu Jidad—the modus vivendi achieved in Algiers soon collapsed. He also explained to the StB that Abu Nidal no longer wanted to organize terrorist attacks: "We must liquidate terrorism but not the struggle against our enemy. Our adversary must not find out that we have laid down our arms."[70]

Abu Bakr's lengthy monologue, effectively a mixture of apologia, confession, and business pitch, was also designed to show that the ANO and the Soviet Bloc stood on the same side of the Cold War. In fact, he detailed how his boss recently took on their joint adversary—the United States. In a 1986 exclusive interview with the American television network NBC, Abu Nidal openly challenged Washington by detailing its "terrorist campaign" in Nicaragua and the Iran-Contra affair—a complicated scheme designed by a group of US government officials to finance anti-Marxist Nicaraguan rebels with money earned by selling weapons to Iran. To warn one of the key protagonists of the Iran-Contra affair, Oliver North, that the ANO was aware of his involvement in these "terrorist" campaigns, Abu Nidal admitted to sending the controversial government official a warning note.

The monologue was also, however, riddled with inconsistencies. Abu Bakr was adamant that the ANO was in fact not the recipient of any state support—"which makes it the only independent [Palestinian] organization." This was unlike the PLO chairman who, Abu Bakr maintained, oscillated between the USSR and the US, saying that "Y. Arafat wears an ushanka hat [a traditional Russian fur headpiece] but one of an American make." Soon, however, he flipped, arguing that several Arab states and companies had provided funding to the ANO. In return, Abu Nidal agreed not to attack them.[71] By this time, Prague had enough intelligence about the terrorist outfit to know that it was indeed dependent on state support and had, over the years, found powerful backers in Iraq, Syria, and later Libya.

Using this as a segue for his pitch, Abu Bakr told the StB that in case Prague felt threatened by the West or any Arab organizations, the ANO was happy to provide assistance. In fact, it would also be willing to help in other ways—either by assisting in case Czechoslovak envoys got kidnapped in the Middle East or by providing information about the Mossad or the West German BND. Perhaps assuming that Prague was interested in expanding its analysis of the wider terrorist underground, Abu Bakr provided the StB with a unique insight into the landscape of the ANO's partnership with other terrorist organizations. Recently it had held negotiations with the female leader of the Japanese Red Army, discussing possible joint operations against the United States, he told the StB. The Belgian Communist Combatant Cells were also inclined to cooperate on joint operations in the future. Although the ANO had held negotiations with the Greek revolutionary organization 17 November and was a sympathizer, the potential for cooperation was likely to be problematic due to Abu Nidal's connections to the Greek government, which viewed 17 November as a terrorist group.

Remarkably, Abu Bakr revealed where the ANO's red lines were with regard to terrorist alliances. Supposedly, his boss kept the Italian Red Brigades at arm's length due to their close ties to the Mafia and Israel. Furthermore, he also found the Baader-Meinhof Gang unsuitable because it was said to be fragmented and riddled with BND agents. There was no cooperation between the ANO and the Carlos Group—perhaps understandably as they were the main competitors in the increasingly privatized terror industry. Although the ANO sympathized with some of these groups, it considered them somewhat aimless in comparison to Palestinian organizations, which, he argued, were a "hundred times more powerful because they know what they are fighting for and have political objectives." "Terrorist organizations in Western Europe," he resumed, "were made up of women and children from bourgeois families. They are also penetrated by many agents of special services of Western countries, and these organizations are now on the edge of collapse." Overall, they were not here to stay.[72]

This fascinating tour d'horizon of international terror was not without its ironies. Having firmly asserted that the ANO had turned its back on terror, Abu Bakr had then calmly narrated plans and plots with the world's most wanted villains. After he was done with boasting about his group's strength and contacts, he assured Prague that the ANO was not going to use Czechoslovak territory for planning its operations as he was aware of Czechoslovakia's links to the official PLO and respected its international standing. Using this opportunity, however, he proposed they retain a clandestine channel to "exchange ideas in the future."[73] The Palestinian effectively asked for Prague to open the door for future dialogue.

The StB was not surprised by this offer. In fact, it had diligently prepared for this very moment. By now, Czechoslovak spies had interacted with enough Cold War jackals to know that they never arrived without a list of requests. Accordingly, a day prior to the meeting, the StB laid out its options and drew red lines: while it would be open to retaining contact with Abu Bakr, it refused to be in touch with other ANO representatives. The StB also flat-out rejected official recognition or contact. In fact, any other forms of agreement with the group were also out of the question; it certainly was not going to allow it to organize or reside on Czechoslovak territory. It appears that StB was primarily interested in Abu Bakr as a source, not as a partner. In preparation for the encounter, it agreed to hold the meeting "in a friendly atmosphere" so as not to aggravate him and his security detail and hence his organization's stance toward Prague.[74]

And so when Abu Bakr made his humble pitch, the StB reacted in a friendly, positive tone. It agreed to keeping open a clandestine communication channel, emphasizing that it must remain clandestine and "in no way be confused with any form of political recognition." The StB's key reason seemed to be its effort to secure the state by staying informed about any impending operations against Czechoslovakia or other socialist states. Overall, in a postmortem it considered the meeting a success, concluding that "the contact fully met its purpose." It helped the StB verify intelligence it had collected on the Abu Nidal enterprise and other Palestinian factions. Crucially, the security men were relieved to hear that the terrorist group was not a threat to Czechoslovakia.[75]

On the following day, the ANO envoy and his entourage quietly left Czechoslovakia. Based on what we know, the Prague–Abu Bakr communication channel was never employed for what it was intended. Abu Bakr never used it to warn Prague of potential threats. In the summer of 1989, however, he sent a distress signal through one of its contacts, pleading with Prague to come to his rescue.

## KNOCKING ON HAVEN'S DOOR

In July 1989 an StB asset asked for an emergency meeting with his handlers. It was immediately clear that this was no routine briefing. The Palestinian living in Prague had received a worrying phone call from a dear friend based in Tripoli. He was in trouble and asked for an urgent message to be delivered to the Czechoslovak state security service.[76]

The friend was none other than Atif Abu Bakr. After four years at the side of the erratic Abu Nidal, he had called it quits. A month earlier, the spokesperson had defected from the violent organization. He was allegedly opposed to the terrorist operations Abu Nidal was famous for and had failed to draw the ANO leader onto a more political path.

The circumstances of his desertion were truly dramatic. Defecting from Abu Nidal was a matter of life and death. The terrorist leader was famous for ruthlessly executing traitors and opponents. Most recently, in 1987 the increasingly paranoid Abu Nidal had ordered almost three hundred ANO members killed in mass executions in Lebanon and Libya.[77] Moreover, Abu Bakr did not go quietly. Together with other top-level ANO defectors, he challenged Abu Nidal and set up his own rival organization. To add insult to injury, Abu Bakr's new outfit was actively trying to poach Abu Nidal's members as well as his money deposited in Swiss and Austrian banks under the names of his family members. Finally, Abu Bakr also tried to take away the most fundamental ingredient of Abu Nidal's success—state support. He pressed Muammar Qaddafi to cease his support of the increasingly drunk and manic Abu Nidal. Abu Bakr was allegedly so bold as to have blackmailed the Libyan leader into letting Abu Nidal go. If Qaddafi refused, he would leak information of Abu Nidal's mass murders to the West, which would mark Libya as an accomplice of these gruesome killings.[78]

Ultimately, however, after his defection, Abu Bakr found himself without significant political backing and therefore vulnerable. In his hour of need, he turned to Prague, first requesting asylum through an official channel—the Czechoslovak embassy in Tripoli. When this failed, he pleaded with Prague via the Palestinian intermediary. Abu Bakr wanted the StB to provide a temporary shelter for him and his family—effectively asking for sanctuary. In return he was ready to provide the StB with invaluable information on ultra-leftist Palestinian terrorist organizations and help uncover activities of terrorist organizations in socialist countries. However, the StB was not open to this. From Prague's perspective, his membership in the ANO was a stain Abu Bakr could not easily wash away. Without an explicit agreement from Arafat's men, Prague would not be able to contemplate even a short-term stay on its territory.[79]

Czechoslovakia never took Abu Bakr in. Perhaps this was due to the preoccupations of the communist regime, which crumbled only months after the Palestinian's desperate request. Or perhaps it was because it wanted nothing to do with an unpredictable diplomat who had spent years at the side of one of the most feared Cold War jackals. We do know, however, that eventually his previous employer, Fatah, took the petrified Palestinian back under its wing and helped him resettle in Algeria. This may have been part of a bigger plan designed by Yasser Arafat's security chief, Abu Iyad, who—upon seeing Abu Nidal massacre dissidents from his own organization—designed a cunning scheme to lure disillusioned Abu Nidal members away from the extremist organization and reintegrate them into the PLO. Many thanked Abu Iyad by sharing insider knowledge of the ANO, Fatah's most lethal opponent.[80]

Remarkably, the PLO attempted to draw Czechoslovakia into its campaign of managing ANO defections. In mid-November 1989, days before the Czechoslovak communist regime started crumbling under the weight of the Velvet Revolution, top Palestinian security officials pressed on Prague to serve as a temporary haven for Abu Nidal defectors. In fact, they claimed that some ex-ANO members were already on Czechoslovak territory. Were they allowed to stay, this would increase their chances of survival. Moreover, they could help lure other ANO members currently residing in Central Europe to defect from the organization. In turn, the Palestinians would pass this information on to their Soviet Bloc allies—the StB included.[81]

As far as we know, the postcommunist Czechoslovak government was not eager to follow in its predecessor's footsteps. In fact, over the coming months, the new democratic government started gradually cutting its ties with its Palestinian allies. It soon put an end to its training program for third world cadets, including those from the PLO. Palestinian envoys at the PLO Office in Prague also struggled to get through to the new government and set up ties with Prague's postcommunist kingmakers. The days of the Czechoslovak-PLO alliance were now effectively over. Nevertheless, the successor of the StB's domestic directorates, the Office for the Protection of the Constitution and Democracy (Úřad pro ochranu ústavy a demokracie), did not cut its links to the Palestinians entirely. After the Cold War's end, it continued to closely work with its Arab agentura and watch jackals, old and new.[82]

## THE FINAL SHOWDOWN

While the world was changing, so was the ANO. In the early 1990s the outfit's activity was diminishing. This, however, did not mean that Arafat's most ruthless challenger and his remaining loyalists would go down quietly.

On January 14, 1991, several hours before the US-led coalition confronted Saddam Hussein's Iraq in what became known as Operation Desert Storm, an agitated Abu Iyad, Yasser Arafat's security chief, arrived at the house of his close associate Abu al-Hol in his bulletproof Mercedes. His host had just returned from Baghdad where, alongside Arafat, they begged Saddam to withdraw from Kuwait, which he had recently invaded, before a United Nations ultimatum ran out. Abu Iyad was keen to hear about the charged meeting in Baghdad and eager to prepare the PLO for the impeding war, which they desperately were trying to prevent.[83]

As the two men discussed the imminent military confrontation in a villa located in a leafy suburb of Tunis, a quarrel broke out outside the front door. Soon afterward, one of the dozen or so security guards stationed in the building's vicinity rang the doorbell. When the maid let him in, all hell broke loose. In a short moment, Abu Iyad was shot dead, and Abu al-Hol was lying in a pool of his own blood, soon to die on an operating table. The assailant took Abu al-Hol's family hostage in an upstairs room. Throughout the night-long drama, he insisted that the Tunisian police bring over none other than Atif Abu Bakr. The assailant was clearly on a revenge killing spree, and the high-ranking Abu Nidal defector was on his hit list.[84]

Abu Bakr was never brought in, and the attacker was eventually pacified. A subsequent PLO investigation revealed that the embittered and depressed PLO security guard turned killer was most likely recruited by the ANO in the latter part of the 1980s, when he spent almost two years roaming around Prague and other Soviet Bloc capitals. After his return to Tunis, he was employed at the al-Hol family villa where he ultimately carried out the lethal vendetta against Abu Nidal's fiercest opponents. As he later confessed, his recruiter told him that Abu Iyad was the source of all PLO corruption and had to die for the Palestinian revolution to live.[85]

For the next decade, Abu Nidal could enjoy the warm feeling that he had sent Abu Iyad—his friend turned rival—to his grave first. The 1990s were, however, marked by personal and professional difficulties. Abu Nidal's organization all but collapsed, and he was gradually pushed to oblivion, with other bad actors taking his place. By 2002, when yet another war was looming over Iraq, Abu Nidal found himself living in Baghdad. He had been allowed to settle there several years earlier by Saddam, the aging dictator presiding over the final years of his rule. Although not much is known about Abu Nidal's final years, he seemed to have lived a solitary life marked by health complications.

It thus came as a surprise when, in August 2002, he died a violent death. His sudden and mysterious passing invited myriad theories. According to former Nidalists, a terminal illness forced him to take his own life. A biographer, Yossi Melman, suggested he may have been killed by a rival group or Iraqi security services that worried he knew too much.[86] After all, during this time Baghdad was under intense scrutiny, not least due to its links to international terrorism.

However, the head of Iraqi intelligence offered a different, much simpler explanation for Abu Nidal's death. He claimed that the aging terrorist took his life when he was about to be arrested by Iraqi security officers for illegally entering the country. Upon hearing the news, Abu Nidal allegedly went to his room, locked the door, and shot himself with a Smith & Wesson pistol. Although the intelligence chief told the press that they found false identity cards, weapons, and suitcases containing dynamite in his flat, he failed to explain how the infamous terrorist managed to incur multiple gunshot wounds as a result of his own suicide.[87]

Unlike his former associates, Atif Abu Bakr did not die a violent death. Following his defection, he settled down in Tunisia and later Algeria. Although he was never entirely safe there—a fact underscored by murders of his fellow defectors—the poet-diplomat outlived all his notorious bosses. As time passed, he came out of the shadows. With fewer curls and extra weight, he embarked on his third career as a commentator on Middle Eastern affairs and a narrator of his days as a Cold War jackal.[88]

## NOTES

1. "Poznatky k organizaci Abu Nidal," n.d., ABS-38165/3.
2. Seale, *Abu Nidal*, 56–57.
3. "Poznatky k organizaci Abu Nidal," n.d., ABS-38165/3.
4. Seale, *Abu Nidal*, 27.
5. Jean-Louis Bruguière, interview with the author, September 22, 2022.
6. "North on His Family's Safety and Meeting Abu Nidal," Understanding the Iran-Contra Affair, Brown University, July 8, 1987, https://www.brown.edu/Research/Understanding_the_Iran_Contra_Affair/v-on8.php.
7. Seale, *Abu Nidal*, 57–58.
8. Melman, *Master Terrorist*, 52–56.
9. Seale, *Abu Nidal*, 62–65.
10. Seale, 65–66.
11. Seale, 66–67.
12. Seale, 69–70.
13. Melman, *Master Terrorist*, 60–62.
14. Seale, *Abu Nidal*, 70, 77–78.
15. Melman, *Master Terrorist*, 71–72; Seale, *Abu Nidal*, 78, 80.
16. Seale, *Abu Nidal*, 84.
17. Arguably, the attack also had other, more strategic goals. See more on this in Seale, 91–92.
18. Sládečko (II.S/6), "Vyhodnocení," April 15, 1986; "Poznatky k organizaci Abu Nidal," n.d., ABS-38165/3.
19. The original sum was $150,000.
20. The original sum was $15 million.
21. Seale, *Abu Nidal*, 100.
22. "Poznatky k organizaci Abu Nidal," n.d., ABS-38165/3.
23. Seale, *Abu Nidal*, 6–7.
24. "Poznatky k organizaci Abu Nidal," n.d., ABS-38165/3.
25. Sládečko (II.S/6), "Vyhodnocení," April 15, 1986, ABS-38165/3; Seale, *Abu Nidal*, 6–7.
26. Josef Dynžík, "Teroristická organizace Abu Nidal—zpráva," December 2, 1985, ABS-38165/3; Seale, *Abu Nidal*, 6–7, 19.
27. "Poznatky k organizaci Abu Nidal," n.d., ABS-38165/3.
28. D. B. Goodsir (Security Department, Foreign and Commonwealth Office), "Abu Nidal," November 11, 1982, TNA-FCO 8/4730.

29. Sládečko (II.S/6), "Vyhodnocení," April 15, 1986, ABS-38165/3.
30. Seale, *Gun for Hire*, 275.
31. Gastold, "Polish Military Intelligence," 88–89.
32. "Poznatky k organizaci Abu Nidal," n.d., ABS-38165/3.
33. Václav Pokorný (X.S), November 13, 1978, "Jednání operativ. Pracovníka 3. Odboru X.S-FMV s vedoucím Organizace pro osvobození Palestiny /OOP/—záznam," ABS-19324/2.
34. V. Pokorný (X.S), November 23, 1978, "ABU BAKER ATEF, vedoucí Organizace pro osvobození Palestiny /OOP/ v ČSSR. Zpráva o jeho názorech," ABS-19324/2; Sládečko (II.S/6), "Vyhodnocení," April 15, 1986, ABS-38165/3.
35. "INFORMACE pro ministra vnitra ČSSR soudruha Vratislava VAJNARA," May 28, 1984, ABS-19324/4.
36. Vítězslav Kába (zást. náč. XIV.S) "Návrh opatření k plánované akci teroristické skupiny Abu Nidala," February 16, 1983, ABS-38165/3.
37. "Informace pro ministra vnitra ČSSR soudruha Vratislava Vajnara," March 18, 1985, ABS-38165/3.
38. Seale, *Gun for Hire*, 151.
39. Karel Fiřt (Náč.II.S)–V. Zamykal (Náč.sekr. I.Nám. MV ČSSR), May 31, 1985, "Stanovisko," ABS-24113/6.
40. Josef Novák, "Informace č. 27," April 29, 1986, ABS-38165/3.
41. Ivan Voleš (Vedoucí 8.t.o. FMZV), May 8, 1986, ABS-24113/6.
42. II.S/4, "Informace," December 8, 1988, ABS-38160/5.
43. V. Rampa (II.S/2), "Interview Abu Nidala," November 18, 1985, ABS-38165/3; Seale, *Gun for Hire*, 144.
44. The original sum was $5 million.
45. J. Dynžík (II.S/5), "TALÁD MAKDAD YACOUB—zpráva," July 25, 1988, ABS-38165/3; "Teroristická organizace "Revoluční rada—Al Fatah" (Abu Nidal)," n.d., ABS-38165/3.
46. Dynžík.
47. "Informace," n.d., ABS-38165/3.
48. "Informace."
49. Karel Sochor (Náč.I.S)–Karel Fiřt (Náč.II.S), "Návštěva vedoucího mezinárodního oddělení palestinské organizace Al Fatah-Revoluční rada v Praze," April 7, 1987, ABS-38165/3.
50. J. Dynžík (II.S/5), "Záznam o vytěžení TS JIRKY po návratu z Libye," May 5, 1988, ABS-38165/3.
51. Dynžík.
52. The original sum was $200. Dynžík.
53. Dynžík.
54. Dynžík.
55. "Jirka," ABS-30327.
56. J. Dynžík (II.S/5), "Poznatky ke kanceláři teroristické organizace Revoluční rada Fatáhu /Abu Nidal/ v Tripolisu," May 16, 1988; J. Dynžík (II.S/5), "Záznam o vytěžení TS JIRKY po návratu z Libye," May 5, 1988, ABS-38165/3.
57. J. Dynžík (II.S/5), "Poznatky ke kanceláři teroristické organizace Revoluční rada Fatáhu /Abu Nidal/ v Tripolisu," May 16, 1988; J. Dynžík (II.S/5), "Záznam o vytěžení TS JIRKY po návratu z Libye," May 5, 1988, ABS-38165/3.

58. J. Dynžík (II.S/5), "Poznatky ke kanceláři teroristické organizace Revoluční rada Fatáhu /Abu Nidal/ v Tripolisu," May 16, 1988; J. Dynžík (II.S/5), "Záznam o vytěžení TS JIRKY po návratu z Libye," May 5, 1988, ABS-38165/3.
59. J. Dynžík (II.S/5), "TS JIRKA dopis od ved. TO Abu Nidala," July 22, 1988, ABS-38165/3.
60. J. Dynžík (II.S/5), "Obsah odesílané zprávy pro TO Abu Nidala v Libyi," September 20, 1988, ABS-38165/4.
61. Dynžík.
62. Ladislav Csipák (II.S ZNB Bratislava/1), "Arabské politické organizácie—ich činnosť na území ČSSR," November 9, 1988, ABS-38165/4.
63. J. Dynžík (II.S/5), "TALÁD MAKDAD YACOUB—schůzka se členem TO Abu Nidala v Praze-zpráva," December 19, 1988, ABS-38165/4.
64. The original sum was $1,200.
65. In early November 1989 they renewed their contact with their two men in Prague and asked them to distribute pamphlets and statements by the leadership of this new Palestinian enterprise. Overall, however, the network never delivered much apart from the first weeks of its operations. J. Dynžík (II.S/5), "Poznatky k teroristické organizaci Abu Nidala," November 14, 1989; J. Dynžík (II.S/5), "KIFAH ABU BAKR-člen TO Abu Nidala—zpráva," December 20, 1988, ABS-38165/4.
66. Dynžík, "KIFAH ABU BAKR-člen."
67. II.S/4, December 21, 1988, "Záznam ze spravodajského vytěžení osoby ATEF ABU BAKR," 38165/5.
68. II.S/4.
69. II.S/4.
70. II.S/4.
71. II.S/4.
72. II.S/4.
73. II.S/4.
74. Milan Beluský (II.S/4), "Návrh na kontakt s členem vedení teroristické organizace Revoluční Rada Fatah /ABU NIDAL/," December 12, 1988, 38165/4.
75. II.S/4, December 21, 1988, "Záznam ze spravodajského vytěžení osoby ATEF ABU BAKR," 38165/5.
76. J. Dynžík (II.S/5), "Záznam," July 26, 1989, ABS-38165/4.
77. III.S/GŠ 3, "Vztah vedení Libye k hnutí Abu Nidala," November 9, 1989, ABS-38165/4.
78. J. Dynžík (II.S/5), "Poznatky k teroristické organizaci Abu Nidala," November 14, 1989, ABS-38165/4; "Poznatky k organizaci Abu Nidal," n.d., ABS-38165/3.
79. J. Dynžík (II.S/5), "Záznam," July 26, 1989; Skydánek, "Telegram z TRIPOLI," July 12, 1989, ABS-38165/4; Ján Nagy (Náč. odboru FMNO A GŠ ČSLA)–4-II.S, January 1, 1989, "Věc: Poznatky k velvyslanci PLO (FATAH) v ČSSR—zaslání," ABS-38165/5.
80. The author's private archive. See also mention of this in Jonathan C. Randal, "Abu Nidal Battles Dissidents," *Washington Post*, June 10, 1990.
81. The author's private archive.
82. "Informace," May 18, 1990, ABS-38165/5.
83. Seale, *Gun for Hire*, 34–35.
84. Seale, 34–35.

85. Seale, 36–39.
86. Ewen MacAskill and Richard Nelsson, "Mystery Death of Abu Nidal, Once the World's Most Wanted Terrorist," *Guardian*, August 20, 2002, https://www.theguardian.com/world/2002/aug/20/israel.
87. "Iraqi Authorities Explain Circumstances around Abu Nidal's Death," AP Archive, August 21, 2002, https://www.youtube.com/watch?v=P5UEsuB_dfU.
88. "Informace," May 18, 1990, ABS-38165/5; "How Did the Iraqis Get Rid of Abu Nidal?" (كيف تخلص العراقيون من أبو نضال؟), n.d., Al Arabiya, https://www.youtube.com/watch?v=Qmby1U6xtlw; "Reviews with Atef Abu Bakr," April 28, 2011 (مراجعات مع عاطف ابو بكر), Al Hiwar TV, https://www.youtube.com/watch?v=U7OvJ7EOPpY.

# 15

# Anxious Hosts

During the last two decades of the Cold War, the most radical of the jackals represented a challenge for Czechoslovakia's security system. When the likes of Abu Daoud, Carlos, or Abu Bakr flocked to Prague, the old-style StB designed to quell state threats and local dissidents struggled to keep up with them. This left the country exposed to uncontrollable terrorists and revolutionaries.

Gradually, however, Prague developed a set of new tools to address this challenge. It adopted a variety of approaches for watching, infiltrating, blocking, and eventually expelling those it feared the most. But how successful was Prague's policy and practice toward these violent nonstate actors? Did its Swiss Army Knife approach work? What hurdles did the mammoth StB have to overcome when deploying the various tools available to its officers? And was Czechoslovakia's multifarious approach to Middle Eastern Cold War jackals fundamentally different from that of Western states?

## WATCH AND WAIT

When the jackals descended on Czechoslovakia, the communist country quickly realized that it knew little about these mercurial actors. Accordingly, it was keen to find out who they were, which faction they belonged to, why they had come to Prague, and whether there was any risk associated with their stay. To achieve this, the StB adopted the careful watch-and-wait approach, characterized by full-spectrum surveillance.

Watching terrorists and revolutionaries, however, proved to be an arduous task for Prague's security community. Much like those of other authoritarian security organizations, the StB's domestic departments—the Second Directorate and Fourteenth Directorate—were designed around an old-style surveillance system focused primarily on two types of enemies: dissidents and adversarial states. Accordingly, its goals, methods, and processes were geared to surveilling its own population and weeding out so-called internal enemies—dissidents, intellectuals, students, minorities, and religious communities.[1] The

StB was intimately familiar with who these opponents were and how and where they operated, and it clamped down on them with much success.

The StB also had ample experience with monitoring the diplomatic outposts of adversarial states—chiefly those of the United States, the United Kingdom, and West Germany—which, the regime thought, were stationed there to subvert the communist regime. In addition to NATO member states, third world diplomatic missions suspected of subversive activity were also closely watched by Prague's spies.[2] With varied success, StB managed to penetrate some of their defenses. To surveil and infiltrate these institutions, Prague's security personnel recruited local embassy employees, installed technical surveillance devices, conducted secret technical inspections in their offices and homes, took secret videos and photographs, and monitored correspondence.[3] These were familiar targets, and the StB had a well-tested plan for keeping them under control.

Watching Middle Eastern jackals represented a new challenge to this old-style surveillance system. Thanks to their foreign and capricious nature coupled with good tradecraft skills, they often made the StB look inept and out of depth. There were several reasons for this. To stay under the radar, the jackals embraced frequent identity changes and carried a variety of travel documents, which enabled them to slip through Czechoslovakia's heavily guarded borders without much effort. This complicated the StB's work as it often learned about the arrival of infamous terrorists days after the fact.

The StB also struggled with understanding these groups' alliances, goals, and plans. The various factions often split and adopted new names, which made affiliations and loyalties difficult to establish. Accordingly, mistakes were often made. For years, Czechoslovak counterintelligence officers tasked with the terror agenda thought Abu Daoud was a member of the Carlos Group, when in fact his original affiliation was with the PLO faction Fatah and the enigmatic Black September.[4] In 1980, when Carlos had already visited Prague more than five times, the StB still referred to the Venezuelan as an "Arab terrorist."[5]

This had as much to do with the nebulous nature of these jackals as it did with who the terrorist watchers were. The domestic officers deployed to pursue them were not the most experienced of spies. Contrary to our current view of terrorism as a high-profile security subject, in the 1970s and 1980s the agenda of monitoring terrorist activities and networks was not a popular career path. As Ladislav Csipák, a former StB officer who worked on the Arab agenda in Bratislava, recalled, "To tell you the truth, the terror agenda was somewhat of an 'orphan.' When I, as a 'greenhorn,' was given this agenda, everyone was happy that they did not receive this new task. They were relieved because they all had been working on different agendas for years, and this was something that needed to be built from scratch." There was also little training that would ease the new recruits into the job, recalls Csipák. "They threw me into the

Anxious Hosts    295

ILLUSTRATION 15.1. Surveillance photo of Abu Daoud walking the streets of Prague, probably in the early 1980s. *ABS, f. Správa sledování SNB–svazky (SL), a.č. SL-5037 MV*

water and told me to swim." Moreover, regional offices tasked with monitoring terrorism were even worse off, as their closest supervisors were based in Prague, and they rarely saw them face-to-face and so received little guidance in this unfamiliar area.[6]

The StB's lack of competence in this area also had to do with its hiring policy. Following the suppression of the Prague Spring—which led to purges within the Communist Party as well as the StB—the regime significantly altered its recruitment standards. Instead of hiring the best and the brightest, it recruited the most loyal. These dutiful officers lacked long-term tradecraft experience, had limited education and language capabilities, and lacked knowledge of foreign cultures. Having spent most of their lives in the rather closed communist system, members of Prague's domestic state security apparatus represented the antithesis of cosmopolitanism. This inward-looking security culture rendered them ill-suited for surveilling elusive foreign targets who communicated in "exotic" languages and engaged in unpredictable alliances. According to Peter P., former head of the Counterterrorism Department in postcommunist Czechoslovakia, "they were no Middle East experts. What they knew they largely learned from their Arab agentura."[7]

The so-called Arab agentura was fundamental to the watch-and-wait approach. It was mostly made up of the large Middle Eastern student community living in Czechoslovakia and diplomats and local employees working at Middle Eastern embassies in Prague, including the PLO Office. To the StB's domestic directorates, which lacked experts on the Middle East, these sources were pivotal to understanding who their targets were and what their business in Czechoslovakia was. According to Miroslav Belica, a former Czechoslovak diplomat stationed in Damascus and Libya, the Palestinians at home and abroad were "good informants"—a valuable source of information. They knew the environment and politics of the region very well, and many of them had an outlook on politics similar to that of the Soviet Bloc.[8]

Nevertheless, the quality of human intelligence provided by this agentura varied significantly. On one hand, this widely cast web of informants enabled the StB to navigate through the unfamiliar and dynamic landscape of relations within the Arab community and the international terrorist milieu. On the other, however, reliability was often an issue. According to Peter P., "in terms of sources they [the StB] were often hostages to their informants' individual interests. Their assets often provided conflicting information and rarely supplied their handlers with information acquired directly from the source. Much of what they fed the StB was based on hearsay or secondhand information."[9]

Their loyalties were also constantly in question. According to Csipák, who recruited and handled Arab agents in the late 1980s, one had to be aware that these informants were often doubles. "Of course, we knew who each Palestinian we recruited worked for—be it the PLO, Al Saiqa, the PFLP, or the Abu Nidal Organization. We knew that these people were effectively intelligence officers with allegiances to these particular groups, but they also worked for us. Being in touch with [an informant] was an advantage even though we knew he was a double."[10] In other words, the StB grew accustomed to the fact that their agentura mixed genuine information with disinformation.

Despite these known deficiencies, the Arab agentura seemed to have been the steadiest way of obtaining information about the StB's most nebulous surveillance targets. Gradually, the StB found ways of rewarding or even blackmailing its agents into sharing valuable information. "Our main goal in respect to this agentura was to find out whether there was any threat of terrorist attacks," recalls Csipák. Soon he and his colleagues found ways to push their contacts into cooperating. "I recruited and nailed down several people when they began to have visa issues or when their permanent student residency permit was about to expire." It was at this point, he recalls, that he would make a pitch: "Listen, I can fix you a permanent work permit, but I need some information from you. . . . So, I gave him the most basic permit possible, and if he fulfilled my expectations, then I had no problem extending his stay."[11]

In its pursuit of the jackals, the StB also activated its "hotel agentura," the ubiquitous StB agents based in hotels across the country. To keep these foreign subjects "under control," the state security placed hotel managers, waiters, receptionists, and cleaners on their payroll. These reported on a regular basis and were helpful when it came to supplying the StB with information on the arrival and departure of terrorists and revolutionaries, together with the content of conversations they held with staff. They were also essential when it came to accommodating the jackals in rooms that were equipped with listening devices. When it came to the detailed discussions held during clandestine meetings, however, the usefulness of this agentura proved limited. Such rendezvous were often held in hotel rooms and safe houses, where the StB had to rely on informants embedded in the Arab community or on technical surveillance.

While technical collection often compensates for failings and biases of human intelligence, this was not entirely the case with regard to the jackals. Although high-class hotels in Prague had some rooms equipped with surveillance technology, it was not always easy for the hotel agentura to ensure that key targets would check into those rooms. For instance, at times the security-sensitive Carlos refused to check into rooms he had been allocated.[12] In these instances, the StB was forced to swiftly install bugging devices into his room during his stay—a highly risky maneuver, especially as Carlos and his associates were known for being security aware and thus rarely leaving their hotel rooms unattended.[13]

Even in those cases when the hotel agentura managed to check surveillance targets into a room with permanent surveillance equipment, things could go wrong. In August 1979 when the Carlos Group held a mini terrorist summit in several rooms of the Intercontinental, the hotel agentura succeeded in checking them into rooms with the appropriate technical surveillance equipment. Everything was set up for the StB to listen in on their plans. The technology failed, however, and the StB was left guessing what these individuals were up to.[14] When they eventually did manage to make the recording device work, the StB was again left disappointed. Much of the recorded conversation was found to be unintelligible and difficult to attribute to the many actors attending the meeting.[15]

Even if technology did not fail, acquiring translation and analysis of transcripts was a complicated endeavor. Members of Carlos's outfit and their associates were a cosmopolitan, multilingual crowd. The StB's domestic security officers rarely spoke foreign languages, and securing translations from English, French, and especially Arabic was a challenge. What is more, the jackals spoke Arabic's various forms and dialects, difficult to grasp even for those with fluency in one. Due to this lack of expertise, the StB had to send transcripts to Moscow for Arabic translation and further analysis. This significantly delayed StB efforts to assess what were deemed high-risk gatherings.[16]

In addition to the StB's shortcomings, the jackals were genuinely hard targets. As most jackals had at least basic countersurveillance training, Prague's watchers often struggled to surveil these smooth operators, who moved among the city's streets, bars, hotels, and safe houses with much ease. During his walks through downtown Prague, Carlos often stopped in front of shop windows to use them as mirrors—a long-tested surveillance-detection technique. Furthermore, the StB also suspected that during some of his visits, the Carlos Group had its own security team monitoring the hotel for people who expressed "undue interest" in its boss.[17]

When it came to the most sensitive meetings, top jackals rarely held them in public. They reserved their most intimate conversations for safe houses typically provided by allied Middle Eastern diplomatic missions. Locating these places could be as complicated as it was dangerous. For instance, in August 1979 an StB surveillance officer followed Carlos and his associates to a Prague safe house. To avoid suspicion, he got off the lift at a higher floor of the building than his surveillance targets. Soon, however, he was cornered by Carlos's associates in the staircase, asked to show his ID, and forcibly prevented from leaving. After some consultation among them in Arabic, which the officer did not speak, he was let go. Having his cover blown, following the incident the officer had to be reassigned to other targets.[18] This was bold and unprecedented behavior toward the StB, which typically instilled fear and compliance in the local population.

Finally, StB standard operating procedures were not well geared to monitoring meetings between the jackals, diplomats, arms dealers, and their other associates, often held late into the morning hours. In everyday life, the routine of StB's surveillance teams tended toward "clockwatching" and adhering to strict shift schedules. When the terrorists convened in private safe houses for long hours, StB surveillance personnel often left their positions before the meetings were over because they had finished their shift.[19]

## BLOCK AND PREVENT

While watching the jackals was arduous, keeping them off Czechoslovak territory was a next-level challenge. The StB opted for the more proactive block-and-prevent approach—characterized by a set of measures designed to keep the jackals out—in instances when these foreigners were deemed to be radical, disruptive, or presenting a potential stain on the country's reputation. Over the course of the 1970s and 1980s, Prague became increasingly worried about having these controversial jackals on its territory. This anxiety was triggered by a complex mixture of factors.

Major geopolitical shifts were pivotal. The 1970s marked the era of détente—an easing of tensions between the West and Warsaw Pact countries—

characterized by increased political negotiations, improvement in economic relations, and the signing of nuclear arms treaties. Washington and Moscow opted for this relaxation due to the heavy economic costs of the long-term arms race during the Cold War. In 1975 both sides also committed to the Helsinki Process, an initiative that put additional emphasis on East-West cooperation and on adherence to human rights.[20]

While this did not turn Moscow and its satellites into beacons of democracy, the modus vivendi reached in Helsinki made Prague more cautious about engaging in controversial conduct and alliances. According to Czechoslovakia's deputy foreign minister for the developing world, Dušan Ulčák, détente and the Helsinki Process were key reasons why Prague was nervous about having the likes of Carlos on its territory.[21] Vladimír Nergl, the veteran StB officer tasked with tracking jackals on Czechoslovak territory, also saw the Helsinki Process as a turning point for Prague with regard to international terrorism. It was then that the communist regime started becoming more attuned to this phenomenon and made it a part of the StB's agenda.[22]

Prague arguably had good reasons to keep the jackals out even when détente waned. Throughout the 1980s Czechoslovakia adhered to this more careful approach due to fear of isolation, argues Gen. Andor Šándor, a communist-trained military intelligence officer who later rose to become head of the Czech Republic's foreign military intelligence. According to him, in the closing decade of the Cold War, Czechoslovakia did not want to further detach itself from the West in terms of travel, foreign currency, and goods.[23] It perhaps learned this lesson from the 1960s, when—thanks to participating in Cuba's global revolutionary training enterprise—Prague faced fierce international criticism, cutting of diplomatic ties, security threats, and economic boycotts.

While the determination was there, preventing these mercurial individuals and groups from entering Czechoslovak territory was no easy feat. Although Prague diligently put those Cold War jackals it wanted to keep out on its persona non grata list, most managed to artfully slip through the system's cracks. This was largely due to their constant identity changes and tradecraft skills as well as the abundance of travel documents at their disposal. These visas and passports were issued on fake identities—names, occupations, and purpose of travel—and sported photographs of jackals' altered appearances.

As the StB and the country's border police painfully learned, the jackals typically carried multiple false documents issued by mostly Middle Eastern and North African states—Iraqi, Kuwaiti, Lebanese, South Yemeni, and Syrian being most popular. Some countries provided them in large quantities. According to a former South Yemen deputy minister of the interior, his country had given out so many passports to "the Palestinians" that it had simply lost track of how many passports they issued.[24]

ILLUSTRATION 15.2. Carlos's request for a Czechoslovak diplomatic visa under assumed South Yemeni identity. *ABS, f. H, a.č. H-720/4*

The StB was acutely aware of this problem because it surfaced with regard to each group they were tracking. Members of Arafat's Force 17 came to Czechoslovakia under false Lebanese passports, Wadi Haddad's disciples traveled on South Yemeni documents, and Carlos carried a new passport during each one of his stays.[25] If confronted, these terrorists were not shy about discussing their deceitful practices for traveling the world. When Abu Daoud was being expelled in November 1982, he rather arrogantly told the StB that there was no point in forcing him to leave Czechoslovakia as he could easily return under another identity whenever he wished—boasting that he had four different Arab passports in his luggage.[26]

In most cases, these were not forgeries but genuine documents issues by Prague's Middle Eastern allies. In fact, the StB found that many jackals carried genuine diplomatic passports issued on fake names and identities. Diplomatic immunity gave the straitlaced Soviet Bloc border officers little wiggle room, even if the person in question seemed suspicious or resembled one of the notorious figures. This was very much the case when the self-proclaimed "good person," Carlos the Jackal, made three attempts to cross the Czechoslovak-GDR border. Despite his suspect behavior, his diplomatic passport disarmed East Berlin's border officials.[27] Not letting in diplomats from friendly countries could lead to political repercussions that security services did not want to have to shoulder.

Prague's attempts to keep the jackals out were further exasperated by technical issues and competency gaps. According to Csipák, who recalls such passports being "widely available" and relatively easy to acquire, even the more diligent of officers would have struggled with assessing the veracity of Arab travel documents. At the time, personal details in most Arab passports were often illegible: "The grammar and spelling was atrocious. They did not use typewriters to fill in personal data; it was all written by hand, in ink."[28] This also enabled the jackals to slip in and out of Czechoslovak territory with relative ease and often unnoticed.

Therefore, the StB often learned about their visits only retrospectively or once they had checked into Prague's luxurious hotels or settled into tucked-away safe houses. A prime example of this was the 1988 visit of Atif Abu Bakr, whose presence in Prague was undetected until he himself called Czechoslovak Communist Party representatives to effectively report his arrival. Moreover, Abu Daoud's first visit to Prague, which coincided with the meeting of the International Olympic Committee, was only discovered by the StB weeks after his departure.[29]

While communist borders seemed impenetrable for the everyday person, international terrorists and revolutionaries managed to navigate their way around with relative ease. As it tried to prevent and block their entry to the communist state, Czechoslovakia's security apparatus was coming to terms with emerging globalization, which allowed the jackals to leverage the space between jurisdictions.

## INFILTRATE AND MANIPULATE

Prague eventually learned there was no way its State Security Service could keep unwanted jackals off its territory entirely. It was thus forced to develop alternative approaches that would enable the StB to better understand these individuals and their organizational goals with regard to Czechoslovakia and the Soviet Bloc but, crucially, also impact their behavior. This would involve recruiting core members of these groups or placing plants in these organizations.

From the jackals' first visits, which commenced in the latter part of the 1970s, Prague did indeed manage to recruit agents who brushed shoulders with them. These were often Palestinian students living in Czechoslovakia and Middle Eastern diplomats and envoys. While, as we saw, the so-called Arab agentura was not always entirely reliable and often harbored mixed loyalties, at times it did deliver insight that the StB would otherwise not acquire via other means. This was particularly the case when it came to understanding the links between the more moderate Palestinian groups, such as Fatah, and international terrorism. This strategy was distinctly rewarding when the StB artfully infiltrated the PLO Office in Prague by recruiting some of Arafat's top envoys there. This gave it unprecedented insight not just into the mission's workings but also into terror links of the likes of Abu Hisham and others.

Plants in terrorist organizations could also help the StB understand the inner operations of these enigmatic groups. Perhaps the most successful of the StB's efforts in this regard was when it succeeded in planting two of its informants—Jirka and Denis—in the ANO. As Prague knew that Abu Nidal and the ANO's spokesperson, Abu Bakr, repeatedly attempted to recruit future members on Czechoslovak territory, the StB adopted a more aggressive strategy by tasking its two informants with infiltrating the lethal organization. While ultimately they did not rise up the ranks or join training—which would have enabled them to provide more insight from within the organization—they were nevertheless able to report back on the organization's recruitment and disinformation operations in Czechoslovakia.

Infiltration was no doubt an asset when it came to intelligence collection. Nevertheless, as a tool, it is perhaps most powerful if deployed in a way that allows the service to exert control over its targets. Prague never had a breakthrough with regard to manipulating these villainous players and changing their behavior. While the StB planned to infiltrate the PFLP by recruiting the scared spokesperson Bassam Abu Sharif, even after a six-year effort this proved unsuccessful. Although the well-placed Palestinian did indeed help Prague place anti-Western propaganda in Palestinian newspapers, the StB rezident gradually realized that Abu Sharif did not envision himself as an agent of a foreign power but rather as a liaison partner. Prague was ultimately unable to get closer to the well-connected Palestinian, to turn him into its asset within the PFLP. Hence, while the StB had on a number of occasions successfully infiltrated the nonstate actors it cooperated with or feared, it fell short of using these assets to effectively manipulate their behavior to suit Czechoslovak security or policy objectives.

## TRICK AND OUST

While Prague watched the jackals, introduced rules to manage their arrivals, and devised ways to infiltrate their organizations, none of these approaches seemed to have the desired effect—keeping radical terrorists off its territory. Accordingly, in the early 1980s, the StB decided to up the ante. At the start of the decade, it developed a new strategy aimed at pushing the Cold War's most villainous jackals out. Acutely aware that its border defenses were porous and its security system overwhelmed, it added a daring new tool to the Swiss Army Knife that was the StB.

The trick-and-oust approach enabled Prague's security men to quietly push those it deemed dangerous out and deter them from returning. Employed only in a handful of cases, this strategy typically saw StB officers confront those individuals it considered extremist face-to-face and request that they leave the country with immediate effect. While in some cases the StB used a false pretext to push select jackals out, in others its approach was much less delicate: the designated spies did not beat around the bush and bluntly told the terrorists to pack up and leave.

Prague deployed this strategy against those jackals who, in StB eyes, presented either physical or reputational hazard. The Munich massacre commander, Abu Daoud, was the first of the few to be ejected from Czechoslovak territory as part of this approach. In 1982 the StB took him in for questioning, a move designed to deliver the verdict to the potentially dangerous Palestinian in a controlled environment. There the battle-hardened Abu Daoud was told to leave the country "in the interest of his own security." Although this was a thinly veiled trick and left the Palestinian furious, it fulfilled its goal. Abu Daoud flew out of the country the next morning, never to return. Three years later, the StB tested this approach again when it conducted a surprise search of the hotel room of Carlos's close associate Kamal al-Issawi and took him in for questioning. Despite his vocal resistance, he was bluntly expelled and put on a flight out of the country the following morning.

One of the most high-profile cases of ousting was the summer 1986 expulsion of the combustible Carlos and his two associates. In this instance, the StB used a well-crafted ruse. It tricked the terrorist into leaving by alleging that the French knew about his whereabouts, implying they might confront him on Czechoslovak territory. While their intervention clearly infuriated the Venezuelan, the tall tale of an impending French intervention helped bring him back down again and facilitated the trio's immediate departure. Eventually, less well-known figures were also subjected to this treatment. Six months after Carlos's ousting, the StB tried this daring move on one of Wadi Haddad's disciples, Nabil Wahbi Hussein, in what it called Operation Visitor (Akce Návštevník). From the StB's perspective, Hussein's close allegiance to the group that had not only attacked the Mossad but also fueled Palestinian infighting warranted this escalation.[30]

To succeed, trick and oust required close coordination with various actors. In some cases, such as that of Abu Daoud, the StB first tried to use an Iraqi intermediary to make the Palestinian leave. It graduated to direct expulsion only after this indirect strategy had failed. In other cases, such as that of representatives of Force 17 and the Carlos Group, top diplomats were brought in to reason with and pressure Middle Eastern envoys based in Prague into cutting their ties with these radical forces. Pushing the Carlos Group out was an all-regime effort, which saw Prague exert diplomatic pressure on the Syrian embassy not to extend its false-identity visa and a set of high-profile visitors to the PLO Office to request Abu Hisham's collaboration in pushing them out.

Despite careful preparation, these operations were as suspenseful as they were challenging. None of the jackals took Prague's "invitations" to leave lightly. Abu Daoud was furious at the StB for asking him to leave and confining him in the Hotel Intercontinental prior to his expulsion. Carlos's deputy, al-Issawi, directly threatened the officers, telling them that had he been questioned in one of the capitalist countries, which his group considered as their principal enemies, he would have already gunned them down or arranged to have them liquidated.[31] A year later, his boss made numerous frantic attempts to prevent what was effectively deportation by engaging the Syrian embassy and lashing out at the StB officers who came to ask him to leave. Wadi Haddad's disciple was also not keen to cut short what, he told the StB officer who came to oust him, was a Christmas shopping trip. Ultimately, although furious, he left Czechoslovakia shortly thereafter, vowing to never return.

Prague was anxious about expelling the jackals as it feared this approach might lead to bloodshed. The regime was aware that these temperamental individuals were all armed, well trained, and ready to shoot if put under pressure. If violence broke out in one of Prague's public places, this would expose their stay in the communist country and arguably invite international condemnation and perhaps even retribution. Alternatively, even if they remained composed during the ousting, Prague feared they could return with a vengeance, attacking Czechoslovak targets at home or abroad at a later stage.

Nevertheless, Prague had good reasons to overcome this anxiety and take measures to push them out. If the jackals continued to visit, this would provide ample opportunity for Western states to expose and perhaps exaggerate their links with Czechoslovakia. The StB and its masters were mindful that during the 1980s, the pressure on states that were seen as "terror sponsors" was being stepped up.[32] Any public shaming of the Central European nation could have serious repercussions on its global diplomatic and business ties.

Prague was also happy to push them out because it understood that there was limited utility to allying with these controversial figures who by the 1980s largely conducted terrorism for personal or monetary reasons and not in the name of "revolution," "liberation," or "anti-imperialism." In other words, they lacked the political gravitas that had led Prague to align with Yasser Arafat's Fatah. Finally, it feared that they might spark intra-Palestinian violence on Czechoslovak soil, not least by confronting some of the more mainstream Palestinian factions.

Prague was also keen to see these bad actors go because they irritated the regime and were hard to control. According to General Šándor, countries of all persuasions—authoritarian or democratic—are reluctant to have unruly terrorists, over whom they do not exercise control, on their territory. This was why Prague gradually started pushing them out.[33] Bruguière seconds this, arguing that this was particularly evident in the case of Carlos: "Soviet Bloc countries were eventually all afraid of him because he was unpredictable, aggressive, and ruthless. He also manipulated them by claiming to have an alliance with Moscow and the KGB. Hence, their most powerful weapon against people like him was expulsion. The inability of the Soviet Bloc states to control the likes of Carlos coupled with their often erratic behavior put these old-style services outside their comfort zone and caused them to take steps to push them out."[34]

Furthermore, in the 1980s Prague also upped the ante because socialist countries began viewing terrorism as a phenomenon that could pose a threat to them. According to Csipák, in the mid-1980s "myriad terrorist organizations and factions emerged that could also strike against Prague. It was at this time that they became serious about terrorism."[35] Moreover, other less known and unpredictable terrorist groups driven by religion more than politics began to appear, adding to the sense of danger. Newly emerging factions of the Muslim Brotherhood and Hezbollah, which attempted to hit Soviet targets in the Middle East, were a case in point.[36]

Finally, by the 1980s Prague's kingmakers also wanted the jackals out. According to Ivan Voleš, who was central to Prague's trick-and-oust strategy, a number of key high-ranking Communist Party members loathed being associated with international terrorists, with the president and party secretary, Gustáv Husák, allegedly being one of them. According to Voleš, "after 1968 Czechoslovakia, as a country occupied by the Soviets, was seen by many in the West as Moscow's puppet. They [communist leaders] did not want us to be seen this way, [hence] we were a lot more risk-avoidant than before. We were ready to provide assistance but did not want to be accused of sponsoring terrorism."[37]

This insistence on keeping a clean slate with regard to Cold War jackals was also evident following the 1988 downing of Pan Am Flight 103 over Lockerbie by operatives of the Qaddafi regime. As Voleš recalled almost three decades later, when investigators found that Prague had sold Libya a significant amount of Semtex, the explosive most likely responsible for downing the aircraft, the then deputy minister of foreign affairs was furious that Czechoslovakia had been dragged into the mess.[38] The government did not want Prague to be propelled onto the front pages of international newspapers for involvement in atrocities of the magnitude of Lockerbie.

Overall, despite the multitude of complications and the risk associated with this strategy, the trick-and-oust approach largely worked. Direct confrontations by Prague's security officers seemed to have sent an unequivocal message to Cold War jackals that they were not welcome in Czechoslovakia. As far as the StB knew, none of the expelled jackals ever returned.

## SOVIET BLOC LIAISON

International terrorism blurred established boundaries between domestic and foreign security. It eventually became clear that liaison was crucial to tracking, blocking, infiltrating, and ultimately ousting these international terrorists from communist territory. In 1977 Moscow shared a three-hundred-page photo album of terrorists with its Warsaw Pact allies, encouraging them to use this "database" for operative purposes. This was a remarkably complex list, which included members of Palestinian hijacking commandos, the German Red Army Faction, and the Japanese Red Army as well as the Carlos Group.[39] This not only provided the smaller services with photos and helpful biographical data of key terrorists but also gave satellites an indication of whom the KGB considered a terrorist. In August 1977 Moscow sent its allies a brief on the "international terrorist Ilich Ramirez." While this did not contain any suggestions or orders for Moscow's junior partners, it made it clear to them that Carlos was considered a foe, not a friend.[40]

At the end of that year, in the run-up to the 1980 Moscow Olympics, Soviet Bloc allies set up a joint electronic database designed to streamline such exchanges. Called the System of Joint Acquisition of Enemy Data, it enabled partner services to share information about those they deemed a threat. While especially the junior services shared numerous terrorism-related signals via this channel, the information did not always flow the other way. It was also considered difficult to use, and entering details of many threats that often failed to materialize was not seen as a priority.[41]

On a more strategic level, the Soviet Bloc boasted two multilateral landmark conferences. The first international consultation of representatives of the Warsaw Pact counterintelligence services on the issue of terrorism was held in Prague in April 1979. It was not, however, until November 1987 that the counterterrorism chiefs of the socialist states met again in this format to discuss the bloc's "fight against terrorism," in the Bulgarian seaside resort of Varna. Ultimately, the meetings' main utility was keeping the allies on the same page.

Although the Warsaw Pact counterterrorism conference in Prague did not produce a unified Soviet Bloc policy on international terrorism, some progress was made. Specific targets were discussed in Prague. For instance, Moscow asked the junior partners' services to collect information about terrorists during the run-up to the 1980 Moscow Olympic Games, arguably accelerating further information exchange on Carlos.[42] Moreover, the conference seems to have increased some allied investment into building an effective national security apparatus, ready to face challenges brought about by terrorism. For instance, Polish counterintelligence agreed to provide a blueprint to Prague for setting up a counterterrorism unit.[43] By 1981 Prague sported its own unit, which it could

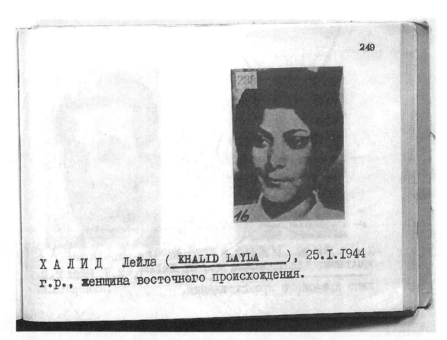

ILLUSTRATION 15.3. Moscow's *Album of Terrorists* listed hundreds of people, including the surviving 1972 Munich Olympic massacre commandos Ali Hassan Salameh (a.k.a. the Red Prince) and, here, Layla Khaled, who was one of Wadi Haddad's earliest hijackers. *ABS-20968*

now use in case Cold War jackals decided to strike on its territory or when they were being ousted from the Czechoslovak capital.[44]

Moreover, the meeting presented ample opportunities to build confidence and accelerate bilateral liaison. While at the conference, the StB planned to consult its allies about a number of sensitive issues linked to key terrorists. The Czechoslovak officers intended to meet with counterparts from the KGB and brief their powerful partner service "about the [Carlos] group of terrorists and their presence on our territory, including their contacts with employees of the Cuban embassy." Moreover, Prague was keen to tap into Moscow's knowledge of the Carlos Group. Accordingly, it planned to inquire about its goals, addresses, financial sources, sources of arms, and links to enemy intelligence agencies and embassies of Arab countries. Crucially, Prague wanted Moscow's assessment of whether the Carlos Group would carry out terrorist attacks in socialist countries.[45]

Much like in the West, operational intelligence liaison was largely done bilaterally. The presence of Carlos on Soviet Bloc territory represented a test case for Central-Eastern European liaison. In the late 1970s Soviet Bloc allies began passing around information and photographs of Carlos—indicating where he would travel next, under what identity and diplomatic cover, and whom he was likely to meet with while in Berlin, Prague, or Budapest.[46] This crucial information often enabled Prague to find out about the jackals' presence on its territory, albeit at times this came with a days-long delay.

Nevertheless, Prague thought it could do better and engage in more in-depth liaison. With cooperation among counterintelligence agencies mostly focused on exchanging lists of terrorists and information about individuals, Prague lamented that partners could instead share their analyses of the goals, methods, and nature of the terrorist organizations. Although most of the services knew who the key players in the most prominent as well as the more obscure terrorist outfits were, not much was known about how these organizations functioned, the StB argued. More strategic analysis, they proposed, would make counterterrorism among Soviet Bloc partners more effective.[47] This was a symptom of a wider problem of these communist services, which were not set up to provide critical assessments for policy support but rather designed to help secure the regime in power.

Soviet Bloc liaison related to the jackals was inherently imperfect. Despite popular belief that these states were well-synchronized machines, allies were not always on the same page when it came to Cold War jackals. The Carlos Group was the first real test case for Central European counterterrorism liaison. In 1979, when this activity began, there were considerable discrepancies between different partners on how to address the group. Although bilaterally the various state security services agreed on intelligence exchange, each alliance member had a different view of what level of support should be extended to Carlos. Remarkably, the GDR sought to transfer risk to allies such as Czechoslovakia. By 1982, however, as the tide turned against Carlos, the attitudes of the three key services who had suffered the presence of Carlos on their territory began to align. Carlos was increasingly eccentric and engaged in planning top-level assassinations of key Middle Eastern politicians, which the Soviet Bloc nations wanted nothing to do with.

Furthermore, when it came to operational liaison in the Soviet Bloc, information mostly flowed in the direction of Moscow. While the satellites gradually learned to exchange information on the jackals, Moscow's role in this was clearly that of a hegemon: while at times it did share basic intelligence related to targets and threats, it rarely reciprocated with information of strategic or operational value. According to Nergl, this was very much a one-way street.[48]

\*\*\*

Overall, terrorists and revolutionaries were challenging targets for the StB's surveillance apparatus. This was due to their ever-changing identities and documents, the amorphous nature of their alliances and affiliations, the lack of formal hierarchy, and the counterintelligence measures these actors employed. This in turn reflected the fact that they were routinely used to playing against top-level opponents such as the Mossad, which made these Cold War jackals not only security conscious but also forced them to adapt and develop sophisticated survival strategies.

While the StB and its partners faced a variety of obstacles and challenges with regard to the jackals, they gradually developed a set of approaches that enabled the old-style security system to quell or eventually push the most dangerous of the jackals out. Czechoslovakia's approach, however, lacked the ultimate finale—that of arresting these internationally wanted criminals. Prague had a number of pragmatic reasons for this.

First, it did not want to alienate the PLO and its close allies in the Middle East and North Africa, who maintained intimate ties with many of these groups. Arresting their jackals would likely expose terrorist links to and infuriate the strategically important Hafez al-Assad or the cash-rich Muammar Qaddafi. Second, not being a member of the International Criminal Police Organization (INTERPOL), Czechoslovakia felt no formal pressure to arrest individuals who perpetrated attacks in the West. Arguably, it also had limited legal means to do so, unless they broke local law. When in the Soviet Bloc, apart from passport forgery and carrying unauthorized weapons, the jackals stayed away from trouble.[49]

Finally, Prague drew the line at arrests because it operated in an ideologically polarized world where exchanges of such high-profile prisoners with adversaries were inconceivable. Although the Soviet Bloc states may have been increasingly irritated by the jackals, they would not collaborate with the West on their indictment or arrest. This red line diligently copied that of the Cold War ideological divide. The politics of the time did not allow it.[50]

## EAST-WEST PARALLELS

Czechoslovakia and other Soviet Bloc countries were not alone in facing challenges associated with the Cold War jackals. As primary targets, throughout the 1970s and 1980s, Western European states felt a clear need to address these terror threats and the groups that mounted them. The Cold War wave of international terrorism, however, caught the West by surprise. Accordingly, it took time for these states to develop dedicated and effective mechanisms for addressing the threats. While doing so, countries such as France, the United Kingdom, and Germany faced many of the dilemmas encountered by their counterparts in Czechoslovakia and, in some cases, adopted similar solutions.[51]

Keeping the jackals off countries' territory and tracking their movements proved to be a challenge across the board. Sir Martin Furnival Jones, the director general of the United Kingdom's Security Service (MI5) during the 1960s, was skeptical about being able to keep terrorists out of UK territory: "It is not difficult for terrorists previously unidentified . . . to gain entry to Britain for short periods, possibly carrying explosives with them. There are a large number of pro-Arab supporters of different nationalities in Britain, including many Arab students, who would be prepared, or could be induced, to give help in minor ways or provide cover."[52] Prague grappled with the same problem for most of the latter part of the Cold War.

In the early years of Cold War international terrorism, counterterrorism liaison was imperfect, and states struggled to keep up with the jackals. After the 1972 Munich massacre, MI5 lamented in a letter to Home Secretary Robert Carr, "It is difficult to predict the likelihood of terrorist operations in the UK. We do not control directly the amount and quality of intelligence we receive about Arab terrorist plans and intentions." According to MI5, the intelligence the UK received from liaison services was "usually imprecise as regards targets, timing and the identities of those involved. It is in any case the practice of terrorists to travel on false passports."[53]

Much like in the East, jackals sporting various identities and travel documents often slipped through Western defenses. This represented a challenge when it came to all the high-profile terrorists of the era. For instance, in 1977 Abu Daoud traveled to France under a fake Iraqi identity as part of an official delegation hosted at the country's Ministry of Foreign Affairs. It was only thanks to an Israeli tip-off that France realized whom they were hosting.[54] Carlos was also an elusive target for the French and the British.[55] This problem persisted throughout the last two decades of the Cold War.

The challenges both the East and West faced with regard to monitoring Cold War jackals seemed remarkably similar, and so were some of the approaches to countering them. While in the 1970s some countries—such as Israel—adopted assertive counterterrorism strategies early on,[56] most Western states were slow to develop effective ways of countering these threats. This was caused by the fact that many Western European nations, as well as the United States, then perceived international terrorism as a short-lived, "politically unattractive" problem that could be waited out. Furthermore, as many in Western capitals believed that the Soviet Bloc was actively using international terrorism as a weapon against them, they saw it as a small part of a much bigger, geostrategic problem that had the full attention of the policymakers.[57] In other words, terrorism, as such, was initially not seen as a problem of its own, worthy of a dedicated long-term strategy for countering it.

Accordingly, many Western capitals were quite selective about which international terrorists it pursued and which it let go.[58] While, for instance, the United Kingdom and France made attempts to arrest the infamous Carlos and his accomplices, who had staged numerous attacks on their soil and murdered three policemen in Paris, not all Cold War jackals were hunted with such passion.[59] This selective reluctance of Western governments was led by the belief that arrests often provoked further attacks and hijackings.

Examples of this approach are many. For instance, in 1970 London, urged on by Washington, exchanged one of the most famous female terrorists—Layla Khaled—for the safe return of one of Britain's hijacked airliners. Less than two months after the 1972 Munich massacre, another group of terrorists hijacked a West German plane in an effort to free three of the surviving attackers from Munich. Remarkably, West Germany swiftly gave in to the hijackers' demands and released the three arrested terrorists.[60] In 1977 Abu Daoud was arrested in Paris while attending the funeral of an assassinated colleague. Although Israel and West Germany filed extradition requests during the visit, in a matter of weeks, thanks to Iraqi intervention, Abu Daoud was a free man.[61] Furthermore, in those cases when the jackals were indeed arrested and convicted, many served relatively modest sentences.[62] This showed that they seemed to exercise significant bargaining and deterrent power over major states as a result of high-profile attacks.

There was perhaps another reason for this reluctance to keep the jackals behind bars. According to Judge Bruguière, when looking to prosecute, states tend to focus on their immediate threats—terrorist or other—and are not keen to open new fronts. "Much like the United Kingdom," which Bruguière worked closely with, "when it was fighting the IRA, it was not keen to open a new front with groups which were less of a threat. So overall cooperation with the British on CT cases was good, but sometimes when we wanted to extradite people it was difficult due to politics or reluctance to provoke." Without attempting to judge, he added that "dealing with terrorists is a complicated game because the priority is the security of the state."[63]

There were, however, also bigger strategic reasons for why some Western European states decided not to arrest and prosecute most Cold War jackals associated with the Palestinian cause. Much like in the East, they feared that harsh measures adopted against these actors could instigate opposition or even repercussion from oil-rich Arab states, with which many Western capitals had good relations or close business dealings.[64] As Baghdad, Damascus, or Tripoli had close ties with the various factions or offshoots of the PLO, including the enfants terribles, they protested against incarcerations of prominent jackals not only east but also west of the Iron Curtain.[65] This worried Western states, which in such cases had to weigh longer-term strategic interests against their more immediate security concerns.

In those instances when states were not able to arrest top jackals due to political or other reasons, their spies pursued other ways of undermining the groups. One way to weaken these nonstate actors was to force their state backers to withdraw support. As traditional diplomatic pressure often failed, some Western intelligence agencies opted for what could be best described as "counterterrorism by disclosure." For instance, in the 1980s, when the US démarches aimed at pushing Middle Eastern states into disassociating with Abu Nidal failed to deliver, the CIA's Center for Counterterrorism (CTC) in conjunction with the State Department issued what became known as *The Abu Nidal Handbook*—an encyclopedia of the group's crimes and organizational information, including names of key operatives and addresses of ANO companies. According to Duane Clarridge, who led the CTC and the anti-ANO effort at the time, the operation achieved its goal. As a result of this disclosure, many governments known for their links to the group—not just Arab ones—severed their ties.[66]

Another way to undermine the jackals was to try to break up their outfits from within by infiltrating, disrupting, or manipulating them. Although details of these highly clandestine operations ran by Western services remain scarce, the little evidence we do have suggests that in the 1980s the CIA and the British SIS made considerable efforts to infiltrate the ANO. Arguably, these were more successful than those attempted by the StB in the late 1980s. Clarridge recalls celebrating this success years later in London's Oriental Club over pink gin with an SIS colleague.[67]

In some cases, the jackals themselves came to the Western agencies. Former CIA officer Douglas London, who hunted the Nidalists in the closing decade of the Cold War, recalls ANO members being "very dangerous and volatile. Their members were generally hardened, violent personalities." As the organization kept on splitting, this created opportunities: "Those who sought to turn to the other side were generally disgruntled and looking for revenge against their organization or a particular person in it. Or perhaps they did something bad within their organization and needed help or a lifeboat fearing they might be caught. One agent came to us after killing someone in their own organization."[68]

Such attempts at infiltration had an important side effect—instilling paranoia into the organization as well as into the mind of an already suspicious leader. In the case of Abu Nidal, increased pressure and interference by Western intelligence as well as, as we saw, Fatah's Joint Security Service under Abu Iyad's command ultimately led the organization to implode. Abu Nidal started seeing traitors everywhere and striking against them with unprecedented cruelty—most notably in the fall of 1987 when almost two hundred ANO members were killed in one night. Operations by his adversaries aimed to infiltrate, manipulate, and disrupt ultimately had the desired effect, albeit this was not immediate and often took years to see results.

Talking to the jackals was also not out of the question. There is now growing evidence that Western countries engaged in conversations with some of the terrorists who attacked the West. According to London, "There is always an advantage in talking to your enemies. You never know what you will achieve at these meetings, and sometimes such contact represents an opportunity to develop and nurture relationships—a.k.a. recruit representatives of the adversarial party who I am not otherwise getting the chance to talk to. As a spy, I will talk to almost anybody as long as physical security is guaranteed." Talking to the jackals could have thus been a way of getting an in, recruiting agents, penetrating, and perhaps even splitting or weakening the organization as such. As London added,

> at a minimum, it provides an opportunity to better learn about your adversary, explain your own country's policy, and allows a discreet means out of public view to make compromises, convey messages, and release steam. Moreover, personal contact also demystifies the preconceived stereotypes. Even if something tangible does not come out of it, the hope is that I would be able to at least plant a seed of doubt or curiosity in their minds, which could make the target consider cooperation, or influence a more constructive outcome within their own organization based on firsthand impressions.[69]

Striking deals with terrorists was another way to lessen the threat. We now know that numerous Western states tried to appease the jackals in the form of unwritten nonaggression pacts, which would allow terrorists to reside or operate on their territory in exchange for peace. France allegedly adopted a so-called sanctuary doctrine, which enabled international terrorists to operate with impunity as long as they refrained from attacking French targets.[70] In the mid-1980s France's domestic security service allowed an Abu Nidal envoy to settle down there and set up a clandestine communication channel with Paris.[71] According to journalist and the first Carlos biographer, Colin Smith, French security often treated its dealings with terrorists as a "gentlemen's affair." They "exuded their usual neutral air of 'we wish you would please go away and fight your battles somewhere else, gentlemen.'"[72] When asked about this doctrine, Judge Bruguière quickly replied, "In the field of intelligence, all is possible!" After a brief chuckle, he added, "The role of intelligence is to make possible what is impossible and to achieve it by another way."[73]

There is now growing evidence that other Western European countries looked for "another way" of engaging with the jackals. This suggests that

Belgium, West Germany, Austria, Switzerland, and Italy all forged nonaggression pacts with various terrorists and revolutionaries. Some of this evidence has been uncovered in archives, but most is based on interviews or the memoirs of former West European government officials.[74] This growing narrative of Western countries' nonaggression pacts with Cold War terrorists mirrors that of Czechoslovakia, which cared strongly about security and order on its own territory but was less worried by intergroup political violence or terrorist attacks carried out at a safe distance from its borders. This suggests that under pressure from the jackals, states on both sides of the Iron Curtain made concessions that they would never admit to publicly. Perhaps Western states could, in a way, also be viewed as anxious hosts.

This raises the question of ideology when interpreting government policies toward terrorism. Warped by Cold War biases, the debate about international terrorism has largely been binary, portraying Western states as the fierce antiterrorist forces of their time, while framing Soviet Bloc countries as a monolithic group of active supporters of terrorism, oblivious to or immune from challenges posed by modern terrorism. This artificial divide into those that "support" terrorism and those that "fight it" (the "good guys" and the "bad guys") ignores what constituted an important emerging trend—namely, an inherent clash between old-fashioned security states and nebulous foreign nonstate actors.

Given recent archival findings, the new image of Cold War counterterrorism looks rather different from the picture that has prevailed over the last thirty years. The divisions were in fact less between East and West and instead more between state and nonstate actors—with anarchists and extremists reviled almost everywhere. Given the common means, goals, and challenges violent nonstate actors posed for Western democracies and communist countries during the Cold War, the congruence in surveillance practices across diverse states is perhaps not entirely surprising. Certainly, empirical contours vary to some degree across national contexts, most prominently in the fact that the communist states never attempted to arrest the terrorists and revolutionaries they feared. Nevertheless, this suggests that these concepts have broad applicability and can be helpful in identifying the surveillance variation along a continuum.

Overall, this brief expedition into Western governments' challenges and approaches to Cold War jackals shows that regardless of ideology, counterterrorism is a dilemmatic exercise determined by geopolitical as well as national state interests. Moreover, it demonstrates that security and intelligence agencies were not omnipotent bureaucracies capable of monitoring or averting threats as they pleased. They operated within distinct political, cultural, and structural contexts, which determined the nature as well as the success of their work. Moreover, they relied on human agents and technology that were far from infallible. From the 1970s onward, with the ascent of international terrorism, this context changed rapidly and found old-fashioned states both east and west of the Iron Curtain to be unprepared. Both camps were perplexed when facing similar challenges: monitoring and "controlling" these unfamiliar actors. In all cases, the security agencies of allies exchanged intelligence hesitantly and imperfectly. This shows that the study of communist regimes and their intelligence and surveillance strategies remains highly relevant not only as a path to understanding undemocratic states but also their democratic contemporaries.

## NOTES

1. Protection of the Czechoslovak economy was also among the top three counterintelligence priorities.
2. RMV ČSSR, December 21, 1977, "Základné zameranie služobnej činnosti Zboru národnej bezpečnosti a vojsk ministerstva vnútra na rok 1978," *Ústav pamäti národa*, Rozkazy ministrov vnútra 1948–1989, č. 32/1977, http://www.upn.gov.sk/data/projekty/rozkazy-mv/RMV_32_77.pdf.
3. Peter Blažek and Pavel Žáček, "Czechoslovakia," in *A Handbook of the Communist Security Apparatus in East Central Europe, 1944–1989*, ed. K. Persak and L. Kamiński (Warsaw: Institute of National Remembrance, 2005), 123–24.
4. Milan Solnický (II.S/6), November 15, 1982, "Záznam," ABS-728008 MV.
5. Jiří Jíra (Náč.II.S/5), August 17, 1979, "ZPRÁVA o jednání mezi delegacemi MStB NDR a II.Správy SNB v Praze uskutočněné ve dnech 16.–17.8.1979," ABS-19324/1.
6. Ladislav Csipák, interview by the author, September 4, 2017.
7. Peter P., interview by the author, August 29, 2017.
8. Miroslav Belica, interview by the author, August 18, 2015.
9. Peter P., interview by the author, August 29, 2017.
10. Csipák, interview by the author, September 4, 2017.
11. Csipák.
12. Vítězslav Kába (Náč.II.S/7)–IV.S/5, July 31, 1980, "Organizace CARLOS—žádost o provedení opatření," ABS-24613/4.
13. Informant Rudolf, August 16, 1979, "Favaz Adil Ahmed, nar. 1949, jemenský st. příslušník ubytován v hotelu IHC -poznatky," ABS-16987.
14. Zdeněk Němec (Náč.XIV.S)–Ján Kováč (I.nám. MV ČSSR), August 20, 1985, "Akce 'CARLOS'—Informace," ABS-24113/4; Z. Němec (Náč.XIV.S)–J. Kováč (I.nám. MV ČSSR), November 11, 1985, "Plnění úkolů vyplývajících z operativní porady u s. I. náměstka MV ČSSR do akce 'CARLOS' ze dne 22.8.1985—informace," ABS-24113/4; J. Kováč (I.nám. MV ČSSR), September 2, 1985, "Zápis z operativní porady do akce 'CARLOS' dne 22.8.1985," ABS-24113/4.
15. J. Jíra (Náč.II.S/5), August 16, 1979, "Informace o pobytu arabských teroristů na území ČSSR," ABS-19324/1.
16. II.S, March 31, 1980, "ZÁZNAM k vyhodnocení úkonu TA-122 nasazeného v akci 'BAK' č.sv. 16987," ABS-19324/1.
17. "FAVAZ Ahmed-zpráva do akce BAK," August 24, 1979, "FAVAZ Ahmed-zpráva do akce BAK," ABS-16987.
18. L. Šmíd (IV.S/4), August 22, 1979, "Úřední záznam," ABS-SL-454 MV.

19. IV.S, August 14–15, 1979, "Akce BAK-sledování," ABS-SL-454 MV.
20. Martin Klimke, Reinhild Kreis, and Christian Ostermann, eds., *Trust, but Verify: The Politics of Uncertainty and the Transformation of the Cold War Order, 1969–1991* (Washington, DC: Woodrow Wilson Center Press, 2016); Békés, "Warsaw Pact and Helsinki Process."
21. Dušan Ulčák, interview by the author, September 8, 2015.
22. Vladimír Nergl, interview by the author, January 9, 2018.
23. Andor Šándor, interview by the author, July 29, 2015.
24. J. Jíra (Náč. II.S/5), May 8, 1980, "INFORMACE—styky ministerstva vnitra JLDR s teroristickou skupinou 'RUCE SVĚTOVÉ REVOLUCE,'" ABS-19324/1.
25. Josef Vlček (OMS MV ČSSR)–V. Stárek (Náč.X.S), May 21, 1979, "AHMED-ADIL-FAWAZ-sdělení," ABS-24613/5.
26. M. Solnický (Náč.II.S/6), November 16, 1982, "INFORMACE," ABS-24751.
27. Vedoucí OMV MV ČSSR–Karel Vrba (Náč.II.S), March 4, 1980, "Skupina kolem CARLOSE—informace z NDR," ABS-19324/1; J. Jíra (Náč.II.S/5)–X.S/3, October 25, 1979, "Informace o činnosti arabských teroristů na území ČSSR—zaslání," ABS-19324/1.
28. Csipák, interview by the author, September 4, 2017.
29. Václav Pokorný (X.S/3), August 8, 1979, "Návrh na zavedení svazku signální: Abu Daoud," ABS-728008 MV.
30. ABS-KR-816986.
31. Vladimír Nergl (Náč.II.S/6), August 20, 1985, "ZÁZNAM o provedení ZTÚ ANALÝZA v akci CARLOS čís.sv.24613," ABS-24113/4; Němec (Náč.XIV.S)–Kováč (Zást. Ministra vnitra ČSSR), August 20, 1985, ABS-24113/4; V. Nergl, August 21, 1985, "Záznam o opatření v akci CARLOS čís.sv.24613," ABS-24113/4; Němec—Odbor pro mezinárodní styky kanceláře MV ČSSR, August 20, 1985, "OBADI AHMED Saleh—informace pro přátele MV PLR," ABS-24113/4.
32. Náč. odboru pro mezinárodní styky kanceláře MV ČSSR–Karel Fiřt (Náč.II.S), "Akcie Sýrie proti organizaci Abu Nidala," August 7, 1987, ABS-38165.
33. Šándor, interview by the author, July 29, 2015.
34. Jean-Louis Bruguière, interview by the author, September 22, 2022.
35. Csipák, interview by the author, September 4, 2017.
36. II.S/5, January 29, 1980, "Současná situace a charakteristika mezinárodního terorismu a hlavní úkoly orgánů po linii II.S-SNB," ABS-19324/1.
37. Ivan Voleš, interview by the author, September 2, 2015.
38. Voleš.
39. F. Rezek (Náč. Zpravodajské správy HS PS OSH)–X.S, April 7, 1977, "Seznam teroristů, dokumentace a opatření," ABS-HFSB, a.č. H-720/5.
40. "СПРАВКА," August 8, 1977, ABS-HFSB, a.č. H-720/2.
41. Orbán-Schwarzkopf, "Hungarian State Security," 129.
42. J. Vlček (Náč. OMS MV ČSSR)–V. Stárek (Náč.X.S), May 11, 1979, "HASSAN SALEH ALI-sdělení," ABS-24613/5.
43. Jaroslav Hrbáček (Náč.II.S)–V. Stárek (Náč.X.S), August 14, 1979, "Důvodová zpráva k návrhu nařízení ministra vnitra ČSSR pro činnost SNB a HS PS OSH na úseku boje proti terorismu," ABS-24613/3.
44. Lucie Hanáčková, "Útvar zvláštního určení v letech 1981–1985" (master's diss., Masarykova University, 2014), https://is.muni.cz/th/yg9oz/Utvar_zvlastniho_urceni_v_letech_1981-1985_pdf_Archive.pdf?kod=Ze0048.

45. II.S, March 27, 1979, "Náměty na jednání při dvoustranných rozhovorech se spřátelenými kontrarozvědkami k problému terorizmu," ABS-16987/1.
46. J. Vlček (Náč. OMS MV ČSSR)–V. Stárek (Náč.X.S), September 19, 1977, "Ramirec Iljič-informace z BLR," ABS-24613/2; J. Hrbáček (Náč.II.S)–OMS MV ČSSR, March 22, 1979, "ADIH FAWAZ Ahmed, člen teroristické skupiny," ABS-16987/1; "Informace k pobytu člena teroristické skupiny na území ČSSR," March 28, 1979, ABS-16987/1.
47. II.S, March 28, 1979, "Zpráva o situaci na úseku boje proti terorismu organizovaný v rámci II. Správy FMV," ABS-24613/2.
48. Nergl, interview by the author, January 9, 2018
49. Jan Musil, former officer of the StB's Second Directorate, and Vladimír Nergl, interview by the author, January 9, 2018.
50. Bruguière, interview by the author, September 22, 2022.
51. During the Cold War, the United States largely faced international terrorism abroad, where various jackals targeted its diplomatic missions, envoys, and troops, and hence faced few of the dilemmas that plagued states attacked by terrorists in their homeland, such as France, West Germany, and the United Kingdom.
52. Andrew, *Defence of the Realm*, 601–2.
53. Andrew, 613.
54. Thomas E. Carbonneau, "The Provisional Arrest and Subsequent Release of Abu Daoud by French Authorities," *Virginia Journal of International Law* 17, no. 3 (1977).
55. Reeve, *One Day in September*, 209–10. Our knowledge of the United Kingdom's pursuit and investigation of key crimes committed by the jackals is limited because most documents remain classified, such as documents in the National Archives in Kew detailing Carlos's role in the attempted murder of Joseph Sieff, which at the time of writing is set to remain closed until 2058.
56. A prime example of this approach was Israel's Operation Wrath of God, the decades-long assassination campaign triggered by the 1972 Munich Olympics massacre and designed to kill prominent Palestinians, many of whom had direct links to the infamous terrorist attack. See Bergman, *Rise and Kill First*. Since 9/11, the United States has also opted for an assassination approach to terrorism—via more traditional means or drones. On the evolution of US counterterrorism, see Naftali, *Blind Spot*.
57. Wyn Rees and Richard J. Aldrich, "Contending Cultures of Counterterrorism: Transatlantic Divergence or Convergence?," *International Affairs* 81, no. 5 (2005): 905–23; Naftali, *Blind Spot*.
58. Their approach to countering Arab/Palestinian perpetrators of international terrorist attacks campaigns should not be confused with Western countries' responses to their domestic challengers, who often used sabotage and terrorism against Western capitals. With regard to the IRA, ETA, and FLN, the West typically adopted harsh responses.
59. Dobson and Payne, *Terror!*, 70.
60. Follain, *Jackal*, 26–27. See also Neil Tweedie, "Desert Hostages Put a Strain on Relations with US," *Telegraph*, January 1, 2001.
61. Reeve, *One Day in September*, 209–10.
62. Seale, *Abu Nidal*, 272.
63. Bruguière, interview by the author, September 22, 2022.

64. For more on French and German anxieties about upsetting Arab partners, see Carbonneau, "Provisional Arrest and Subsequent Release," 501–2.
65. In cases when Western states chose to prosecute, concerns about relations were also present. For instance, in the run-up to the trial of ANO members who attacked the Israeli ambassador to the United Kingdom, Shlomo Agrov, London was worried about Iraq's response, especially if links with the terrorist organizations were discussed in court. See documents in file TNA-FCO 8/4730.
66. Duane R. Clarridge, *A Spy for All Seasons: My Life in the CIA* (New York: Scribner, 1997), 334–35.
67. Clarridge, 335–36.
68. Douglas London, interview by the author, September 13, 2022.
69. London, interview by the author, September 13, 2022.
70. Jeremy Shapiro and Bénédicte Suzan, "The French Experience of Counterterrorism," *Survival* 45, no. 1 (2003): 67–98; Kim Willsher, "Ex-French spy chief admits 1980s pact with Palestinian terrorists" Guardian, August 9, 2019, https://www.theguardian.com/world/2019/aug/09/we-made-a-deal-ex-french-spy-chief-admits-1983-pact-with-fatah-terrorists.
71. Seale, *Abu Nidal*, 269–71.
72. Smith, *Carlos*, 123–24.
73. Bruguière, interview by the author, September 22, 2022.
74. A rare case of documents detailing such an arrangement is the so-called Wischnewski Protocol discussed by Matthias Dahlke in Hänni, Riegler, and Gasztold, *Terrorism in the Cold War*, vol. 2, 175–91. Interview-based evidence of Western states' alleged pacts is further discussed by Tobias Hof in Hänni, Riegler, and Gasztold, vol. 2, 153–73; and Marcel Gyr in Hänni, Riegler, and Gasztold, vol. 2, 63–88.

# Conclusion

The story of Prague's engagement with Cold War jackals represents a crucial chapter in Cold War history and invites a number of reflections on the nature of statecraft and spycraft within the context of state interactions with violent nonstate actors.

Overall, this book has attempted to show that state relations with violent nonstate actors are fluid and complex. They vary from group to group and metamorphose over time—usually as a consequence of numerous strategic and tactical considerations or the eccentricities of particular players. They may be entirely overt, entirely covert, or a mixture of the two. At times these interactions can also be paradoxical. While pursuing liaison with a group, states might simultaneously attempt to manipulate and infiltrate the very same nonstate allies and, in some cases, seek to counter or expel their most radical components. With regard to terrorist foes, governments might seek to open a channel of communication even with those they fear and despise.

In the closing decades of the Cold War, international terrorists and revolutionaries descended on Prague and other Soviet Bloc capitals largely uninvited. While some were there on business—to meet their Middle Eastern supporters, plot further attacks, liaise, or request support from communist leaders—others flocked to the region to lie low and escape the intense political environments they typically operated in, pursue education and training, or seek medical treatment. Their arrival forced communist states to carefully consider their posture toward these foreign players: to decide who to align with and who to leave out in the cold.

Prague closely watched the jackals and gradually drew red lines. It learned to distinguish between those it deemed moderate and wished to align with and those it considered too extremist. Accordingly, by the mid-1970s, it had created a long-term political alliance with the PLO and its key faction, Fatah. Several years later, this partnership developed a strong security and intelligence component characterized by weapon sales, security training, information exchange, active-measures collaboration, and consideration of joint operations. Czechoslovak kingmakers also gradually warmed up to the controversial Rejectionist factions, Arafat's rivals. In the last decade of the Cold War, they established semiofficial relations with the likes of George Habash and his PFLP, which enabled them to engage in limited liaison but to avoid formal recognition. While following this thaw Rejectionists did receive some military and security support, this was somewhat limited and arguably introduced to show Prague's goodwill rather than to increase capacity.

Prague, however, refused to strike similar alliances with the extremist elements of the wider Palestinian resistance movement, such as Abu Daoud's or Wadi Haddad's disciples, as well as with the enfants terribles. Aware of the questionable revolutionary credentials of the likes of Carlos and Abu Nidal, their limited strategic utility, and fearing possible reputational damage, Czechoslovakia resisted creating partnerships with these capricious and violent players. It eventually developed measures to counter them.

Prague's heterogeneous approach to the jackals was determined by a combination of factors. The Soviet Bloc's, and hence Prague's, strategic foreign policy goals in the Middle East had a profound effect on whether it aligned with a particular group and, if so, on what level. The bloc's ambition to maintain a foothold in the Middle East, to play a key role in a future Israeli-Arab peace deal, and to keep the West out led Moscow and its allies to partner with the PLO and its dominant Fatah faction when they embraced diplomacy and rose to international prominence. The Soviets and Czechoslovaks were hopeful that one day, when the PLO controlled a recognized state, their early overt and covert support for Arafat's organization would pay off.

It was these very strategic interests that prevented Prague from creating an official alliance with the more controversial Palestinian groups. Although the leaders of key Rejectionist factions were ideologically closer to Prague than Arafat, their groups simply never offered the weight and gravitas that the Palestinian umbrella organization commanded. In fact, until the late 1970s, Prague refused to establish direct ties. By the time Carlos the Jackal and Abu Nidal asked Prague for support, it was quite clear to the communist country that their strategic utility was almost zero. Although Carlos claimed to be a Marxist and Abu Nidal a defender of Palestinian interests, Prague considered them to be loose cannons or mercenaries motivated by personal vendettas and financial interests.

It was, however, not all about strategic interests. Prague's interaction with these groups was also led by intelligence motivations. The StB had few Middle Eastern experts among its ranks and a limited understanding of international terrorism. Accordingly, Prague was eager for the PLO to provide knowledge and information about important players and targets across the Middle East, to which Palestinian representatives—diplomats, fighters, and spies—had much better access. In exchange, Czechoslovakia provided Arafat's men with diplomatic support and material aid and helped build their capacity by sharing know-how—namely, via security and intelligence training of Palestinians on Czechoslovak soil. Nevertheless, this was not a simple quid pro quo affair. Even when the PLO failed to deliver valuable intelligence, Czechoslovak support continued in the hope that Arafat's envoys and spies would deliver more once they regained their foothold in the Middle East. Furthermore, they learned more about and from each other as StB officers and Palestinian security representatives worked together through various crises and challenges.

Group agendas and dynamics mattered. From the very beginning of their alliance with Arafat, the Soviet Union and Czechoslovakia were concerned about the internal politics of the PLO—primarily about Palestinian unity. According to the wisdom of the times, the more united the Palestinians were, the more relevant actors they were considered to be. Moreover, if united, various factions would not seek support from Arab reactionary states, which were thorns in the side of the Soviet Bloc.

Crucially, the jackals' tactics were of great concern. While in the 1960s strategic interests in the third world and the ethos of the decolonization era led Prague to take more risks—most notably by training African revolutionaries in sabotage and allowing Latin American revolutionaries to use its territory as a gateway to Cuba—by the 1970s it displayed considerably more caution. In the last two decades of the Cold War, Prague was much more concerned about reckless violence and questionable revolutionary credentials. It thus consistently discouraged its Fatah allies from using terrorist and sabotage-like tactics and refused to provide them with so-called terrorist training. Similar concerns kept it from creating a partnership with the likes of Carlos the Jackal and Abu Nidal.

Prague's approach to tactics matured not due to the softening of its feelings toward the West but simply because the stakes became too high. With the Reagan administration increasingly spinning its narrative of the Soviet-terror plot, Prague was acutely aware that any association with jackals involved in terrorism could have wide-reaching reputational, diplomatic, and even economic consequences.

The foreign and domestic branches of the StB were crucial to managing these relations and guarding Prague's red lines. The Communist Party, Czechoslovakia's key decision-making force, deployed its spies much like a Swiss Army Knife—as a multitool device designed to carry out its multifaceted approach to Cold War jackals.

Accordingly, in the case of Arafat's Fatah, Prague deployed its case officers to liaise with the faction's representatives across the Middle East—a dangerous region where alliances were often put to the test during times of crisis. During these postings, Prague's case officers often took substantial risks to meet their contacts and had to learn to navigate the complicated terrain of local civil conflicts. The StB's domestic directorates were tasked with liaising with the Palestinians on Czechoslovak territory. Here they participated in high-level negotiations, helped train their cadres, and attempted to partner with the PLO Office in an effort to counter extremist Middle Eastern groups.

When it came to the Rejectionists, StB officers were deployed by the regime when official contacts were out of the question. Before the country set up direct relations with Arafat's key opponents, they used their spies to keep close contact with a key PFLP figure. While this "gray zone" arrangement lacked a formal footing and proved to be challenging, it helped Prague gain insight into Palestinian politics and pursue modest covert policies in the region. Czechoslovak leaders also used the StB as their first line of defense and a risk-mitigation tool against the most radical of the jackals. The regime deployed its domestic officers to watch, block, infiltrate, and, in some cases, also oust these villainous figures—often at great personal risk.

Overall, the StB was not the ideational and functional monolith it is often made out to be. When deployed to deal with the jackals, the organization emerged as a complex ecosystem made up of officers of various aptitudes and capabilities. Disagreements between departments and individuals were also not uncommon. When it came to controversial operations or decisions, StB officers engaged in testy debates about the risks and benefits of various scenarios. The old-style institution that was the StB had to adapt and reform at a time when it seemed that the terrorist threat was all too close and ready to cross the Iron Curtain. For over two decades, Prague and its State Security Service balanced precariously on a narrow ledge in its dealings with Middle Eastern revolutionaries and terrorists who sought refuge, arms, training, money, and political support.

In all its forms, interactions between Prague and the Cold War jackals were inherently uncomfortable and anxious. Despite shared rhetoric about "revolutions" and the potential of mutual utility, they lacked trust. In fact, when it came to the orderly Soviet Bloc countries, liaisons with violent, unstable, and controversial nonstate entities, often entangled in internecine rivalry, did not sit well. Communist states revered revolutionaries in theory but struggled when having to associate with them in practice, not least because of their disorderly and anarchic practices.

Accordingly, the Czechoslovak-PLO diplomatic, security, and intelligence alliance was no symbiotic relationship. It was characterized by dissonance—a mismatch in expectations, objectives, and preferred tactics. Arguably, Czechoslovakia sought an ideologically and politically reliable partner to fight the imperialists in the Middle East—not a group that engaged in internal revolutionary rivalry and messy operations that alienated the public and whose members repeatedly tried to defect to the West. The PLO and its many factions often searched for rich and reckless sponsors. This they failed to find in

Czechoslovakia as the communist state proved to be more cautious in its dealings with these groups than they had hoped. Accordingly, the Czechoslovak-Palestinian security and intelligence alliance never matured into a well-rounded operational partnership.

This uneasiness also extended to Prague's perspective on the enfants terribles. Above all, the communist state feared the unpredictable Carlos the Jackal as well as other extremists associated with the Palestinian cause. They disliked their tempers, were skeptical of their Marxist credentials, and disapproved of their indiscriminately violent methods. This fear was further amplified by the changing counterterrorism environment in Europe, which especially in the 1980s led to increased international pressure and thus reputational hazards for states engaging with revolutionaries and terrorists.

To disassociate with these controversial actors, in the last decade of the Cold War Czechoslovakia developed its own way of countering extremists it deemed dangerous. While it had its own tempo when applied to each group, in most cases Prague first adopted a subtle watch-and-wait approach, which entailed deploying long-term, full-scale surveillance of a particular target. If the target was deemed dangerous, suspected of organizing terrorist activity, or would persistently return to the Central European nation under false identity, Prague's watchers escalated their approach to block and prevent, a strategy that entailed adding the individual to the country's persona non grata list. In select cases, the StB adopted the infiltrate-and-manipulate approach, in an effort to better understand and attempt to control the jackals. Finally, if all failed, Prague devised complicated plans to expel the most dangerous jackals from its territory as part of its trick-and-oust strategy.

Czechoslovakia's multistage strategy designed to counter the jackals could be best described as a risk-management-centered counterterrorism style. This was an inward-looking and devious model of counterterrorism aimed at chasing the problem away rather than solving it. Although its ousting strategy typically worked and deterred the jackals from returning, the three less aggressive approaches generated long-term problems for the Czechoslovak security services, which found themselves repeatedly surveilling individuals and then blocking them from their territory as well as reforming their border-control and surveillance mechanisms, desperate to avoid reputational damage. These groups clandestinely descending on the socialist country's territory in many ways outpaced the plodding watchers of the StB. In the last decade of the Cold War, this struggle for control over these unpredictable groups led Prague to engage in what emerged to be an embryonic regional counterterrorist network aimed at surveilling violent nonstate actors.

Counterterrorism was as challenging in the East as it was in the West. In fact, during this formative era of European counterterrorism, the two ideological blocs were arguably faced with profoundly similar challenges and in some instances adopted analogous approaches to Cold War international terrorism. On both sides of the Iron Curtain, it took some time to develop strategies and practices that would enable states to keep up with the dynamic and elusive nonstate actors. Counterterrorism showed itself as an inherently imperfect exercise regardless of ideology.

\*\*\*

The story of Prague's interactions with Cold War jackals also tells us much about the nature of Cold War terrorism. It shows that these allegedly well-coordinated networks of terrorists were often happenstance alliances of individuals who had ideological and personal differences. The underground life of revolutionaries and terrorists was a precarious one, characterized by unpredictable and frequent infighting and splits, everchanging alliances with host states, and questionable characters led by their own egos. Like other collective human endeavors, it was marked by competition and conflict between groups—often caused by such mundane things as overstepping boundaries or personal anomalies. This was a contested space where collaboration was tried but often failed. The Cold War terrorist underworld was a far cry from what Claire Sterling called *The Terror Network*.

Crucially, this story shows that the Soviet Bloc was far from a monolithic supporter of Cold War terrorism. While Czechoslovakia, like most Soviet Bloc states, supported the PLO and its main faction, Fatah, it had a much more cautious and, in some cases, hostile relationship with other Cold War jackals. Furthermore, its approach often diverged from that of other Soviet Bloc allies that may have been more adventurous in their support for these villainous figures. These findings should encourage us to step outside the simplistic binary narrative of Soviet sponsorship of terror, which for decades unhelpfully divided states between those who support and those who oppose terror. The truth is more complicated and indeed often convoluted.

The story also highlights the advantages of adopting Tony Smith's pericentric approach to studying the Cold War. By showing the agency of Prague as well as the jackals, it confirms that the contest between the East and the West can indeed be better understood if we appreciate the role of junior partners—state and nonstate alike. By zooming in on the interaction between Czechoslovakia and terrorists and revolutionaries, we can see how the more peripheral players of the Cold War contributed to building alliances, strengthening each other's capacity, and developing nuanced counterterrorism methods.

Moreover, it shows the complicated legacy of such figures as Yasser Arafat, Gustáv Husák, Vasiľ Biľak, and Ilich Ramírez Sánchez, who all played a role in the epic Cold War struggle—often adding more color and complexity to the central dynamics of the conflict than previously appreciated. Cold War jackals as a collective also emerge as an important driver of superpower involvement and competition in the Middle East—especially when their daring terrorist attacks forced superpowers to negotiate or, in some cases, go to war. They also proved to be fiercely independent actors, who Prague—despite its efforts—simply failed to control.

This ultimately begs a final reflection on Michael Herman's important notion of intelligence as a form of power.[1] In its dealings with Cold War jackals, was intelligence used as a form of power? Did it help Prague achieve its goals when it came to those with whom it partnered as well as those it firmly opposed? Or did the tail wag the dog? Intelligence liaison with nonstate actors contributed to Prague's understanding of its Palestinian partners and the wider Middle East and enabled subtle propaganda campaigns. The StB also helped demonstrate the country's power by monitoring, blocking, and in some cases ousting dangerous individuals from Czechoslovak territory when diplomatic and political interventions had proven ineffective. Ultimately, however, Prague's intelligence and security apparatus failed to control its nonstate partners and foes. Intelligence was thus not used here to project power but rather to mitigate and negotiate risk. The StB was there to save face, avoid embarrassment, and prevent retribution from the Cold War jackals.

## NOTE

1. Michael Herman, *Intelligence Power in Peace and War* (Cambridge: Cambridge University Press, 1996).

# AFTERWORD

*A Note on Sources*

Czechoslovak communist-era intelligence and state security documents are at the core of this book. Thanks to them, we are now able to explore the fascinating world of Czechoslovakia's secret state and provide a fresh interpretation of some of the key events that unfolded during the Cold War. Today the vast majority of StB documents are in the Czech Republic. The general public and researchers were first given significant access to StB documents in 2007. This was the result of a set of laws that enabled access to all documents in their original form, without redaction, and blanket declassification of all communist-era security and intelligence documents established prior to the dissolution of Czechoslovakia on December 31, 1992. This legislation also led to the establishment of the Institute for the Study of Totalitarian Regimes (Ústav pro studium totalitních režimů, or ÚSTR), a research outfit dedicated to the study of the Nazi occupation of the Czech lands (1938–45) and the Czechoslovak communist regime (1948–89),[1] as well as the ABS (Archiv bezpečnostních složek), which became the main repository for all security and intelligence files pertinent to these periods.[2]

The volume of declassifications of security and intelligence material in Prague has been unprecedented. This scale and speed were facilitated by the fact that the ABS was set up primarily as a mechanism of reconciling with Czechoslovakia's totalitarian past. At the time of writing, the archive holds the vast majority of all civilian and military documents produced by Prague's law enforcement, security, and intelligence organizations during the two periods of totalitarian rule. According to estimates by official historians of the Czech foreign intelligence service, to date their service, the Office for Foreign Relations and Information (Úřad pro zahraniční styky a informace, or ÚZSI), has released 99 percent of all communist-era intelligence StB documents and retains only a fraction—140 files—of all secret-collaborator files.[3]

The Czech approach to handling communist secret service files arguably makes the country's legislation the most liberal in postcommunist Europe. First, researchers are given access to virtually all declassified files, including personal files of StB targets, unlike in Germany or Slovakia, where only subjects of personal files are given full access. Second, unlike in the United States, none of the documents in the ABS are redacted, unless they pertain to the period following the dissolution of Czechoslovakia on December 31, 1992. This means that they contain levels of unprecedented detail—including all officers' and agents' names, addresses, biographies, operations, and training details. This enables researchers of the StB to not only analyze the entire content of these files but also to "follow the trail" to other files that may provide additional content and context. Third, First Directorate (foreign intelligence) files, generally considered more sensitive than files of domestic intelligence services, have—unlike in the East German case—in many cases survived, and most have now been made available to researchers.[4] Fourth, the archive provides online aids that not only enable researchers to search existing databases of files but, as of November 2022, also access and word-search many files online.[5]

Documents housed in the ABS have, however, also suffered from several plagues: routine and end-of-regime destruction, theft, and controversy. How have files on the Middle East, terrorists, and revolutionaries been impacted? Any final assessments are hard to make because Prague's interactions with the jackals stretched across four decades of the Cold War and unfolded in Czechoslovakia as well as abroad. Nevertheless, some preliminary conclusions on the state of affairs are possible.

Not all StB and military intelligence files pertinent to the jackals and the countries they operated in have indeed survived. Much like many other services, the StB shredded files periodically. Some documents detailing StB rezidenturas in key Middle Eastern capitals became victims of this routine destruction as, years after they were set up, they were no longer judged to be of use. End-of-regime destruction also had an impact on the file collection used for this book. Immediately after the November 1989 Velvet Revolution, StB officers were given orders to destroy some of the most sensitive documents. While this hasty destruction of files was primarily aimed at erasing the Soviet footprint, ongoing operations against the principal adversary and Czechoslovak dissidents as well as files on international terrorism were not hard hit.[6] Although some files of foreign informants—largely Middle Eastern—working for the StB were destroyed, the larger thematic files were generally preserved as they were thought possibly to be useful in years to come.

Arguably, by destroying these "live" personal files of key agents, the StB not only sought to cover up its own tracks but also aimed to protect some of its key assets. Perhaps it anticipated that some of its foreign-national collaborators were likely to suffer harsh repercussions in their countries of origin (Syria, Libya, or Lebanon) were they found to have worked for foreign security or intelligence.

Core files on international terrorism face an additional set of problems. Some documents listed in core file registers are clearly missing. We can only speculate when and why they were taken out. They could have been removed during the communist period, especially in the 1980s when the "international terror agenda" was repeatedly shifted from directorate to directorate due to bureaucratic reshuffles.[7] We also know that the files related to this agenda were not always kept as tidy as StB management would have desired. However, they also could have been removed in the early 1990s, when documents deemed highly relevant to the new democratic Czechoslovak intelligence services were extracted from the original communist-era files and put into new "select files on international terrorism."[8] Having been released for the first time in January 2018, these select files are incorporated into this book and enable us to present the most holistic interpretation of Prague's take on international terrorism to date.

There are several imbalances with respect to the nature of StB archival records that further complicated this investigation. We know more about the 1980s than we do about the early stages of Prague's interactions with international terrorism and nonstate actors. Core StB files were only set up at the end of the 1970s and thus mostly focus on the period thereafter (although they do contain some documents from earlier eras). Furthermore, we have more tactical than strategic documents. To a historian, such an abundance of tactical data helps reconstruct the narrative of a particular operation and allows the StB's own assessment of particular episodes to be put to the test.

Nevertheless, the lack of strategic documents—decisions and orders—regarding different violent nonstate actors is problematic. Although we can observe changes in policy or approach without them, we are often left without a clear record of why such decisions were taken and in fact who decided on a particular course of action. Some interviewees and written records suggest that sensitive orders such as those to expel Carlos the Jackal and Abu Daoud from Czechoslovakia (and those allowing their stay in the first place) were never put on paper. Furthermore, records show that when discussing setting up a direct liaison contact with the PLO in Beirut, oral orders were preferred.[9]

While written records are key to understanding and interpreting the past, prominent scholars have warned of historians becoming hostage to their sources—a trap Richard Drayton termed "a kind of intellectual Stockholm Syndrome."[10] In other words, it is tempting for the historian to trust and view newly declassified material as "true facts." Interviews have therefore been a crucial element of historical inquiries into the secret state as they help provide wider context, evaluate archival records critically, and often provide the missing backstory.

Elite and oral history interviews have thus been an important part of this inquiry especially in its initial stages. While locating former communists, diplomats, and spies was an arduous task, this book is informed by over two dozen unstructured, in-depth interviews with subjects from the Czech Republic,

Slovakia, France, the United Kingdom, and the United States. While some of the interviewees wished to remain anonymous, most spoke on record, often providing crucial detail, context, or anecdotes that added color to the narrative.

Regretfully, we are thus far missing the Arab angle to the narrative presented in this book. Access to Palestinian and Arab documents on security and intelligence is problematic. Although this book utilizes a number of memoirs by top Palestinian figures and we do have some documents from PLO archives, captured by Israeli forces during their 1982 invasion of Lebanon,[11] this is but the tip of the iceberg. There is no equivalent of the ABS for Palestinian Cold War security and intelligence papers. Moreover, Palestinian subjects were reluctant to go on record. Although approaches were made to several members of the Arab community living in the Czech Republic and Slovakia, these individuals either denied involvement in security or intelligence matters or have simply refused to talk.

Hopefully, in the future we will be able to cover this fascinating story also from the vantage point of the key Palestinian figures who engaged with Czechoslovak communists, diplomats, and spies. Until then, this book can serve as a road map to understanding the complexity of these interactions from the Czechoslovak perspective.

## NOTES

1. "Council of the Institute for the Study of Totalitarian Regimes," *Ústav pro studium totalitních režimů*, http://www.ustrcr.cz/en. A segment of records pertinent to the StB's work, most crucially that of its branches in Slovakia, is managed by the ÚSTR's Slovak equivalent, the Archive of the Nation's Memory Institute (*Ústav pamäti národa*), a.k.a. the ÚPN Archive.
2. The ABS manages civilian documents as well as those related to military intelligence and security, the Ministry of Justice, and law enforcement. Petr Kaňák, "Cesta ke zpřístupnění dokumentace československé rozvědky," the author's private archive, unpublished, 2023; "Zákon o Ústavu pro studium totalitních režimů a o Archivu bezpečnostních složek a o změně některých zákonů," Sbírka zákonů, Zákony pro lidi, https://www.zakonyprolidi.cz/cs/2007-181.
3. Kaňák, "Cesta ke zpřístupnění dokumentace"; Koura and Kaňák, "Czechoslovak Foreign Intelligence Files."
4. For instance, the Stasi archive mostly holds collections of East Germany's internal security services. The majority of foreign intelligence files were destroyed in the last days of the communist regime. Joachim Gauck and Martin Fry, "Dealing with a Stasi Past," *Daedalus*, 123 (January 1994).
5. eBadatelna, Archiv bezpečnostních složek, https://www.abscr.cz/ebadatelna/.
6. R. Schovánek, "Svazek Dialog. StB versus Pavel Kohout," http://www.ludvikvaculik.cz/index.php?pid=121&sid=149.
7. Zdeněk Němec (Náč. XIV.S-SNB)–Ján Kováč (I. Nám. ministra vnitra), November 11, 1985, "Plnění úkolů vyplývajících z operativní porady u s. I. náměstka MV ČSSR do akce 'CARLOS' ze dne 22.8.1985—informace," ABS-24113/6.

8. A good example of such files is ABS-OBŽ-38165.
9. As one particular document on liaison with the PLO clearly states, "The rest of the orders will be given to you personally by the first deputy minister of the interior." Dezider Hronec (Náč. sekr. I. NMV ČSSR)–Karel Vrba (Náčelník II.S-SNB), November 15, 1979, ABS-19324/1.
10. Richard Drayton, "Where Does the World Historian Write From? Objectivity, Moral Conscience, and the Past and Present of Imperialism," *Journal of Contemporary History* 46, no. 3 (2011): 672.
11. Israeli, *PLO in Lebanon*.

# BIBLIOGRAPHY

PRIMARY SOURCES

Archival Sources

All references to primary documents in the endnotes are from the following archives:

- Archiv bezpečnostních složek (ABS), Czech Republic
- Archiv Ministerstva zahraničních věcí (AMZV), Czech Republic
- Národní archiv (NA), Czech Republic
- National Archives (TNA), United Kingdom
- Ústav pamäti národa (UPN), Slovak Republic
- Vojenský historický archív (VHA), Czech Republic

Interviews by the Author

Belica, Miroslav. Prague. August 18, 2015.
Bruguière, Jean-Louis. Paris. June 2, 2016; September 22, 2022.
Csipák, Ladislav. Bratislava. September 4, 2017.
Goodman, Melvin A. Washington, DC. June 29, 2016.
K., Maroš. Prague. January 8, 2018.
K., Milan. Dunajská Lužná. September 13, 2017.
Krejčí, Josef. Prague. September 16, 2015; July 13, 2017.
Kropáček, Luboš. Prague. August 13, 2015.
Kukan, Eduard. Bratislava. August 24, 2017.
London, Douglas. Online. September 13, 2022.
Musil, Jan. Prague. January 9, 2018.
Nergl, Vladimír. Prague. January 9, 2018.
P., Peter. Southwestern Czech Republic. September 4, 2015; January 3, 2016.
Šándor, Andor. Prague. July 29, 2015.
Schwarcz, Petr. Prague. September 7, 2015.
Ulčák, Dušan. Ostrava. September 8, 2015.
Voleš, Ivan. Prague. September 2, 2015; August 28, 2017.
Wiant, Jon. Baltimore. February 24, 2017.

## Speeches, Government, and NGO Reports

Arafat, Yasser. "Speech to the UN General Assembly in New York." November 13, 1974. https://al-bab.com/documents-section/speech-yasser-arafat-1974.

Federal Chancellery. *Events of September 28th and 29th 1973: A Documentary Report*. Vienna: Federal Chancellery, 1973.

Federální ministerstvo vnitra. *Základy bezpečnostní služby II: Základní úkoly StB*. Prague: Federální ministerstvo vnitra, 1981.

Jenkins, Brian M., and Janera A. Johnson. *International Terrorism: A Chronology, 1968–1974*. R-1597-DOS/ARPA. Santa Monica, CA: RAND, March 1975. https://www.rand.org/content/dam/rand/pubs/reports/2007/R1597.pdf.

———. *International Terrorism: A Chronology (1974 Supplement)*. R-1909-1-ARPA. Santa Monica, CA: RAND, February 1976. http://www.dtic.mil/dtic/tr/fulltext/u2/a043758.pdf.

Roosevelt, Franklin D., and Winston S. Churchill. "The Atlantic Charter." August 14, 1941, Avalon Project, Yale Law School, https://avalon.law.yale.edu/wwii/atlantic.asp.

## SECONDARY SOURCES

### Video, Audio, and Live Seminars

Andrew, Christopher. "Speech at Cambridge Intelligence Seminar." Corpus Christi College, October 13, 2017.

"How Did the Iraqis Get Rid of Abu Nidal?" [كيف تخلص العراقيون من أبو نضال؟]. *Al Arabiya*, n.d. https://www.youtube.com/watch?v=Qmby1U6xtlw.

"Reviews with Atef Abu Bakr" [مراجعات مع فطاع وبا بكر]. Al Hiwar TV, April 28, 2011. https://www.youtube.com/watch?v=U7OvJ7EOPpY.

"Synd 27/03/73 Interview Guerilla Leader Abu Daoud on Black September." AP Archive, March 3, 1973. https://www.youtube.com/watch?v=MF4AYcS337w.

"Tajné akce StB—Akce Asanace." Česká televize, 2008. https://www.youtube.com/watch?v=iFajS19aYb4.

### Written Secondary Sources

Abarbanell, Oded. "Hijacking to Algiers—Part 1." In *Stories of My Family and from the Fawn of Flight in Israel* (blog), May 8, 2013. https://odedabarbanell.wordpress.com/2013/03/08/hijacked-to-algiers-part-1/.

Abu Sharif, Bassam, and Uri Mahnaimi. *Best of Enemies: The Memoirs of Bassam Abu-Sharif and Uri Mahnaimi*. Boston: Little, Brown, 1995.

Adamec, Jan. "Czechoslovak-Syrian Relations during the Cold War." In *Syria during the Cold War: The East European Connection*, edited by Przemyslaw Gasztold-Sen, Massimiliano Trenin and Jan Adamec, 67–89. Fife, UK: University of St Andrews Centre for Syrian Studies, 2014.

Aldrich, Richard J., and Rory Cormac. *The Black Door: Spies, Secret Intelligence and British Prime Ministers*. London: Collins, 2016.

Anderson, Sheldon. *A Cold War in the Soviet Bloc: Polish–East German Relations, 1945–1962*. London: Routledge, 2018.

Andrew, Christopher. *The Defence of the Realm: The Authorized History of MI5*. London: Penguin, 2009.

Andrew, Christopher, and David Dilks. *The Missing Dimension: Governments and Intelligence Communities in the Twentieth Century.* London: Macmillan, 1984.
Andrew, Christopher, and Vasili Mitrokhin. *The Mitrokhin Archive: The KGB in Europe and the West.* London: Allen Lane / Penguin, 1999.
———. *The World Was Going Our Way: The KGB and the Battle for the Third World.* New York: Basic Books, 2005.
Baev, Jordan. "Infiltration of Non-European Terrorist Groups in Europe and Antiterrorist Responses in Western and Eastern Europe (1969–1991)." In *Counter Terrorism in Diverse Communities*, edited by Siddik Ekici, 58–74. Amsterdam: IOS Press, 2011.
Bar-Zohar, Michael and Eitan Haber. *The Quest for the Red Prince.* London: Weidenfeld & Nicolson, 1983.
Becker, Jillian. *The PLO: The Rise and Fall of the Palestine Liberation Organization.* 2nd ed. Bloomington, IN: AuthorHouse, 2014.
Békés, Csaba. "The Warsaw Pact and the Helsinki Process, 1965–1970." In *The Making of Détente: Eastern and Western Europe in the Cold War, 1965–75*, edited by Wilfried Loth and Georges-Henri Soutou, 20120. London: Routledge, 2010.
Bergman, Ronen. *Rise and Kill First: The Secret History of Israel's Targeted Assassinations.* London: Hachette UK, 2018.
Bezci, Egemen. *Turkish Intelligence and the Cold War: The Turkish Secret Service, the US and the UK.* London: Bloomsbury, 2019.
Biľak, Vasiľ. *Až po mé smrti.* Prague: BVD, 2014.
———. *Paměti Vasila Biľaka: Unikátní svědectví ze zákulisí KSČ.* Prague: Agentura Cesty, 1991.
Bird, Kai. *The Good Spy: The Life and Death of Robert Ames.* New York: Broadway Books, 2014.
Bittman, Ladislav. *The KGB and Soviet Disinformation: An Insider's View.* Washington, DC: Pergamon-Brassey's, 1985.
Blažek, Petr, and Pavel Žáček. "Czechoslovakia." In *A Handbook of the Communist Security Apparatus in East Central Europe 1944–1989*, edited by Krzysztof Persak and Łukasz Kamiński, 87–100. Warsaw: Institute of National Remembrance, 2005.
Blumenau, Bernhard. *The United Nations and Terrorism: Germany, Multilateralism, and Antiterrorism Efforts in the 1970s.* Basingstoke, UK: Palgrave Macmillan, 2014.
Brennan, James R. "The Secret Lives of Dennis Phombeah: Decolonization, the Cold War, and African Political Intelligence, 1953–1974." *International History Review* 43, no. 1 (2021): 153–69.
Březinová, Kateřina. "Turbines and Weapons for Latin America Czechoslovak Documentary Film Propaganda in the Cold War Context, 1948–1989." In Mitchell Belfer and Kateřina Březinová, "Cold War Engagements. Czechoslovakia and Latin America 1948–1989." Special issue, *Central European Journal of International and Security Studies* 7, no. 3 (September 2013): 38–58.
Byman, Daniel. *Deadly Connections: States That Sponsor Terrorism.* Cambridge: Cambridge University Press, 2005.
Cajthaml, Petr. "Profesionální lháři: Aktivní opatření čs. rozvědky do srpna 1968." *Sborník Archivu Ministerstva vnitra* 4 (2006): 9–41.
Carbonneau, Thomas E. "The Provisional Arrest and Subsequent Release of Abu Daoud by French Authorities." *Virginia Journal of International Law* 17, no. 3 (1977): 496–514.
Carolla, Mark A. "Operation 'Magic Fire': A Case Study in Collaborative Threat Assessments and Risk Analysis of the German Bundesgrenzschutz GSG-9 Rescue of the

Lufthansa Boeing 737-200 'Landshut' Hostages in Mogadishu, October 1977." Diss., George Washington University, 2007.

Cassen, Robert, ed. *Soviet Interests in the Third World*. London: Sage Publications, 1985.

Chamberlin, Paul Thomas. *The Global Offensive: The United States, the Palestine Liberation Organization, and the Making of the Post–Cold War Order*. Oxford: Oxford University Press, 2012.

———. "Schönau and the Eagles of the Palestinian Revolution: Refugees, Guerillas, and Human Rights in the Global 1970s." *Cold War History* 12, no. 4 (2012): 595–614.

Clarridge, Duane R. *A Spy for All Seasons: My Life in the CIA*. New York: Scribner, 1997.

Cline, Ray S., and Yonah Alexander. *Terrorism: The Soviet Connection*. New York: Crane Russak, 1984.

Cobban, Helena. *The Palestinian Liberation Organisation: People, Power and Politics*. Cambridge: Cambridge University Press, 1984.

Council of the Institute for the Study of Totalitarian Regimes. *Ústav pro studium totalitních režimů*. http://www.ustrcr.cz/en.

Crenshaw, Martha. "The Subjective Reality of the Terrorist: Ideological and Psychological Factors in Terrorism." In *Current Perspectives on International Terrorism*, edited by Robert O. Slater and Michael Stohl, 12–46. London: Palgrave Macmillan.

Crump, Laurien. *The Warsaw Pact Reconsidered: International Relations in Eastern Europe, 1955–1969*. London: Routledge, 2015.

Cummings, Richard H. *Cold War Radio: The Dangerous History of American Broadcasting in Europe, 1950–1989*. Jefferson, NC: McFarland, 2009.

Dannreuther, Roland. *The Soviet Union and the PLO*. London: Macmillan, 1998.

De la Calle, Luis, and Ignacio Sánchez-Cuenca. "What We Talk about When We Talk about Terrorism." *Politics & Society* 39, no. 3 (2011): 451–72.

Dobson, Christopher. *Black September: Its Short, Violent History*. London: Macmillan, 1974.

Dobson, Christopher, and Ronald Payne. *Terror! The West Fights Back*. London: Macmillan, 1982.

———. *The Terrorists: Their Weapons, Leaders and Tactics*. New York: Facts on File, 1982.

Drake, Richard. "The Aldo Moro Murder Case in Retrospect." *Journal of Cold War Studies* 8, no. 2 (2006): 114–25.

Drayton, Richard. "Where Does the World Historian Write From? Objectivity, Moral Conscience, and the Past and Present of Imperialism." *Journal of Contemporary History* 46, no. 3 (2011): 671–85.

Dufek, Jiří, and Vladimír Šlosar. "Československá materiálně technická pomoc Izraeli." In *Československo a Izrael v letech 1947–1951: Studie*, edited by Jiří Dufek, 108–89. Brno: Ústav pro soudobé dějiny AV ČR v nakl. Doplněk, 1993.

Dvořáček, Petr. "Ústav zahraničního studia Vysoké školy Sboru národní bezpečnosti a jeho role ve vzdělávacím systému ministerstva vnitra." *Marginalia Historica* 3, no. 2 (2012): 114–15.

Dvořáková, Jiřina, Zdeňka Jurová, and Petr Kaňák. *Československá rozvědka a pražské jaro*. Prague: Ústav pro studium totalitních režimů, 2016.

Eisenberg, Laurie. "History Revisited or Revamped? The Maronite Factor in Israel's 1982 Invasion of Lebanon." *Israel Affairs* 15, no. 4 (2009): 372–96.

Foley, Frank. *Countering Terrorism in Britain and France: Institutions, Norms and the Shadow of the Past*. Cambridge: Cambridge University Press, 2013.

Follain, John. *Jackal: The Complete Story of the Legendary Terrorist, Carlos the Jackal.* New York: Arcade, 1998.
Forsyth, Frederick. *The Day of the Jackal.* London: Hutchinson, 1971.
Francev, Vladimír. *Československé zbraně ve světě: V míru i za války.* Prague: Grada, 2015.
Francis, Samuel T. *The Soviet Strategy of Terror.* Washington, DC: Heritage Foundation, 1981.
Frolik, Josef. *The Frolik Defection: The Memoirs of a Czech Intelligence Agent.* London: Leo Cooper, 1975.
Gasztold-Seń, Przemysław. "Between Geopolitics and National Security: Polish Intelligence and International Terrorism during the Cold War." In *Need to Know: Eastern and Western Perspectives: Studies in Intelligence and Security*, edited by Władysław Bułhak and Thomas Wegener Friis, 137–62. Odense: University Press of Southern Denmark, 2014.
———. "Międzynarodowi terroryści w PRL-historia niewymuszonej współpracy." *Pamięć i Sprawiedliwość* 21 (2013): 275–315.
———. "Warsaw and the Fedayeen: Wars in the Middle East, Secret Arms Deals and Polish Relations with the Palestine Liberation Organisation, 1967–1976." *Cold War History* 24 no. 2 (2024): 161–86.
———. *Zabójcze układy: Służby PRL i międzynarodowy terroryzm.* Warsaw: Wydawnictwo Naukowe PWN, 2017.
Gauck, Joachim, and Martin Fry. "Dealing with a Stasi Past." *Daedalus*, 123 (January 1994): 277–84.
Geiger, Tim. "'Landshut' in Mogadischu: Das Außenpolitische Krisenmanagement der Bundesregierung Angesichts der Terroristischen Herausforderung 1977." *Vierteljahrshefte Fur Zeitgeschichte* 3 (2009): 413–56.
George, Alexander, ed. *Western State Terrorism.* Cambridge: Polity, 1991.
Golan, Galia. "Moscow and Third World National Liberation Movements: The Soviet Role." *Journal of International Affairs* 40, no. 2 (Winter/Spring 1987): 303–24.
———. *Soviet Policies in the Middle East: From World War Two to Gorbachev.* Vol. 2. Cambridge: Cambridge University Press, 1990.
———. *The Soviet Union and National Liberation Movements in the Third World.* Routledge: London, 1988.
———. *The Soviet Union and the Palestine Liberation Organization: An Uneasy Alliance.* New York: Praeger, 1980.
Golani, Motti. "The Historical Place of the Czech-Egyptian Arms Deal, Fall 1955." *Middle Eastern Studies* 31, no. 4 (1995): 803–27.
Goodman, Melvin A. *Failure of Intelligence: The Decline and Fall of the CIA.* Lanham, MD: Rowman & Littlefield, 2008.
Goren, Roberta. *The Soviet Union and Terrorism.* London: Allen & Unwin, 1984.
Guevara, Che. *The African Dream: The Diaries of the Revolutionary War in the Congo.* New York: Random House, 2001.
Guttmann, Aviva. "Turning Oil into Blood: Western Intelligence, Libyan Covert Actions, and Palestinian Terrorism (1973–74)." *Journal of Strategic Studies* 45, nos. 6–7 (2022): 993–1020.
Hanáčková, Lucie. "Útvar zvláštního určení v letech 1981–1985." Bachelor's thesis, Masarykova University, 2014.
Hanhimäki, Jussi M., and Bernhard Blumenau, eds. *An International History of Terrorism: Western and Non-Western Experiences.* Abingdon, UK: Routledge, 2013.

Hänni, Adrian. "When Casey's Blood Pressure Rose: A Case Study of Intelligence Politicization in the United States." *Intelligence and National Security* 31, no. 7 (2016): 963–77.

Hänni, Adrian, Thomas Riegler, and Przemyslaw Gasztold, eds. *Terrorism in the Cold War: State Support in Eastern Europe and the Soviet Sphere of Influence*. Vol. 1. London: Bloomsbury, 2021.

———, eds. *Terrorism in the Cold War: State Support in the West, Middle East and Latin Americac*. Vol. 2. London: Bloomsbury, 2021.

Hannová, Daniela. "Problémoví elegáni: Arabští studenti v Praze v 50. a 60. letech 20. století." *Auc Historia Universitatis Carolinae Pragensis* 54, no. 2 (2016): 105–25.

Harper, Lauren. "The Merchant of Death's Account Book." National Security Archive, February 23, 2015. https://nsarchive2.gwu.edu/NSAEBB/NSAEBB502/.

Harrison, Hope M. *Driving the Soviets up the Wall: Soviet–East German Relations, 1953–1961*. Princeton, NJ: Princeton University Press, 2011.

Herf, Jeffrey. *Undeclared Wars with Israel: East Germany and the West German Far Left, 1967–1989*. New York: Cambridge University Press, 2016.

Herman, Edward S. *The Real Terror Network: Terrorism in Fact and Propaganda*. Montreal: South End, 1982.

Herman, Edward S., and Gerry O'Sullivan. *The Terrorism Industry: The Experts and Institutions That Shape Our View of Terror*. New York: Pantheon, 1989.

Herman, Michael. *Intelligence Power in Peace and War* (Cambridge: Cambridge University Press, 1996).

Hirst, David. *Beware of Small States: Lebanon, Battleground of the Middle East*. London: Faber, 2011.

Hoffman, Bruce. *Inside Terrorism*. New York: Columbia University Press, 2006.

Israeli, Raphael, ed. *PLO in Lebanon: Selected Documents*. London: Weidenfeld & Nicolson, 1983.

Iyad, Abu, and Eric Rouleau. *My Home, My Land: A Narrative of the Palestinian Struggle*. New York: Times Books, 1981.

Jacobson, Sidney, and Ernie Colón. *Che: A Graphic Biography*. New York: Hill & Wang, 2009.

Jašek, Peter. *Biľak: Zradca alebo kolaborant?* Bratislava: Marenčín PT, 2018.

Jersild, Austin. "The Soviet State as Imperial Scavenger: 'Catch Up and Surpass' in the Transnational Socialist Bloc, 1950–1960." *American Historical Review* 116, no. 1 (2011): 109–32.

Kalinovsky, Artemy M., and Sergey Radchenko, eds. *The End of the Cold War and the Third World*. London: Routledge, 2011.

Kaňák, Peter. "Cesta ke zpřístupnění dokumentace československé rozvědky." Unpublished manuscript, 2023.

Katsakioris, Constantin. "The Lumumba University in Moscow: Higher Education for a Soviet–Third World Alliance, 1960–91." *Journal of Global History* 14, no. 2 (2019): 281–300.

Khalidi, Rashid. *Under Siege: PLO Decisionmaking during the 1982 War*. New York: Columbia University Press, 2013.

Kim, Samuel S., ed. *China and the World: Chinese Foreign Relations in the Post–Cold War Era*. Boulder, CO: Westview, 1994.

Klein, Aaron J. *Protiúder: Mníchov*. Bratislava: Slovenský spisovateľ, 2005.
Klimke, Martin, Reinhild Kreis, and Christian Ostermann, eds. *Trust, but Verify: The Politics of Uncertainty and the Transformation of the Cold War Order, 1969–1991*. Washington, DC: Woodrow Wilson Center Press, 2016.
Kolář, Pavel, and Michal Pullmann. *Co byla normalizace? Studie o pozdním socialismu*. Prague: NLN, ÚSTR, 2017.
Koura, Jan. "A Prominent Spy: Mehdi Ben Barka, Czechoslovak Intelligence, and Eastern Bloc Espionage in the Third World during the Cold War." *Intelligence and National Security* 36, no. 3 (2020): 318–39.
Koura, Jan, and Petr Kaňák. "Czechoslovak Foreign Intelligence Files," *International Journal of Intelligence and CounterIntelligence* 37, no. 2 (2024): 450–81.
Koura, Jan, and Robert Anthony Waters. "'Africanos' versus 'Africanitos': The Soviet-Czechoslovak Competition to Protect the Cuban Revolution." *International History Review* 43, no. 1 (2021): 72–89.
Krátká, Lenka. "'Astounding It Is, What Lidice Carries': The Transport of Czechoslovak Weapons for the Algerian National Liberation Front in 1959." *International Journal of Maritime History* 33, no. 1 (2021): 54–69.
Laron, Guy. "Logic Dictates That They May Attack When They Feel They Can Win: The 1955 Czech-Egyptian Arms Deal, the Egyptian Army, and Israeli Intelligence." *Middle East Journal* 63, no. 1 (Winter 2009): 69–84.
Levin, Nora. *The Jews in the Soviet Union since 1917: Paradox of Survival*. Vols. 1 and 2. New York: NYU Press, 1990.
Macháček, Michal. *Gustáv Husák*. Prague: Vyšehrad, 2017.
Maeke, Lutz. *DDR und PLO: Die Palästinapolitik des SED-Staates*. Berlin: De Gruyter Oldenbourg, 2017.
Melman, Yossi. *The Master Terrorist: The True Story of Abu-Nidal*. New York: Adama Books, 1986.
Muehlenbeck, Philip. *Czechoslovakia in Africa, 1945–1968*. New York: Palgrave Macmillan, 2016.
Muehlenbeck, Philip E., and Natalia Telepneva, eds. *Warsaw Pact Intervention in the Third World: Aid and Influence in the Cold War*. London: I. B. Tauris, 2018.
Naftali, Timothy. *Blind Spot: The Secret History of American Counterterrorism*. New York: Basic Books, 2005.
Nehring, Christopher. "Umbrella or Pen? The Murder of Georgi Markov: New Facts and Old Questions." *Journal of Intelligence History* 16, no. 1 (2017): 47–58.
Pacner, Karel. *Československo ve zvláštních službách. Díl IV*. Prague: Themis, 2002.
"Palestine Chronology, 16 August–15 November 1986." *Journal of Palestine Studies* 16, no. 2 (Winter 1987): 215–32.
Pešta, Mikuláš. "Reluctant Revolutionaries: Czechoslovak Support of Revolutionary Violence between Decolonization and Détente." *Intelligence and National Security* (2022): 1–17.
Piškula, Jiří. "Roque Dalton García: Básník, bohém a partyzán očima tří tajných služeb." *Paměť a dějiny* 1 (January 2014): 108–16.
Possony, Stefan, and L. Francis Bouchey. *International Terrorism: The Communist Connection*. Washington, DC: American Council for World Freedom, 1978.
Raab, David. *Terror in Black September: The First Eyewitness Account of the Infamous 1970 Hijackings*. New York: St. Martin's, 2007.

Ra'anan, Uri, Robert L. Pfaltzgraff Jr., Richard H. Shultz, Ernst Halperin, and Igor Lukes, eds. *Hydra of Carnage: International Linkages of Terrorism; The Witnesses Speak*. Lexington, MA: Lexington Books, 1986.

Ramsay, Gilbert. "Why Terrorism Can, but Should Not Be Defined." *Critical Studies on Terrorism* 8, no. 2 (2015): 211–28.

Rapoport, David. "The Four Waves of Rebel Terror and September 11." *Anthropoetics* 8, no. 1 (Spring/Summer 2002). http://anthropoetics.ucla.edu/ap0801/terror/.

Rees, Wyn, and Richard J. Aldrich. "Contending Cultures of Counterterrorism: Transatlantic Divergence or Convergence?" *International Affairs* 81, no. 5 (2005): 905–23.

Reeve, Simon. *One Day in September: The Full Story of the 1972 Munich Olympics Massacre and the Israeli Revenge Operation "Wrath of God."* New York: Arcade, 2000.

Richterova, Daniela. "The Anxious Host: Czechoslovakia and Carlos the Jackal, 1978–1986." *International History Review* 40, no. 1 (2018): 108–32.

———. "Terrorists and Revolutionaries: The Achilles Heel of Communist Surveillance." *Surveillance & Society* 16, no. 3 (2018): 277–97.

Richterova, Daniela, Mikuláš Pešta, and Natalia Telepneva. "Banking on Military Assistance: Czechoslovakia's Struggle for Influence and Profit in the Third World, 1955–1968." *International History Review* 43, no. 1 (2021): 90–108.

Richterova, Daniela, Peter Rendek, and Radek Schovanek. "Covert Measures in Peace and War: The Czechoslovak Way." In *Covert Action: National Approaches to Unacknowledged Intervention*, edited by Magda Long, Rory Cormac, Genevieve Lester, Mark Stout, and Damien Van Puyvelde. Washington, DC: Georgetown University Press, forthcoming 2025.

Riegler, Thomas. "When Modern Terrorism Began: The OPEC Hostage Taking of 1975." In *Handbook of OPEC and the Global Energy Order: Past, Present and Future Challenges*, edited by Dag Harald Claes and Giuliano Garavini, 290–99. London: Routledge, 2020.

Rimington, Stella. *Open Secret: The Autobiography of the Former Director-General of MI5*. London: Arrow Books, 2001.

Ronen, Yehudit. "Libya's Qadhafi and the Israeli–Palestinian Conflict, 1969–2002." *Middle Eastern Studies* 40, no. 1 (2004): 85–98.

Rubin, Barry, and Judith Colp Rubin. *Yasir Arafat: A Political Biography*. New York: Oxford University Press, 2003.

Sayigh, Yezid. *Armed Struggle and the Search for State: The Palestinian National Movement, 1949–1993*. Oxford: Clarendon, 1997.

Scheuer, Thomas. "Ich brachte die Waffen nach München." *Focus*, no. 24 (June 14, 1999). http://www.focus.de/politik/deutschland/deutschland-ich-brachte-die-waffen-nach-muenchen_aid_177704.html.

———. "Jedenfalls lebe ich noch." *Focus*, no. 4 (January 23, 2006). http://www.focus.de/politik/deutschland/olympia-72-jedenfalls-lebe-ich-noch_aid_214369.html.

Schovánek, Radek. "Atentát na Pelikána." Minulost.cz, June 6, 2015. https://www.minulost.cz/cs/atentat-na-pelikana.

———. "Svazek Dialog: StB versus Pavel Kohout." http://www.ludvikvaculik.cz/index.php?pid=121&sid=149.

Seale, Patrick. *Abu Nidal: A Gun for Hire*. New York: Random House, 1992.

Sejna, Jan. *We Will Bury You*. London: Sidgwick & Jackson, 1982.

Shain, Yossi. *The Frontier of Loyalty: Political Exiles in the Age of the Nation-State*. Ann Arbor: University of Michigan Press, 1989.

Shapiro, Jeremy, and Bénédicte Suzan. "The French Experience of Counterterrorism." *Survival* 45, no. 1 (2003): 67–98.
Silke, Andrew, ed. *Routledge Handbook of Terrorism and Counterterrorism*. London: Routledge, 2019.
Skřivan, Aleš. "Zbrojní výroba a vývoz meziválečného Československa." *Ekonomická revue* 9, no. 3 (2006): 19–31.
Smíšek, Martin. *Czechoslovak Arms Exports to the Middle East*. Vol. 1. Warwick, UK: Helion, 2021.
Smith, Colin. *Carlos: Portrait of a Terrorist*. London: Deutsch, 1995.
Smith, Tony. "New Bottles for New Wine: A Pericentric Framework for the Study of the Cold War." *Diplomatic History* 24, no. 4 (2000): 567–91.
Stampnitzky, Lisa. *Disciplining Terror: How Experts Invented "Terrorism."* Cambridge: Cambridge University Press, 2013.
Steinhoff, P. G. "Portrait of a Terrorist: An Interview with Kozo Okamoto." *Asian Survey* 16, no. 9 (1976): 830–45.
Sterling, Claire. *The Terror Network: The Secret War of International Terrorism*. New York: Berkley Books, 1981.
———. *The Time of the Assassins*. New York: Holt, Rinehart & Winston, 1983.
Taylor, Peter. *States of Terror: Democracy and Political Violence*. London: BBC Books, 1993.
Telepneva, Natalia. "'Code Name SEKRETÁŘ': Amílcar Cabral, Czechoslovakia and the Role of Human Intelligence during the Cold War." *International History Review* 42, no. 6 (2020): 1257–73.
———. *Cold War Liberation: The Soviet Union and the Collapse of the Portuguese Empire in Africa, 1961–1975*. Chapel Hill: University of North Carolina Press, 2022.
———. "Mediators of Liberation: Eastern-Bloc Officials, Mozambican Diplomacy and the Origins of Soviet Support for Frelimo, 1958–1965." *Journal of Southern African Studies* 43, no. 1 (2017): 67–81.
"Tesař, Jan." Courage: Connecting Collections. http://cultural-opposition.eu/registry/?lang=en&uri=http://courage.btk.mta.hu/courage/individual/n91011&type=people.
Thatcher, Margaret. *The Downing Street Years*. London: HarperCollins, 1993.
Tofan, Liviu. *Şacalul securităţii: Teroristul Carlos în solda spionajului românesc*. Iaşi, Rom.: Polirom, 2013.
Tomek, Prokop. "Akce MANUEL." *Securitas Imperii* 9 (2002): 325–32.
———. "Czechoslovakia: The Czech Path between Totalitarianism and Democracy." In *The Handbook of European Intelligence Cultures*, edited by Bob de Graaff and James M. Nyce, 81–94. Lanham, MD: Rowman & Littlefield, 2016.
———. "Dům, v němž bydlel i Guevara." *Paměť a dějiny*, March 2016.
———. "*Objekt Alfa*": *Československé bezpečnostní složky proti Rádiu Svobodná Evropa*. Prague: Úřad dokumentace a vyšetřování zločinů komunismu, 2006.
Vrána, Karel, Jakub Szántó, and Pavel Novotný. "Československý ministr plánoval s arabskými teroristy atentát, který překazila až StB." Reportéři, Česká televize, May 20, 2017. http://www.ceskatelevize.cz/ct24/domaci/2127858-ceskoslovensky-ministr-planoval-s-arabskymi-teroristy-atentat-ktery-prekazila-az-stb.
Walker, Tony, and Andrew Gowers, *Arafat: The Biography*. London: Virgin, 2003.
Weinberg, Leonard. *The End of Terrorism?* New York: Routledge, 2012.
Westad, Odd Arne. *The Global Cold War: Third World Interventions and the Making of Our Times*. Cambridge: Cambridge University Press, 2007.

Wilkinson, Paul. *Terrorism versus Democracy: The Liberal State Response*. 3rd ed. London: Routledge, 2011.

Williams, Kieran, and Dennis Deletant. *Security Intelligence Services in New Democracies: The Czech Republic, Slovakia and Romania*. Studies in Russia and East Europe. London: Palgrave, 2000.

Willsher, Kim. "Ex-French spy chief admits 1980s pact with Palestinian terrorists." *Guardian*. August 9, 2019. https://www.theguardian.com/world/2019/aug/09/we-made-a-deal-ex-french-spy-chief-admits-1983-pact-with-fatah-terrorists.

Witte, Joan. "Violence in Lenin's Thought and Practice: The Spark and the Conflagration." *Terrorism and Political Violence* 5, no. 3 (1993): 135–203.

Wolf, Markus, and Anne McElvoy. *Man without a Face: The Autobiography of Communism's Greatest Spymaster*. London: Jonathan Cape, 1999.

Woodward, Bob. *Veil: The Secret Wars of the CIA, 1981–1987*. London: Simon & Schuster, 1987.

Zabetakis, Stanley G., and John F. Peterson. "The Diyarbakir Radar." *Studies in Intelligence* 8, no. 4 (Fall 1964): 41–47.

Žáček, Pavel. "Military Intelligence from Libya and Terrorism." *Behind the Iron Curtain* 2 (2012).

———. *Ruce světové revoluce: Carlos, mezinárodní terorismus a Státní bezpečnost, 1976–1989. Edice dokumentů*. Prague: Akademia, 2022.

"Zákon o Ústavu pro studium totalitních režimů a o Archivu bezpečnostních složek a o změně některých zákonů." Sbírka zákonů, Zákony pro lidi. https://www.zakonyprolidi.cz/cs/2007-181.

Zídek, Petr. *Československo a francouzská Afrika, 1948–1968*. Prague: Libri, 2006.

Zídek, Petr, and Karel Sieber. *Československo a Blízký východ v letech, 1948–1989*. Prague: Ústav mezinárodních vztahů, 2009.

———. *Československo a subsaharská Afrika v letech, 1948–1989*. Prague: Ústav mezinárodních vztahů, 2007.

Zourek, Michal. "Czechoslovakia and Latin America's Guerrilla Insurgencies: Secret Services, Training Networks, Mobility, and Transportation." In *Towards a Global History of Latin America's Revolutionary Left*, edited by Tanya Harmer and Alberto Martín Álvarez, 27–66. Gainesville: University of Florida Press, 2021.

———. "Operation MANUEL: Prague as a Transit Hub of International Terrorism." *Central European Journal of International & Security Studies* 9, no. 3 (2015): 78–98.

———. "Zusammenarbeit tschechoslowakischer und kubanischer Geheimdienste: Der geheime Aufenthalt von Ernesto Che Guevara." Prague Papers on the History of International Relations, Univerzita Karlova, Filozofická fakulta, 2018, 69–83. https://praguepapers.ff.cuni.cz/wp-content/uploads/sites/16/2018/10/Michal_Zourek_69-83.pdf.

# INDEX

Note: page numbers in italics indicate figures.

Abbas, Abu, 143
Abdulla, Muslah Owni, *156*, 156–57
ABS. *See* Archiv bezpečnostních složek (ABS, Security Services Archive)
Abu Nidal Organization (ANO), 3, 7–8, 15, 66–67, 85, 163–64, 173, 191, 271–87
*Achille Lauro*, 143
Action Directe, 58
Afghanistan, 33, 40, 122, 148, 253
African National Congress (ANC), 6, 9, 25, 27, 30, 38–39
African Party of Independence of Portuguese Guinea and Cape Verde Islands (PAIGC), 29, 32–33, 35
al-Ali, Naji, 190
al-Assad, Hafez, xiv, 10, 101, 106, 115, 248, 273, 309
al-Banna, Sabri, 268. *See also* Nidal, Abu
Algeria, 37, 41, 58, 109
al-Hadithi, Anwar, 245
al-Hadithi, A. S. Qadir, 252
al-Hawari. *See* al-Natour, Mahmoud
al-Hol, Abu, 287
Ali, Mohammad, 25, 40
al-Issawi, Kamal, 243, *256*, 258
al-Kassar, Monzer, 234
al-Natour, Mahmoud, 190–91
al-Qaddumi, Faruq, 88, 121
al-Qaeda, 60
al-Qasim, Rihab, 244

Al Saiqa, 70, 89
al-Shuqayri, Ahmad, 78–79, 81
al-Tal, Wasfi, 180
al-Wazir, Khalil, 62
Amal, 105
Ames, Bob, 86
Amman Accord, 87–89, 105–6, 160, 274
Amr, Talib Hamud, 173
ANC. *See* African National Congress (ANC)
Andrawes, Souhaila, 245, 259
Andrew, Christopher, 12–13
Andropov Institute, 151
Angola, 9, 29, 36–38, 40, 247
ANM. *See* Arab Nationalist Movement (ANM)
ANO. *See* Abu Nidal Organization (ANO)
Antonín Zápotocký Military Academy (Vojenská akademie Antonín Zápotockého, or VAAZ), 33–36, *34*, 39, 147
Arab League, 82, 85, 118, 121, 180
Arab Liberation Front, 62
Arab Nationalist Movement (ANM), 202, 233
Arafat, Yasser, xiv, xv, 3, 51, *83*, 87, 91, *96*, *207*, 324–25; Ahmad Mustafa Ahmed Mohammad and, 159; Amman Accord and, 90, 105–6; assassination attempts against, 68; background of, 61–62; Bakr and, 274; Black September and,

343

Arafat, Yasser (*continued*)
    64, 182, 195n4; Carlos the Jackal and, 248; Daoud and, 186; Force 17 and, 190; Husák and, 77, *78*; International Union of Socialist Youth and, 113; Iran and, 119; Iyad and, 99; Lebanon and, 100–101; Lenin and, 151–54; in Moscow, 79–81; Nidal and, 271, 275, 280, 283; Pelikán and, 122; Traboulsi and, 176; at United Nations, 65; US politicians meeting with, 86
Archiv bezpečnostních složek (ABS, Security Services Archive), xiii, 11–13, 327, 330n2
archives, 11–13, 327–30
Argentina, 41, 44, 47, 247
Argov, Shlomo, 272
Armenian Secret Army for the Liberation of Armenia (ASALA), 58
Arm of the Arab Revolution, 242
Army of Communist Combat, 6
Austria, 113, 117, 169, 272, 286
Ayman, Abu, 98–104, 109, 115–16, 121, 127–29, 140–41

Baader, Andreas, *59*, 65
Baader-Meinhof Gang, 58, *59*, 235, 284
Ba'ath Party, 269
Bakr, Atif Abu, 164–70, *168*, 186, 273–82, *282*, 282–84, 286, 301
Bakr, Kifah Abu, 280
Barrientos, René, 49
Begin, Menachem, 114, 120, 241
Belica, Miroslav, 296
Biľak, Vasiľ, 82, *83*, 211, *214*, 282, 324–25
Black September, xiv, 64, 99, 180–87, 195n4, 245, 269–70, 294
Bolivia, 45, 49–50
Brandt, Willy, 86
Brazil, 44–46
Brožovský, Jiří, 219–20, 222–25
Bruguière, Jean-Louis, 267–68, 311, 313
Bseiso, Atif, 175, 186

Bulgaria, 7–8, 12, 101, 274, 306
Bunke, Tamara, 49
Bush, George H. W., 247

Cabral, Amílcar, 32–33
Cambodia, 26
Carlos Group, 242–46, 254–56, 258, 294, 303–4
Carlos the Jackal, xiv, 3–4, *241*, *251*, *256*, *300*, 320; Andrawes and, 245; Arafat and, 248; becoming, 240–42; Daoud and, 187; German Democratic Republic and, 7; Hisham and, 259–60; Hungary and, 8, 256–57; Iraq and, 243–44; Joint Security Service and, 97; liaising against, 252–57; OPEC hostages and, 66; ouster of, 257–62; Sadat and, 248; Soviet Bloc and, 239–40; Soviet Union and, 253–54; State Security Service and, 245–46, 249–51, 253, 260–61; Syria and, 244; as threat, 247–48
Carr, Robert, 310
Casey, William J., 6
Castro, Fidel, 41, *42*, 50
Ceaușescu, Nicolae, 7, 126, 254
Central Intelligence Agency (CIA), xiii, 312
Chaí Soler, Carlos, 40–41
Chalid, Walid, 277
Charter 77, 125
Chile, 26
China, 30, 86, 150, 222, 224, 271
Chňoupek, Bohuslav, 82, 88
Churchill, Winston, 58
CIA. *See* Central Intelligence Agency (CIA)
*Codebreakers, The* (Kahn), 150
Colombia, 41, 44, 71n8
cryptography, 150
Csipák, Ladislav, xiv, 294–95, 301, 305
Cuba, 9, 33, 40–46, 48–49, 71n2
Cuban Missile Crisis, 41–42, 51
Cuban Revolution, 28

Dalton, Roque, 56n83
Daoud, Abu, xiv, 1, 15, 183–90, *184, 188, 295*, 303, 310; Black September and, 182, 269; Carlos Group and, 246, 294; Carlos the Jackal and, 164; Munich Olympics and, 245; Mušír and, 175; Nidal and, 165, 270; uproar over release of, 196n14
David, Václav, 79
*Day of the Jackal, The* (Forsyth), 2
Dearlove, Richard, 6
Democratic Front for the Liberation of Palestine (DFLP), 62, 88–89, 141, 201–2, 204, 206–11
Democratic Republic of Congo (DRC), 26
developing world, 19n31, 26–28
DFLP. *See* Democratic Front for the Liberation of Palestine (DFLP)
Dominican Republic, 44
Drayton, Richard, 329
DRC. *See* Democratic Republic of Congo (DRC)
Dubček, Alexander, 122–23, 148
Dzasokhov, Aleksandr, 81

East Germany. *See* German Democratic Republic (GDR)
Ecuador, 41, 44
Egypt, 33, 40, 67, 99, 108, 114, 144n2, 155
Egyptian Islamic Jihad, 118
Eisenmenger, Johann Andreas, 116
El Al Flight 426, 57, 60, 63, 202
El Salvador, 44
Ensslin, Gudrun, *59*
Eritreans, 27, 44
Eshkol, Levi, 269
ETA. *See* Euskadi Ta Askatasuna (ETA)
Ethiopia, 148
European Community, 31
Euskadi Ta Askatasuna (ETA), 244
explosives, 141–42, 305. *See also* weapons

Falklands War, 247
Fallah, Fuad, 194
false flags, 127–29
Fatah, 7, 15, 64, 88–89, 95–96, 137–39, 319–22, 324; Ahmad Mustafa Ahmed Mohammad in, 157–58; CIA and, 86; Force 17 and, 190–91; founding of, 62; Muslah Owni Abdulla in, 156; Nidal and, 270–71, 275; PLO and, 87; Qaddafi and, 120; Rejectionists and, 202; Ten Point Program and, 201; weapons and, 141
Fatah-Revolutionary Council, 267. *See also* Abu Nidal Organization (ANO)
Fattah, Samir Abdul, 170. *See also* Hisham, Abu
FCD Red Banner Institute, 151
Federal Republic of Germany (FDR), 1, 31, 64–66, 92n27, 127–29, 156, 181, 193, 203, 240–45, 284, 294, 311, 317n51
First Intifada, 89, 280
FLN. *See* Front de libération nationale (FLN, Algerian National Liberation Front)
FLOSY. *See* Front for the Liberation of Occupied South Yemen (FLOSY)
Force 17, 190–94, 300
Forsyth, Frederick, 2
France, 58, 241–42, 270, 309
FRELIMO. *See* Liberation Front of Mozambique (FRELIMO)
Front de libération nationale (FLN, Algerian National Liberation Front), 30, 37, 41, 58
Front for the Liberation of Occupied South Yemen (FLOSY), 30
Fulbright, William, 86

Gagarin, Yuri, *123*
GDR. *See* German Democratic Republic (GDR)
Gemayel, Bashir, 101
General Union of Palestinian Students, 62

German Democratic Republic (GDR), 7, 9–10, 84, 97, 142, 239, 254–55, 330n4
Germany. *See* Federal Republic of Germany (FDR); German Democratic Republic (GDR)
*Global Cold War, The* (Westad), 9
Goldenberg, Chez Jo, 272
Gomez, José, 49
Gott, Karel, *114*
Guatemala, 41, 44–45
Guevara, Ernesto "Che," 47–50, *48*, 218
Guinea, 33
Guinea-Bissau, 157

Habash, George, 69, 85, 89, 141, 202–13, *203*, 227–29, 232–33, 271, 320
Habib, Philip C., 114
Haddad, Wadi, 65, 232–36, 241, 300, 304
Haig, Alexander, 5–6, 114
Haiti, 44
Hamdun, Ragheb, 192
Hammami, Said, 167
Havel, Václav, 127
Hawatmeh, Nayef, 141, 201, *207*, 207–8, 212–13, 215
Helsinki Accords, 133n46
Helsinki Conference, 123
Helsinki Process, 299
Herranz, Jean, 242
Hezbollah, 104–5, 305
hijacking, 57, 59–60, 62–64, *63*, 66, 71n2, 143, 245, 272
Hillo, Zakki, 233–35
Hisham, Abu, 95–99, 147, 166, 170–76, *171*, 192–94, 213, 259–60
Hoffman, Bruce, 65
Honduras, 44
Hotel Kosodrevina, 25, 40
Hrušecký, Vladimír, 124
Hula, Abu, 190
Hungary, 8, 157, 254–57, 259, 264n34
Husák, Gustáv, 77, *78*, 81, 106, *114*, 148, *171*, 324–25

Hussein, Nabil Wahbi, 235–36, 303
Hussein, Saddam, xiv, 244, 247, 272, 287

Indonesia, 33
Institute for Foreign Studies, 147–48, *150*, 154–57
Institute for the Study of Totalitarian Regimes (Ústav pro studium totalitních režimů, or ÚSTR), 11, 327
International Olympic Committee, 1
International Union of Socialist Youth, 113
interviews, 11–13
Iran, 26, 66, 119
Iran-Contra affair, 283
Iran-Iraq War, 118–19, 247, 272
Iraq, xiv, 67, 138, 144n2, 243–44
Ireland, 58, 71n7
Irgun Zvai Le'umi (National Military Organization), 58
Irish Republican Army, 17n6
Israel, 57–58, 61–68, 79, 90, 96–100, 103, 114; Black September and, 180–81; Daoud and, 196n14; Lebanon and, 140–41; Operation Wrath of God, 65, 185, 190, 317n56; Soviet Union and, 206. *See also* Mossad; Zionism
Italy, 58, 60, 244
Iyad, Abu, 62, 88–89, 95–99, *96*, 101–3, 108, 113–14, 120–24; Arafat and, 99; Black September and, 181–82; Carlos the Jackal and, 245; Force 17 and, 192; Nidal and, 270, 288; Tesař and, 125–26

Jabar, Abdul Rahman Abu, 178n23
Japanese Red Army (JRA), 69, 128–29, 205, 218, 306
Jawad, Ahmed, 191–93
Jenkins, Brian, 60
Jordan, 12, 64, 99–100, 105–6, 114, 155, 180–81, 203–4
Jordanian Civil War, 137, 181
JRA. *See* Japanese Red Army (JRA)

Kahn, David, 150
KANU. *See* Kenya African National Union (KANU)
Kenya African National Union (KANU), 30, 36
KGB, 8, 31, 43
Khalaf, Salah, 62
Khaled, Layla, 311
Khomeini, Ayatollah Ruhollah, 119
Khrushchev, Nikita, 26–27, 41
Kissinger, Henry, 115
Kopp, Magdalena, 243, 247, 251, 254, 259
Kreisky, Bruno, 86
Krejčí, Jaroslav, 49
Krejčí, Josef, 82, 211–12
Kukan, Edward, 340
Kurdistan Workers' Party (PKK), 127–28
Kurds, 27
Kuruc, Ján, 101–2, *102*, 108, 127, 227
Kuwait, 138–39

Lebanese Civil War, 139–40, 222
Lebanon, 12, 100–106, 129, 140
Lehi/Stern Gang, 58
Lenin, Vladimir, 151–54
Liberation Front of Mozambique (FRELIMO), 29–30
Libya, xiv, 67, 118–21, 144n2, 257
*Lidice*, 37
Lohamei Herut Yisrael, 58
London, Douglas, 86, 312–13
Lumumba, Patrice, 47–48

M-19, 71n8
Makeba, Miriam, 50
Mandela, Nelson, 39
Mareček, Tomáš, 137–39
Markov, Georgi, 125
McGovern, George, 86
Meinhof, Ulrike, 65
Meir, Golda, 65, 185
MI5, xiii, 310. *See also* Secret Intelligence Service (SIS)

MI6, xiii, 17n6. *See also* Secret Intelligence Service (SIS)
MK. *See* uMkhonto we Sizwe (MK)
Mohammad, Ahmad Mustafa Ahmed, 157–59, *159*
Moravec, František, xiii
Morávek, August, 137–39
Moro, Aldo, 60
Morocco, 109, 155
Moscow Olympics, 306
Mossad, 65, 89, 96, 117, 185, 233, 278, 281
Moukharbal, Michel, 241
Mozambique, 27, 29
MPLA. *See* People's Movement for the Liberation of Angola (MPLA)
Mubarak, Hosni, 118
Munich Olympics, xiv, 1, 64–65, 68–69, 96, 164, 180–81, 183
Musa, Abu, 172, 187
Muslim Brotherhood, 61–62, 273, 305

Nasser, Gamal Abdel, 80, 205
Nasser, Kamal, *207*
national liberation movements, 6, 27–28, 37–38, 40
NATO. *See* North Atlantic Treaty Organization (NATO)
Nergl, Vladimír, 257, 299, 308
"New Bottles for New Wine" (Smith), 9
Nicaragua, 45, 247, 283
Nidal, Abu, xiv, 85, *268*, 312–13, 320; as "apostle of Palestinian violence," 267–89; Arafat and, 271, 275, 280, 283; attempts at liaison with, 275–77; background of, 268–69; Bakr and, 282–83, 286; Black September and, 270; Daoud and, 165, 270; Fatah and, 270–71, 275; German Democratic Republic and, 7; Iyad and, 270, 288; name of, 269–70; propaganda and, 278; from radical to terrorist, 268–73; State Security Service and, 273, 279. *See also* Abu Nidal Organization (ANO)

Non-Aligned Movement, 8, 121
normalizace, 51, 148, 154
North, Oliver, 268, 283
North Atlantic Treaty Organization (NATO), 31, 60, 113, 121, 155, 294
Northern Ireland, 58, 71n7

OAS. *See* Organization of American States (OAS)
Obzina, Jaromír, 97–98, 113, *114*
Office for Foreign Relations and Information, 327
Olympic Games, 60, 306
Olympics, attack on Munich, xiv, 1, 64–65, 68–69, 96, 164, 180–81, 183
OPEC. *See* Organization of the Petroleum Exporting Countries (OPEC)
Operation Asanace, 133n46
Operation Desert Storm, 287
Operation Harbor, 154
Operation Manuel, 43–48, 51
Operation Pelikán, 122, 124
Operation Ramadan, 44, 47
Operation Visitor, 303
Operation Wrath of God, 65, 185, 190, 317n56
Organization of American States (OAS), 45
Organization of the Petroleum Exporting Countries (OPEC), 59–60, 66, 233
Oudeh, Mohammad Daoud. *See* Daoud, Abu

Pahlavi, Mohammed Reza, 119
PAIGC. *See* African Party of Independence of Portuguese Guinea and Cape Verde Islands (PAIGC)
Palestine, 58, 60–67
Palestinian cadets, in Institute for Foreign Studies, 154–57
Palestinian Liberation Organization (PLO), xv, 3, 77, 103; beginnings of alliance with, 78–82; countering extremists of, 180–95; flaws in alliance with, 106–9; Joint Security Service, 95, 97, 99–103, 108, 122, 126, 129, 140, 165; Lebanon and, 101, 103–6; liaising with office of, 164–67; liaison in crisis and war, 99–104; as national liberation movement, 6, 27; official alliance with, 95–99; Soviet bloc and, 7; stumbling blocks in relationship with, 85–88; terrorism and, 15, 61–65, 68; training, 149–51
Palestinian National Council, 62, 280
Palestinian Resistance Movement, 204
Palestinian Secret Organization, 269
Palmer, Mark, 261
Panama, 44
Pan Am Flight 103, 141, 305
Paraguay, 44
Pelikán, Jiří, 122–27, *123*
People's Movement for the Liberation of Angola (MPLA), 29, 36, 38, 40
Percy, Charles, 86
Peru, 41, 44, 71n8
PFLP. *See* Popular Front for the Liberation of Palestine (PFLP)
Pineiro Losada, Manuel, 43
PIRA. *See* Provisional Irish Republican Army (PIRA)
PKK. *See* Kurdistan Workers" Party (PKK)
plausible deniability, 37–40
PLO. *See* Palestinian Liberation Organization (PLO)
Poland, 7, 12, 69, 125, 173, 234–35, 273, 306
Popular Front for the Liberation of Palestine (PFLP), 69, 71n2, 137, 205–6, 210, 212, 302, 320, 322; creation of, 202; El Al Flight 426 and, 57; Fatah and, 62; Kuruc and, 227–28; Sharif and, 219–20, 222–24; terrorism and, 62–66
Portugal, 29, 37–38, 41
Prague Spring, 51, 56n106, 122, 125, 147, 207, 295
Prima Linea, 244
Proll, Thorwald, *59*

Provisional Irish Republican Army (PIRA), 58, 71n7, 244

Qaddafi, Muammar, xiv, 103, 119–21, 142, 144, 205, 248, 283, 286
Qalaq, Ezzedine, 167

Radio Free Europe, 126, 133n52, 255
"Ramadanists," 153–54
Ramírez Sánchez, Ilich, 66, 240, 267, 324
Reagan, Ronald, 5, 120
Red Army Faction, 5, 58, 59, 65, 306
Red Brigades, 58, 60, 129, 244
Rejectionists, 201–2, 206–14, 227, 232, 271, 320, 322
revolutions, 40–47. *See also* national liberation movements
Riafaat, Nassri, 276–77
Rivonia Trial, 39
Rocard, Michel, 96
Romania, 7, 254–55, 257
Roosevelt, Franklin, 58

Sadat, Anwar, 114, 118, *119*, 248
Salameh, Ali Hassan, 86, 183, 190, *191*
Salim, Abu, 233–34
Šándor, Andor, 299, 304–5
Sarkis, Sarkis Fareed, 246–47
Saudi Arabia, 66, 114, 212
Sayeret Matkal, 66
Sayigh, Yezid, 17n6
Schwarcz, Petr, 148, 154
Seale, Patrick, 267, 273
2 June Movement, 58
Secret Intelligence Service (SIS), 6. *See also* MI6
Semtex, 120, 141–42, 305
Sendero Luminoso, 71n8
Seychelles, 154, 158
Sharif, Abu Bassam, 204, 218–29, *221*, *226*, 301
Shigenobu, Fusako, *128*
Sieff, Joseph, 317n55
SIS. *See* Secret Intelligence Service (SIS)

Six Day War, 57, 61, 67, 79, 202, 206, 218, 233
Skyjack Sunday, 63, 68, 202–3, 233
Smith, Colin, 313
Smith, Tony, 9, 324
Sochor, Karel, 235
Söhnlein, Horst, 59
Somalia, 66
Somoza Debayle, Anastasio, 247
Soghanalian, Sarkis, 246–47
sources. *See* archives
South Africa, 25, 29, 36, 38–40
South Yemen, 157, 248, 300
Soviet Union: Arafat and, 151–54; Carlos the Jackal and, 253–54; Israel and, 206; Libya and, 120; national liberation movements and, 80; Palestinian Liberation Organization and, 7; as terrorism sponsor, 5–8; third world and, 26–28
Spain, 244
State Security Service (Státní bezpečnost StB): Abu Bakr and, 165; Carlos the Jackal and, 245–46, 249–51, 253, 260–61; Daoud and, 1, 187–89; file destruction by, 12; files, 328–29; First Directorate, 11, 29, 31, 46, 101–2, 108–9, 115–17, 121, 124–26, 130, 210–11, 219, 225, 328; materials from, 11; Nidal and, 273, 279; Operation Asanace and, 133n46; Operation Manuel and, 43–44, 46; Palestinian spies and, 174–77; Red Brigades and, 129; Soghanalian and, 246–47; Traboulsi and, 176; train hijacking and, 73n51
Sterling, Claire, 6
Štrougal, Lubomír, 45, 214
Syria, xiv, 3, 6, 9–12, 115, 144n2, 243–44; Antonín Zápotocký Military Academy and, 33; Israel and, 69–70; Iyad and, 97; Jawad and, 192–93; Jordan and, 64; Mohammad and, 157; PLO and, 80, 88, 99, 103, 172; threat landscape and, 67

Syrian Social Nationalist Party, 101
System of Joint Acquisition of Enemy
    Data, 306

Tanzania, 32, 39
Tawari, Tawfiq, 104–5
Taysir, Quba, 220, 228
Ten Point Program, 201
terminology, 13–16
terrorism, xiv; 1960s wave of, 1–2, 14,
    57–58; defining, 14, 16; domestic,
    14; ideologies of counterterrorism,
    323–24; as international, 14–15,
    59–60; networking and, 127–29;
    Palestinian, 15, 60–67; Popular Front
    for the Liberation of Palestine and,
    202–4; Soviet-sponsored, 5–8; tactics
    in, 58–59
*Terror Network, The* (Sterling), 6
Tesař, Jan, 125–26
Thatcher, Margaret, 18n19
third world. *See* developing world
threat landscape, 67–70
Toubi, Tawfiq, 89
Traboulsi, Beshara, 102–3, 136, 142–43,
    149, *150*, 172, 193, 274
Tunisia, 90, 109, 288
Tupamaros, 71n8
Turkey, 118, 127, 158

Uganda, 33, 66
Ulčák, Dušan, 209, 299
uMkhonto we Sizwe (MK), 25, 29, 36,
    38–39
United Kingdom, xiii, 18n19, 31, 58, 294,
    309–11, 317n55

United Nations, 37, 65, 89
Uruguay, 71n8
ÚSTR. *See* Institute for the Study of
    Totalitarian Regimes (Ústav pro
    studium totalitních režimů, or ÚSTR)

VAAZ. *See* Antonín Zápotocký Military
    Academy (Vojenská akademie Antonín
    Zápotockého, or VAAZ)
Velvet Revolution, 151, 287
Venezuela, 41, 44–45, 59, 66, 260
Vietnam, 9, 28
Vietnam War, 58
Voleš, Ivan, 170, 193, 209, 305

Wattar, Walid, 258–59
weapons, 32, 135–44, *136*, 144n2,
    213–14, 223, 248, 271
Weather Underground, 58
Weinberger, Caspar, 114
Weinrich, Johannes, 243, 254, 259–60
Westad, Arne, 9, 26
West Germany. *See* Federal Republic of
    Germany (FDR)
Wischnewski Protocol, 318n74
Wolf, Markus, 27

Yassin, Ali, 167
Yemen, 67, 155, 157, 248, 299–300
Yugoslavia, 8

Zimbabwe, 27
Zimbabwe African People's Union
    (ZAPU), 29–30, 32
Zionism, 67, 113, 116, 134, 153–54, 247
Zourek, Michal, 44

# ABOUT THE AUTHOR

**DR. DANIELA RICHTEROVA** is an associate professor of intelligence studies at the Department of War Studies, King's College London. A leading expert among a new generation of intelligence and security scholars, she specializes in the history of Cold War espionage and state relations with terrorists and revolutionaries. She regularly publishes in prestigious academic and media outlets, including *International Affairs* and *Foreign Policy*. She is codirector of the King's Centre for the Study of Intelligence and coconvenor of the Cambridge Intelligence Seminar.